Graphing Calculator Keystroke Guide: Algebra

Benjamin N. Levy
and
Laurel Technical Services

Houghton Mifflin Company   Boston   New York

Sponsoring Editor: Jack Shira
Senior Associate Editor: Maureen Brooks
Managing Editor: Cathy Cantin
Associate Editor: Michael Richards
Assistant Editor: Carolyn Johnson
Supervising Editor: Karen Carter
Art Supervisor: Gary Crespo
Marketing Manager: Sara Whittern
Marketing Manager: Ros Kane
Marketing Assistant: Carrie Lipscomb

Trademark acknowledgments: TI is a registered trademark of
Texas Instruments Incorporated. Casio is a registered trademark
of Casio, Inc. Sharp is a registered trademark of Sharp Electronics
Corporation. Hewlett-Packard is a registered trademark.

Printed in the United States of America.

ISBN: 0-395-87777-6

123456789-VG-01 00 99 98 97

Graphing Calculator Keystroke Guide
Algebra

Contents

Chapter Key
$x = 1$ Texas Instruments TI-80
$x = 2$ Texas Instruments TI-81
$x = 3$ Texas Instruments TI-82
$x = 4$ Texas Instruments TI-85
$x = 9$ Texas Instruments TI-83
$x = 10$ Texas Instruments TI-86

Detailed Contents for
Casio, Sharp, and Hewlett Packard Calculators

Chapter Key

$x = 5$ Casio fx-7700GE and fx-9700GE
$x = 6$ Casio CFX-9800G
$x = 7$ Hewlett Packard HP 38G
$x = 8$ Sharp EL-9200/9300

Graphing Calculator Keystroke Guide
Algebra

Introduction

This *Guide* provides keystroke-level commands and instructions so that you may begin using your graphing calculator as a problem-solving tool with exercises in the Larson/Hostetler *Elementary Algebra* and *Intermediate Algebra* textbooks. It is not intended to be a comprehensive guide to all the capabilities of your calculator. To learn about other features your calculator may have, refer to the manual that came with it.

In the chapters that follow, we shall use different typefaces to distinguish *keystrokes* that you press from the *text* of this guide. Thus MATH and ENTER will represent the labels on your calculator's keys.

Some calculators have function keys that assume different behavior in different contexts. To clarify the effect expected from depressing a function key, we sometimes write F1 *[COMMAND]*, where F1 names the key and *[COMMAND]* represents its corresponding functions in the current menu.

For convenience and simplicity, when you are asked to type a *number*, say 345.67, we shall express the keystrokes as 345.67, without any spaces between the individual keys, instead of writing 3 4 5 . 6 7.

Chapter 1

Texas Instruments TI-80 Graphics Calculator

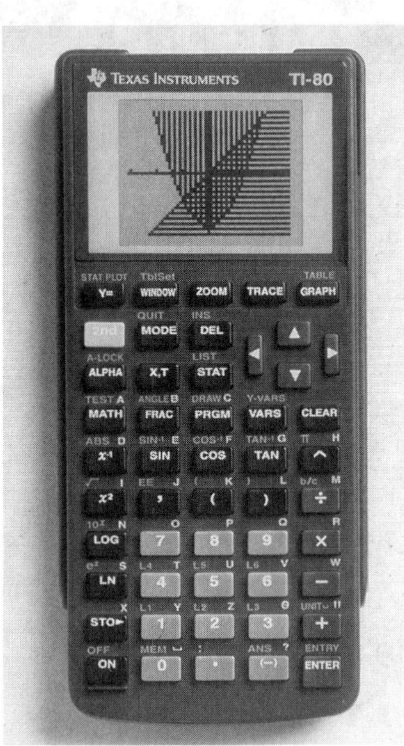

1.1.1 Basics: Press the **ON** key to begin using your TI-80 calculator. If you need to adjust the display contrast, first press 2nd, then press and hold ▲ (the *up* arrow key) to increase the contrast or ▼ (the *down* arrow key) to decrease the contrast. As you press and hold ▲ or ▼, an integer between 0 (lightest) and 9 (darkest) appears in the upper right corner of the display. When you have finished with the calculator, turn it off to conserve battery power by pressing 2nd and then **OFF**.

Check the TI-80's settings by pressing **MODE**. If necessary, use the arrow keys to move the blinking cursor to a setting you want to change. Press **ENTER** to select a new setting. To start with, select the options along the left side of the **MODE** menu as illustrated in Figure 1.1: normal display, floating decimals, radian measure, mixed numbers, automatically simplify, function graphs, connected lines, and sequential plotting. Details on alternative options will be given later in this guide. For now, leave the **MODE** menu by pressing **CLEAR**.

Figure 1.1: MODE menu

Figure 1.2: Home screen

1.1.2 Editing: One advantage of the TI-80 is that up to 8 lines are visible at one time, so you can *see* a long calculation. For example, type this sum (see Figure 1.2):

$$1 + 2 + 3 + 4 + 5 + 6 + 7 + 8 + 9 + 10 + 11 + 12 + 13 + 14 + 15 + 16 + 17 + 18 + 19 + 20$$

Then press **ENTER** to see the answer, too.

Often we do not notice a mistake until we see how unreasonable an answer is. The TI-80 permits you to re-display an entire calculation, edit it easily, then execute the *corrected* calculation.

Suppose you had typed 12 + 34 + 56 as in Figure 1.2 but had *not* yet pressed **ENTER**, when you realize that 34 should have been 74. Simply press ◀ (the *left* arrow key) as many times as necessary to move the blinking cursor left to 3, then type 7 to write over it. On the other hand, if 34 should have been 384, move the cursor back to 4, press 2nd INS (the cursor changes to a blinking underline) and then type 8 (inserts at the cursor position and other characters are pushed to the right). If the 34 should have been 3 only, move the cursor to 4 and press DEL to delete it.

Even if you had pressed **ENTER**, you may still edit the previous expression. Press 2nd and then **ENTRY** to *recall* the last expression that was entered. Now you can change it. In fact, the TI-80 retains many prior entries in a "last entry" storage area. Press 2nd **ENTRY** repeatedly until the previous line you want replaces the current line.

Technology Tip: When you need to evaluate a formula for different values of a variable, use the editing feature to simplify the process. For example, suppose you want to find the balance in an investment account if there is now $5000 in the account and interest is compounded annually at the rate of 8.5%. The formula for the balance is $P\left(1+\frac{r}{n}\right)^{nt}$, where P = principal, r = rate of interest (expressed as a decimal), n = number of times interest is compounded each year, and t = number of years. In our example, this becomes $5000(1+.085)^{t}$. Here are the keystrokes for finding the balance after $t = 3$, 5, and 10 years.

Years	*Keystrokes*	*Balance*
3	5000 (1 + .085) ^ 3 ENTER	$6386.45
5	2nd ENTRY ◀ 5 ENTER	$7518.28
10	2nd ENTRY ◀ 10 ENTER	$11,304.92

Figure 1.3: Editing expressions

Then to find the balance from the same initial investment but after 5 years when the annual interest rate is 7.5%, press these keys to change the last calculation above: 2nd ENTRY ◀ DEL ◀ 5 ◀ ◀ ◀ ◀ ◀ 7 ENTER.

1.1.3 Key Functions: Most keys on the TI-80 offer access to more than one function, just as the keys on a computer keyboard can produce more than one letter ("g" and "G") or even quite different characters ("5" and "%"). The primary function of a key is indicated on the key itself, and you access that function by a simple press on the key.

To access the *second* function indicated to the *left* above a key, first press 2nd (the cursor changes to a blinking ↑) and *then* press the key. For example, to calculate $\sqrt{25}$, press 2nd √ 25 ENTER.

When you want to use a letter or other character printed to the *right* above a key, first press ALPHA (the cursor changes to a blinking **A**) and then the key. For example, to use the letter K in a formula, press ALPHA K. If you need several letters in a row, press 2nd A-LOCK, which is like Caps Lock on a computer keyboard, and then press all the letters you want. Remember to press ALPHA when you are finished and want to restore the keys to their primary functions.

1.1.4 Order of Operations: The TI-80 performs calculations according to the standard algebraic rules. Working outwards from inner parentheses, calculations are performed from left to right. Powers and roots are evaluated first, followed by multiplications and divisions, and then additions and subtractions.

Note that the TI-80 distinguishes between *subtraction* and the *negative sign*. If you wish to enter a negative number, it is necessary to use the (-) key. For example, you would evaluate $-5-(4\cdot-3)$ by pressing (-) 5 - (4 × (-) 3) ENTER to get 7.

Enter these expressions to practice using your TI-80.

Expression	*Keystrokes*	*Display*
$7-5\cdot3$	7 - 5 × 3 ENTER	-8
$(7-5)\cdot3$	(7 - 5) × 3 ENTER	6
$120-10^2$	120 - 10 x² ENTER	20
$(120-10)^2$	(120 - 10) x² ENTER	12100

$$\frac{24}{2^3} \qquad\qquad \text{24} \div \text{2} \wedge \text{3 ENTER} \qquad\qquad 3$$

$$\left(\frac{24}{2}\right)^3 \qquad\qquad (\text{ 24} \div \text{2)} \wedge \text{3 ENTER} \qquad\qquad 1728$$

$$(7--5)\cdot-3 \qquad\qquad (\text{ 7 - (-) 5)} \times \text{(-) 3 ENTER} \qquad\qquad -36$$

1.1.5 Algebraic Expressions and Memory: Your calculator can evaluate expressions such as $\dfrac{N(N+1)}{2}$ *after* you have entered a value for N. Suppose you want $N = 200$. Press 200 STO ▸ ALPHA N ENTER to store the value 200 in memory location N. Whenever you use N in an expression, the calculator will substitute the value 200 until you make a change by storing *another* number in N. Next enter the expression $\dfrac{N(N+1)}{2}$ by typing ALPHA N (ALPHA N + 1) ÷ 2 ENTER. For $N = 200$, you will find that $\dfrac{N(N+1)}{2} = 20100$.

The contents of any memory location may be revealed by typing just its letter name and then ENTER. And the TI-80 retains memorized values even when it is turned off, so long as its batteries are good.

1.1.6 Repeated Operations with ANS: The result of your *last* calculation is always stored in memory location ANS and replaces any previous result. This makes it easy to use the answer from one computation in another computation. For example, press 30 + 15 ENTER so that 45 is the last result displayed. Then press 2nd ANS ÷ 9 ENTER and get 5 because $\frac{45}{9} = 5$.

With a function like division, you press the ÷ key *after* you enter an argument. For such functions, whenever you would start a new calculation with the previous answer followed by pressing the function key, you may press just the function key. So instead of 2nd ANS ÷ 9 in the previous example, you could have pressed simply ÷ 9 to achieve the same result. This technique also works for these functions: + - × x^2 $\wedge$ x^{-1}.

Here is a situation where this is especially useful. Suppose a person makes \$5.85 per hour and you are asked to calculate earnings for a day, a week, and a year. Execute the given keystrokes to find the person's incomes during these periods (results are shown in Figure 1.4):

Pay period	*Keystrokes*	*Earnings*
8-hour day	5.85 × 8 ENTER	\$46.80
5-day week	× 5 ENTER	\$234
52-week year	× 52 ENTER	\$12,168

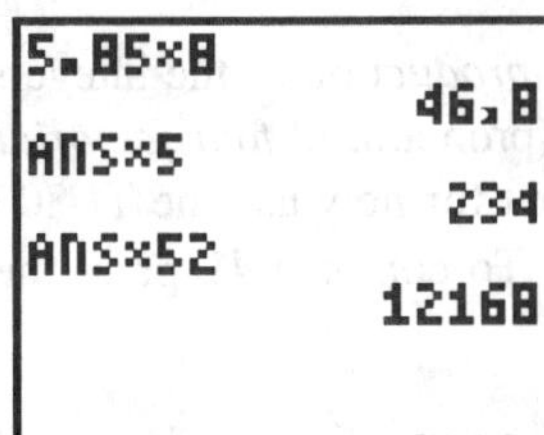

Figure 1.4: ANS variable

1.1.7 The MATH Menu: Operators and functions associated with a scientific calculator are available either immediately from the keys of the TI-80 or by 2nd keys. You have direct key access to common arithmetic operations (x^2, 2nd $\sqrt{}$, x^{-1}, $\wedge$, 2nd ABS), exponential and logarithmic functions (LOG, 2nd 10^x, LN, 2nd e^x), and a famous constant (2nd π).

A significant difference between the TI-80 and many scientific calculators is that the TI-80 requires the argument of a function *after* the function, as you would see a formula written in your textbook. For example, on the TI-80 you calculate $\sqrt{16}$ by pressing the keys 2nd $\sqrt{}$ 16 in that order.

The TI-80 has two special keys, 2nd b/c for creating fractions and 2nd UNIT ˷ for the integer part of a mixed number. To enter a fraction such as $\tfrac{2}{5}$, press 2 2nd b/c 5 ENTER. To enter a mixed number like $2\tfrac{3}{4}$, press 2 2nd UNIT ˷ 3 2nd b/c 4 ENTER. Press FRAC 2 to display this as an improper fraction ($2\tfrac{3}{4}$ to $\tfrac{11}{4}$); FRAC 3 to convert an improper fraction to a mixed number; and FRAC 5 to write a number in its decimal form.

Here are keystrokes for basic mathematical operations. Try them for practice on your TI-80.

Expression	Keystrokes	Display
$\sqrt{3^2+4^2}$	2nd $\sqrt{}$ (3 x^2 + 4 x^2) ENTER	5
$2\tfrac{1}{3}$	2 2nd UNIT ˷ 1 2nd b/c 3 FRAC 5 ENTER	2.333333333
$\lvert -5 \rvert$	2nd ABS (-) 5 ENTER	5
$\log 200$	LOG 200 ENTER	2.301029996
$2.34 \cdot 10^5$	2.34 × 2nd 10^x 5 ENTER	234000

Additional mathematical operations and functions are available from the MATH menu (Figure 1.5). Press MATH to see the various options. You will learn in your mathematics textbook how to apply many of them. As an example, calculate $\sqrt[3]{7}$ by pressing MATH and then *either* 4 *or* ▾ ▾ ▾ ENTER; finally press 7 ENTER to see 1.912931183. To leave the MATH menu and take no other action, press 2nd QUIT or just CLEAR.

Figure 1.5: MATH menu

The *factorial* of a non-negative integer is the *product* of *all* the integers from 1 up to the given integer. The symbol for factorial is the exclamation point. So 4! (pronounced *four factorial*) is $1\cdot2\cdot3\cdot4 = 24$. You will learn more about applications of factorials in your textbook, but for now use the TI-80 to calculate 4! The factorial command is located in the MATH menu's PRB sub-menu. To compute 4!, press these keystrokes: 4 MATH ◂ 4 ENTER *or* 4 MATH ◂ ▾ ▾ ▾ ENTER ENTER.

Note that you can select a sub-menu from the MATH menu by pressing either ◂ or ▸. It is easier to press ◂ once than to press ▸ twice to get to the PRB sub-menu.

1.2   Functions and Graphs

1.2.1 Evaluating Functions: Suppose you receive a monthly salary of \$1975 plus a commission of 10% of sales. Let x = your sales in dollars; then your wages W in dollars are given by the equation $W = 1975 + .10x$. If your January sales were \$2230 and your February sales were \$1865, what was your income during those months?

Here's how to use your TI-80 to perform this task. Press the Y= key at the top of the calculator to display the function editing screen (Figure 1.6). You may enter as many as four different functions for the TI-80 to use at one time. If there is already a function Y1, press ▲ or ▼ as many times as necessary to move the cursor to Y1 and then press CLEAR to delete whatever was there. Then enter the expression $1975 + .10x$ by pressing these keys: 1975 + .10 X,T. (The X,T key lets you enter the variable X easily without having to use the ALPHA key.) Now press 2nd QUIT to return to the main calculations screen.

Figure 1.6: Y= screen

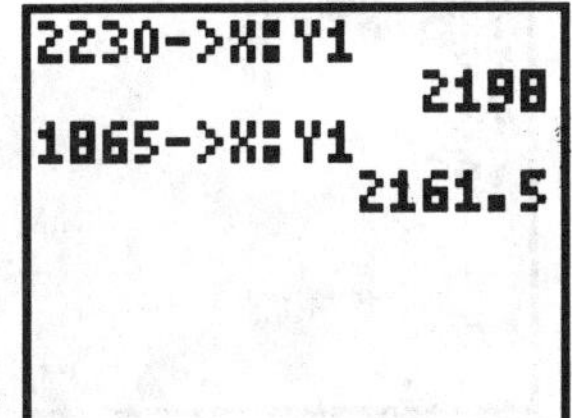

Figure 1.7: Evaluating a function

Assign the value 2230 to the variable x by these keystrokes (see Figure 1.7): 2230 STO ▶ X,T. Then press 2nd : to allow another expression to be entered on the same command line. Next press the following keystrokes to evaluate Y1 and find January's wages: 2nd Y-VARS 1 ENTER.

It is not necessary to repeat all these steps to find the February wages. Simply press 2nd ENTRY to recall the entire previous line and change 2230 to 1865. Each time the TI-80 evaluates the function Y1, it uses the *current* value of x.

Like your textbook, the TI-80 uses standard function notation. So to evaluate $Y_1(2230)$ when $Y_1(x) = 1975 + .10x$, press 2nd Y-VARS 1 (2230) ENTER (see Figure 1.8). Then to evaluate $Y_1(1865)$, press 2nd ENTRY to recall the last line and change 2230 to 1865.

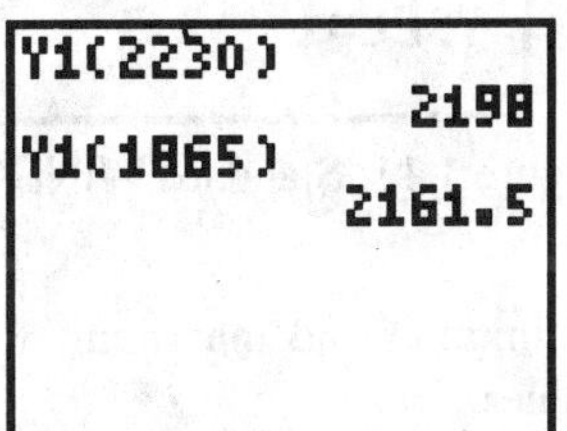

Figure 1.8: Function notation

Technology Tip: The TI-80 does not require multiplication to be expressed between variables, so xxx means x^3. It is often easier to press two or three x's together than to search for the square key or the cube operation. Of course, expressed multiplication is also not required between a constant and a variable. Hence to enter $2x^3 + 3x^2 - 4x + 5$ in the TI-80, you might save keystrokes and press just these keys: 2 X,T X,T X,T + 3 X,T X,T - 4 X,T + 5.

1.2.2 Functions in a Graph Window: Once you have entered a function in the Y= screen of the TI-80, just press GRAPH to see its graph. The ability to draw a graph contributes substantially to our ability to solve problems.

For example, here is how to graph $y = -x^3 + 4x$. First press Y= and delete anything that may be there by moving with the arrow keys to Y1 or to any of the other lines and pressing CLEAR wherever necessary. Then, with the cursor on the top line Y1, press (-) X,T MATH 3 + 4 X,T to enter the function (as in Figure 1.9). Now press GRAPH and the TI-80 changes to a window with the graph of $y = -x^3 + 4x$.

While the TI-80 is calculating coordinates for a plot, it displays a busy indicator at the top right of the graph window.

Your graph window may look like the one in Figure 1.10 or it may be different. Since the graph of $y = -x^3 + 4x$ extends infinitely far left and right and also infinitely far up and down, the TI-80 can display only a piece of the actual graph. This displayed rectangular part is called a *viewing rectangle*. You can easily change the viewing rectangle to enhance your investigation of a graph.

Figure 1.9: Y= screen

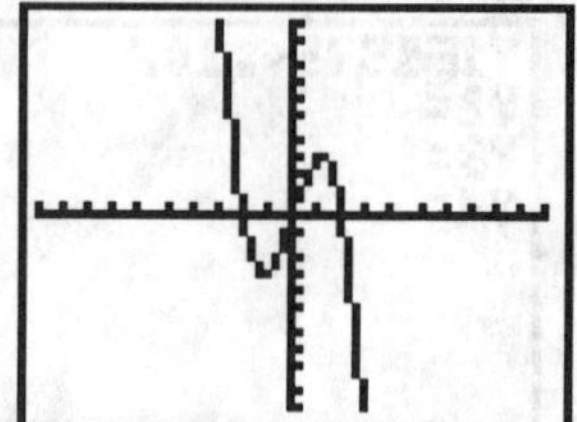

Figure 1.10: Graph of $y = -x^3 + 4x$

The viewing rectangle in Figure 1.10 shows the part of the graph that extends horizontally from -10 to 10 and vertically from -10 to 10. Press WINDOW to see information about your viewing rectangle. Figure 1.11 shows the WINDOW screen that corresponds to the viewing rectangle in Figure 1.10. This is the *standard* viewing rectangle for the TI-80.

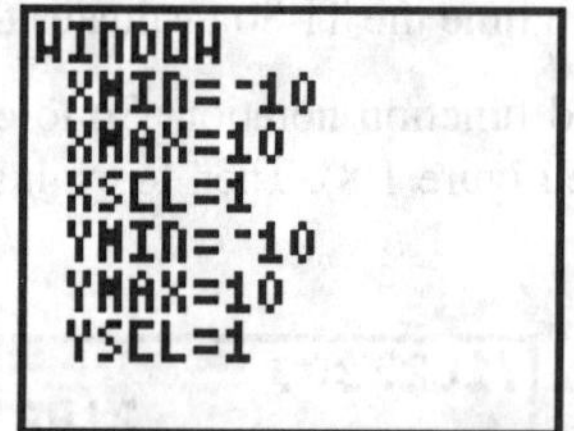

Figure 1.11: Standard WINDOW

The variables XMIN and XMAX are the minimum and maximum x-values of the viewing rectangle; YMIN and YMAX are its minimum and maximum y-values.

XSCL and YSCL set the spacing between tick marks on the axes.

Use the arrow keys ▲ and ▼ to move up and down from one line to another in this list; pressing the ENTER key will move down the list. Press CLEAR to delete the current value and then enter a new value. You may also edit the entry as you would edit an expression. Remember that a minimum *must* be less than the corresponding maximum or the TI-80 will issue an error message. Also, remember to use the (-) key, not - (which is subtraction), when you want to enter a negative value. Figures 1.10-11, 1.12-13, and 1.14-15 show different WINDOW screens and the corresponding viewing rectangle for each one.

TI-80 Graphics Calculator

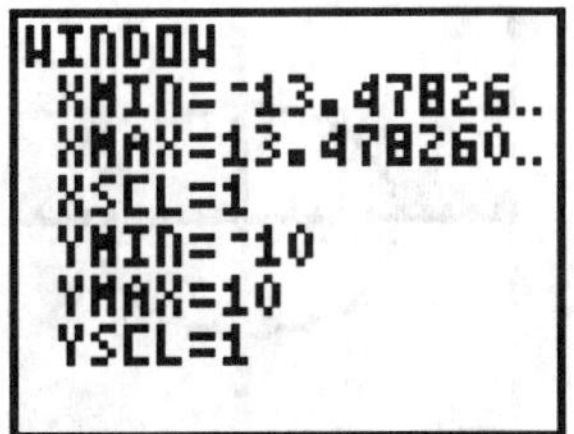

Figure 1.12: Square window

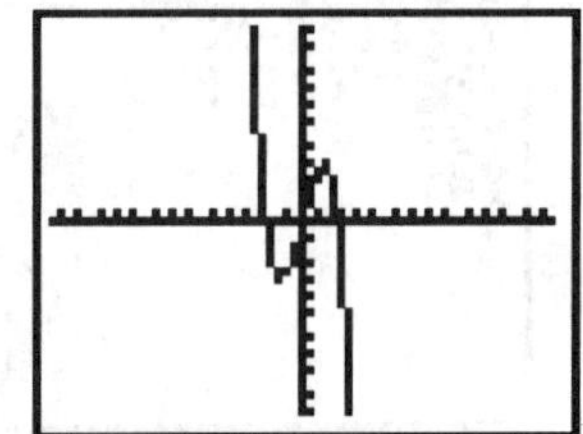

Figure 1.13: Graph of $y = -x^3 + 4x$

To set the range quickly to standard values (see Figure 1.11), press ZOOM 6. To set the viewing rectangle quickly to a square (Figure 1.12), press ZOOM 5. More information about square windows is presented later in Section 1.2.3.

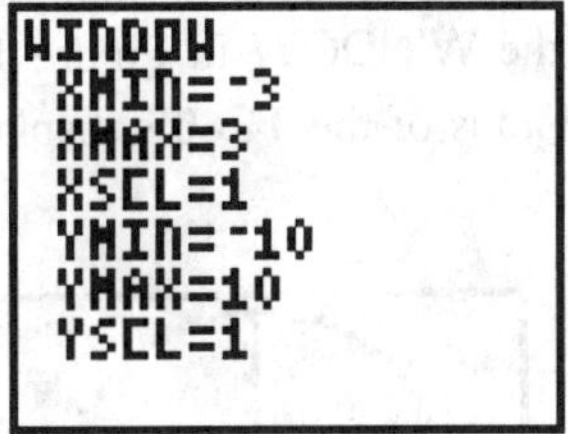

Figure 1.14: Custom window

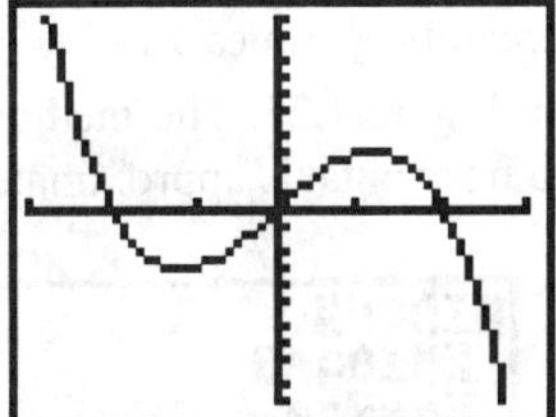

Figure 1.15: Graph of $y = -x^3 + 4x$

Sometimes you may wish to display grid points corresponding to tick marks on the axes. This option may be changed by pressing 2nd DRAW to display the DRAW menu (Figure 1.16); use arrow keys to move the blinking cursor way down to GridOn in the 9th line and press ENTER. The quicker way to accomplish this is to press DRAW 9. Then press ENTER to put this into effect and GRAPH to redraw the graph. Figure 1.17 shows the same graph as in Figure 1.15 but with the grid turned on. In general, you'll want the grid turned *off*, so make it that way now by pressing DRAW 0 ENTER.

Figure 1.16: DRAW menu

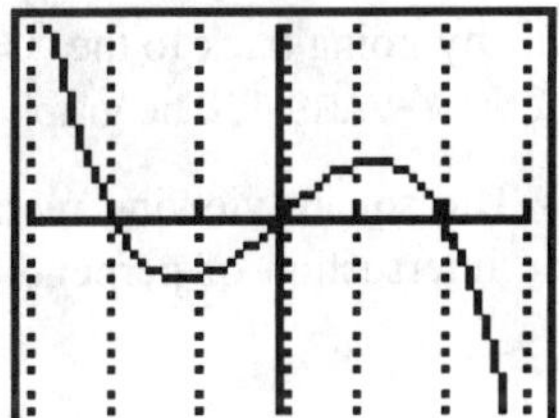

Figure 1.17: Grid turned on for $y = -x^3 + 4x$

1.2.3 Graphing a Circle: Here is a useful technique for graphs that are not functions, but that can be "split" into a top part and a bottom part, or into multiple parts. Suppose you wish to graph the circle whose equation is $x^2 + y^2 = 36$. First solve for y and get an equation for the top semicircle, $y = \sqrt{36 - x^2}$, and for the bottom semicircle, $y = -\sqrt{36 - x^2}$. Then graph the two semicircles simultaneously.

The keystrokes to draw this circle's graph follow. Enter $\sqrt{36 - x^2}$ as Y1 and $-\sqrt{36 - x^2}$ as Y2 (see Figure 1.18) by pressing Y= CLEAR 2nd $\sqrt{\ }$ (36 - X,T x²) ENTER CLEAR (-) 2nd $\sqrt{\ }$ (36 - X,T x²). Then press GRAPH to draw them both.

Figure 1.18: Two semicircles

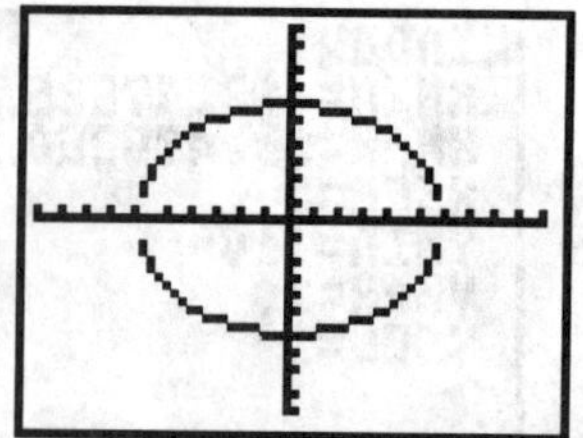

Figure 1.19: Circle's graph - standard view

If your range were set to the standard viewing rectangle, your graph would look like Figure 1.19. Now this does *not* look like a circle, because the units along the axes are not the same. This is where the square viewing rectangle is important. Press ZOOM 5 and see a graph that appears more circular.

Technology Tip: Another way to get a square graph is to change the range variables so that the value of YMAX - YMIN is approximately $\frac{3}{4}$ times XMAX - XMIN. For example, see the WINDOW in Figure 1.20 and the corresponding graph in Figure 1.21. The method works because the dimensions of the TI-80's display are such that the ratio of vertical to horizontal is approximately $\frac{3}{4}$.

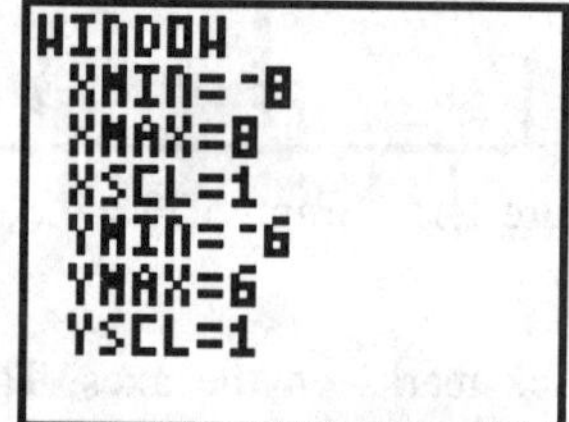

Figure 1.20: $\frac{\text{vertical}}{\text{horizontal}} = \frac{6}{8} = \frac{3}{4}$

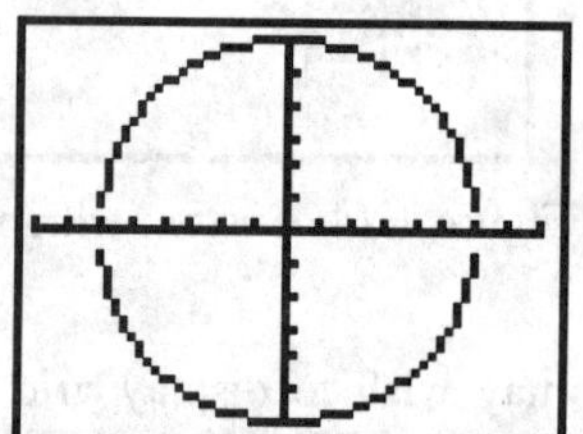

Figure 1.21: A "square" circle

The two semicircles in Figure 1.21 do not meet because of an idiosyncrasy in the way the TI-80 plots a graph.

Back when you entered $\sqrt{36 - x^2}$ as Y1 and $-\sqrt{36 - x^2}$ as Y2, you could have entered -Y1 as Y2 and saved some keystrokes. Try this by going back to the Y= menu and pressing the arrow key to move the cursor down to Y2. Then press CLEAR (-) 2nd Y-VARS 1. The graph should be just as it was before.

Technology Tip: The square viewing rectangle is also important when you want to judge whether two lines are perpendicular. The intersection of perpendicular lines will always *look* like a right angle in a square viewing rectangle.

1.2.4 TRACE: Graph $y = -x^3 + 4x$ in the standard viewing rectangle. Press any of the arrow keys ▲ ▼ ◀ ▶ and see the cursor move from the center of the viewing rectangle. The coordinates of the cursor's location are displayed at the bottom of the screen, as in Figure 1.22, in floating decimal format. This cursor is called a *free-moving cursor* because it can move from dot to dot *anywhere* in the graph window.

Remove the free-moving cursor and its coordinates from the window by pressing GRAPH or CLEAR. Now press an arrow key and the free-moving cursor will move again from the point where you left it.

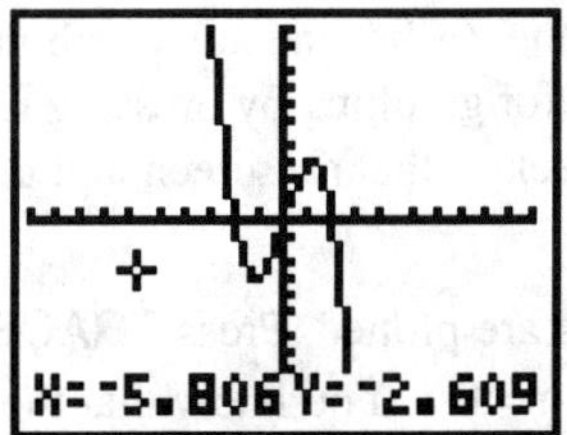

Figure 1.22: Free-moving cursor

Press **TRACE** to enable the left ◄ and right ► arrow keys to move the cursor along the function. The cursor is no longer free-moving, but is now constrained to the function. The coordinates that are displayed belong to points on the function's graph, so the y-coordinate is the calculated value of the function at the corresponding x-coordinate.

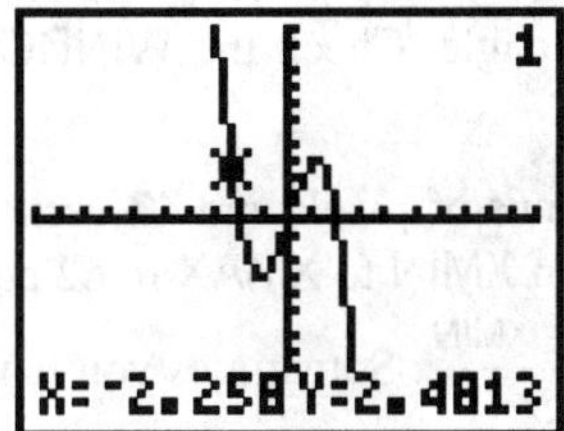

Figure 1.23: Trace on $y = -x^3 + 4x$

Now plot a second function, $y = -.25x$, along with $y = -x^3 + 4x$. Press **Y=** and enter $-.25x$ for Y2, then press **GRAPH**.

Figure 1.24: Two functions

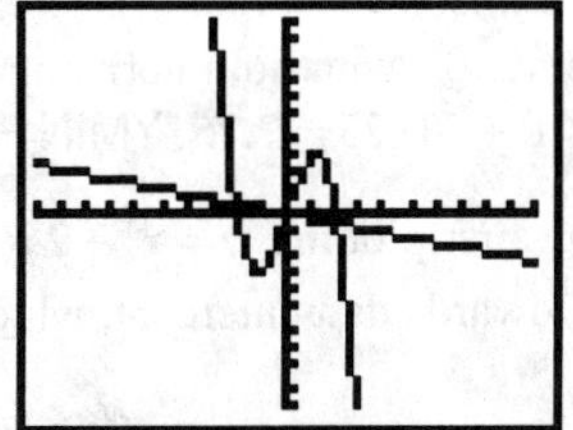

Figure 1.25: $y = -x^3 + 4x$ and $y = -.25x$

Note in Figure 1.24 that the equal signs next to Y1 and Y2 are *both* highlighted. This means *both* functions will be graphed. In the **Y=** screen, move the cursor directly on top of the equal sign next to Y1 and press **ENTER**. This equal sign should no longer be highlighted (see Figure 1.26). Now press **GRAPH** and see that only Y2 is plotted (Figure 1.27).

Figure 1.26: Y= screen with only Y2 active

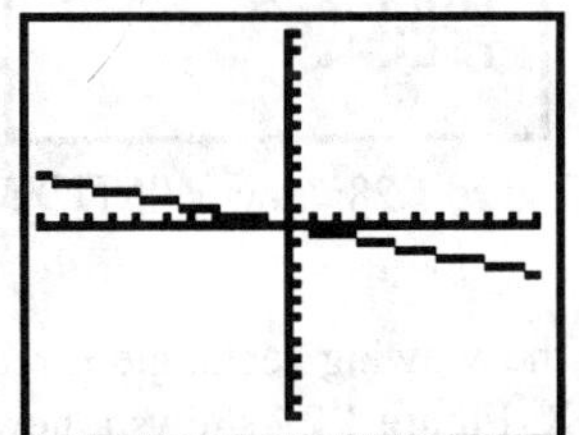

Figure 1.27: Graph of $y = -.25x$

Many different functions may be stored in the Y= list and any combination of them may be graphed simultaneously. You can make a function active or inactive for graphing by pressing ENTER on its equal sign to highlight (activate) or remove the highlight (deactivate). Go back to the Y= screen and do what is needed in order to graph Y1 but not Y2.

Now activate Y2 again so that both graphs are plotted. Press TRACE and the cursor appears first on the graph of $y = -x^3 + 4x$ because it is higher up in the Y= list. You know that the cursor is on this function, Y1, because of the numeral 1 that is displayed in the upper right corner of the window (see Figure 1.23). Press the up ▲ or down ▼ arrow key to move the cursor vertically to the graph of $y = -.25x$. Now the numeral 2 is displayed in the top right corner of the window. Next press the right and left arrow keys to trace along the graph of $y = -.25x$. When more than one function is plotted, you can move the trace cursor vertically from one graph to another in this way.

Technology Tip: By the way, trace along the graph of $y = -.25x$ and press and hold either ◀ or ▶. Eventually you will reach the left or right edge of the window. Keep pressing the arrow key and the TI-80 will allow you to continue the trace by panning the viewing rectangle. Check the WINDOW screen to see that XMAX and XMAX are automatically updated.

The TI-80's display has 63 horizontal columns of pixels and 47 vertical rows. So when you trace a curve across a graph window, you are actually moving from XMIN to XMAX in 62 equal jumps, each called Δx. You would calculate the size of each jump to be $\Delta x = \dfrac{\text{XMAX} - \text{XMIN}}{62}$. Sometimes you may want the jumps to be friendly numbers like .1 or .25 so that, when you trace along the curve, the x-coordinates will be incremented by such a convenient amount. Just set your viewing rectangle for a particular increment Δx by making XMAX = XMIN + 62·Δx. For example, if you want XMIN = -5 and Δx = .3, set XMAX = -5 + 62·.3 = 13.6. Likewise, set YMAX = YMIN + 46·Δy if you want the vertical increment to be some special Δy.

To center your window around a particular point, say (h, k), and also have a certain Δx, set XMIN = h - 31·Δx and XMAX = h + 31·Δx. Likewise, make YMIN = k - 23·Δy and YMAX = k + 23·Δy. For example, to center a window around the origin, (0, 0), with both horizontal and vertical increments of .25, set the range so that XMIN = 0 - 31·.25 = -7.75, XMAX = 0 + 31·.25 = 7.75, YMIN = 0 - 23·.25 = -5.75, and YMAX = 0 + 23·.25 = 5.75.

See the benefit by first plotting $y = x^2 + 2x + 1$ in a standard graphing window. Trace near its y-intercept, which is (0, 1), and move towards its x-intercept, which is (-1, 0). Then press ZOOM 4 and trace again near the intercepts.

1.2.5 ZOOM: Plot again the two graphs, for $y = -x^3 + 4x$ and for $y = -.25x$. There appears to be an intersection near $x = 2$. The TI-80 provides several ways to enlarge the view around this point.

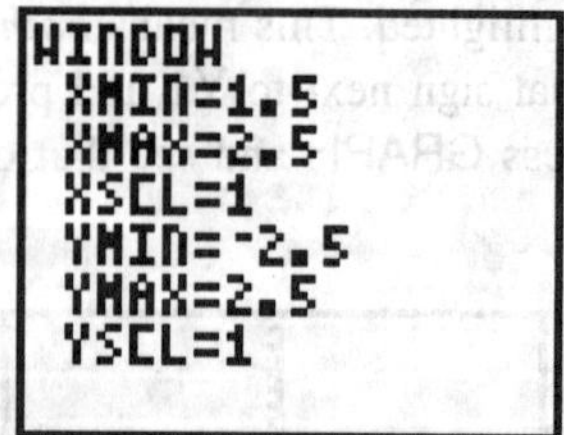

Figure 1.28: New WINDOW

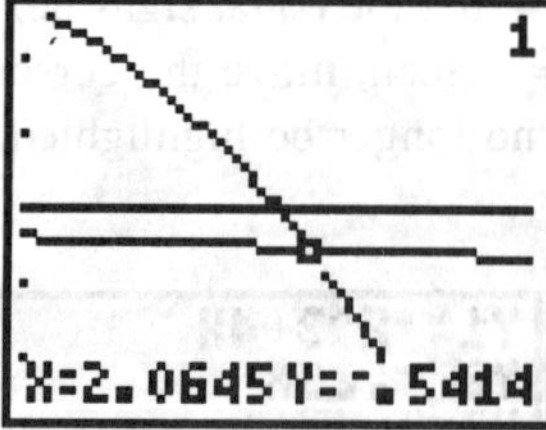

Figure 1.29: Closer view

You can change the viewing rectangle directly by pressing WINDOW and editing the values of XMIN, XMAX, YMIN, and YMAX. Figure 1.29 shows a new viewing rectangle for the range displayed in Figure 1.28. The cursor has been moved near the point of intersection; move your cursor closer to get the best approximation possible for the coordinates of the intersection.

A more efficient method for enlarging the view is to draw a new viewing rectangle with the cursor. Start again with a graph of the two functions $y = -x^3 + 4x$ and $y = -.25x$ in a standard viewing rectangle (press ZOOM 6 for the standard window, from -10 to 10 along both axes).

Figure 1.30: ZOOM menu

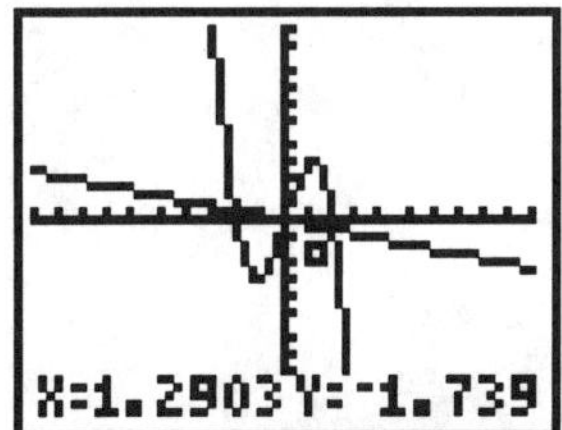

Figure 1.31: One corner selected

Now imagine a small rectangular box around the intersection point, near $x = 2$. Press ZOOM 1 (Figure 1.30) to draw a box to define this new viewing rectangle. Use the arrow keys to move the cursor, whose coordinates are displayed at the bottom of the window, to one corner of the new viewing rectangle you imagine.

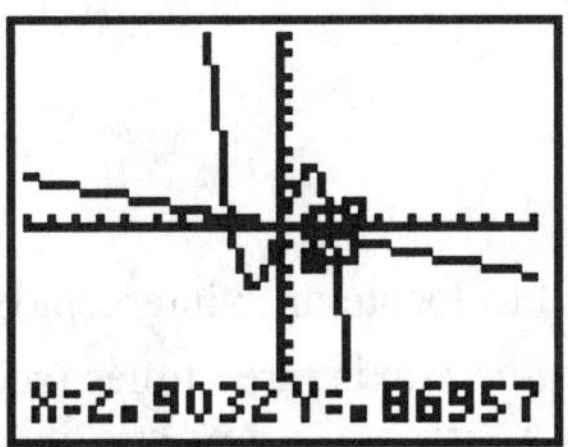

Figure 1.32: Box drawn

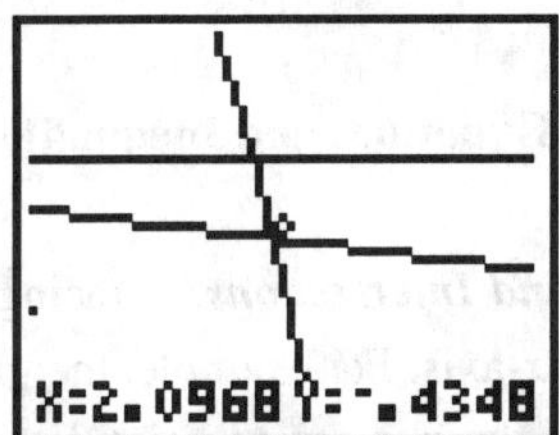

Figure 1.33: New viewing rectangle

Press ENTER to fix the corner where you have moved the cursor; it changes shape and becomes a blinking square (Figure 1.31). Use the arrow keys again to move the cursor to the diagonally opposite corner of the new rectangle (Figure 1.32). If this box looks all right to you, press ENTER. The rectangular area you have enclosed will now enlarge to fill the graph window (Figure 1.33).

You may interrupt the zoom any time *before* you press this last ENTER. Press ZOOM once more and start over. Press CLEAR or GRAPH to cancel the zoom, or press 2nd QUIT to cancel the zoom and return to the home screen.

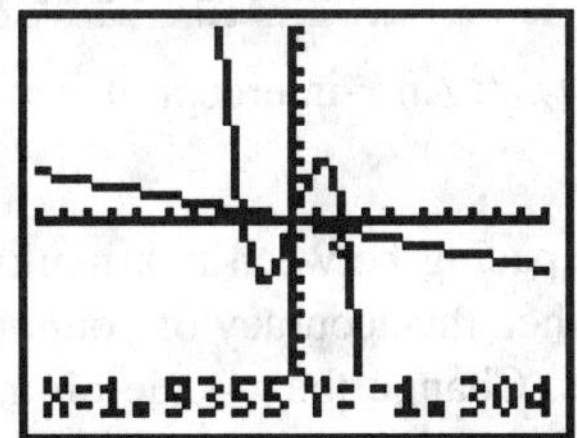

Figure 1.34: Before a zoom in

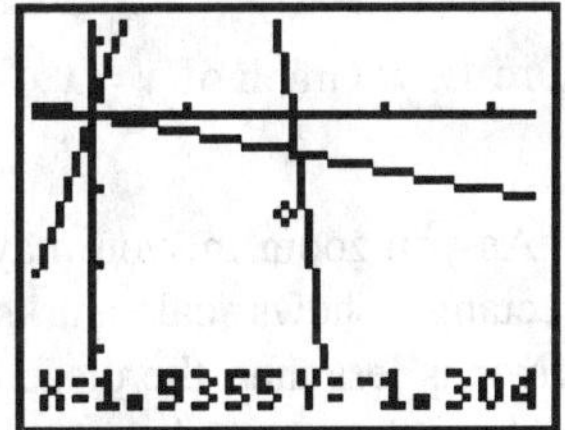

Figure 1.35: After a zoom in

You can also gain a quick magnification of the graph around the cursor's location. Return once more to the standard window for the graph of the two functions $y = -x^3 + 4x$ and $y = -.25x$. Press ZOOM 2 and then press arrow keys to move the cursor as close as you can to the point of intersection near $x = 2$ (see Figure 1.34). Then press ENTER and the calculator draws a magnified graph, centered at the cursor's position (Figure 1.35). The range variables are changed to reflect this new viewing rectangle. Look in the WINDOW menu to verify this.

As you see in the ZOOM menu (Figure 1.30), the TI-80 can ZOOM IN (press ZOOM 2) or ZOOM OUT (press ZOOM 3). Zoom out to see a larger view of the graph, centered at the cursor position. You can change the horizontal and vertical scale of the magnification by assigning values to the variables XFACT and YFACT, the horizontal and vertical magnification factors. For example, to set XFACT equal to 2, go to the home screen and press 2 STO VARS 1 9.

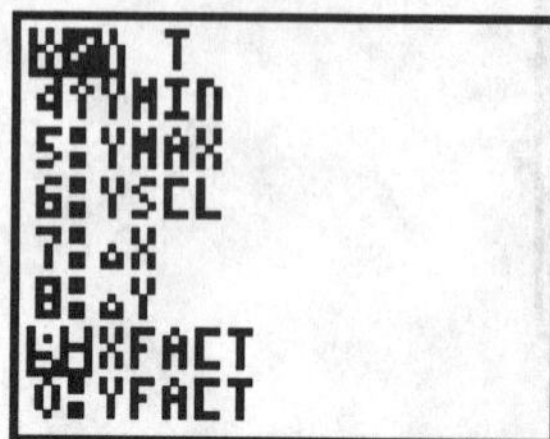

Figure 1.36: VARS, then WINDOW..., for zoom factors

The default zoom factor is 4 in both directions. It is not necessary for XFACT and YFACT to be equal. Sometimes, you may prefer to zoom in one direction only, so the other factor should be set to 1.

1.3   Solving Equations and Inequalities

1.3.1 Intercepts and Intersections: Tracing and zooming are also used to locate an x-intercept of a graph, where a curve crosses the x-axis. For example, the graph of $y = x^3 - 8x$ crosses the x-axis three times (see Figure 1.37). After tracing over to the x-intercept point that is furthest to the left, zoom in (Figure 1.38). Continue this process until you have located all three intercepts with as much accuracy as you need. The three x-intercepts of $y = x^3 - 8x$ are approximately -2.828, 0, and 2.828.

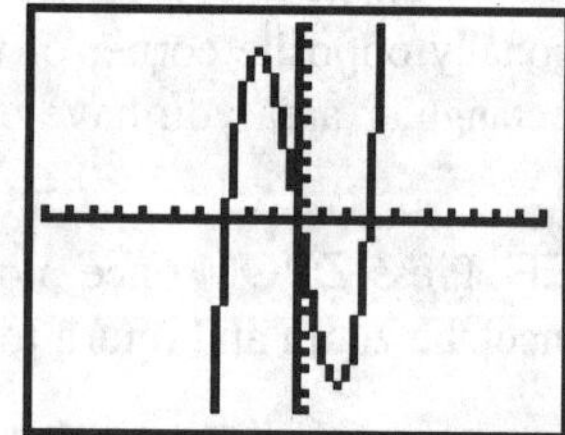

Figure 1.37: Graph of $y = x^3 - 8x$

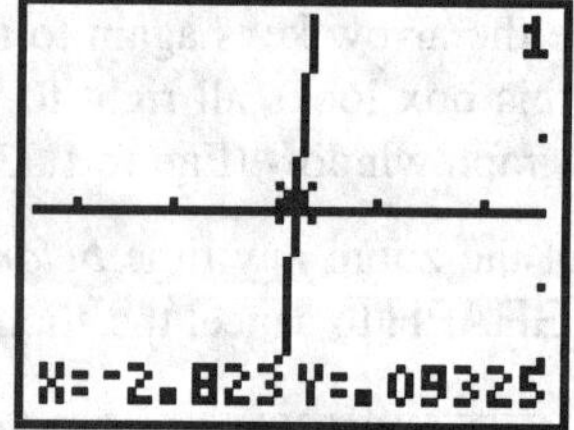

Figure 1.38: An x-intercept of $y = x^3 - 8x$

Technology Tip: As you zoom in, you may also wish to change the spacing between tick marks on the x-axis so that the viewing rectangle shows scale marks near the intercept point. Then the accuracy of your approximation will be such that the error is less than the distance between two tick marks. Change the x-scale on the TI-80 from the WINDOW menu. Move the cursor down to XSCL and enter an appropriate value.

TRACE and ZOOM are especially important for locating the intersection points of two graphs, say the graphs of $y = -x^3 + 4x$ and $y = -.25x$. Trace along one of the graphs until you arrive close to an intersection point. Then press ▲ or ▼ to jump to the other graph. Notice that the x-coordinate does not change, but the y-coordinate is likely to be different (see Figures 1.39 and 1.40).

When the two y-coordinates are as close as they can get, you have come as close as you now can to the point of intersection. So zoom in around the intersection point, then trace again until the two y-coordinates are as close as possible. Continue this process until you have located the point of intersection with as much accuracy as necessary.

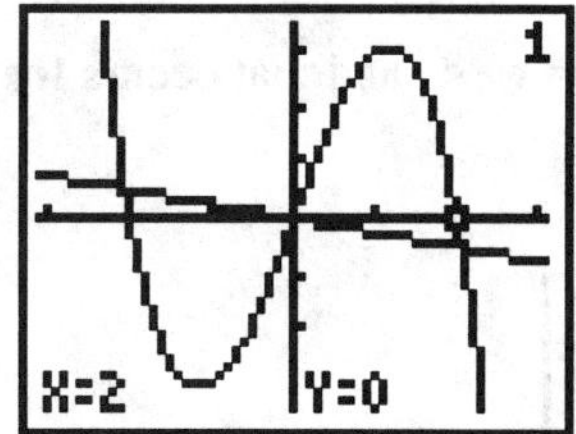

Figure 1.39: Trace on $y = -x^3 + 4x$

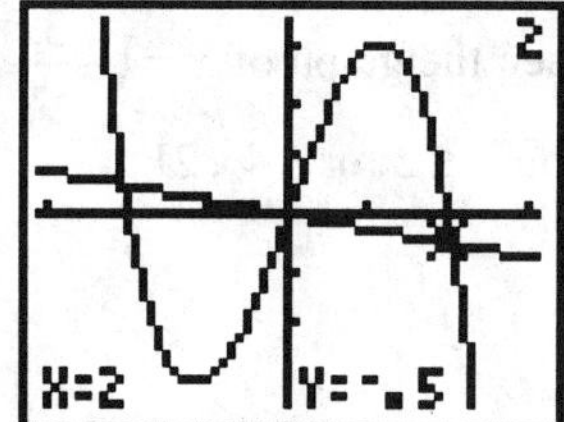

Figure 1.40: Trace on $y = -.25x$

1.3.2 Solving Equations by Graphing: Suppose you need to solve the equation $24x^3 - 36x + 17 = 0$. First graph $y = 24x^3 - 36x + 17$ in a window large enough to exhibit *all* its x-intercepts, corresponding to all the equation's roots. Then use trace and zoom to locate each one. In fact, this equation has just one solution, approximately $x = -1.414$.

Remember that when an equation has more than one root, it may be necessary to change the viewing rectangle a few times to locate all of them.

Technology Tip: To solve an equation like $24x^3 + 17 = 36x$, you may first transform it into standard form, $24x^3 - 36x + 17 = 0$, and proceed as above. However, you may also graph the *two* functions $y = 24x^3 + 17$ and $y = 36x$, then zoom and trace to locate their point of intersection.

1.3.3 Solving Systems by Graphing: The solutions to a system of equations correspond to the points of intersection of their graphs (Figure 1.41). For example, to solve the system $y = x^2 - 3x - 4$ and $y = x^3 + 3x^2 - 2x - 1$, first graph them together. Then zoom and trace to locate their point of intersection, approximately (-2.17, 7.25).

You must judge whether the two current y-coordinates are sufficiently close for $x = -2.17$ or whether you should continue to zoom and trace to improve the approximation.

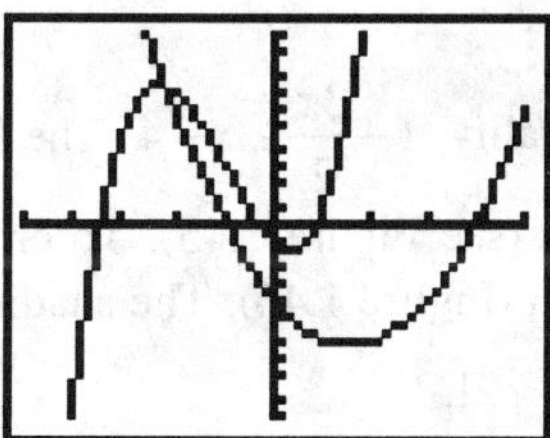

Figure 1.41: Solving a system of equations

The solutions of the system of two equations $y = x^3 + 3x^2 - 2x - 1$ and $y = x^2 - 3x - 4$ correspond to the solutions of the single equation $x^3 + 3x^2 - 2x - 1 = x^2 - 3x - 4$, which simplifies to $x^3 + 2x^2 + x + 3 = 0$. So you may also graph $y = x^3 + 2x^2 + x + 3$ and find its x-intercepts to solve the system.

1.3.4 Solving Inequalities by Graphing: Consider the inequality $1 - \frac{3x}{2} \geq x - 4$. To solve it with your TI-80, graph the two functions $y = 1 - \frac{3x}{2}$ and $y = x - 4$ (Figure 1.42). First locate their point of intersection, at $x = 2$. The inequality is true when the graph of $y = 1 - \frac{3x}{2}$ lies *above* the graph of $y = x - 4$, and that occurs for $x < 2$. So the solution is the half-line $x \leq 2$, or $(-\infty, 2]$.

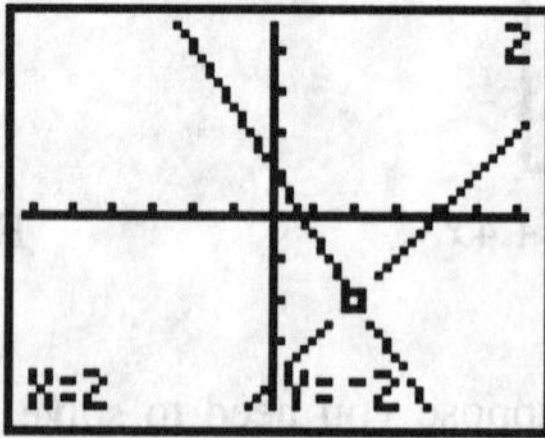

Figure 1.42: Solving $1 - \frac{3x}{2} \geq x - 4$

The TI-80 is capable of shading the region above or below a graph or between two graphs. For example, to graph $y \geq x^2 - 1$, first graph the function $y = x^2 - 1$ as Y1. Then press 2nd DRAW 6 2nd Y-VARS 1 ENTER (see Figure 1.43). These keystrokes instruct the TI-80 to shade the region *above* $y = x^2 - 1$. The result is shown in Figure 1.44. To clear the shading, press 2nd DRAW 1.

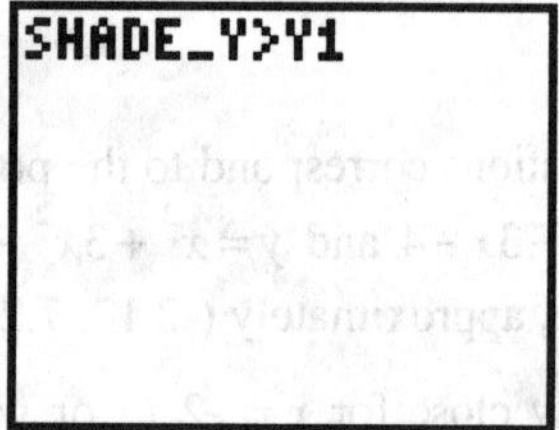

Figure 1.43: SHADE_Y> command

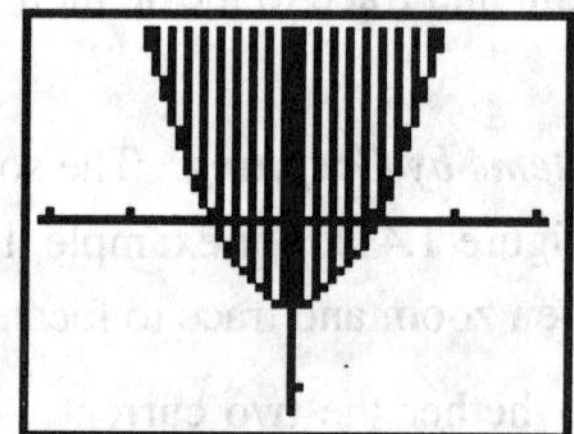

Figure 1.44: Graph of $y \geq x^2 - 1$

Now use shading to solve the previous inequality, $1 - \frac{3x}{2} \geq x - 4$. The function whose graph forms the *lower* boundary is named *first* in the SHADE command (see Figure 1.45). To enter this in your TI-80, press these keys: 2nd DRAW 8 X,T - 4 , 1 - 3 X,T ÷ 2 , 2) ENTER (Figure 1.46). The shading extends left from $x = 2$, hence the solution to $1 - \frac{3x}{2} \geq x - 4$ is the half-line $x \leq 2$, or $(-\infty, 2]$.

Figure 1.45: DRAW Shade command

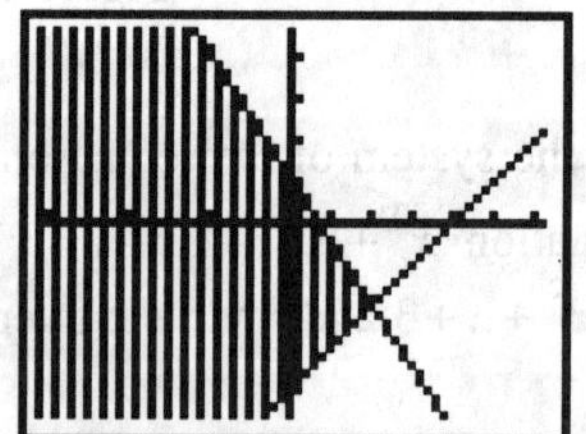

Figure 1.46: Graph of $1 - \frac{3x}{2} \geq x - 4$

TI-80 Graphics Calculator

More information about the DRAW menu is in the TI-80 manual.

1.4   Matrices

The TI-80 calculator does not perform matrix operations.

1.5   Additional Topics

1.5.1 Iteration: The ANS feature enables you to perform iterations to evaluate a function repeatedly. As an example, calculate $\dfrac{n-1}{3}$ for $n = 27$. Then calculate $\dfrac{n-1}{3}$ for n = the answer to the previous calculation. Continue to use each answer as n in the *next* calculation. Here are keystrokes to accomplish this iteration on the TI-80 calculator (see the results in Figure 1.47). Notice that when you use ANS in place of n in a formula, it is sufficient to press ENTER to continue an iteration.

Iteration	*Keystrokes*	*Display*
1	27 ENTER	27
2	(2nd ANS - 1) ÷ 3 ENTER	8.666666667
3	ENTER	2.555555556
4	ENTER	.5185185185
5	ENTER	-.1604938272

Figure 1.47: Iteration

Press ENTER several more times and see what happens with this iteration. You may wish to try it again with a different starting value.

1.5.2 Arithmetic and Geometric Sequences: Use iteration with the ANS variable to determine the n-th term of a sequence. For example, find the 18th term of an *arithmetic* sequence whose first term is 7 and whose common difference is 4. Enter the first term 7, then start the progression with the recursion formula, 2nd ANS + 4 ENTER. This yields the 2nd term, so press ENTER sixteen more times to find the 18th term. For a *geometric* sequence whose common ratio is 4, start the progression with 2nd ANS × 4 ENTER.

Of course, you could use the *explicit* formula for the n-th term of an arithmetic sequence, $t_n = a + (n-1)d$. First enter values for the variables a, d, and n, then evaluate the formula by pressing ALPHA A + (ALPHA N - 1) ALPHA D ENTER. For a geometric sequence whose n-th term is given by $t_n = a \cdot r^{n-1}$, enter values for the variables a, r, and n, then evaluate the formula by pressing ALPHA A ALPHA R ^ (ALPHA N - 1) ENTER.

You may also have the TI-80 make a list of values for a sequence. For an example, we'll continue to use the arithmetic sequence whose first term is 7 and whose common difference is 4; its formula is $t_n = 7 + 4 \cdot (n-1)$. So press 2nd LIST 4 (Figure 1.48); enter the formula $7 + 4 \cdot (n-1)$; and continue by pressing , ALPHA N , 1 , 20 , 1) STO▶ 2nd L1 ENTER (see Figure 1.49). These commands create a sequence and store it in the list L1. The sequence command has the format SEQ(*expression*, *variable*, *initial value*, *final value*, *increment*).

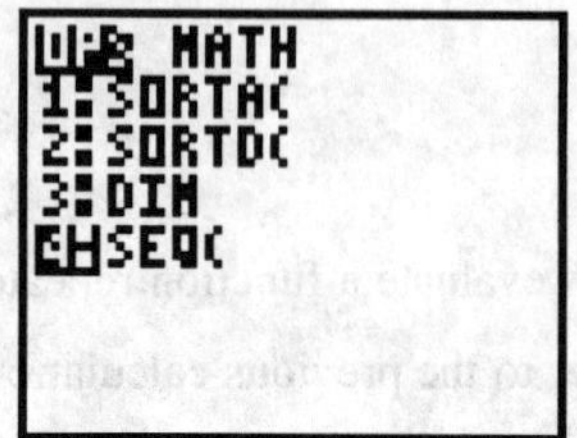

Figure 1.48: LIST options

Figure 1.49: Creating a sequence in a list

A TI-80 list has the format {*element element ... element*}. The list in Figure 1.49 does not display a close brace } so scroll with the right arrow key ▶ to see more of its elements.

Display the 18th term of the sequence stored in list L_1 by using ordinary function notation, $L_1(18)$.

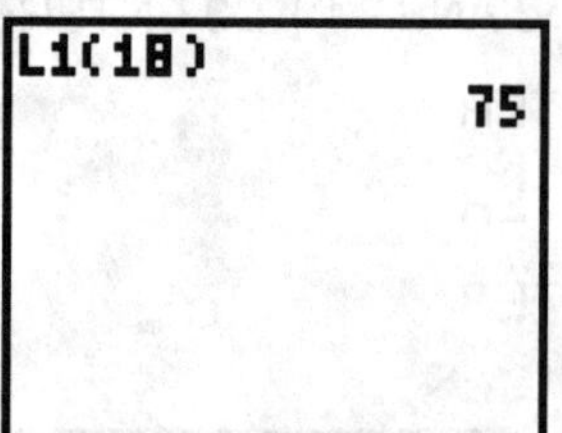

Figure 1.50: Element of a list

1.5.3 Permutations and Combinations: To calculate the number of *permutations* of 12 objects taken 7 at a time, $_{12}P_7$, press 12 MATH ◀ 2 7 ENTER. Thus $_{12}P_7 = 3,991,680$, as shown in Figure 1.51.

For the number of *combinations* of 12 objects taken 7 at a time, $_{12}C_7$, press 12 MATH ◀ 3 7 ENTER. So $_{12}C_7 = 792$.

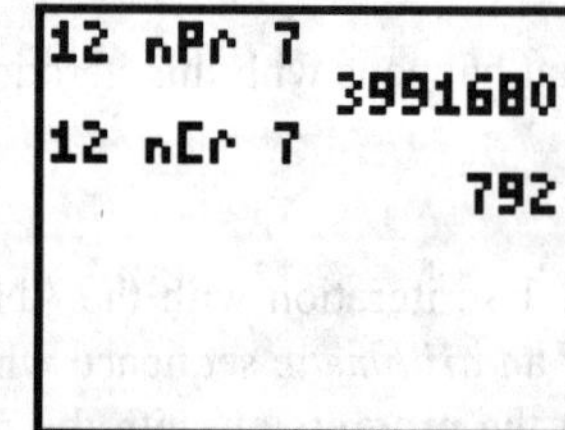

Figure 1.51: $_{12}P_7$ and $_{12}C_7$

1.6 Programming

1.6.1 Entering a Program: The TI-80 is a programmable calculator that can store sequences of commands for later replay. Here's an example to show you how to enter a useful program that solves quadratic equations by the quadratic formula.

Press PRGM to access the programming menu. The TI-80 has space for many programs, each called by a name you give it. Create a new program now, so press PRGM ◀ 1.

For convenience, the cursor is a blinking **A**, indicating that the calculator is set to receive alphabetic characters. Enter a descriptive title of up to seven characters, letters or numerals (but the first character must be a letter). Name this program QUADRAT and press ENTER to go to the program editor.

In the program, each line begins with a colon : supplied automatically by the calculator. Any command you could enter directly in the TI-80's home screen can be entered as a line in a program. There are also special programming commands.

Figure 1.52: Program QUADRAT

Input the program QUADRAT by pressing the keystrokes given in the listing below. You may interrupt program input at any stage by pressing 2nd QUIT. To return later for more editing, press PRGM ▶, move the cursor down to this program's name, and press ENTER.

Program Line	*Keystrokes*
: Disp "ENTER A"	PRGM ▶ 2 2nd A-LOCK " E N T E R ␣ A " ALPHA ENTER

displays the words *Enter A* on the TI-80 screen

: Input A	PRGM ▶ 1 ALPHA A ENTER

waits for you to input a value that will be assigned to the variable A

: Disp "ENTER B"	PRGM ▶ 2 2nd A-LOCK " E N T E R ␣ B " ALPHA ENTER
: Input B	PRGM ▶ 1 ALPHA B ENTER
: Disp "ENTER C"	PRGM ▶ 2 2nd A-LOCK " E N T E R ␣ C " ALPHA ENTER
: Input C	PRGM ▶ 1 ALPHA C ENTER
: B²-4AC → D	ALPHA B x² - 4 ALPHA A ALPHA C STO▶ ALPHA D ENTER

calculates the discriminant and stores its value as D

: If D>0	PRGM 1 ALPHA D 2nd TEST 3 0 ENTER

tests to see if the discriminant is positive

: Then   PRGM 2 ENTER

    in case the discriminant is positive, continues on to the next line;
    if the discriminant is not positive, jumps to the command after Else below

: Disp "TWO REAL   PRGM ▶ 2 2nd A-LOCK " T W O ␣ R E A L ␣ R O O T S "
ROOTS"   ALPHA ENTER

: (-B+√D)/(2A) → M   ((-) ALPHA B + 2nd √ ALPHA D) ÷ (2 ALPHA A)
                             STO▶ ALPHA M ENTER

    calculates one root and stores it as M

: Disp M   PRGM ▶ 2 ALPHA M ENTER

    displays one root

: (-B-√D)/(2A) → N   ((-) ALPHA B - 2nd √ ALPHA D) ÷ (2 ALPHA A)
                             STO▶ ALPHA N ENTER

: Disp N   PRGM ▶ 2 ALPHA N ENTER

: Else   PRGM 3 ENTER

    continues from here if the discriminant is not positive

: If D=0   PRGM 1 ALPHA D 2nd TEST 1 0 ENTER

    tests to see if the discriminant is zero

: Then   PRGM 2 ENTER

    in case the discriminant is zero, continues on to the next line;
    if the discriminant is not zero, jumps to the command after Else below

: Disp "DOUBLE   PRGM ▶ 2 2nd A-LOCK " D O U B L E ␣ R O O T " ENTER
ROOT"

    displays a message in case there is a double root

: -B/(2A) → M   (-) ALPHA B ÷ (2 ALPHA A) STO▶ ALPHA M ENTER

    the quadratic formula reduces to $\dfrac{-b}{2a}$ when $D = 0$

: Disp M   PRGM ▶ 2 ALPHA M ENTER

: Else   PRGM 3 ENTER

    continues from here if the discriminant is not zero

: Disp "COMPLEX   PRGM ▶ 2 2nd A-LOCK " C O M P L E X ␣ R O O T S "
ROOTS"   ALPHA ENTER

    displays a message in case the roots are complex numbers

: Disp "REAL PART"   PRGM ▶ 2 2nd A-LOCK " R E A L ␣ P A R T " ALPHA ENTER

: -B/(2A) → R   (-) ALPHA B ÷ (2 ALPHA A) STO▶ ALPHA R ENTER

    calculates the real part $\dfrac{-b}{2a}$ of the complex roots

: Disp R	PRGM ▶ 2 ALPHA R ENTER
: Disp "IMAGINARY PART"	PRGM ▶ 2 2nd A-LOCK " I M A G I N A R Y ␣ P A R T " ALPHA ENTER
: √-D/(2A) → I	2nd √ (-) ALPHA D ÷ (2 ALPHA A) STO▶ ALPHA I ENTER

calculates the imaginary part $\dfrac{\sqrt{-D}}{2a}$ of the complex roots;
since $D < 0$, we must use $-D$ as the radicand

| : Disp I | PRGM ▶ 3 ALPHA I ENTER |
| : End | PRGM 5 ENTER |

marks the end of an If-Then-Else group of commands

| : End | PRGM 5 |

When you have finished, press 2nd QUIT to leave the program editor.

You may remove a program from memory by pressing 2nd MEM 2 *[Delete...]*. Then move the cursor to the program's name and press ENTER to delete the entire program.

1.6.2 Running a Program: To run the program just entered, from the home screen press PRGM, use the arrow keys to find its name in the alphabetical program listing. then ENTER.

The program has been written to prompt you for values of the coefficients a, b, and c in a quadratic equation $ax^2 + bx + c = 0$. Input a value, then press ENTER to continue the program.

If you need to interrupt a program during execution, press ON.

The instruction manual for your TI-80 gives detailed information about programming. Refer to it to learn more about programming and how to use other features of your calculator.

Chapter 2

Texas Instruments TI-81
Graphics Calculator

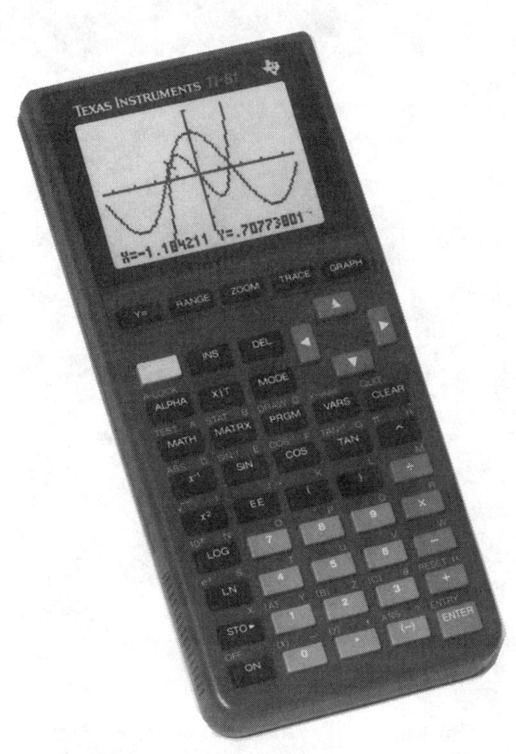

2.1 Getting started with the TI-81

2.1.1 Basics: Press the ON key to begin using your TI-81 calculator. If you need to adjust the display contrast, first press 2nd, then press and hold ▲ (the *up* arrow key) to increase the contrast or ▼ (the *down* arrow key) to decrease the contrast. As you press and hold ▲ or ▼, an integer between 0 (lightest) and 9 (darkest) appears in the upper right corner of the display. When you have finished with the calculator, turn it off to conserve battery power by pressing 2nd and then OFF.

Check the TI-81's settings by pressing MODE. If necessary, use the arrow keys to move the blinking cursor to a setting you want to change. Press ENTER to select a new setting. To start with, select the options along the left side of the MODE menu as illustrated in Figure 2.1: normal display, floating decimals, radian measure, function graphs, connected lines, sequential plotting, grid off, and rectangular coordinates. Details on alternative options will be given later in this guide. For now, leave the MODE menu by pressing CLEAR.

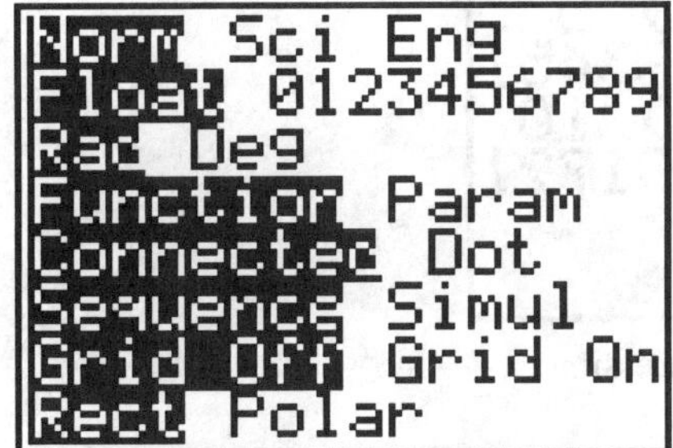

Figure 2.1: MODE menu

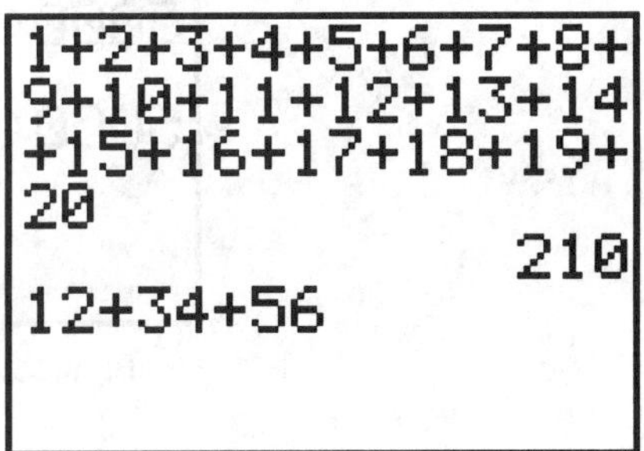

Figure 2.2: Home screen

2.1.2 Editing: One advantage of the TI-81 is that up to 8 lines are visible at one time, so you can *see* a long calculation. For example, type this sum (see Figure 2.2):

$$1 + 2 + 3 + 4 + 5 + 6 + 7 + 8 + 9 + 10 + 11 + 12 + 13 + 14 + 15 + 16 + 17 + 18 + 19 + 20$$

Then press ENTER to see the answer, too.

Often we do not notice a mistake until we see how unreasonable an answer is. The TI-81 permits you to re-display an entire calculation, edit it easily, then execute the *corrected* calculation.

Suppose you had typed 12 + 34 + 56 as in Figure 2.2 but had *not* yet pressed ENTER, when you realize that 34 should have been 74. Simply press ◄ (the *left* arrow key) as many times as necessary to move the blinking cursor left to 3, then type 7 to write over it. On the other hand, if 34 should have been 384, move the cursor back to 4, press INS (the cursor changes to a blinking underline) and then type 8 (inserts at the cursor position and other characters are pushed to the right). If the 34 should have been 3 only, move the cursor to 4 and press DEL to delete it.

Even if you had pressed ENTER, you may still edit the previous expression. Press 2nd and then ENTRY to *recall* the last expression that was entered. Now you can change it. If you have not pressed any key since the last ENTER, you can recall the previous expression by pressing ▲.

Technology Tip: When you need to evaluate a formula for different values of a variable, use the editing feature to simplify the process. For example, suppose you want to find the balance in an investment account if there is now $5000 in the account and interest is compounded annually at the rate of 8.5%. The formula for the balance is $P\left(1 + \frac{r}{n}\right)^{nt}$, where P = principal, r = rate of interest (expressed as a decimal), n = number of times interest is com-

pounded each year, and t = number of years. In our example, this becomes $5000(1+.085)^t$. Here are the keystrokes for finding the balance after $t = 3, 5,$ and 10 years.

Years	*Keystrokes*	*Balance*
3	5000 (1 + .085) ^ 3 ENTER	$6386.45
5	◢ ◁ 5 ENTER	$7518.28
10	◢ ◁ 10 ENTER	$11,304.92

Figure 2.3: Editing expressions

Then to find the balance from the same initial investment but after 5 years when the annual interest rate is 7.5%, press these keys to change the last calculation above: ◢ ◁ DEL ◁ 5 ◁ ◁ ◁ ◁ ◁ 7 ENTER.

2.1.3 Key Functions: Most keys on the TI-81 offer access to more than one function, just as the keys on a computer keyboard can produce more than one letter ("g" and "G") or even quite different characters ("5" and "%"). The primary function of a key is indicated on the key itself, and you access that function by a simple press on the key.

To access the *second* function indicated to the *left* above a key, first press 2nd (the cursor changes to a blinking ↑) and *then* press the key. For example, to calculate $\sqrt{25}$, press 2nd $\sqrt{\ }$ 25 ENTER.

When you want to use a letter or other character printed to the *right* above a key, first press ALPHA (the cursor changes to a blinking **A**) and then the key. For example, to use the letter K in a formula, press ALPHA K. If you need several letters in a row, press 2nd A-LOCK, which is like Caps Lock on a computer keyboard, and then press all the letters you want. Remember to press ALPHA when you are finished and want to restore the keys to their primary functions.

2.1.4 Order of Operations: The TI-81 performs calculations according to the standard algebraic rules. Working outwards from inner parentheses, calculations are performed from left to right. Powers and roots are evaluated first, followed by multiplications and divisions, and then additions and subtractions.

Note that the TI-81 distinguishes between *subtraction* and the *negative sign*. If you wish to enter a negative number, it is necessary to use the (-) key. For example, you would evaluate $-5-(4\cdot-3)$ by pressing (-) 5 - (4 × (-) 3) ENTER to get 7.

Enter these expressions to practice using your TI-81.

Expression	Keystrokes	Display
$7 - 5 \cdot 3$	7 - 5 × 3 ENTER	-8
$(7 - 5) \cdot 3$	(7 - 5) × 3 ENTER	6
$120 - 10^2$	120 - 10 x² ENTER	20
$(120 - 10)^2$	(120 - 10) x² ENTER	12100
$\dfrac{24}{2^3}$	24 ÷ 2 ^ 3 ENTER	3
$\left(\dfrac{24}{2}\right)^3$	(24 ÷ 2) ^ 3 ENTER	1728
$(7 - -5) \cdot -3$	(7 - (-) 5) × (-) 3 ENTER	-36

2.1.5 Algebraic Expressions and Memory: Your calculator can evaluate expressions such as $\dfrac{N(N+1)}{2}$ *after* you have entered a value for N. Suppose you want $N = 200$. Press 200 STO ► N ENTER to store the value 200 in memory location N. (The STO ► key prepares the TI-81 for an alphabetical entry, so it is *not* necessary to press ALPHA also.) Whenever you use N in an expression, the calculator will substitute the value 200 until you make a change by storing *another* number in N. Next enter the expression $\dfrac{N(N+1)}{2}$ by typing ALPHA N (ALPHA N + 1) ÷ 2 ENTER. For $N = 200$, you will find that $\dfrac{N(N+1)}{2} = 20100$.

The contents of any memory location may be revealed by typing just its letter name and then ENTER. And the TI-81 retains memorized values even when it is turned off, so long as its batteries are good.

2.1.6 Repeated Operations with ANS: The result of your *last* calculation is always stored in memory location ANS and replaces any previous result. This makes it easy to use the answer from one computation in another computation. For example, press 30 + 15 ENTER so that 45 is the last result displayed. Then press 2nd ANS ÷ 9 ENTER and get 5 because $\frac{45}{9} = 5$.

With a function like division, you press the ÷ key *after* you enter an argument. For such functions, whenever you would start a new calculation with the previous answer followed by pressing the function key, you may press just the function key. So instead of 2nd ANS ÷ 9 in the previous example, you could have pressed simply ÷ 9 to achieve the same result. This technique also works for these functions: + - × x² ^ x⁻¹.

Here is a situation where this is especially useful. Suppose a person makes \$5.85 per hour and you are asked to calculate earnings for a day, a week, and a year. Execute the given keystrokes to find the person's incomes during these periods (results are shown in Figure 2.4):

Pay period	Keystrokes	Earnings
8-hour day	5.85 × 8 ENTER	\$46.80
5-day week	× 5 ENTER	\$234
52-week year	× 52 ENTER	\$12,168

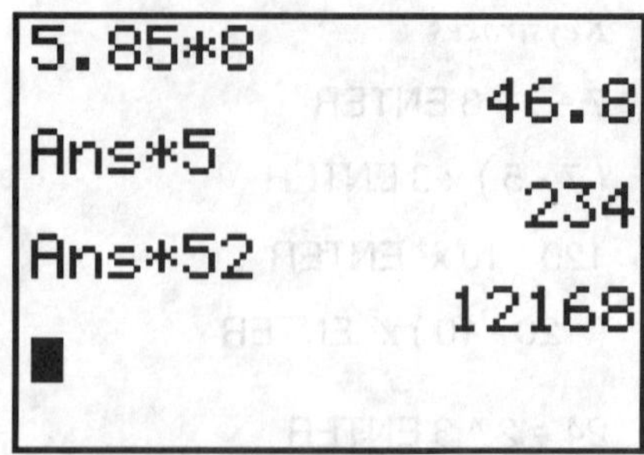

Figure 2.4: ANS variable

2.1.7 The MATH Menu: Operators and functions associated with a scientific calculator are available either immediately from the keys of the TI-81 or by 2nd keys. You have direct key access to common arithmetic operations (x^2, 2nd $\sqrt{}$, x^{-1}, ^, 2nd ABS), exponential and logarithmic functions (LOG, 2nd 10^x, LN, 2nd e^x), and a famous constant (2nd π).

A significant difference between the TI-81 and many scientific calculators is that the TI-81 requires the argument of a function *after* the function, as you would see a formula written in your textbook. For example, on the TI-81 you calculate $\sqrt{16}$ by pressing the keys 2nd $\sqrt{}$ 16 in that order.

Here are keystrokes for basic mathematical operations. Try them for practice on your TI-81.

Expression	Keystrokes	Display
$\sqrt{3^2 + 4^2}$	2nd $\sqrt{}$ (3 x^2 + 4 x^2) ENTER	5
$2\frac{1}{3}$	2 + 3 x^{-1} ENTER	2.333333333
$\lvert -5 \rvert$	2nd ABS (-) 5 ENTER	5
$\log 200$	LOG 200 ENTER	2.301029996
$2.34 \cdot 10^5$	2.34 × 2nd 10^x 5 ENTER	234000

Additional mathematical operations and functions are available from the MATH menu (Figure 2.5). Press MATH to see the various options. You will learn in your mathematics textbook how to apply many of them. As an example, calculate $\sqrt[3]{7}$ by pressing MATH and then *either* 4 *or* ▼ ▼ ▼ ENTER; finally press 7 ENTER to see 1.912931183. To leave the MATH menu and take no other action, press 2nd QUIT or just CLEAR.

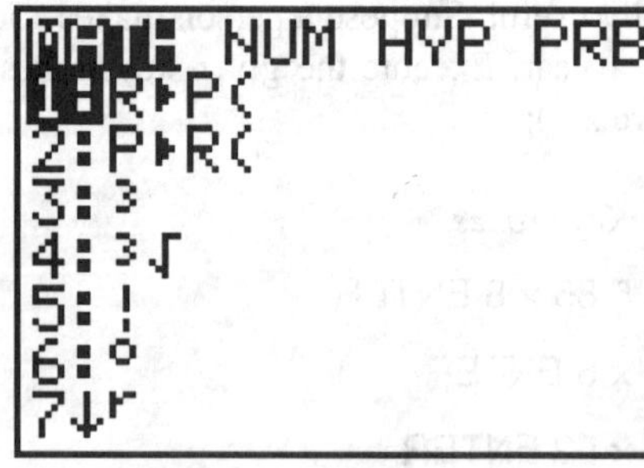

Figure 2.5: MATH menu

The *factorial* of a non-negative integer is the *product* of *all* the integers from 1 up to the given integer. The symbol for factorial is the exclamation point. So 4! (pronounced *four factorial*) is $1 \cdot 2 \cdot 3 \cdot 4 = 24$. You will learn more about applications of factorials in your textbook, but for now use the TI-81 to calculate 4! Press these keystrokes: 4 MATH 5 ENTER *or* 4 MATH ▼ ▼ ▼ ▼ ENTER ENTER.

Note that you can select a sub-menu from the MATH menu by pressing either ◄ or ►. It is easier to press ◄ once than to press ► three times to get to the PRB sub-menu.

2.2   Functions and Graphs

2.2.1 Evaluating Functions: Suppose you receive a monthly salary of $1975 plus a commission of 10% of sales. Let x = your sales in dollars; then your wages W in dollars are given by the equation $W = 1975 + .10x$. If your January sales were $2230 and your February sales were $1865, what was your income during those months?

Here's how to use your TI-81 to perform this task. Press the Y= key at the top of the calculator to display the function editing screen (Figure 2.6). You may enter as many as four different functions for the TI-81 to use at one time. If there is already a function Y_1, press ▲ or ▼ as many times as necessary to move the cursor to Y_1 and then press CLEAR to delete whatever was there. Then enter the expression $1975 + .10x$ by pressing these keys: 1975 + .10 X|T. (The X|T key lets you enter the variable x easily without having to use the ALPHA key.) Now press 2nd QUIT to return to the main calculations screen.

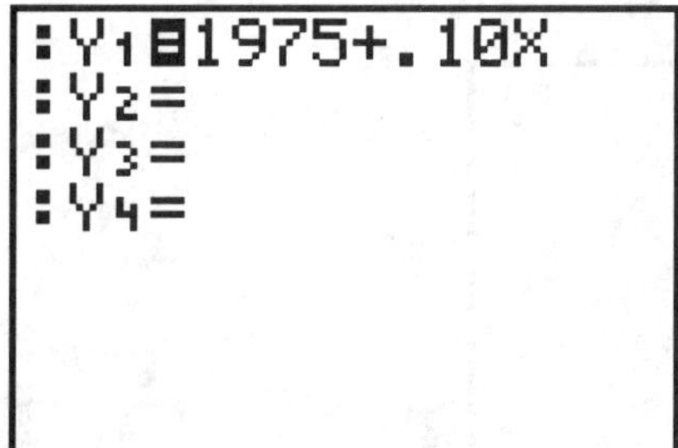

Figure 2.6: Y= screen

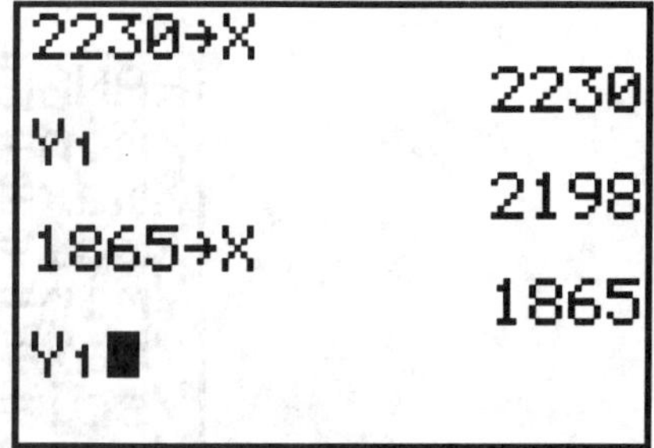

Figure 2.7: Evaluating a function

Assign the value 2230 to the variable x by these keystrokes (see Figure 2.7): 2230 STO ► X|T ENTER. Next press the following keystrokes to evaluate Y_1 and find January's wages: 2nd Y-VARS 1 ENTER. Repeat these steps to find the February wages. Each time the TI-81 evaluates the function Y_1, it uses the *current* value of x.

Technology Tip: The TI-81 does not require multiplication to be expressed between variables, so xxx means x^3. It is often easier to press two or three x's together than to search for the square key or the cube operation. Of course, expressed multiplication is also not required between a constant and a variable. Hence to enter $2x^3 + 3x^2 - 4x + 5$ in the TI-81, you might save keystrokes and press just these keys: 2 X|T X|T X|T + 3 X|T X|T - 4 X|T + 5.

2.2.2 Functions in a Graph Window: Once you have entered a function in the Y= screen of the TI-81, just press GRAPH to see its graph. The ability to draw a graph contributes substantially to our ability to solve problems.

For example, here is how to graph $y = -x^3 + 4x$. First press Y= and delete anything that may be there by moving with the arrow keys to Y_1 or to any of the other lines and pressing CLEAR wherever necessary. Then, with the cursor on the top line Y_1, press (-) X|T MATH 3 + 4 X|T to enter the function (as in Figure 2.8). Now press GRAPH and the TI-81 changes to a window with the graph of $y = -x^3 + 4x$.

Your graph window may look like the one in Figure 2.9 or it may be different. Since the graph of $y = -x^3 + 4x$ extends infinitely far left and right and also infinitely far up and down, the TI-81 can display only a piece of the actual graph. This displayed rectangular part is called a *viewing rectangle*. You can easily change the viewing rectangle to enhance your investigation of a graph.

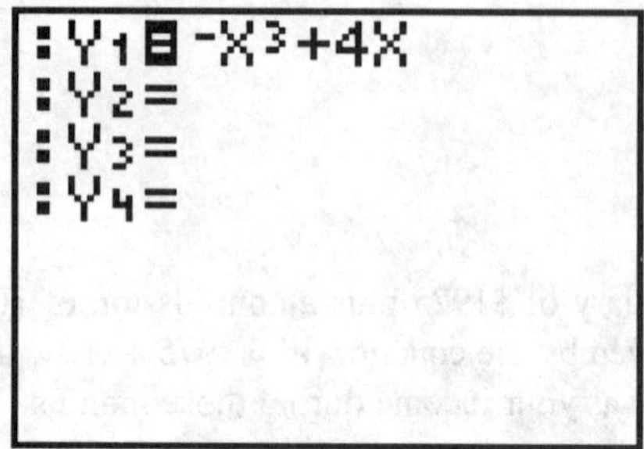

Figure 2.8: Y= screen

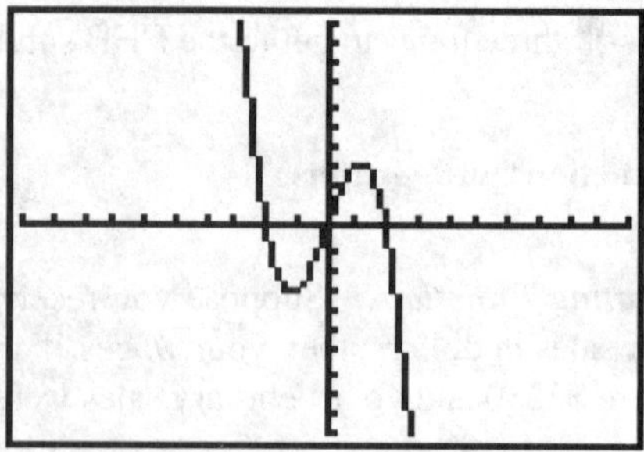

Figure 2.9: Graph of $y = -x^3 + 4x$

The viewing rectangle in Figure 2.9 shows the part of the graph that extends horizontally from -10 to 10 and vertically from -10 to 10. Press RANGE to see information about your viewing rectangle. Figure 2.10 shows the RANGE screen that corresponds to the viewing rectangle in Figure 2.9. This is the *standard* viewing rectangle for the TI-81.

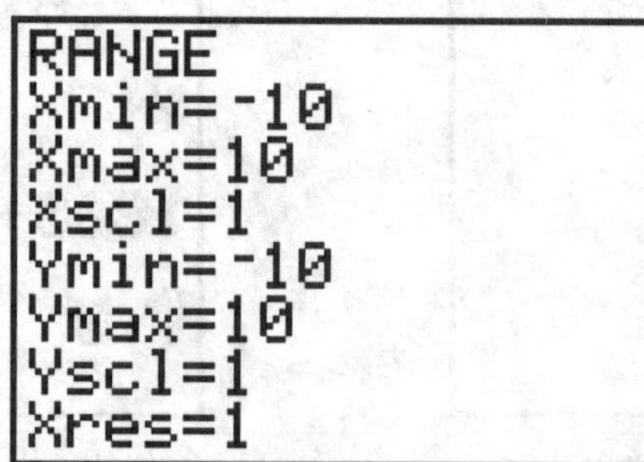

Figure 2.10: Standard RANGE

The variables Xmin and Xmax are the minimum and maximum *x*-values of the viewing rectangle; Ymin and Ymax are its minimum and maximum *y*-values.

Xscl and Yscl set the spacing between tick marks on the axes.

Xres is an integer from 1 to 8 that controls the resolution of the plot and also the speed of plotting. When Xres = 1, the calculator evaluates the function and plots a point 96 times along the *x*-axis. When Xres = 2, the calculator evaluates and plots at every *second* point, 48 times along the *x*-axis. Keep Xres = 1 to have the best resolution for your graphs.

Use the arrow keys ▲ and ▼ to move up and down from one line to another in this list; pressing the ENTER key will move down the list. Press CLEAR to delete the current value and then enter a new value. You may also edit the entry as you would edit an expression. Remember that a minimum *must* be less than the corresponding maximum or the TI-81 will issue an error message. Also, remember to use the (-) key, not - (which is subtraction), when you want to enter a negative value. The following figures show different RANGE screens and the corresponding viewing rectangle for each one.

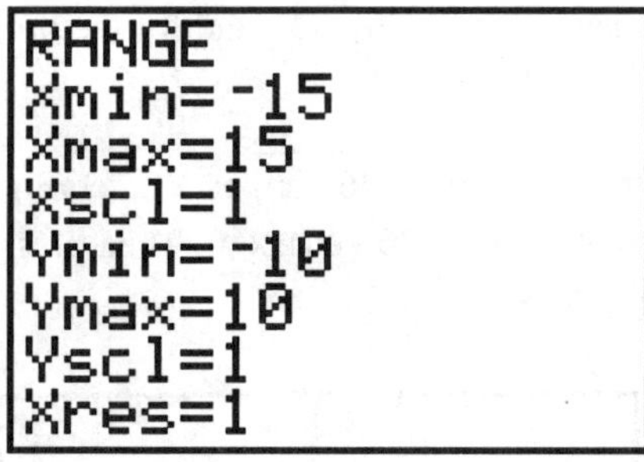

Figure 2.11: Square window

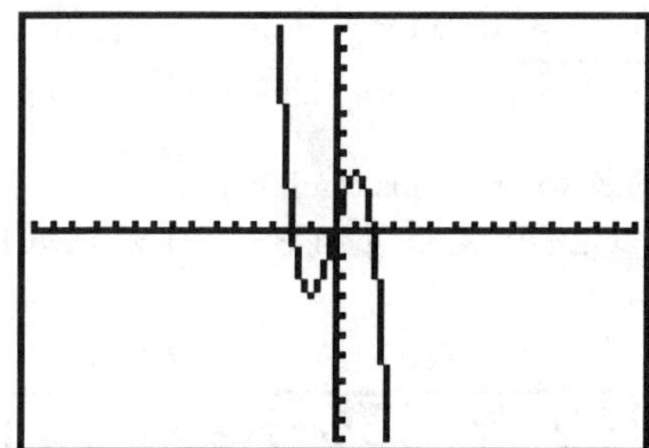

Figure 2.12: Graph of $y = -x^3 + 4x$

To set the range quickly to standard values (see Figure 2.10), press ZOOM 6. To set the viewing rectangle quickly to a square (Figure 2.11), press ZOOM 5. More information about square windows is presented later in Section 2.2.3.

Sometimes you may wish to display grid points corresponding to tick marks on the axes. In the MODE menu (Figure 2.1), use arrow keys to move the blinking cursor to Grid On, then press ENTER and 2nd QUIT GRAPH. Figure 2.15 shows the same graph as in Figure 2.14 but with the grid turned on. In general, you'll want the grid turned *off*, so do that now by pressing MODE, use the arrow keys to move the blinking cursor to Grid Off, and press ENTER.

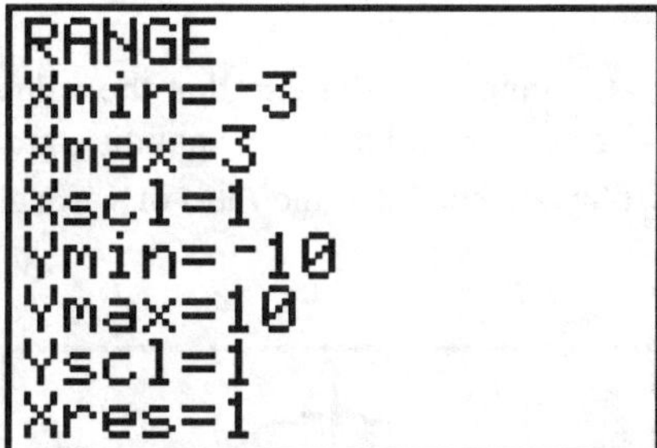

Figure 2.13: Custom window

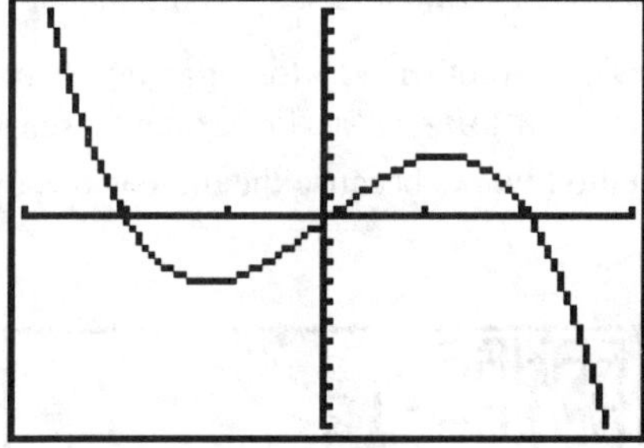

Figure 2.14: Graph of $y = -x^3 + 4x$

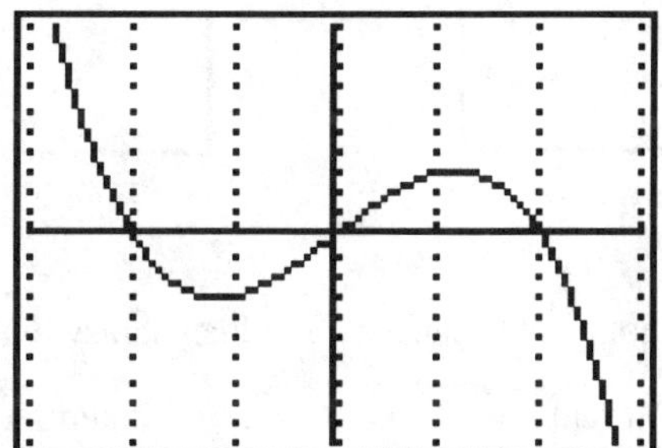

Figure 2.15: Grid turned on for $y = -x^3 + 4x$

2.2.3 Graphing a Circle: Here is a useful technique for graphs that are not functions, but that can be "split" into a top part and a bottom part, or into multiple parts. Suppose you wish to graph the circle whose equation is

$x^2 + y^2 = 36$. First solve for y and get an equation for the top semicircle, $y = \sqrt{36 - x^2}$, and for the bottom semicircle, $y = -\sqrt{36 - x^2}$. Then graph the two semicircles simultaneously.

The keystrokes to draw this circle's graph follow. Enter $\sqrt{36 - x^2}$ as Y_1 and $-\sqrt{36 - x^2}$ as Y_2 (see Figure 2.16) by pressing Y= CLEAR 2nd √ (36 - X|T x²) ENTER CLEAR (-) 2nd √ (36 - X|T x²). Then press GRAPH to draw them both.

Figure 2.16: Two semicircles

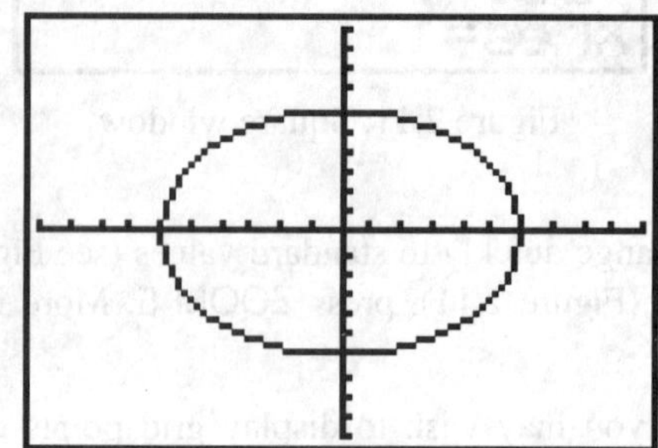

Figure 2.17: Circle's graph - standard view

If your range were set to the standard viewing rectangle, your graph would look like Figure 2.17. Now this does *not* look like a circle, because the units along the axes are not the same. This is where the square viewing rectangle is important. Press ZOOM 5 and see a graph that appears more circular.

Technology Tip: Another way to get a square graph is to change the range variables so that the value of Ymax - Ymin is $\frac{2}{3}$ times Xmax - Xmin. For example, see the RANGE in Figure 2.18 and the corresponding graph in Figure 2.19. The method works because the dimensions of the TI-81's display are such that the ratio of vertical to horizontal is $\frac{2}{3}$.

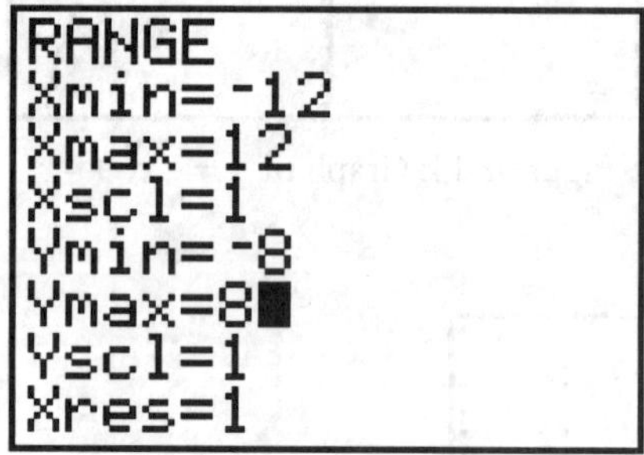

Figure 2.18: $\frac{\text{vertical}}{\text{horizontal}} = \frac{16}{24} = \frac{2}{3}$

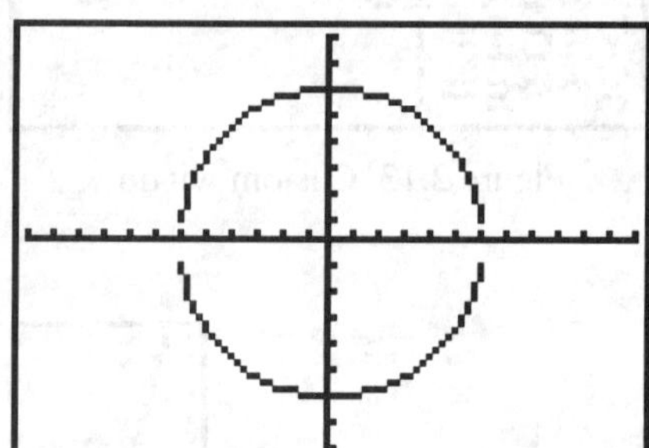

Figure 2.19: A "square" circle

The two semicircles in Figure 2.19 do not meet because of an idiosyncrasy in the way the TI-81 plots a graph.

Back when you entered $\sqrt{36 - x^2}$ as Y_1 and $-\sqrt{36 - x^2}$ as Y_2, you could have entered -Y_1 as Y_2 and saved some keystrokes. Try this by going back to the Y= menu and pressing the arrow key to move the cursor down to Y_2. Then press CLEAR (-) 2nd Y-VARS 1. The graph should be just as it was before.

Technology Tip: The square viewing rectangle is also important when you want to judge whether two lines are perpendicular. The intersection of perpendicular lines will always *look* like a right angle in a square viewing rectangle.

TI-81 Graphics Calculator

2.2.4 TRACE: Graph $y = -x^3 + 4x$ in the standard viewing rectangle. Press any of the arrow keys ▲ ▼ ◄ ►
and see the cursor move from the center of the viewing rectangle. The coordinates of the cursor's location are displayed at the bottom of the screen, as in Figure 2.20, in floating decimal format. This cursor is called a *free-moving cursor* because it can move from dot to dot *anywhere* in the graph window.

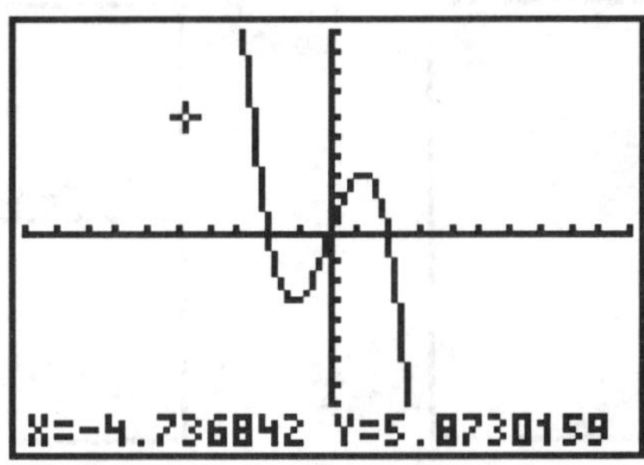

Figure 2.20: Free-moving cursor

Remove the free-moving cursor and its coordinates from the window by pressing GRAPH or ENTER. If you press GRAPH, the next time you press an arrow key the free-moving cursor will appear again from the center of the viewing rectangle. If you press ENTER, the cursor will reappear at the same point you left it.

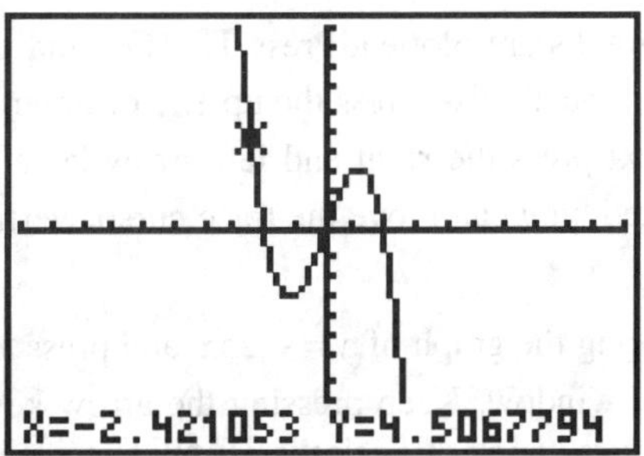

Figure 2.21: Trace on $y = -x^3 + 4x$

Press TRACE to enable the left ◄ and right ► arrow keys to move the cursor along the function. The cursor is no longer free-moving, but is now constrained to the function. The coordinates that are displayed belong to points on the function's graph, so the y-coordinate is the calculated value of the function at the corresponding x-coordinate.

Now plot a second function, $y = -.25x$, along with $y = -x^3 + 4x$. Press Y= and enter $-.25x$ for Y_2, then press GRAPH.

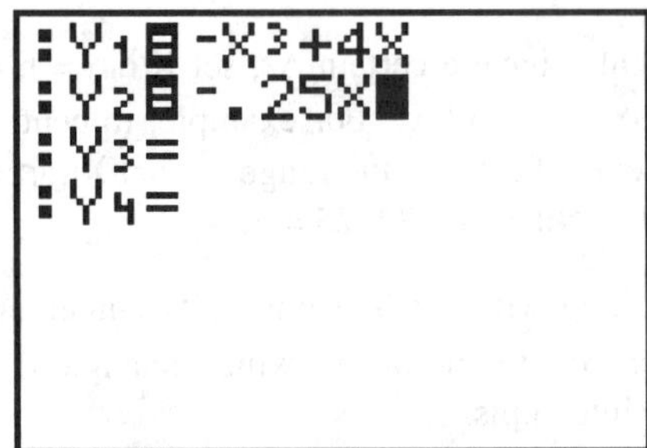

Figure 2.22: Two functions

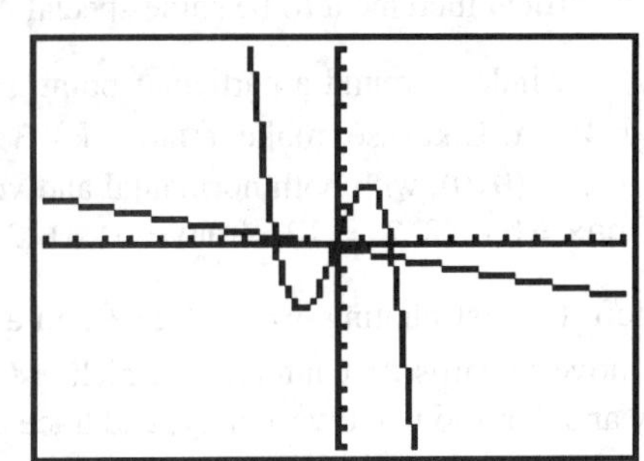

Figure 2.23: $y = -x^3 + 4x$ and $y = -.25x$

Note in Figure 2.22 that the equal signs next to Y_1 and Y_2 are *both* highlighted. This means *both* functions will be graphed. In the Y= screen, move the cursor directly on top of the equal sign next to Y_1 and press ENTER. This equal sign should no longer be highlighted (see Figure 2.24). Now press GRAPH and see that only Y_2 is plotted (Figure 2.25).

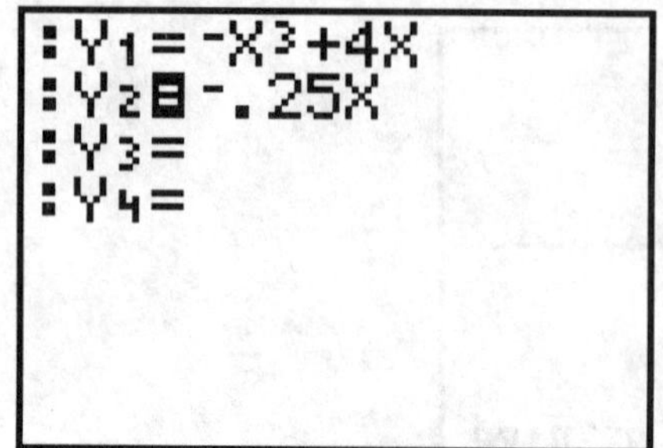

Figure 2.24: Y= screen with only Y_2 active

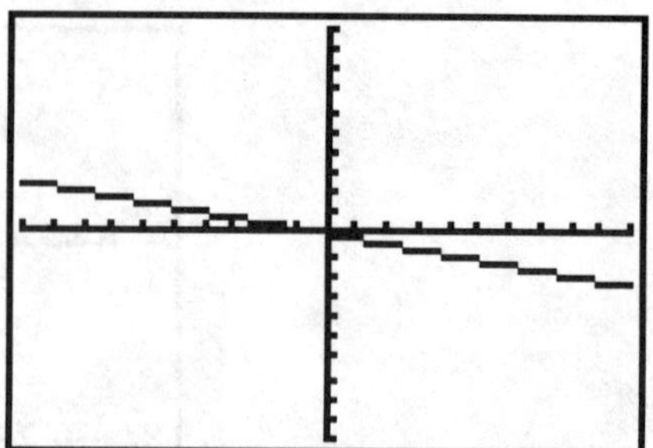

Figure 2.25: Graph of $y = -.25x$

So up to 4 different functions may be stored in the Y= list and any combination of them may be graphed simultaneously. You can make a function active or inactive for graphing by pressing ENTER on its equal sign to highlight (activate) or remove the highlight (deactivate). Go back to the Y= screen and do what is needed in order to graph Y_1 but not Y_2.

Now activate Y_2 again so that both graphs are plotted. Press TRACE and the cursor appears first on the graph of $y = -x^3 + 4x$ because it is higher up in the Y= list. Press the up ▲ or down ▼ arrow key to move the cursor vertically to the graph of $y = -.25x$. Next press the right and left arrow keys to trace along the graph of $y = -.25x$. When more than one function is plotted, you can move the trace cursor vertically from one graph to another in this way.

Technology Tip: By the way, trace along the graph of $y = -.25x$ and press and hold either ◄ or ►. Eventually you will reach the left or right edge of the window. Keep pressing the arrow key and the TI-81 will allow you to continue the trace by panning the viewing rectangle. Check the RANGE screen to see that Xmin and Xmax are automatically updated.

The TI-81's display has 96 horizontal columns of pixels and 64 vertical rows. So when you trace a curve across a graph window, you are actually moving from Xmin to Xmax in 95 equal jumps, each called Δx. You would calculate the size of each jump to be $\Delta x = \dfrac{\text{Xmax} - \text{Xmin}}{95}$. Sometimes you may want the jumps to be friendly numbers like .1 or .25 so that, when you trace along the curve, the x-coordinates will be incremented by such a convenient amount. Just set your viewing rectangle for a particular increment Δx by making Xmax = Xmin + 95·Δx. For example, if you want Xmin = -5 and Δx = .3, set Xmax = -5 + 95·.3 = 23.5. Likewise, set Ymax = Ymin + 63·Δy if you want the vertical increment to be some special Δy.

To center your window around a particular point, say (h, k), and also have a certain Δx, set Xmin = h - 47·Δx and Xmax = h + 48·Δx. Likewise, make Ymin = k - 31·Δy and Ymax = k + 32·Δy. For example, to center a window around the origin, (0, 0), with both horizontal and vertical increments of .25, set the range so that Xmin = 0 - 47·.25 = -11.75, Xmax = 0 + 48·.25 = 12, Ymin = 0 - 31·.25 = -7.75, and Ymax = 0 + 32·.25 = 8.

See the benefit by first plotting $y = x^2 + 2x + 1$ in a standard graphing window. Trace near its y-intercept, which is (0, 1), and move towards its x-intercept, which is (-1, 0). Then change to another viewing rectangle from -9 to 10 horizontally and from -6 to 6.6 vertically, and trace again near the intercepts.

2.2.5 ZOOM: Plot again the two graphs, for $y = -x^3 + 4x$ and for $y = -.25x$. There appears to be an intersection near $x = 2$. The TI-81 provides several ways to enlarge the view around this point. You can change the viewing rectangle directly by pressing RANGE and editing the values of Xmin, Xmax, Ymin, and Ymax. Figure 2.27 shows a new viewing rectangle for the range displayed in Figure 2.26. Trace has been turned on and the coordinates of a point on $y = -x^3 + 4x$ that is close to the intersection are displayed.

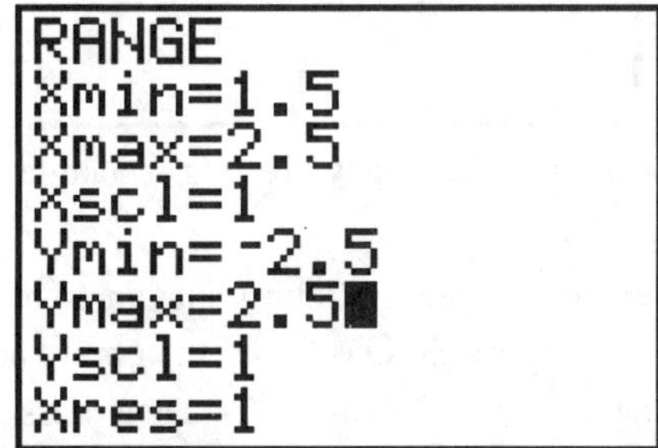

Figure 2.26: New RANGE

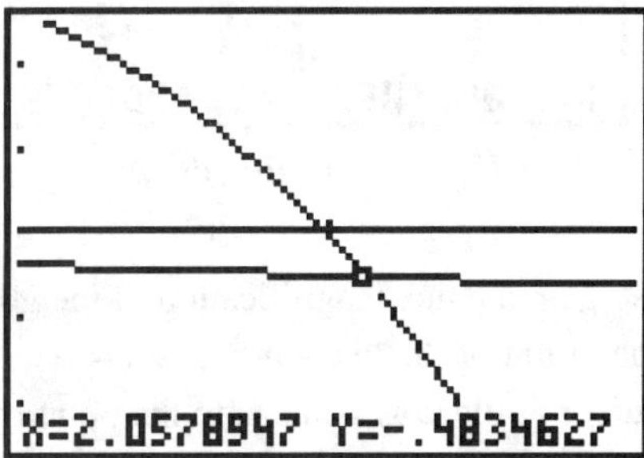

Figure 2.27: Closer view

A more efficient method for enlarging the view is to draw a new viewing rectangle with the cursor. Start again with a graph of the two functions $y = -x^3 + 4x$ and $y = -.25x$ in a standard viewing rectangle (press ZOOM 6 for the standard window, from -10 to 10 along both axes).

Now imagine a small rectangular box around the intersection point, near $x = 2$. Press ZOOM 1 (Figure 2.28) to draw a box to define this new viewing rectangle. Use the arrow keys to move the cursor, whose coordinates are displayed at the bottom of the window, to one corner of the new viewing rectangle you imagine.

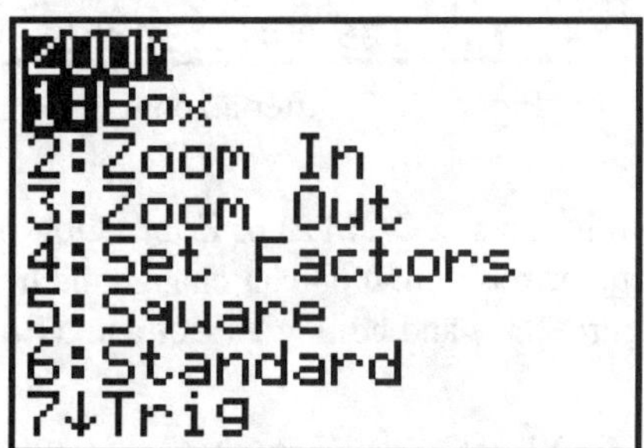

Figure 2.28: ZOOM menu

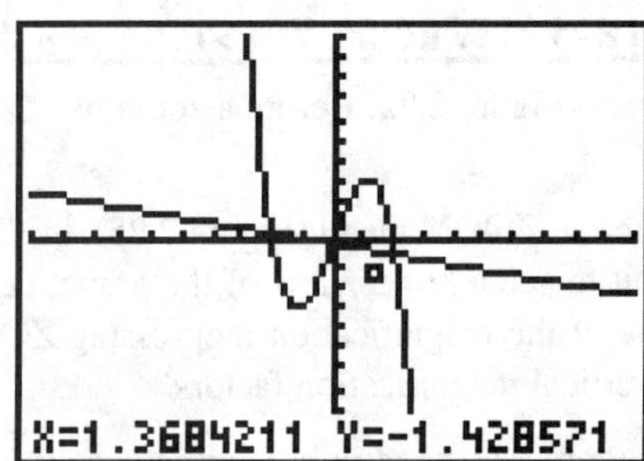

Figure 2.29: One corner selected

Press ENTER to fix the corner where you have moved the cursor; it changes shape and becomes a blinking square (Figure 2.29). Use the arrow keys again to move the cursor to the diagonally opposite corner of the new rectangle (Figure 2.30). If this box looks all right to you, press ENTER. The rectangular area you have enclosed will now enlarge to fill the graph window (Figure 2.31).

You may cancel the zoom any time *before* you press this last ENTER. Press 2nd QUIT to cancel the zoom and return to the home screen, or select another screen by pressing GRAPH or ZOOM and also cancel the zoom.

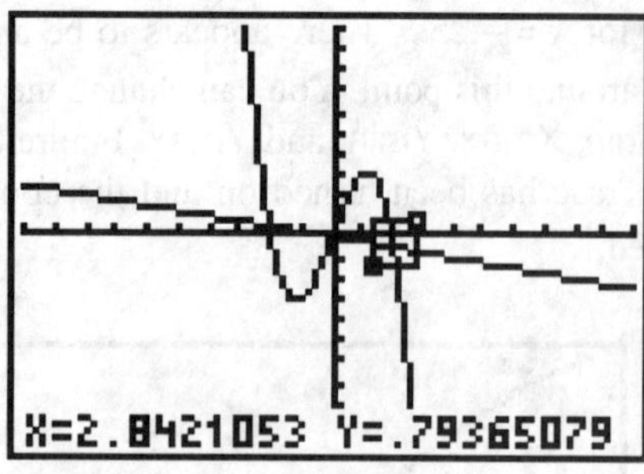

Figure 2.30: Box drawn

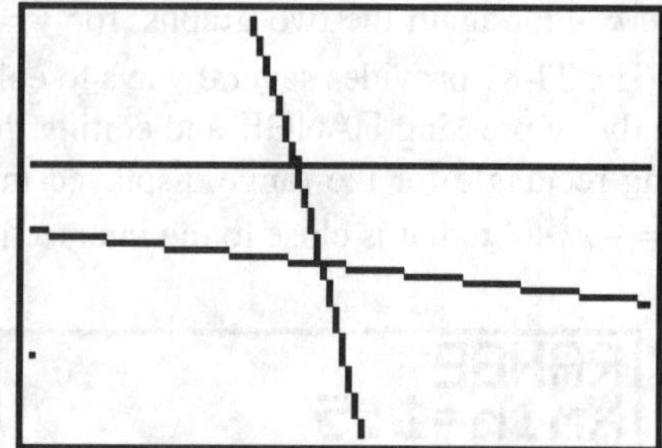

Figure 2.31: New viewing rectangle

You can also gain a quick magnification of the graph around the cursor's location. Return once more to the standard range for the graph of the two functions $y = -x^3 + 4x$ and $y = -.25x$. Press ZOOM 2 and then press arrow keys to move the cursor as close as you can to the point of intersection near $x = 2$ (see Figure 2.32). Then press ENTER and the calculator draws a magnified graph, centered at the cursor's position (Figure 2.33). The range variables are changed to reflect this new viewing rectangle. Look in the RANGE menu to check.

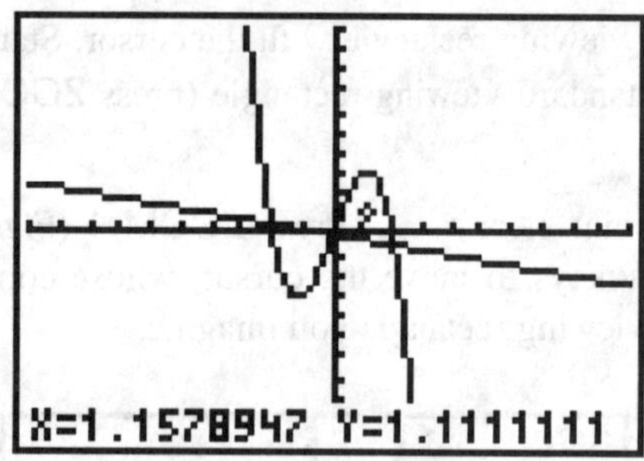

Figure 2.32: Before a zoom in

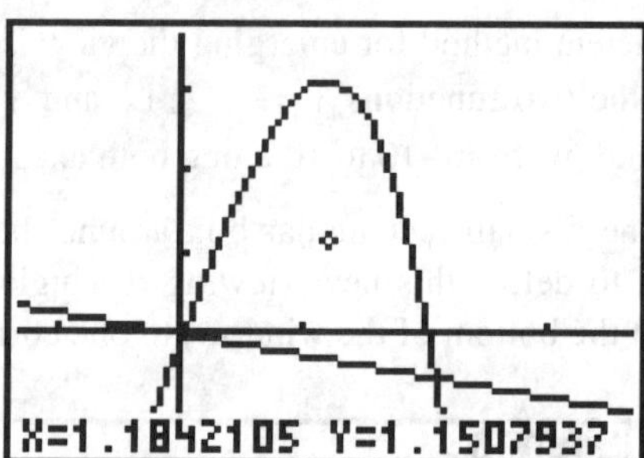

Figure 2.33: After a zoom in

As you see in the ZOOM menu (Figure 2.28), the TI-81 can Zoom In (press ZOOM 2) or Zoom Out (press ZOOM 3). Zoom out to see a larger view of the graph, centered at the cursor position. You can change the horizontal and vertical scale of the magnification by pressing ZOOM 4 (see Figure 2.34) and editing XFact and YFact, the horizontal and vertical magnification factors.

The default zoom factor is 4 in both directions. It is not necessary for XFact and YFact to be equal. Sometimes, you may prefer to zoom in one direction only, so the other factor should be set to 1. As usual, press 2nd QUIT to leave the ZOOM menu.

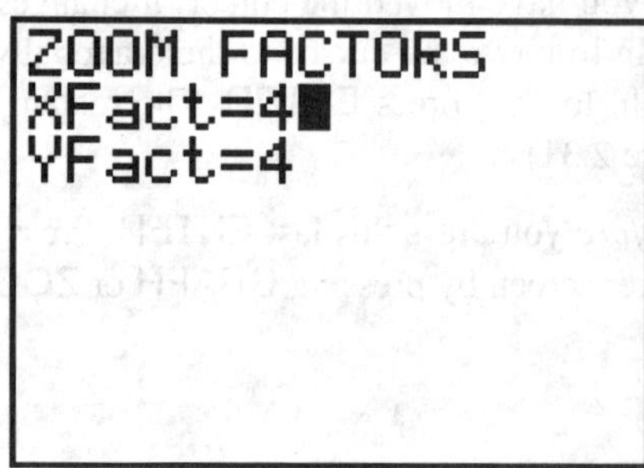

Figure 2.34: Set zoom factors

Technology Tip: If you should zoom in too much and lose the curve, zoom back to the standard viewing rectangle and start over.

2.3   Solving Equations and Inequalities

2.3.1 Intercepts and Intersections: Tracing and zooming are also used to locate an x-intercept of a graph, where a curve crosses the x-axis. For example, the graph of $y = x^3 - 8x$ crosses the x-axis three times (see Figure 2.35). After tracing over to the x-intercept point that is furthest to the left, zoom in (Figure 2.36). Continue this process until you have located all three intercepts with as much accuracy as you need. The three x-intercepts of $y = x^3 - 8x$ are approximately -2.828, 0, and 2.828.

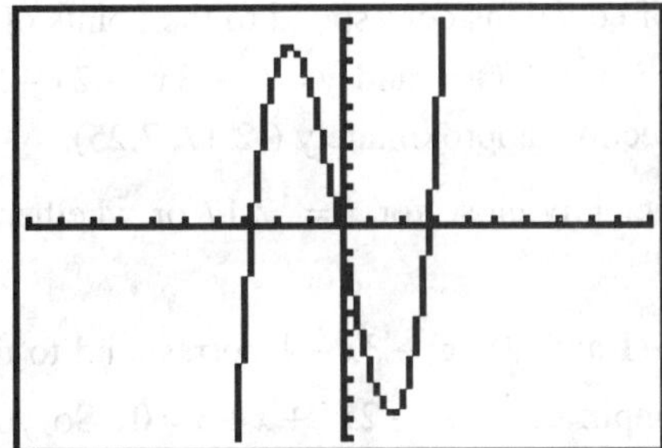

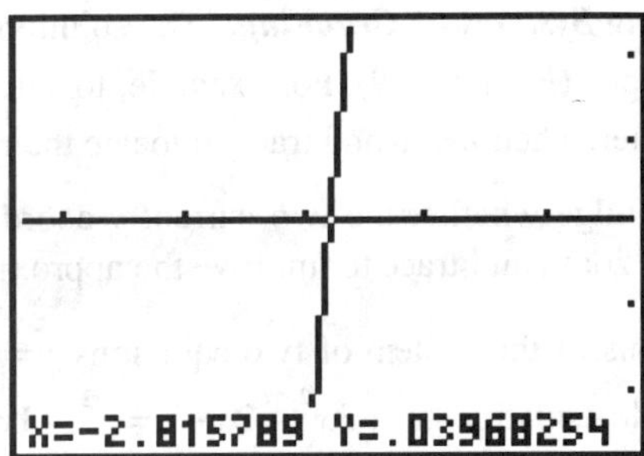

Figure 2.35: Graph of $y = x^3 - 8x$ Figure 2.36: An x-intercept of $y = x^3 - 8x$

Technology Tip: As you zoom in, you may also wish to change the spacing between tick marks on the x-axis so that the viewing rectangle shows scale marks near the intercept point. Then the accuracy of your approximation will be such that the error is less than the distance between two tick marks. Change the x-scale on the TI-81 from the RANGE menu. Move the cursor down to Xscl and enter an appropriate value.

TRACE and ZOOM are especially important for locating the intersection points of two graphs, say the graphs of $y = -x^3 + 4x$ and $y = -.25x$. Trace along one of the graphs until you arrive close to an intersection point. Then press ▲ or ▼ to jump to the other graph. Notice that the x-coordinate does not change, but the y-coordinate is likely to be different (see Figures 2.37 and 2.38).

When the two y-coordinates are as close as they can get, you have come as close as you now can to the point of intersection. So zoom in around the intersection point, then trace again until the two y-coordinates are as close as possible. Continue this process until you have located the point of intersection with as much accuracy as necessary.

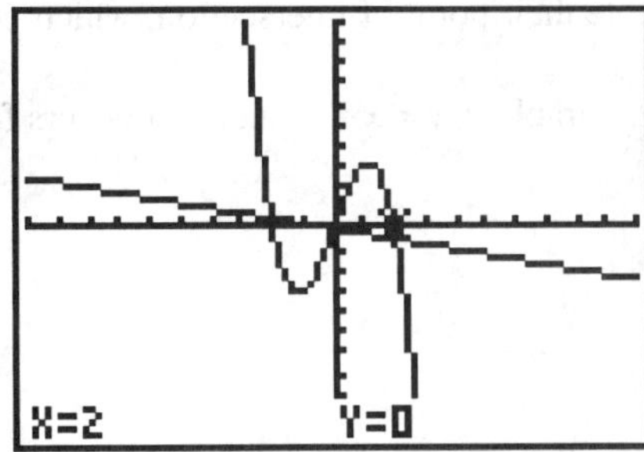

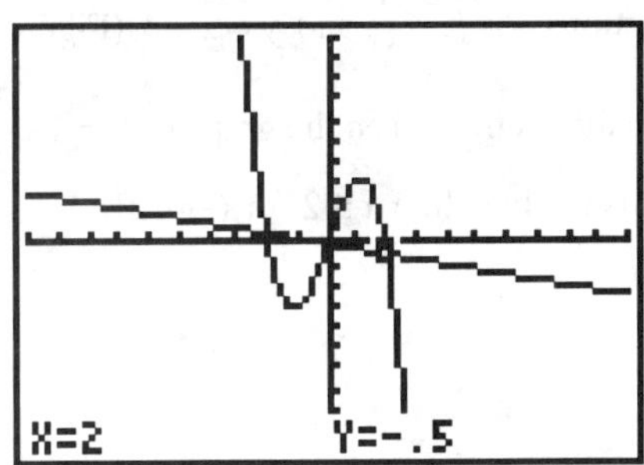

Figure 2.37: Trace on $y = -x^3 + 4x$ Figure 2.38: Trace on $y = -.25x$

2.3.2 Solving Equations by Graphing: Suppose you need to solve the equation $24x^3 - 36x + 17 = 0$. First graph $y = 24x^3 - 36x + 17$ in a window large enough to exhibit *all* its x-intercepts, corresponding to all the equation's roots. Then use trace and zoom to locate each one. In fact, this equation has just one solution, approximately $x = -1.414$.

Remember that when an equation has more than one root, it may be necessary to change the viewing rectangle a few times to locate all of them.

Technology Tip: To solve an equation like $24x^3 + 17 = 36x$, you may first transform it into standard form, $24x^3 - 36x + 17 = 0$, and proceed as above. However, you may also graph the *two* functions $y = 24x^3 + 17$ and $y = 36x$, then zoom and trace to locate their point of intersection.

2.3.3 Solving Systems by Graphing: The solutions to a system of equations correspond to the points of intersection of their graphs (Figure 2.39). For example, to solve the system $y = x^2 - 3x - 4$ and $y = x^3 + 3x^2 - 2x - 1$, first graph them together. Then zoom and trace to locate their point of intersection, approximately (-2.17, 7.25).

You must judge whether the two current y-coordinates are sufficiently close for $x = -2.17$ or whether you should continue to zoom and trace to improve the approximation.

The solutions of the system of two equations $y = x^3 + 3x^2 - 2x - 1$ and $y = x^2 - 3x - 4$ correspond to the solutions of the single equation $x^3 + 3x^2 - 2x - 1 = x^2 - 3x - 4$, which simplifies to $x^3 + 2x^2 + x + 3 = 0$. So you may also graph $y = x^3 + 2x^2 + x + 3$ and find its x-intercepts to solve the system.

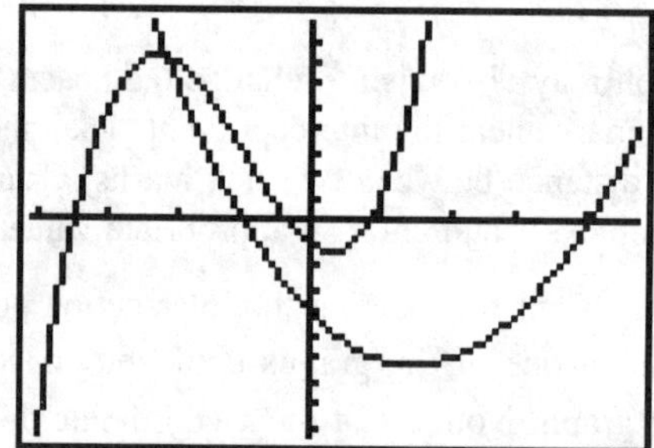

Figure 2.39: Solving a system of equations

2.3.4 Solving Inequalities by Graphing: Consider the inequality $1 - \dfrac{3x}{2} \geq x - 4$. To solve it with your TI-81, graph the two functions $y = 1 - \dfrac{3x}{2}$ and $y = x - 4$ (Figure 2.40). First locate their point of intersection, which occurs at $x = 2$. The inequality is true when the graph of $y = 1 - \dfrac{3x}{2}$ lies *above* the graph of $y = x - 4$, and that occurs for $x < 2$. So the solution is the half-line $x \leq 2$, or $(-\infty, 2]$.

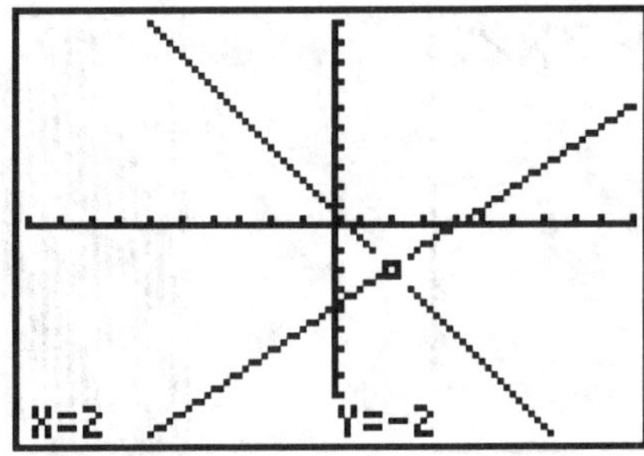

Figure 2.40: Solving $1 - \dfrac{3x}{2} \geq x - 4$

The TI-81 is capable of shading the region above or below a graph or between two graphs. For example, to graph $y \geq x^2 - 1$, first graph the function $y = x^2 - 1$ as Y$_1$. Then press **2nd DRAW 7 2nd Y-VARS 1 ALPHA , 10 ALPHA , 2) ENTER** (see Figure 2.41). These keystrokes instruct the TI-81 to shade the region *above* $y = x^2 - 1$ and *below* $y = 10$ (chosen because this is the greatest y-value in the graph window) with shading resolution value of 2. The result is shown in Figure 2.42.

To clear the shading, press **2nd DRAW 1 ENTER**.

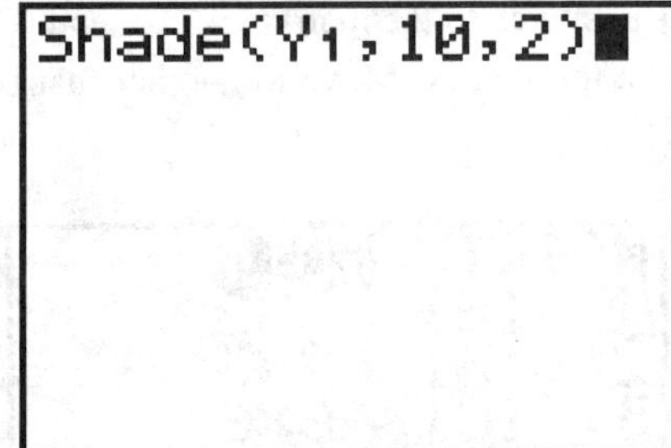

Figure 2.41: **DRAW Shade**

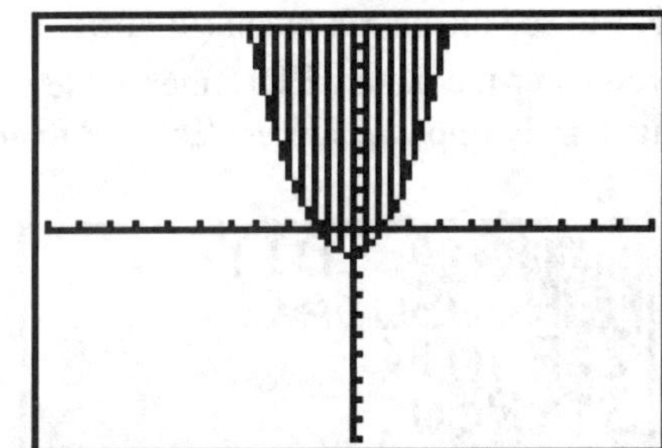

Figure 2.42: Graph of $y \geq x^2 - 1$

Now use shading to solve the previous inequality, $1 - \dfrac{3x}{2} \geq x - 4$.

The function whose graph forms the lower boundary is named *first* in the **SHADE** command (see Figure 2.43). To enter this in your TI-81, press these keys: **2nd DRAW 7 X|T - 4 ALPHA , 1 - 3 X|T ÷ 2 ALPHA , 2) ENTER** (Figure 2.44). The shading extends left from $x = 2$, hence the solution to $1 - \dfrac{3x}{2} \geq x - 4$ is the half-line $x \leq 2$, or $(-\infty, 2]$.

More information about the **DRAW** menu is in the TI-81 manual.

Figure 2.43: DRAW Shade command

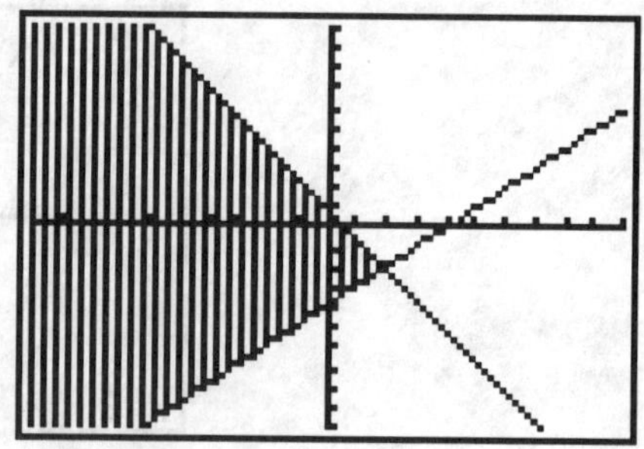

Figure 2.44: Graph of $1 - \dfrac{3x}{2} \ge x - 4$

2.4   Matrices

2.4.1 Making a Matrix: The TI-81 can display and use three different matrices, each with up to six rows and up to

six columns. Here's how to create this 3×4 matrix $\begin{bmatrix} 1 & -4 & 3 & 5 \\ -1 & 3 & -1 & -3 \\ 2 & 0 & -4 & 6 \end{bmatrix}$ in your calculator.

Press MATRX to see the matrix menu (Figure 2.45); then press ▶ to switch to the matrix EDIT menu (Figure 2.46). Whenever you enter the matrix EDIT menu, the cursor starts at the top matrix. Move to another matrix by repeatedly pressing ▼. For now, just press ENTER to edit matrix [A].

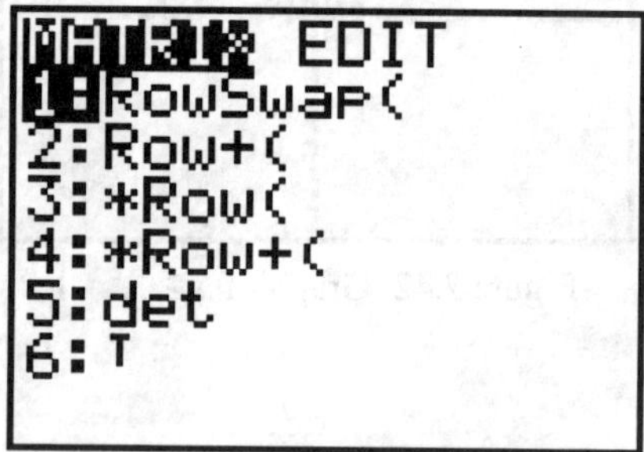

Figure 2.45: MATRX menu

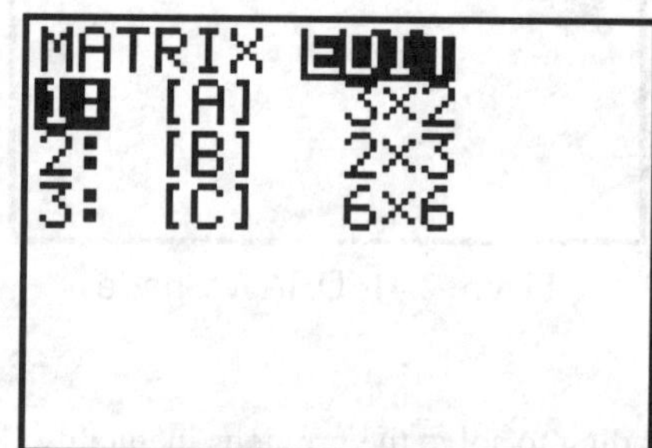

Figure 2.46: Matrix EDIT menu

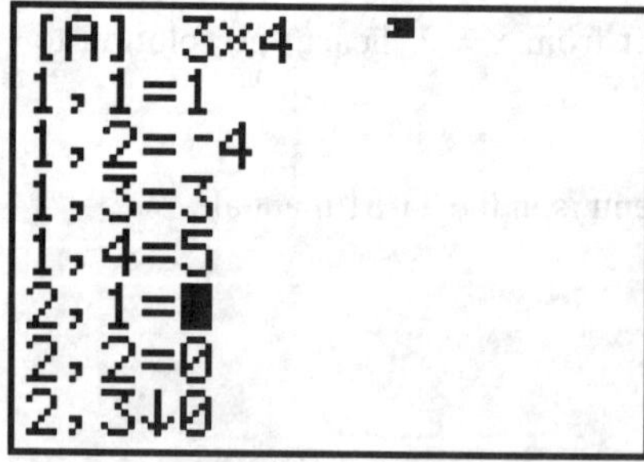

Figure 2.47: Editing the 2nd row, 1st column element

You may now change the dimensions of matrix [A] to 3×4 by pressing 3 ENTER 4 ENTER. Simply press ENTER or an arrow key to accept an existing dimension. As you change the dimensions, a small black rectangle appears at the top of the TI-81 screen, as in Figure 2.47. This rectangle represents the matrix and shows its size and the element where the cursor is positioned.

Use ▲ and ▼ to move the cursor to a matrix element you want to change, and watch the white mark move in the black rectangle to show the cursor's location within the matrix. At the bottom of the screen in Figure 2.47, there is ↓ instead of = to indicate that more elements are below, off the screen. Go to them by pressing ▼ as many times as necessary. The white mark in the black rectangle indicates that the cursor in Figure 2.47 is currently on the element in the second row and first column. Continue to enter all the elements of matrix [A].

Leave the matrix [A] editing screen by pressing 2nd QUIT and return to the home screen.

2.4.2 Row Operations: Here are the keystrokes necessary to perform elementary row operations on a matrix. Your textbook provides more careful explanation of the elementary row operations and their uses.

To interchange the second and third rows of the matrix [A] that was defined above, press MATRX 1 2nd [A] ALPHA , 2 ALPHA , 3) ENTER (see Figure 2.48). The format of this command is RowSwap(*matrix, row1, row2*).

To add row 2 and row 3 and store the results in row 3, press MATRX 2 2nd [A] ALPHA , 2 ALPHA , 3) ENTER. The format of this command is Row+(*matrix, row1, row2*).

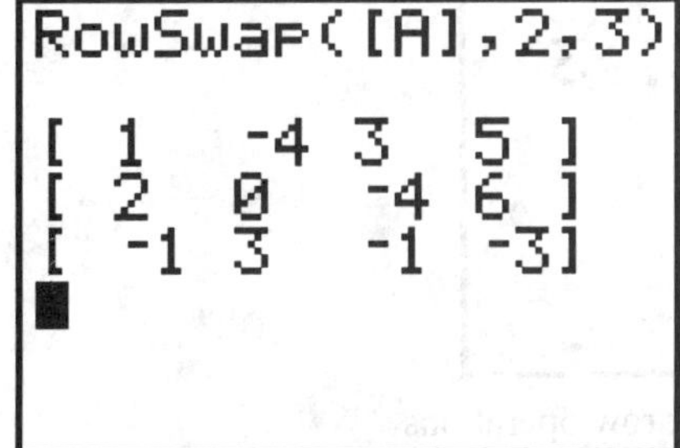

Figure 2.48: Swap rows 2 and 3

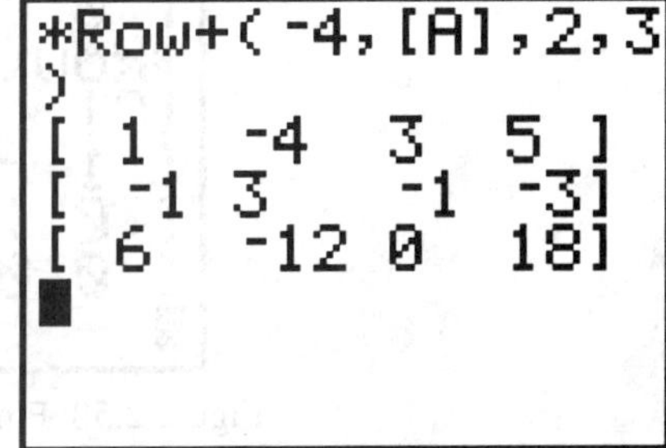

Figure 2.49: Add -4 times row 2 to row 3

To multiply row 2 by -4 and *store* the results in row 2, thereby replacing row 2 with new values, press MATRX 3 (-) 4 ALPHA , 2nd [A] ALPHA , 2) ENTER. The format of this command is ✳Row(*scalar, matrix, row*).

To multiply row 2 by -4 and *add* the results to row 3, thereby replacing row 3 with new values, press MATRX 4 (-) 4 ALPHA , 2nd [A] ALPHA , 2 ALPHA , 3) ENTER (see Figure 2.49). The format of this command is ✳Row+(*scalar, matrix, row1, row2*).

Technology Tip: It is important to remember that your TI-81 does *not* store a matrix obtained as the result of any row operations. So when you need to perform several row operations in succession, it is a good idea to store the result of each one in a temporary place. You may wish to use matrix [C] to hold such intermediate results.

For example, use elementary row operations to solve this system of linear equations:
$$\begin{cases} x - 2y + 3z = 9 \\ -x + 3y = -4 \,. \\ 2x - 5y + 5z = 17 \end{cases}$$

First enter this *augmented matrix* as [A] in your TI-81: $\begin{bmatrix} 1 & -2 & 3 & 9 \\ -1 & 3 & 0 & -4 \\ 2 & -5 & 5 & 17 \end{bmatrix}$. Next store this matrix in [C] (press **2nd**

[A] STO ▶ 2nd [C] ENTER) so you may keep the original in case you need to recall it.

Here are the row operations and their associated keystrokes. At each step, the result is stored in [C] and replaces the previous matrix [C]. The solution is shown in Figure 2.50.

Row Operation	*Keystrokes*
Row+([C], 1, 2)	MATRX 2 2nd [C] ALPHA , 1 ALPHA , 2) STO ▶ 2nd [C] ENTER
✳Row+(-2, [C], 1, 3)	MATRX 4 (-) 2 ALPHA , 2nd [C] ALPHA , 1 ALPHA , 3) STO ▶ 2nd [C] ENTER
Row+([C], 2, 3)	MATRX 2 2nd [C] ALPHA , 2 ALPHA , 3) STO ▶ 2nd [C] ENTER
✳Row(½, [C], 3)	MATRX 3 1 ÷ 2 ALPHA , 2nd [C] ALPHA , 3) STO ▶ 2nd [C] ENTER

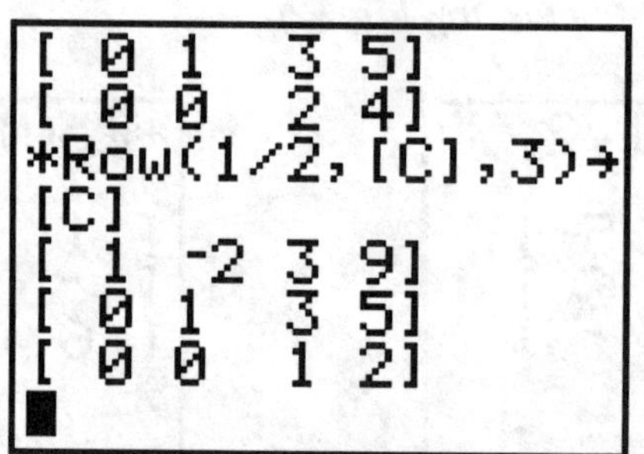

Figure 2.50: Final matrix after row operations

Thus $z = 2$, so $y = -1$ and $x = 1$.

2.4.3 Determinants: Enter this 3×3 square matrix as [A]: $\begin{bmatrix} 1 & -2 & 3 \\ -1 & 3 & 0 \\ 2 & -5 & 5 \end{bmatrix}$. To calculate its determinant, $\begin{Vmatrix} 1 & -2 & 3 \\ -1 & 3 & 0 \\ 2 & -5 & 5 \end{Vmatrix}$, press **MATRX 5 2nd [A] ENTER**. You should find that $\begin{vmatrix} [A] \end{vmatrix} = 2$.

2.5   Additional Topics

2.5.1 Iteration: The ANS feature enables you to perform iterations to evaluate a function repeatedly. As an example, calculate $\dfrac{n-1}{3}$ for $n = 27$. Then calculate $\dfrac{n-1}{3}$ for $n =$ the answer to the previous calculation. Continue to use each answer as n in the *next* calculation. Here are keystrokes to accomplish this iteration on the TI-81 calculator (see the results in Figure 2.51). Notice that when you use ANS in place of n in a formula, it is sufficient to press ENTER to continue an iteration.

Iteration	Keystrokes	Display
1	27 ENTER	27
2	(2nd ANS - 1) ÷ 3 ENTER	8.666666667
3	ENTER	2.555555556
4	ENTER	.5185185185
5	ENTER	-.1604938272

Press ENTER several more times and see what happens with this iteration. You may wish to try it again with a different starting value.

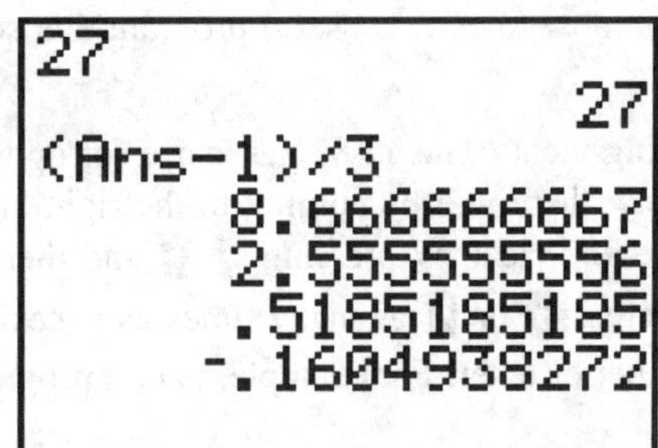

Figure 2.51: Iteration

2.5.2 Arithmetic and Geometric Sequences: Use iteration with the ANS variable to determine the n-th term of a sequence. For example, find the 18th term of an *arithmetic* sequence whose first term is 7 and whose common difference is 4. Enter the first term 7, then start the progression with the recursion formula, 2nd ANS + 4 ENTER. This yields the 2nd term, so press ENTER sixteen more times to find the 18th term. For a *geometric* sequence whose common ratio is 4, start the progression with 2nd ANS × 4 ENTER.

Of course, you could also use the *explicit* formula for the n-th term of an arithmetic sequence, $t_n = a + (n-1)d$. First enter values for the variables a, d, and n, then evaluate the formula by pressing ALPHA A + (ALPHA N - 1) ALPHA D ENTER. For a geometric sequence whose n-th term is given by $t_n = a \cdot r^{n-1}$, enter values for the variables a, r, and n, then evaluate the formula by pressing ALPHA A ALPHA R ^ (ALPHA N - 1) ENTER.

2.5.3 Permutations and Combinations: To calculate the number of *permutations* of 12 objects taken 7 at a time, $_{12}P_7$, press 12 MATH ◄ 2 7 ENTER. Then $_{12}P_7 = 3{,}991{,}680$, as shown in Figure 2.52.

For the number of *combinations* of 12 objects taken 7 at a time, $_{12}C_7$, press 12 MATH ◄ 3 7 ENTER. So $_{12}C_7 = 792$.

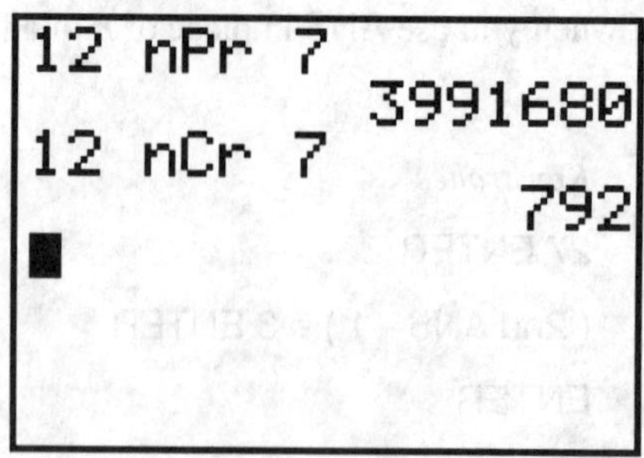

Figure 2.52: $_{12}P_7$ and $_{12}C_7$

2.6　Programming

2.6.1 Entering a Program:　The TI-81 is a programmable calculator that can store sequences of commands for later replay. Here's an example to show you how to enter a useful program that solves quadratic equations by the quadratic formula.

Press PRGM to access the programming menu. The TI-81 has space for up to 37 programs, each named by a number or letter. If a program area is empty, there will be nothing to the right of its name in the PRGM window. You may ERASE a program area to make one clear by pressing ▶ ▶ and then the number or letter of the program. When you see a clear program area, press ▶ or ◀ as many times as necessary to move the cursor to EDIT; then press the key corresponding to its number or letter. For example, to edit program 5, press 5; to edit program B, press ALPHA B.

For convenience, the cursor is now a blinking **A**, indicating that the calculator is set to receive alphabetic characters. Enter a descriptive title of up to eight characters, letters or numerals, and end by pressing ENTER. Let's call this program QUADRAT.

In the program, each line begins with a colon : supplied automatically by the calculator. Any command you could enter directly in the TI-81's home screen can be entered as a line in a program. There are also special programming commands.

Figure 2.53: Program QUADRAT

Enter the program QUADRAT by pressing the keystrokes given in the listing below.

Program Line	*Keystrokes*
: Disp "ENTER A"	PRGM ▶ 1 2nd A-LOCK " E N T E R ␣ A " ENTER

　　　　　　　　displays the words *Enter A* on the TI-81 screen

　　　　　　　　　　　　　　　　　　　　　　TI-81 Graphics Calculator

: Input A   PRGM ▶ 2 ALPHA A ENTER

    waits for you to input a value that will be assigned to the variable *A*

: Disp "ENTER B"   PRGM ▶ 1 2nd A-LOCK " E N T E R ⌴ B " ENTER

: Input B   PRGM ▶ 2 ALPHA B ENTER

: Disp "ENTER C"   PRGM ▶ 1 2nd A-LOCK " E N T E R ⌴ C " ENTER

: Input C   PRGM ▶ 2 ALPHA C ENTER

: B^2-4AC → D   ALPHA B x^2 - 4 ALPHA A ALPHA C STO▶ D ENTER

    calculates the discriminant and stores its value as *D*

: If D<0   PRGM 3 ALPHA D 2nd TEST 5 0 ENTER

    tests to see if the discriminant is negative

: Goto 1   PRGM 2 1 ENTER

    in case the discriminant is negative, jumps to the line Lbl 1 below;
    if the discriminant is not negative, continues on to the next line

: If D=0   PRGM 3 ALPHA D 2nd TEST 5 0 ENTER

    tests to see if the discriminant is zero

: Goto 2   PRGM 2 1 ENTER

    in case the discriminant is zero, jumps to the line Lbl 2 below;
    if the discriminant is not zero, continues on to the next line

: Disp "TWO REAL   PRGM ▶ 1 2nd A-LOCK " T W O ⌴ R E A L ⌴ R O O T S " ENTER
ROOTS"

: (-B+√D)/(2A) → M   ((-) ALPHA B + 2nd √ ALPHA D) ÷ (2 ALPHA A) STO▶ M ENTER

    calculates one root and stores it as *M*

: Disp M   PRGM ▶ 1 ALPHA M ENTER

    displays one root

: (-B-√D)/(2A) → N   ((-) ALPHA B - 2nd √ ALPHA D) ÷ (2 ALPHA A) STO▶ N ENTER

: Disp N   PRGM ▶ 1 ALPHA N ENTER

: End   PRGM 7 ENTER

    stops program execution

: Lbl 1   PRGM 1 1 ENTER

    jumping point for the Goto command above

: Disp "COMPLEX   PRGM ▶ 1 2nd A-LOCK " C O M P L E X ⌴ R O O T S " ENTER
ROOTS"

    displays a message in case the roots are complex numbers

: Disp "REAL PART"   PRGM ▶ 1 2nd A-LOCK " R E A L ⌴ P A R T " ENTER

: -B/(2A) → R	(-) ALPHA B ÷ (2 ALPHA A) STO▶ R ENTER

calculates the real part $\dfrac{-b}{2a}$ of the complex roots

: Disp R	PRGM ▶ 1 ALPHA R ENTER
: Disp "IMAGINARY PART"	PRGM ▶ 1 2nd A-LOCK " I M A G I N A R Y ⎵ P A R T " ENTER
: √-D/(2A) → I	2nd √ (-) ALPHA D ÷ (2 ALPHA A) STO▶ I ENTER

calculates the imaginary part $\dfrac{\sqrt{-D}}{2a}$ of the complex roots;

since $D < 0$, we must use $-D$ as the radicand

: Disp I	PRGM ▶ 1 ALPHA I ENTER
: End	PRGM 7 ENTER
: Lbl 2	PRGM 1 2 ENTER
: Disp "DOUBLE ROOT"	PRGM ▶ 1 2nd A-LOCK " D O U B L E ⎵ R O O T " ENTER

displays a message in case there is a double root

: -B/(2A) → M	(-) ALPHA B ÷ (2 ALPHA A) STO▶ M ENTER

the quadratic formula reduces to $\dfrac{-b}{2a}$ when $D = 0$

: Disp M	PRGM ▶ 1 ALPHA M ENTER
: End	PRGM 7

When you have finished, press 2nd QUIT to leave the program editor.

2.6.2 Running a Program: To run the program just entered, press PRGM and the number or letter that it was named, then ENTER. If you have forgotten its name, use the arrow keys to move through the program listing to find its description QUADRAT, then press ENTER to select this program and ENTER again to run it.

The program has been written to prompt you for values of the coefficients a, b, and c in a quadratic equation $ax^2 + bx + c = 0$. Input a value, then press ENTER to continue the program.

If you need to interrupt a program during execution, press ON.

The instruction manual for your TI-81 gives detailed information about programming. Refer to it to learn more about programming and how to use other features of your calculator.

Chapter 3

Texas Instruments TI-82
Graphics Calculator

3.1 Getting started with the TI-82

3.1.1 Basics: Press the ON key to begin using your TI-82 calculator. If you need to adjust the display contrast, first press 2nd, then press and hold ▲ (the *up* arrow key) to increase the contrast or ▼ (the *down* arrow key) to decrease the contrast. As you press and hold ▲ or ▼, an integer between 0 (lightest) and 9 (darkest) appears in the upper right corner of the display. When you have finished with the calculator, turn it off to conserve battery power by pressing 2nd and then OFF.

Check the TI-82's settings by pressing MODE. If necessary, use the arrow keys to move the blinking cursor to a setting you want to change. Press ENTER to select a new setting. To start with, select the options along the left side of the MODE menu as illustrated in Figure 3.1: normal display, floating decimals, radian measure, function graphs, connected lines, sequential plotting, and full screen display. Details on alternative options will be given later in this guide. For now, leave the MODE menu by pressing CLEAR.

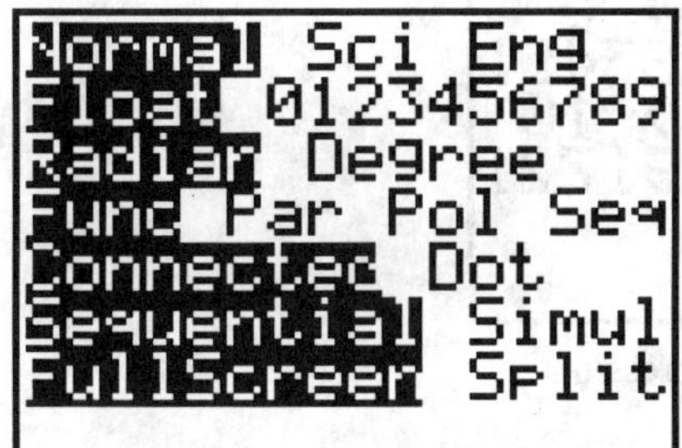

Figure 3.1: MODE menu

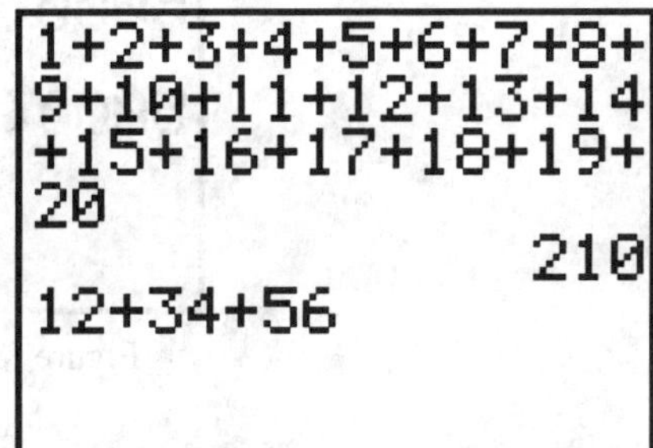

Figure 3.2: Home screen

3.1.2 Editing: One advantage of the TI-82 is that up to 8 lines are visible at one time, so you can *see* a long calculation. For example, type this sum (see Figure 3.2):

$$1 + 2 + 3 + 4 + 5 + 6 + 7 + 8 + 9 + 10 + 11 + 12 + 13 + 14 + 15 + 16 + 17 + 18 + 19 + 20$$

Then press ENTER to see the answer, too.

Often we do not notice a mistake until we see how unreasonable an answer is. The TI-82 permits you to re-display an entire calculation, edit it easily, then execute the *corrected* calculation.

Suppose you had typed $12 + 34 + 56$ as in Figure 3.2 but had *not* yet pressed ENTER, when you realize that 34 should have been 74. Simply press ◄ (the *left* arrow key) as many times as necessary to move the blinking cursor left to 3, then type 7 to write over it. On the other hand, if 34 should have been 384, move the cursor back to 4, press 2nd INS (the cursor changes to a blinking underline) and then type 8 (inserts at the cursor position and other characters are pushed to the right). If the 34 should have been 3 only, move the cursor to 4 and press DEL to delete it.

Even if you had pressed ENTER, you may still edit the previous expression. Press 2nd and then ENTRY to *recall* the last expression that was entered. Now you can change it. In fact, the TI-82 retains many prior entries in a "last entry" storage area. Press 2nd ENTRY repeatedly until the previous line you want replaces the current line.

Technology Tip: When you need to evaluate a formula for different values of a variable, use the editing feature to simplify the process. For example, suppose you want to find the balance in an investment account if there is now \$5000 in the account and interest is compounded annually at the rate of 8.5%. The formula for the balance is $P\left(1+\frac{r}{n}\right)^{nt}$, where P = principal, r = rate of interest (expressed as a decimal), n = number of times interest is com-

pounded each year, and t = number of years. In our example, this becomes $5000(1+.085)^t$. Here are the keystrokes for finding the balance after $t = 3, 5,$ and 10 years.

Years	Keystrokes	Balance
3	5000 (1 + .085) ^ 3 ENTER	$6386.45
5	2nd ENTRY ◀ 5 ENTER	$7518.28
10	2nd ENTRY ◀ 10 ENTER	$11,304.92

Figure 3.3: Editing expressions

Then to find the balance from the same initial investment but after 5 years when the annual interest rate is 7.5%, press these keys to change the last calculation above: 2nd ENTRY ◀ DEL ◀ 5 ◀ ◀ ◀ ◀ ◀ 7 ENTER.

3.1.3 Key Functions: Most keys on the TI-82 offer access to more than one function, just as the keys on a computer keyboard can produce more than one letter ("g" and "G") or even quite different characters ("5" and "%"). The primary function of a key is indicated on the key itself, and you access that function by a simple press on the key.

To access the *second* function indicated to the *left* above a key, first press 2nd (the cursor changes to a blinking ↑) and *then* press the key. For example, to calculate $\sqrt{25}$, press 2nd √ 25 ENTER.

When you want to use a letter or other character printed to the *right* above a key, first press ALPHA (the cursor changes to a blinking A) and then the key. For example, to use the letter K in a formula, press ALPHA K. If you need several letters in a row, press 2nd A-LOCK, which is like Caps Lock on a computer keyboard, and then press all the letters you want. Remember to press ALPHA when you are finished and want to restore the keys to their primary functions.

3.1.4 Order of Operations: The TI-82 performs calculations according to the standard algebraic rules. Working outwards from inner parentheses, calculations are performed from left to right. Powers and roots are evaluated first, followed by multiplications and divisions, and then additions and subtractions.

Note that the TI-82 distinguishes between *subtraction* and the *negative sign*. If you wish to enter a negative number, it is necessary to use the (-) key. For example, you would evaluate $-5-(4\cdot-3)$ by pressing (-) 5 - (4 × (-) 3) ENTER to get 7.

Enter these expressions to practice using your TI-82.

Expression	Keystrokes	Display
$7 - 5 \cdot 3$	7 - 5 × 3 ENTER	-8
$(7 - 5) \cdot 3$	(7 - 5) × 3 ENTER	6
$120 - 10^2$	120 - 10 x² ENTER	20
$(120 - 10)^2$	(120 - 10) x² ENTER	12100
$\dfrac{24}{2^3}$	24 ÷ 2 ^ 3 ENTER	3
$\left(\dfrac{24}{2}\right)^3$	(24 ÷ 2) ^ 3 ENTER	1728
$(7 - -5) \cdot -3$	(7 - (-) 5) × (-) 3 ENTER	-36

3.1.5 Algebraic Expressions and Memory: Your calculator can evaluate expressions such as $\dfrac{N(N+1)}{2}$ *after* you have entered a value for N. Suppose you want $N = 200$. Press 200 STO ▸ ALPHA N ENTER to store the value 200 in memory location N. Whenever you use N in an expression, the calculator will substitute the value 200 until you make a change by storing *another* number in N. Next enter the expression $\dfrac{N(N+1)}{2}$ by typing ALPHA N (ALPHA N + 1) ÷ 2 ENTER. For $N = 200$, you will find that $\dfrac{N(N+1)}{2} = 20100$.

The contents of any memory location may be revealed by typing just its letter name and then ENTER. And the TI-82 retains memorized values even when it is turned off, so long as its batteries are good.

3.1.6 Repeated Operations with ANS: The result of your *last* calculation is always stored in memory location ANS and replaces any previous result. This makes it easy to use the answer from one computation in another computation. For example, press 30 + 15 ENTER so that 45 is the last result displayed. Then press 2nd ANS ÷ 9 ENTER and get 5 because $\frac{45}{9} = 5$.

With a function like division, you press the ÷ key *after* you enter an argument. For such functions, whenever you would start a new calculation with the previous answer followed by pressing the function key, you may press just the function key. So instead of 2nd ANS ÷ 9 in the previous example, you could have pressed simply ÷ 9 to achieve the same result. This technique also works for these functions: + - × x² ^ x⁻¹.

Here is a situation where this is especially useful. Suppose a person makes $5.85 per hour and you are asked to calculate earnings for a day, a week, and a year. Execute the given keystrokes to find the person's incomes during these periods (results are shown in Figure 3.4):

Pay period	Keystrokes	Earnings
8-hour day	5.85 × 8 ENTER	$46.80
5-day week	× 5 ENTER	$234
52-week year	× 52 ENTER	$12,168

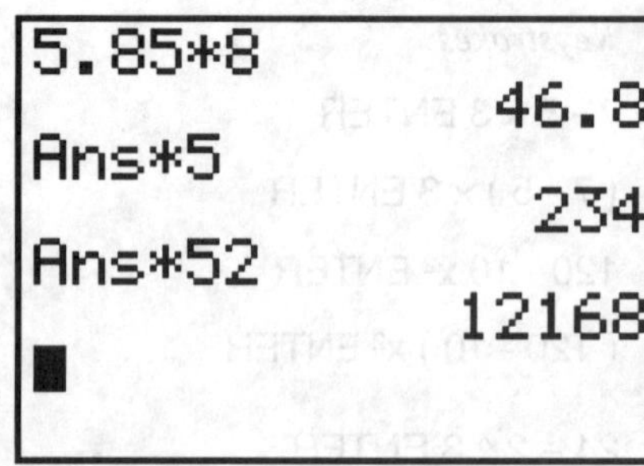

Figure 3.4: ANS variable

3.1.7 The MATH Menu: Operators and functions associated with a scientific calculator are available either immediately from the keys of the TI-82 or by 2nd keys. You have direct key access to common arithmetic operations (x^2, 2nd $\sqrt{}$, x^{-1}, ^, 2nd ABS), exponential and logarithmic functions (LOG, 2nd 10^x, LN, 2nd e^x), and a famous constant (2nd π).

A significant difference between the TI-82 and many scientific calculators is that the TI-82 requires the argument of a function *after* the function, as you would see a formula written in your textbook. For example, on the TI-82 you calculate $\sqrt{16}$ by pressing the keys 2nd $\sqrt{}$ 16 in that order.

Here are keystrokes for basic mathematical operations. Try them for practice on your TI-82.

Expression	*Keystrokes*	*Display*
$\sqrt{3^2 + 4^2}$	2nd $\sqrt{}$ (3 x^2 + 4 x^2) ENTER	5
$2\frac{1}{3}$	2 + 3 x^{-1} ENTER	2.333333333
$\lvert -5 \rvert$	2nd ABS (-) 5 ENTER	5
$\log 200$	LOG 200 ENTER	2.301029996
$2.34 \cdot 10^5$	2.34 × 2nd 10^x 5 ENTER	234000

Additional mathematical operations and functions are available from the MATH menu (Figure 3.5). Press MATH to see the various options. You will learn in your mathematics textbook how to apply many of them. As an example, calculate $\sqrt[3]{7}$ by pressing MATH and then *either* 4 *or* ▼ ▼ ▼ ENTER; finally press 7 ENTER to see 1.912931183. To leave the MATH menu and take no other action, press 2nd QUIT or just CLEAR.

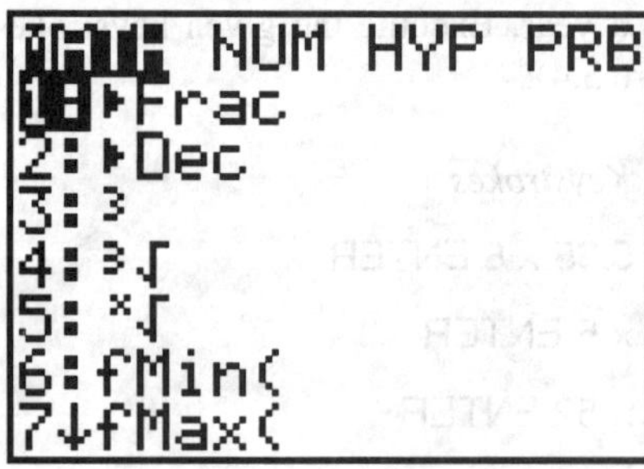

Figure 3.5: MATH menu

The *factorial* of a non-negative integer is the *product* of *all* the integers from 1 up to the given integer. The symbol for factorial is the exclamation point. So 4! (pronounced *four factorial*) is $1 \cdot 2 \cdot 3 \cdot 4 = 24$. You will learn more about applications of factorials in your textbook, but for now use the TI-82 to calculate 4! The factorial command is located in the MATH menu's PRB sub-menu. To compute 4!, press these keystrokes: 4 MATH ◀ 4 ENTER *or* 4 MATH ◀ ▾ ▾ ▾ ENTER ENTER.

Note that you can select a sub-menu from the MATH menu by pressing either ◀ or ▶. It is easier to press ◀ once than to press ▶ three times to get to the PRB sub-menu.

3.2   Functions and Graphs

3.2.1 Evaluating Functions: Suppose you receive a monthly salary of \$1975 plus a commission of 10% of sales. Let x = your sales in dollars; then your wages W in dollars are given by the equation $W = 1975 + .10x$. If your January sales were \$2230 and your February sales were \$1865, what was your income during those months?

Here's how to use your TI-82 to perform this task. Press the Y= key at the top of the calculator to display the function editing screen (Figure 3.6). You may enter as many as ten different functions for the TI-82 to use at one time. If there is already a function Y_1, press ▲ or ▾ as many times as necessary to move the cursor to Y_1 and then press CLEAR to delete whatever was there. Then enter the expression $1975 + .10x$ by pressing these keys: 1975 + .10 X,T,θ. (The X,T,θ key lets you enter the variable X easily without having to use the ALPHA key.) Now press 2nd QUIT to return to the main calculations screen.

Figure 3.6: Y= screen

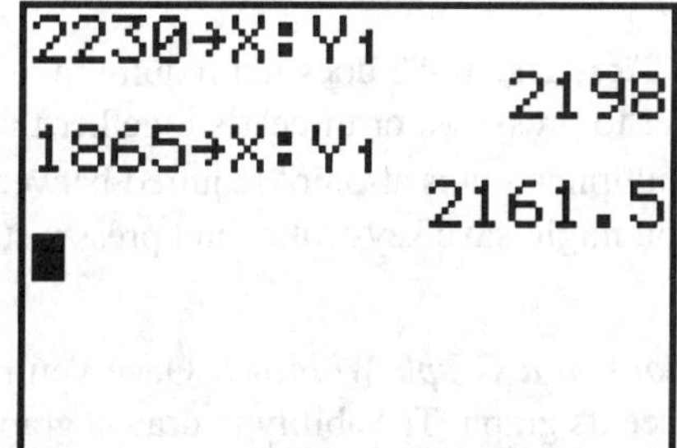

Figure 3.7: Evaluating a function

Assign the value 2230 to the variable x by these keystrokes (see Figure 3.7): 2230 STO ▶ X,T,θ. Then press 2nd : to allow another expression to be entered on the same command line. Next press the following keystrokes to evaluate Y_1 and find January's wages: 2nd Y-VARS 1 1 ENTER.

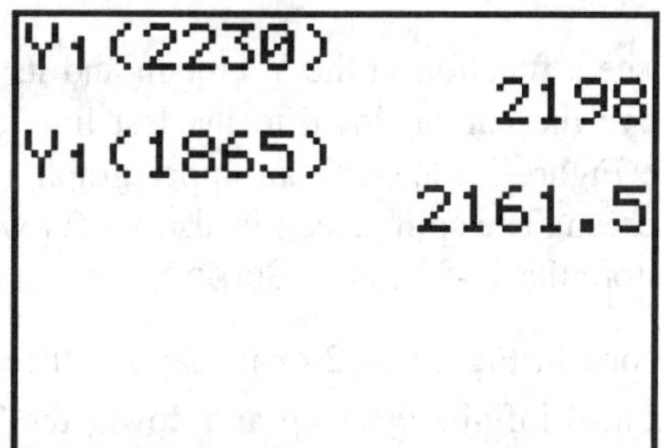

Figure 3.8: Function notation

It is not necessary to repeat all these steps to find the February wages. Simply press 2nd ENTRY to recall the entire previous line and change 2230 to 1865. Each time the TI-82 evaluates the function Y_1, it uses the *current* value of x.

Like your textbook, the TI-82 uses standard function notation. So to evaluate $Y_1(2230)$ when $Y_1(x) = 1975 + .10x$, press 2nd Y-VARS 1 1 (2230) ENTER (see Figure 3.8). Then to evaluate $Y_1(1865)$, press 2nd ENTRY to recall the last line and change 2230 to 1865.

You may also have the TI-82 make a table of values for the function. Press 2nd TblSet to set up the table (Figure 3.9). Move the blinking cursor onto Ask beside Indpnt:, then press ENTER. This configuration permits you to input values for x one at a time. Now press 2nd TABLE, enter 2230 in the x column, and press ENTER (see Figure 3.10). Continue to enter additional values for x and the calculator automatically completes the table with corresponding values of Y_1. Press 2nd QUIT to leave the TABLE screen.

Figure 3.9: TblSet screen

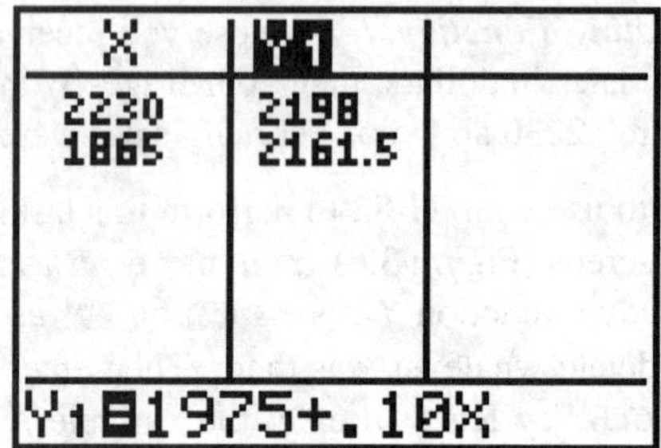

Figure 3.10: Table of values

Technology Tip: The TI-82 does not require multiplication to be expressed between variables, so xxx means x^3. It is often easier to press two or three x's together than to search for the square key or the cube operation. Of course, expressed multiplication is also not required between a constant and a variable. Hence to enter $2x^3 + 3x^2 - 4x + 5$ in the TI-82, you might save keystrokes and press just these keys: 2 X,T,θ X,T,θ X,T,θ + 3 X,T,θ X,T,θ - 4 X,T,θ + 5.

3.2.2 Functions in a Graph Window: Once you have entered a function in the Y= screen of the TI-82, just press GRAPH to see its graph. The ability to draw a graph contributes substantially to our ability to solve problems.

For example, here is how to graph $y = -x^3 + 4x$. First press Y= and delete anything that may be there by moving with the arrow keys to Y_1 or to any of the other lines and pressing CLEAR wherever necessary. Then, with the cursor on the top line Y_1, press (-) X,T,θ MATH 3 + 4 X,T,θ to enter the function (as in Figure 3.11). Now press GRAPH and the TI-82 changes to a window with the graph of $y = -x^3 + 4x$.

While the TI-82 is calculating coordinates for a plot, it displays a busy indicator at the top right of the graph window.

Technology Tip: If you would like to see a function in the Y= menu and its graph in a graph window, both at the same time, open the MODE menu, move the cursor down to the last line, and select Split screen. Your TI-82's screen is now divided horizontally (see Figure 3.11), with an upper graph window and a lower window that can display the home screen or an editing screen. The split screen is also useful when you need to do some calculations as you trace along a graph. For now, restore the TI-82 to FullScreen.

Your graph window may look like the one in Figure 3.12 or it may be different. Since the graph of $y = -x^3 + 4x$ extends infinitely far left and right and also infinitely far up and down, the TI-82 can display only a piece of the actual graph. This displayed rectangular part is called a *viewing rectangle*. You can easily change the viewing rectangle to enhance your investigation of a graph.

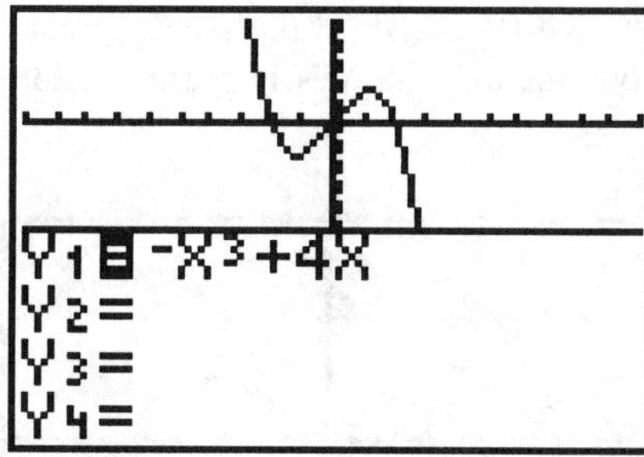

Figure 3.11: Split screen: Y= below

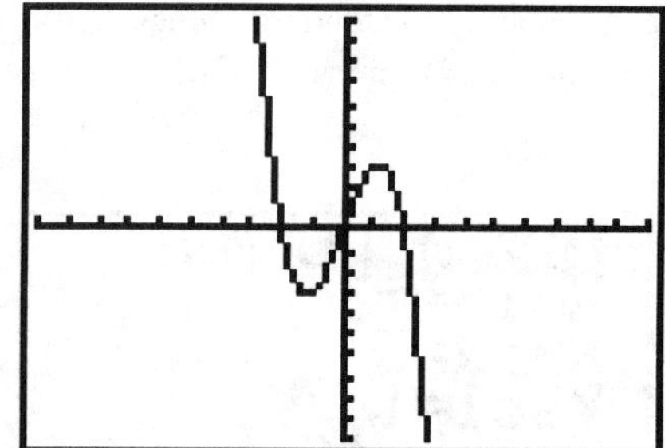

Figure 3.12: Graph of $y = -x^3 + 4x$

The viewing rectangle in Figure 3.12 shows the part of the graph that extends horizontally from -10 to 10 and vertically from -10 to 10. Press **WINDOW** to see information about your viewing rectangle. Figure 3.13 shows the **WINDOW** screen that corresponds to the viewing rectangle in Figure 3.12. This is the *standard* viewing rectangle for the TI-82.

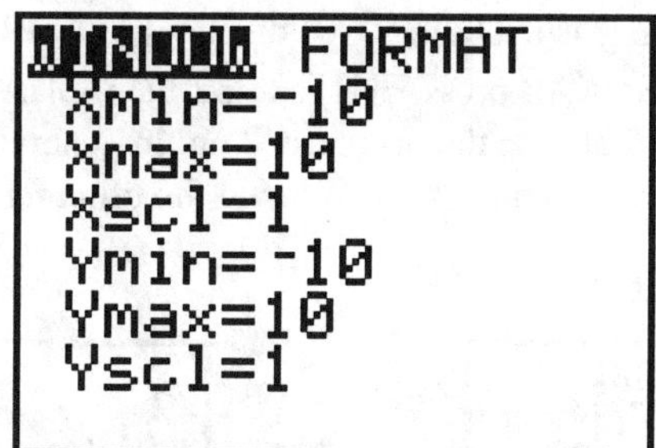

Figure 3.13: Standard **WINDOW**

The variables **Xmin** and **Xmax** are the minimum and maximum *x*-values of the viewing rectangle; **Ymin** and **Ymax** are its minimum and maximum *y*-values.

Xscl and **Yscl** set the spacing between tick marks on the axes.

Use the arrow keys ▲ and ▼ to move up and down from one line to another in this list; pressing the **ENTER** key will move down the list. Press **CLEAR** to delete the current value and then enter a new value. You may also edit the entry as you would edit an expression. Remember that a minimum *must* be less than the corresponding maximum or the TI-82 will issue an error message. Also, remember to use the (-) key, not - (which is subtraction), when you want to enter a negative value. Figures 3.12-13, 3.14-15, and 3.16-17 show different **WINDOW** screens and the corresponding viewing rectangle for each one.

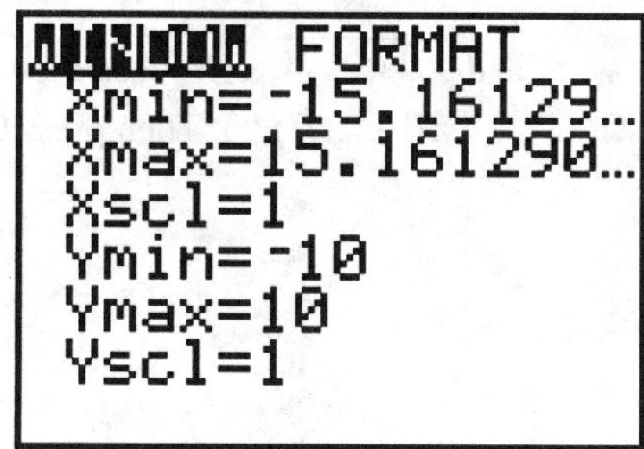

Figure 3.14: Square window

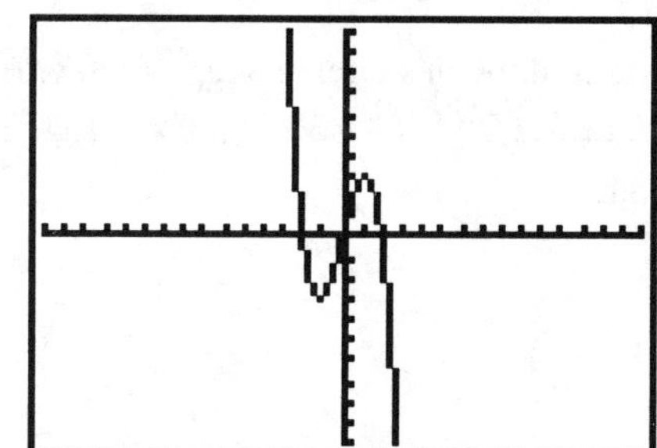

Figure 3.15: Graph of $y = -x^3 + 4x$

To set the range quickly to standard values (see Figure 3.13), press ZOOM 6. To set the viewing rectangle quickly to a square (Figure 3.14), press ZOOM 5. More information about square windows is presented later in Section 3.2.3.

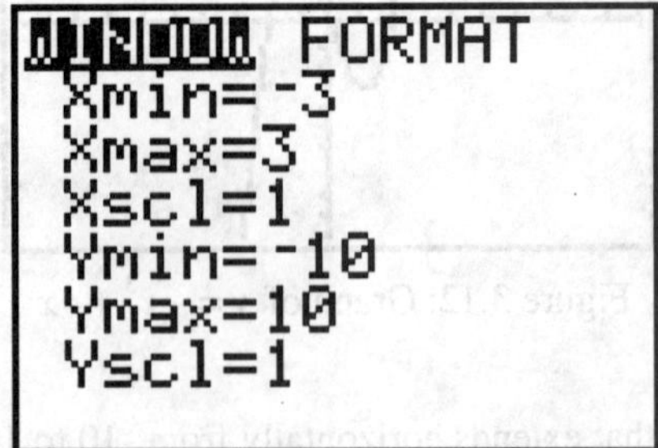

Figure 3.16: Custom window

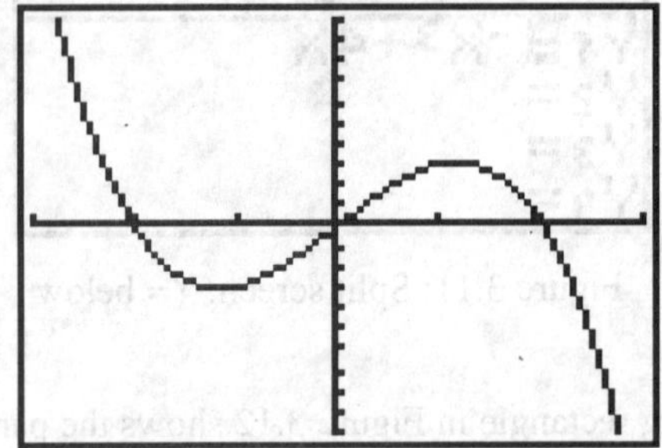

Figure 3.17: Graph of $y = -x^3 + 4x$

Sometimes you may wish to display grid points corresponding to tick marks on the axes. This and other graph format options may be changed by pressing WINDOW ▶ to display the FORMAT menu (Figure 3.18). Use arrow keys to move the blinking cursor to GridOn; press ENTER and then GRAPH to redraw the graph. Figure 3.19 shows the same graph as in Figure 3.17 but with the grid turned on. In general, you'll want the grid turned *off*, so do that now by pressing WINDOW ▶, use the arrow keys to move the blinking cursor to GridOff, and press ENTER and CLEAR.

Figure 3.18: WINDOW FORMAT menu

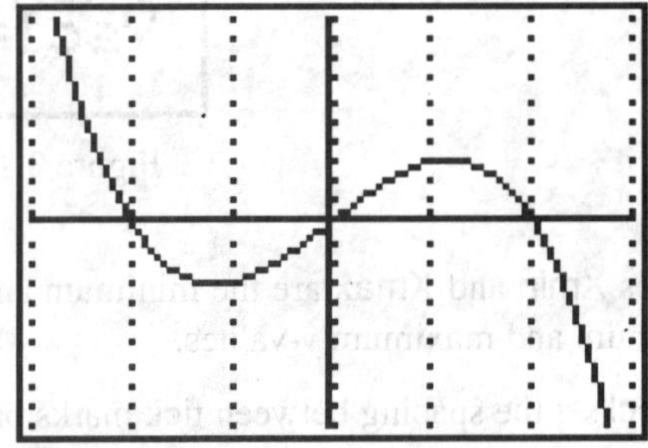

Figure 3.19: Grid turned on for $y = -x^3 + 4x$

3.2.3 Graphing a Circle: Here is a useful technique for graphs that are not functions, but that can be "split" into a top part and a bottom part, or into multiple parts. Suppose you wish to graph the circle whose equation is $x^2 + y^2 = 36$. First solve for y and get an equation for the top semicircle, $y = \sqrt{36 - x^2}$, and for the bottom semicircle, $y = -\sqrt{36 - x^2}$. Then graph the two semicircles simultaneously.

The keystrokes to draw this circle's graph follow. Enter $\sqrt{36 - x^2}$ as Y$_1$ and $-\sqrt{36 - x^2}$ as Y$_2$ (see Figure 3.20) by pressing Y= CLEAR 2nd $\sqrt{}$ (36 - X,T,θ x^2) ENTER CLEAR (-) 2nd $\sqrt{}$ (36 - X,T,θ x^2). Then press GRAPH to draw them both.

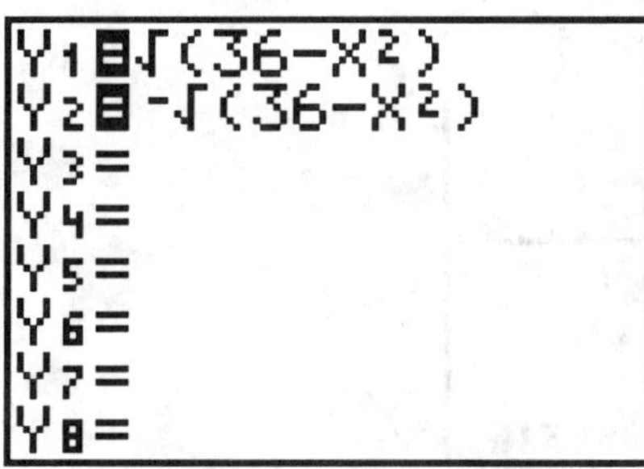

Figure 3.20: Two semicircles

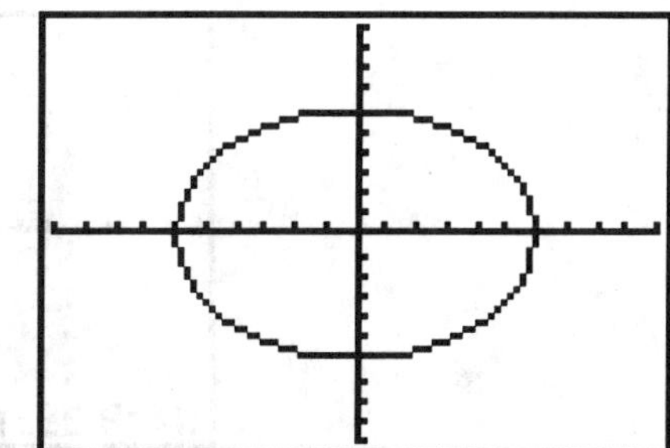

Figure 3.21: Circle's graph - standard view

If your range were set to the standard viewing rectangle, your graph would look like Figure 3.21. Now this does *not* look like a circle, because the units along the axes are not the same. This is where the square viewing rectangle is important. Press ZOOM 5 and see a graph that appears more circular.

Technology Tip: Another way to get a square graph is to change the range variables so that the value of Ymax - Ymin is approximately $\frac{2}{3}$ times Xmax - Xmin. For example, see the WINDOW in Figure 3.22 and the corresponding graph in Figure 3.23. The method works because the dimensions of the TI-82's display are such that the ratio of vertical to horizontal is approximately $\frac{2}{3}$.

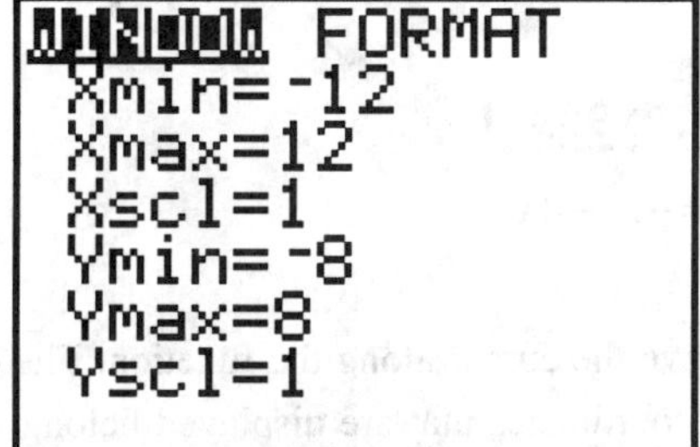

Figure 3.22: $\frac{\text{vertical}}{\text{horizontal}} = \frac{16}{24} = \frac{2}{3}$

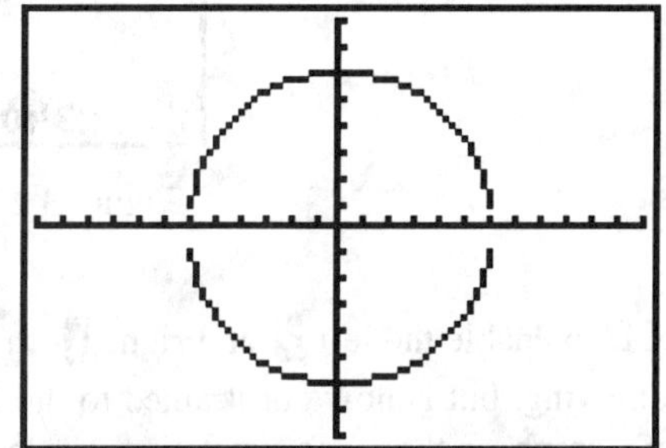

Figure 3.23: A "square" circle

The two semicircles in Figure 3.23 do not meet because of an idiosyncrasy in the way the TI-82 plots a graph.

Back when you entered $\sqrt{36-x^2}$ as Y_1 and $-\sqrt{36-x^2}$ as Y_2, you could have entered -Y_1 as Y_2 and saved some keystrokes. Try this by going back to the Y= menu and pressing the arrow key to move the cursor down to Y_2. Then press CLEAR (-) 2nd Y-VARS 1 1. The graph should be just as it was before.

Technology Tip: The square viewing rectangle is also important when you want to judge whether two lines are perpendicular. The intersection of perpendicular lines will always *look* like a right angle in a square viewing rectangle.

3.2.4 TRACE: Graph $y = -x^3 + 4x$ in the standard viewing rectangle. Press any of the arrow keys ▲ ▼ ◀ ▶ and see the cursor move from the center of the viewing rectangle. The coordinates of the cursor's location are displayed at the bottom of the screen, as in Figure 3.24, in floating decimal format. This cursor is called a *free-moving cursor* because it can move from dot to dot *anywhere* in the graph window.

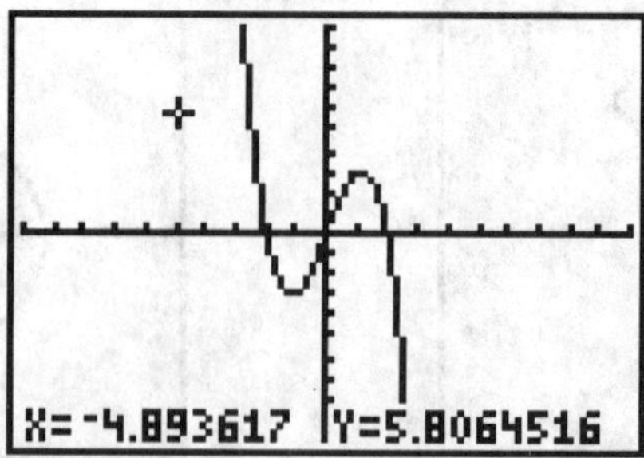

Figure 3.24: Free-moving cursor

Remove the free-moving cursor and its coordinates from the window by pressing GRAPH, CLEAR, or ENTER. Press an arrow key again and the free-moving cursor will reappear at the same point you left it.

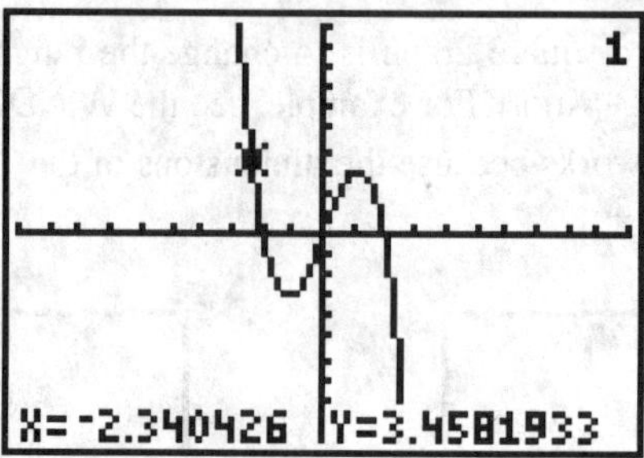

Figure 3.25: Trace on $y = -x^3 + 4x$

Press TRACE to enable the left ◄ and right ► arrow keys to move the cursor along the function. The cursor is no longer free-moving, but is now constrained to the function. The coordinates that are displayed belong to points on the function's graph, so the y-coordinate is the calculated value of the function at the corresponding x-coordinate.

Now plot a second function, $y = -.25x$, along with $y = -x^3 + 4x$. Press Y= and enter $-.25x$ for Y_2, then press GRAPH.

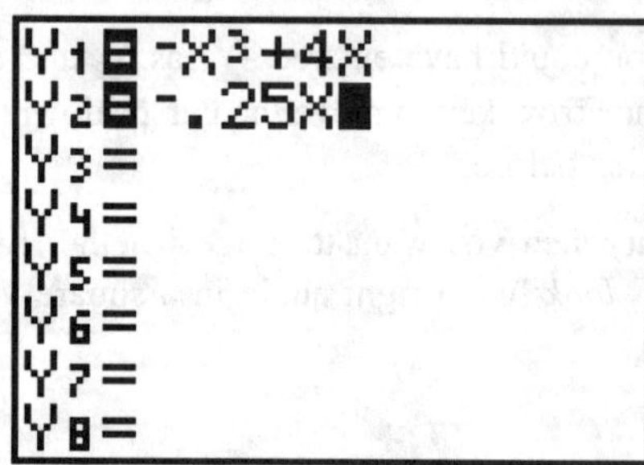

Figure 3.26: Two functions

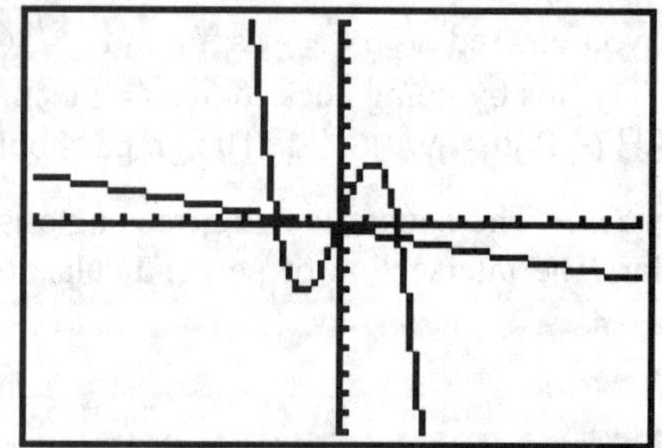

Figure 3.27: $y = -x^3 + 4x$ and $y = -.25x$

Note in Figure 3.26 that the equal signs next to Y_1 and Y_2 are *both* highlighted. This means *both* functions will be graphed. In the Y= screen, move the cursor directly on top of the equal sign next to Y_1 and press ENTER. This equal sign should no longer be highlighted (see Figure 3.28). Now press GRAPH and see that only Y_2 is plotted (Figure 3.29).

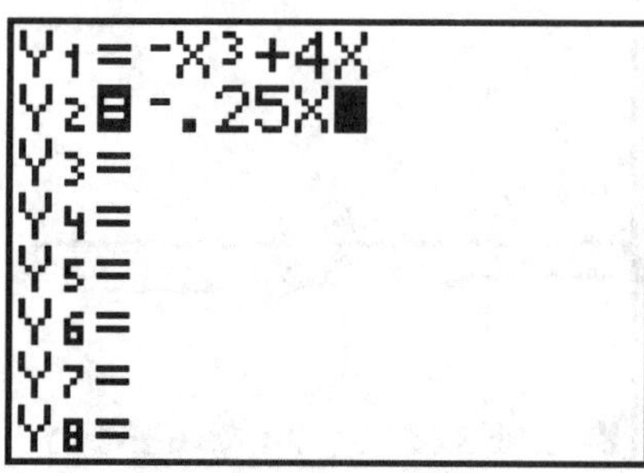

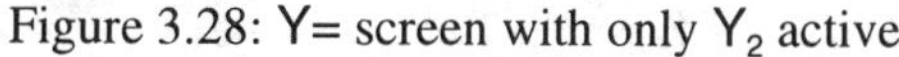

Figure 3.28: Y= screen with only Y$_2$ active

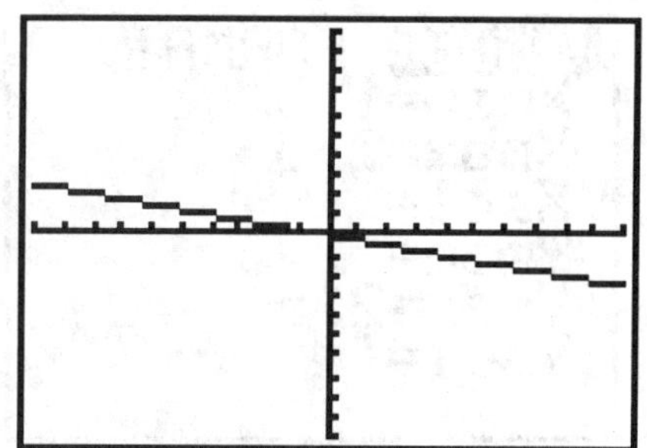

Figure 3.29: Graph of $y = -.25x$

Many different functions may be stored in the Y= list and any combination of them may be graphed simultaneously. You can make a function active or inactive for graphing by pressing ENTER on its equal sign to highlight (activate) or remove the highlight (deactivate). Go back to the Y= screen and do what is needed in order to graph Y$_1$ but not Y$_2$.

Now activate Y$_2$ again so that both graphs are plotted. Press TRACE and the cursor appears first on the graph of $y = -x^3 + 4x$ because it is higher up in the Y= list. You know that the cursor is on this function, Y$_1$, because of the numeral 1 that is displayed in the upper right corner of the window (see Figure 3.25). Press the up ▲ or down ▼ arrow key to move the cursor vertically to the graph of $y = -.25x$. Now the numeral 2 is displayed in the top right corner of the window. Next press the right and left arrow keys to trace along the graph of $y = -.25x$. When more than one function is plotted, you can move the trace cursor vertically from one graph to another in this way.

Technology Tip: By the way, trace along the graph of $y = -.25x$ and press and hold either ◄ or ►. Eventually you will reach the left or right edge of the window. Keep pressing the arrow key and the TI-82 will allow you to continue the trace by panning the viewing rectangle. Check the WINDOW screen to see that Xmin and Xmax are automatically updated.

The TI-82's display has 95 horizontal columns of pixels and 63 vertical rows. So when you trace a curve across a graph window, you are actually moving from Xmin to Xmax in 94 equal jumps, each called Δx. You would calculate the size of each jump to be $\Delta x = \dfrac{\text{Xmax} - \text{Xmin}}{94}$. Sometimes you may want the jumps to be friendly numbers like .1 or .25 so that, when you trace along the curve, the x-coordinates will be incremented by such a convenient amount. Just set your viewing rectangle for a particular increment Δx by making Xmax = Xmin + 94·Δx. For example, if you want Xmin = -5 and Δx = .3, set Xmax = -5 + 94·.3 = 23.2. Likewise, set Ymax = Ymin + 62·Δy if you want the vertical increment to be some special Δy.

To center your window around a particular point, say (h, k), and also have a certain Δx, set Xmin = h - 47·Δx and Xmax = h + 47·Δx. Likewise, make Ymin = k - 31·Δy and Ymax = k + 31·Δy. For example, to center a window around the origin, (0, 0), with both horizontal and vertical increments of .25, set the range so that Xmin = 0 - 47·.25 = -11.75, Xmax = 0 + 47·.25 = 11.75, Ymin = 0 - 31·.25 = -7.75, and Ymax = 0 + 31·.25 = 7.75.

See the benefit by first plotting $y = x^2 + 2x + 1$ in a standard graphing window. Trace near its y-intercept, which is (0, 1), and move towards its x-intercept, which is (-1, 0). Then press ZOOM 4 and trace again near the intercepts.

3.2.5 ZOOM: Plot again the two graphs, for $y = -x^3 + 4x$ and for $y = -.25x$. There appears to be an intersection near $x = 2$. The TI-82 provides several ways to enlarge the view around this point.

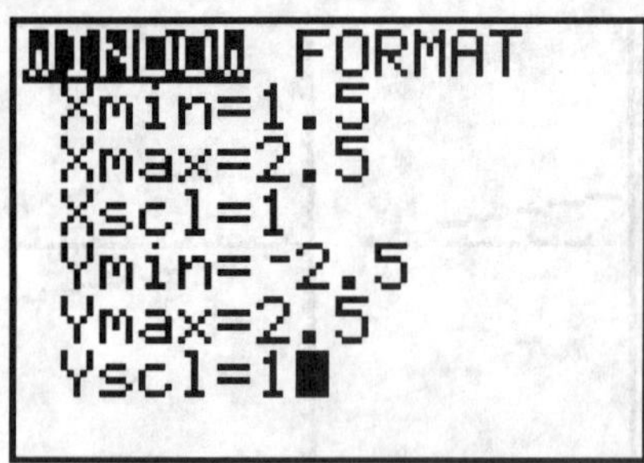

Figure 3.30: New WINDOW

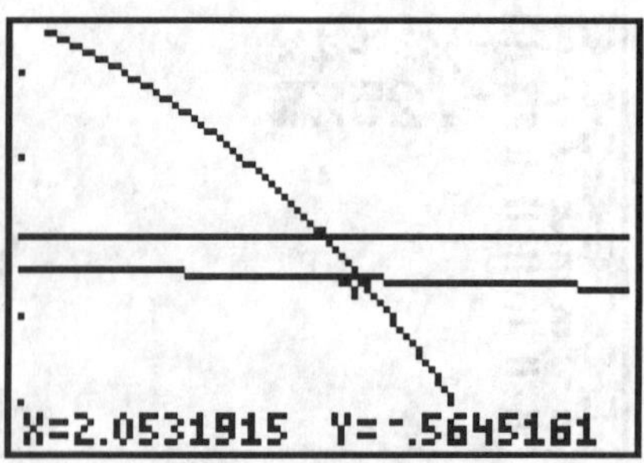

Figure 3.31: Closer view

You can change the viewing rectangle directly by pressing WINDOW and editing the values of Xmin, Xmax, Ymin, and Ymax. Figure 3.31 shows a new viewing rectangle for the range displayed in Figure 3.30. The cursor has been moved near the point of intersection; move your cursor closer to get the best approximation possible for the coordinates of the intersection.

A more efficient method for enlarging the view is to draw a new viewing rectangle with the cursor. Start again with a graph of the two functions $y = -x^3 + 4x$ and $y = -.25x$ in a standard viewing rectangle (press ZOOM 6 for the standard window, from -10 to 10 along both axes).

Figure 3.32: ZOOM menu

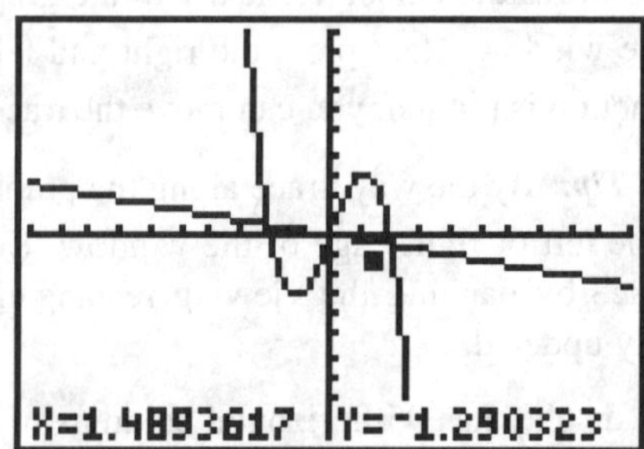

Figure 3.33: One corner selected

Now imagine a small rectangular box around the intersection point, near $x = 2$. Press ZOOM 1 (Figure 3.32) to draw a box to define this new viewing rectangle. Use the arrow keys to move the cursor, whose coordinates are displayed at the bottom of the window, to one corner of the new viewing rectangle you imagine.

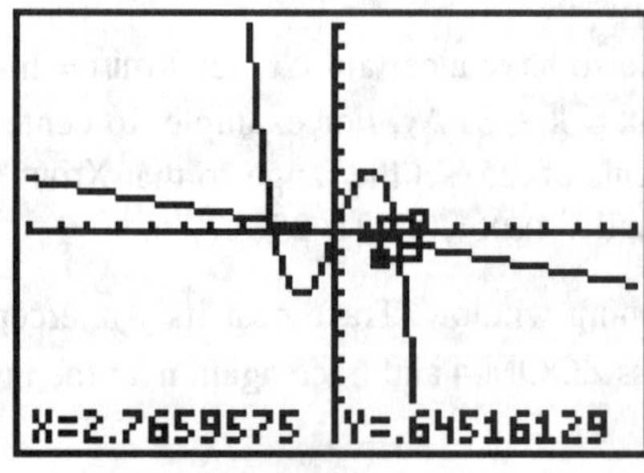

Figure 3.34: Box drawn

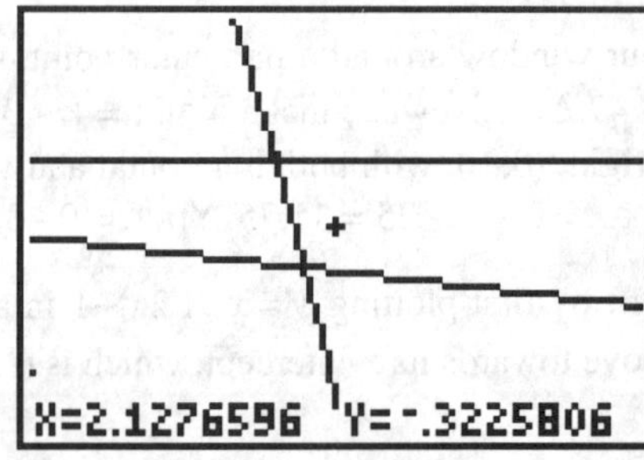

Figure 3.35: New viewing rectangle

Press ENTER to fix the corner where you have moved the cursor; it changes shape and becomes a blinking square (Figure 3.33). Use the arrow keys again to move the cursor to the diagonally opposite corner of the new rectangle

(Figure 3.34). If this box looks all right to you, press ENTER. The rectangular area you have enclosed will now enlarge to fill the graph window (Figure 3.35).

You may interrupt the zoom any time *before* you press this last ENTER. Press ZOOM once more and start over. Press CLEAR or GRAPH to cancel the zoom, or press 2nd QUIT to cancel the zoom and return to the home screen.

You can also gain a quick magnification of the graph around the cursor's location. Return once more to the standard window for the graph of the two functions $y = -x^3 + 4x$ and $y = -.25x$. Press ZOOM 2 and then press arrow keys to move the cursor as close as you can to the point of intersection near $x = 2$ (see Figure 3.36). Then press ENTER and the calculator draws a magnified graph, centered at the cursor's position (Figure 3.37). The range variables are changed to reflect this new viewing rectangle. Look in the WINDOW menu to verify this.

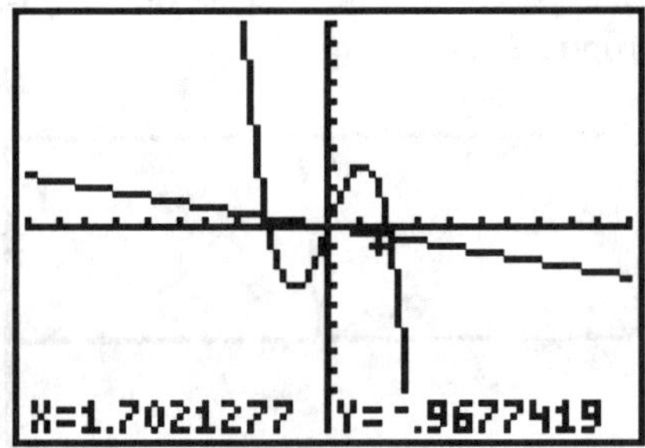

Figure 3.36: Before a zoom in

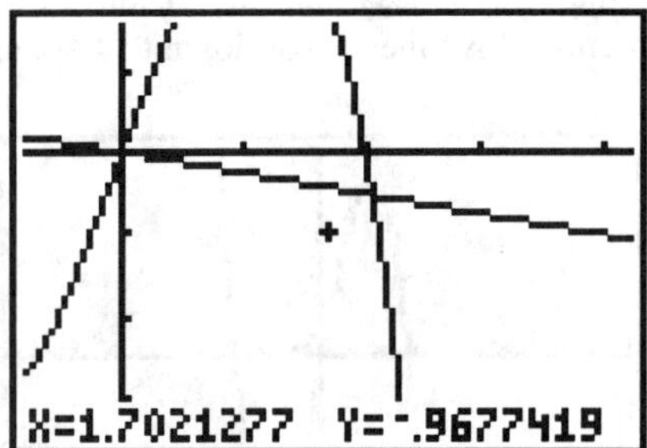

Figure 3.37: After a zoom in

As you see in the ZOOM menu (Figure 3.32), the TI-82 can Zoom In (press ZOOM 2) or Zoom Out (press ZOOM 3). Zoom out to see a larger view of the graph, centered at the cursor position. You can change the horizontal and vertical scale of the magnification by pressing ZOOM ▶ 4 (see Figure 3.39) and editing XFact and YFact, the horizontal and vertical magnification factors.

The default zoom factor is 4 in both directions. It is not necessary for XFact and YFact to be equal. Sometimes, you may prefer to zoom in one direction only, so the other factor should be set to 1. As usual, press 2nd QUIT to leave the ZOOM menu.

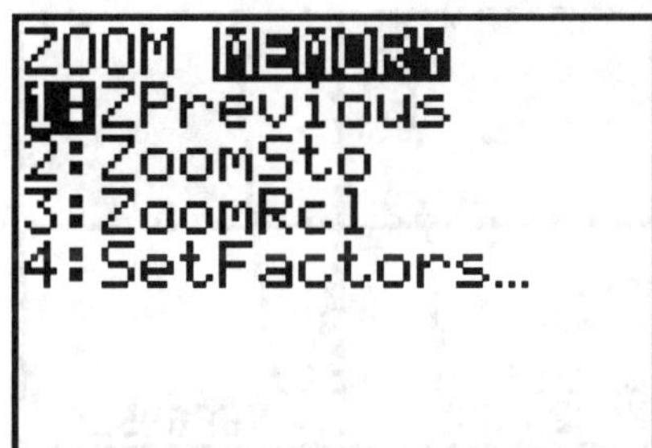

Figure 3.38: ZOOM MEMORY menu

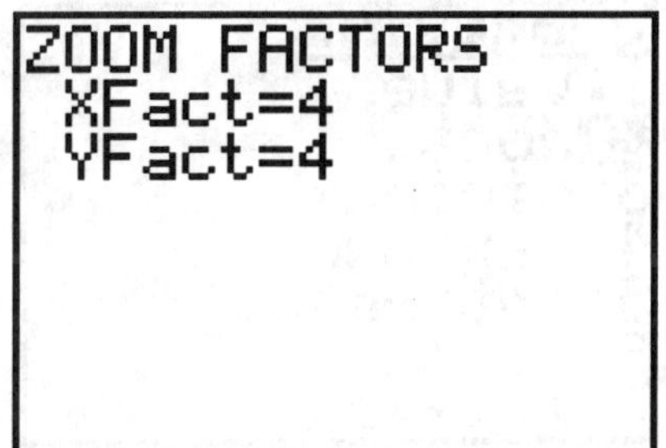

Figure 3.39: ZOOM MEMORY SetFactors...

Technology Tip: The TI-82 remembers the window it displayed before a zoom. So if you should zoom in too much and lose the curve, press ZOOM ▶ 1 to go back to the window before. If you want to execute a series of zooms but then return to a particular window, press ZOOM ▶ 2 to store the current window's dimensions. Later, press ZOOM ▶ 3 to recall the stored window.

3.3.1 Intercepts and Intersections: Tracing and zooming are also used to locate an x-intercept of a graph, where a curve crosses the x-axis. For example, the graph of $y = x^3 - 8x$ crosses the x-axis three times (see Figure 3.40). After tracing over to the x-intercept point that is furthest to the left, zoom in (Figure 3.41). Continue this process until you have located all three intercepts with as much accuracy as you need. The three x-intercepts of $y = x^3 - 8x$ are approximately -2.828, 0, and 2.828.

Technology Tip: As you zoom in, you may also wish to change the spacing between tick marks on the x-axis so that the viewing rectangle shows scale marks near the intercept point. Then the accuracy of your approximation will be such that the error is less than the distance between two tick marks. Change the x-scale on the TI-82 from the WINDOW menu. Move the cursor down to Xscl and enter an appropriate value.

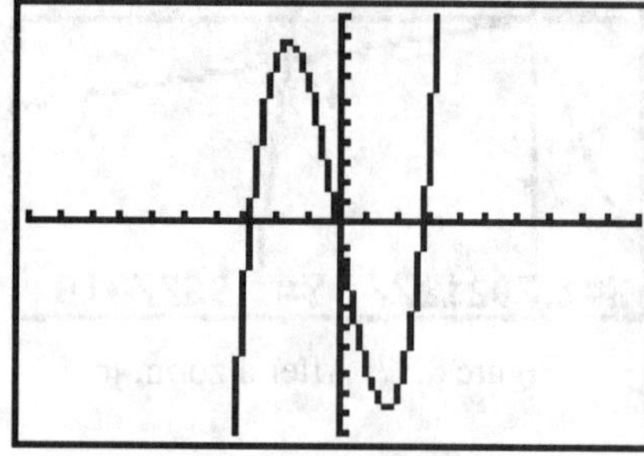

Figure 3.40: Graph of $y = x^3 - 8x$

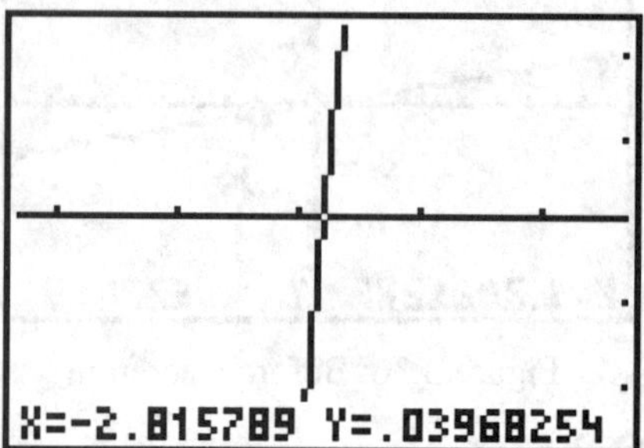

Figure 3.41: An x-intercept of $y = x^3 - 8x$

The x-intercept of a function's graph is a *root* of the equation $f(x) = 0$. And the TI-82 automates the search for roots. Press 2nd CALC to display the CALCULATE menu (Figure 3.42). Choose 2 to calculate the root of the function. You will be prompted to trace the cursor along the graph first to a point *left* of a root (press ENTER to set this *lower bound*). Then move to a point *right* of the root and set an *upper bound* (as in Figure 3.43) and press ENTER. Note the two arrows marking the lower and upper bounds at the top of the display.

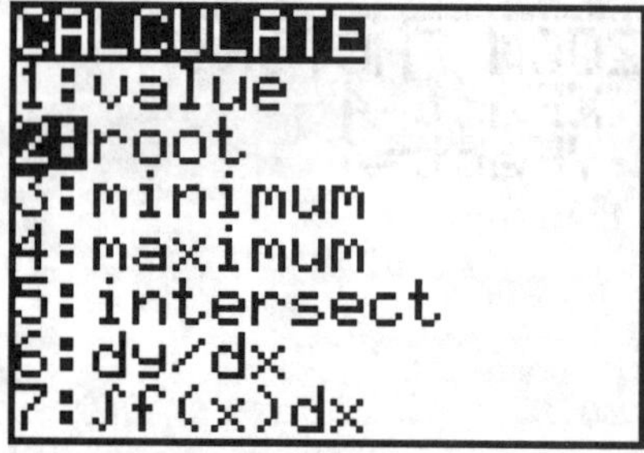

Figure 3.42: CALCULATE menu

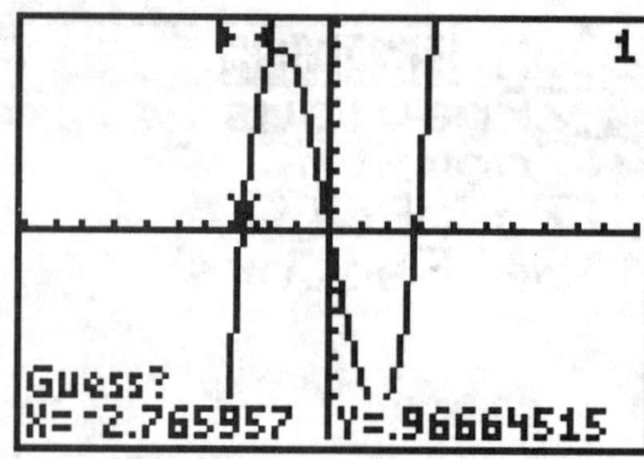

Figure 3.43: Finding a root

Next move the cursor along the graph between the two bounds and as close to the root as you can; this serves as a *guess* for the TI-82 to start its search. Good choices for the lower bound, upper bound, and guess can help the calculator work more efficiently and quickly. Press ENTER and the coordinates of a root will be displayed (see Figure 3.44). Repeat this process to find the coordinates of any other root the function may have.

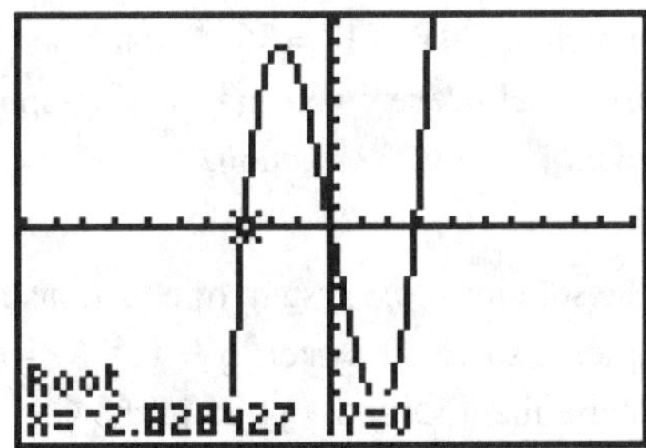

Figure 3.44: A root of $y = x^3 - 8x$

TRACE and ZOOM are especially important for locating the intersection points of two graphs, say the graphs of $y = -x^3 + 4x$ and $y = -.25x$. Trace along one of the graphs until you arrive close to an intersection point. Then press ▲ or ▼ to jump to the other graph. Notice that the x-coordinate does not change, but the y-coordinate is likely to be different (see Figures 3.45 and 3.46).

When the two y-coordinates are as close as they can get, you have come as close as you now can to the point of intersection. So zoom in around the intersection point, then trace again until the two y-coordinates are as close as possible. Continue this process until you have located the point of intersection with as much accuracy as necessary.

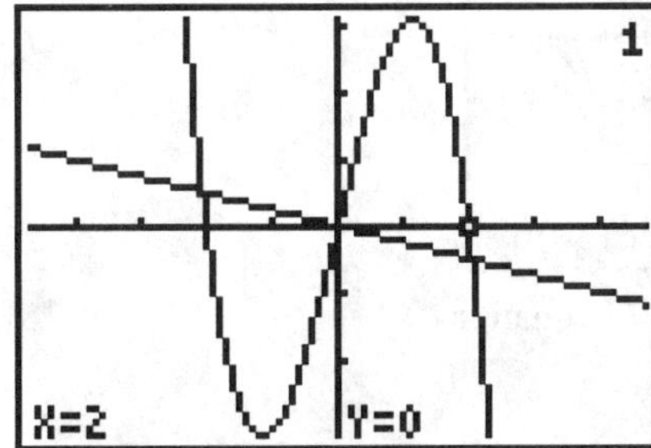

Figure 3.45: Trace on $y = -x^3 + 4x$

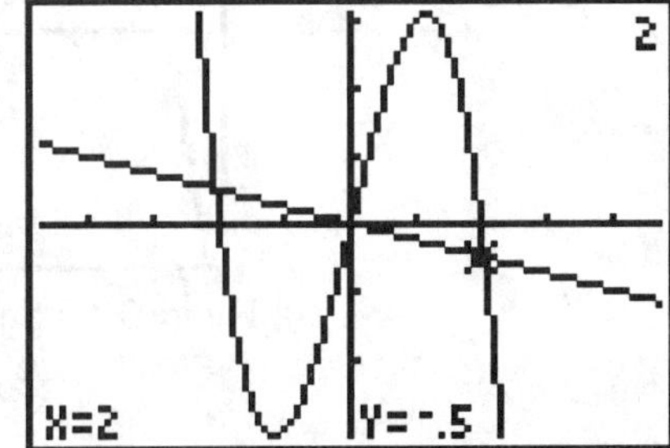

Figure 3.46: Trace on $y = -.25x$

You can also find the point of intersection of two graphs by pressing 2nd CALC 5. Trace with the cursor first along one graph near the intersection and press ENTER; then trace with the cursor along the other graph and press ENTER. Marks + are placed on the graphs at these points. Finally, move the cursor near the point of intersection and press ENTER again. Coordinates of the intersection will be displayed at the bottom of the window.

3.3.2 Solving Equations by Graphing: Suppose you need to solve the equation $24x^3 - 36x + 17 = 0$. First graph $y = 24x^3 - 36x + 17$ in a window large enough to exhibit *all* its x-intercepts, corresponding to all the equation's roots. Then use trace and zoom, or the TI-82's root finder, to locate each one. In fact, this equation has just one solution, approximately $x = -1.414$.

Remember that when an equation has more than one root, it may be necessary to change the viewing rectangle a few times to locate all of them.

Technology Tip: To solve an equation like $24x^3 + 17 = 36x$, you may first transform it into standard form, $24x^3 - 36x + 17 = 0$, and proceed as above. However, you may also graph the *two* functions $y = 24x^3 + 17$ and $y = 36x$, then zoom and trace to locate their point of intersection.

3.3.3 Solving Systems by Graphing: The solutions to a system of equations correspond to the points of intersection of their graphs (Figure 3.47). For example, to solve the system $y = x^2 - 3x - 4$ and $y = x^3 + 3x^2 - 2x - 1$, first graph them together. Then zoom and trace, or use the intersect option in the CALC menu, to locate their point of intersection, approximately (-2.17, 7.25).

You must judge whether the two current y-coordinates are sufficiently close for $x = -2.17$ or whether you should continue to zoom and trace to improve the approximation.

The solutions of the system of two equations $y = x^3 + 3x^2 - 2x - 1$ and $y = x^2 - 3x - 4$ correspond to the solutions of the single equation $x^3 + 3x^2 - 2x - 1 = x^2 - 3x - 4$, which simplifies to $x^3 + 2x^2 + x + 3 = 0$. So you may also graph $y = x^3 + 2x^2 + x + 3$ and find its x-intercepts to solve the system.

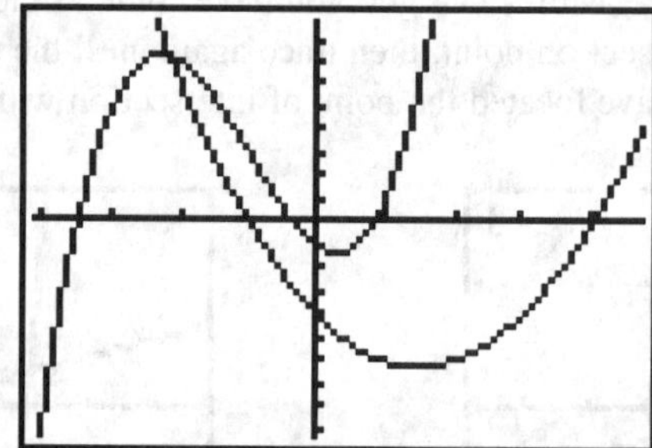

Figure 3.47: Solving a system of equations

3.3.4 Solving Inequalities by Graphing: Consider the inequality $1 - \dfrac{3x}{2} \geq x - 4$. To solve it with your TI-82, graph the two functions $y = 1 - \dfrac{3x}{2}$ and $y = x - 4$ (Figure 3.48). First locate their point of intersection, at $x = 2$. The inequality is true when the graph of $y = 1 - \dfrac{3x}{2}$ lies *above* the graph of $y = x - 4$, and that occurs for $x < 2$. So the solution is the half-line $x \leq 2$, or $(-\infty, 2]$.

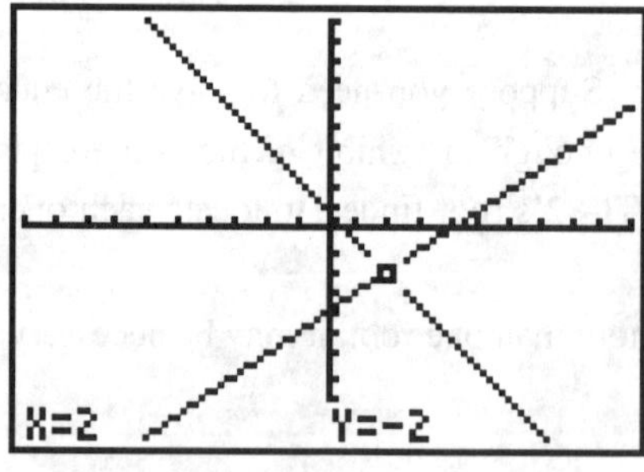

Figure 3.48: Solving $1 - \dfrac{3x}{2} \geq x - 4$

The TI-82 is capable of shading the region above or below a graph or between two graphs. For example, to graph $y \geq x^2 - 1$, first graph the function $y = x^2 - 1$ as Y₁. Then press 2nd DRAW 7 2nd Y-VARS 1 1 , 10 , 2) ENTER (see Figure 3.49). These keystrokes instruct the TI-82 to shade the region *above* $y = x^2 - 1$ and *below* $y = 10$ (chosen because this is the greatest y-value in the graph window) with shading resolution value of 2. The result is shown in Figure 3.50.

To clear the shading, press 2nd DRAW 1.

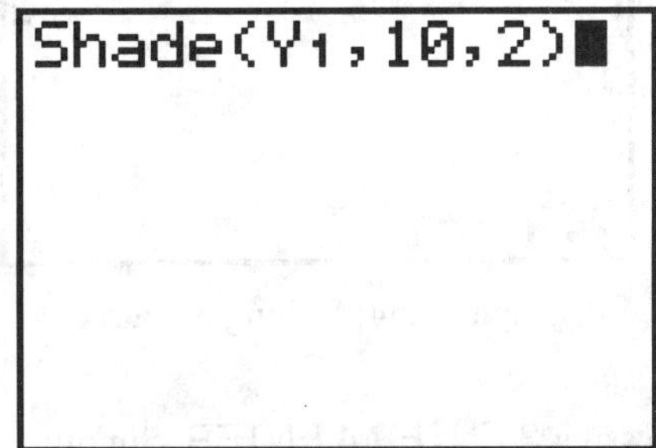

Figure 3.49: DRAW Shade

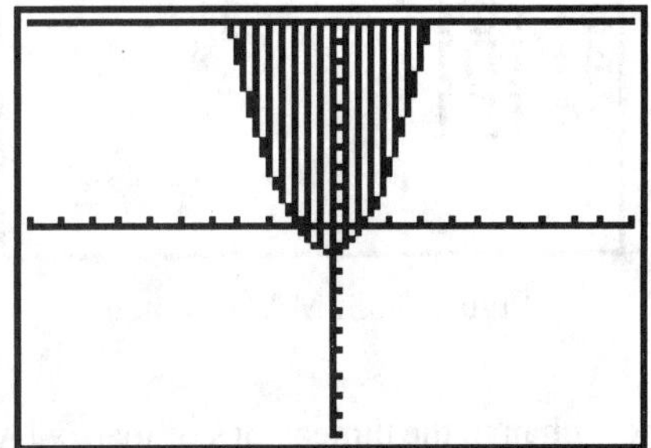

Figure 3.50: Graph of $y \geq x^2 - 1$

Now use shading to solve the previous inequality, $1 - \dfrac{3x}{2} \geq x - 4$. The function whose graph forms the lower boundary is named *first* in the SHADE command (see Figure 3.51). To enter this in your TI-82, press these keys: 2nd DRAW 7 X,T,θ - 4 , 1 - 3 X,T,θ ÷ 2 , 2) ENTER (Figure 3.52). The shading extends left from $x = 2$, hence the solution to $1 - \dfrac{3x}{2} \geq x - 4$ is the half-line $x \leq 2$, or $(-\infty, 2]$.

Figure 3.51: DRAW Shade command

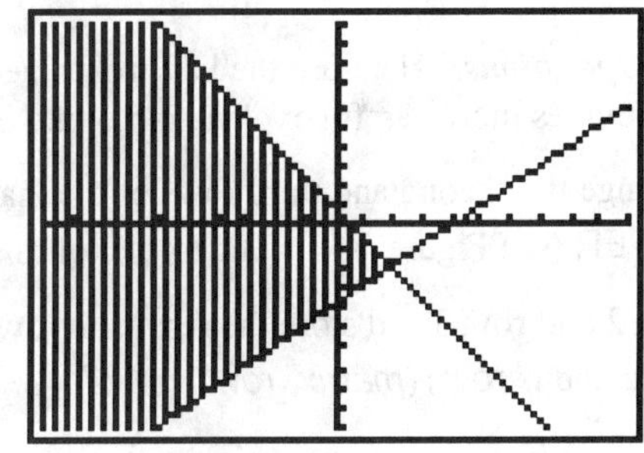

Figure 3.52: Graph of $1 - \dfrac{3x}{2} \geq x - 4$

More information about the DRAW menu is in the TI-82 manual.

3.4   Matrices

3.4.1 Making a Matrix: The TI-82 can display and use five different matrices. Here's how to create this 3×4 matrix
$$\begin{bmatrix} 1 & -4 & 3 & 5 \\ -1 & 3 & -1 & -3 \\ 2 & 0 & -4 & 6 \end{bmatrix}$$ in your calculator.

Press MATRX to see the matrix menu (Figure 3.53); then press ▶ ▶ or just ◀ to switch to the matrix EDIT menu (Figure 3.54). Whenever you enter the matrix EDIT menu, the cursor starts at the top matrix. Move to another matrix by repeatedly pressing ▼ . For now, press ENTER to edit matrix [A].

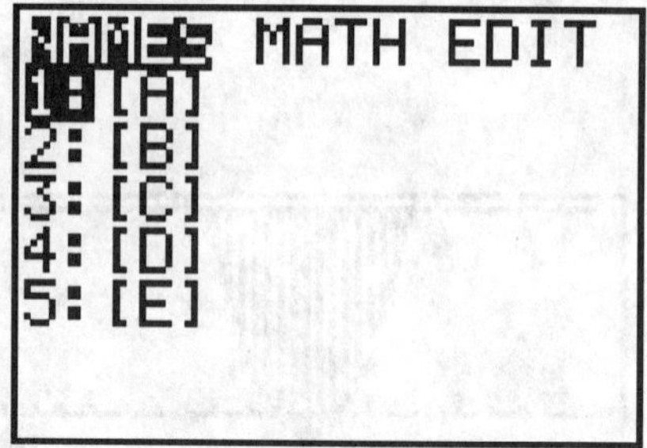

Figure 3.53: MATRX menu

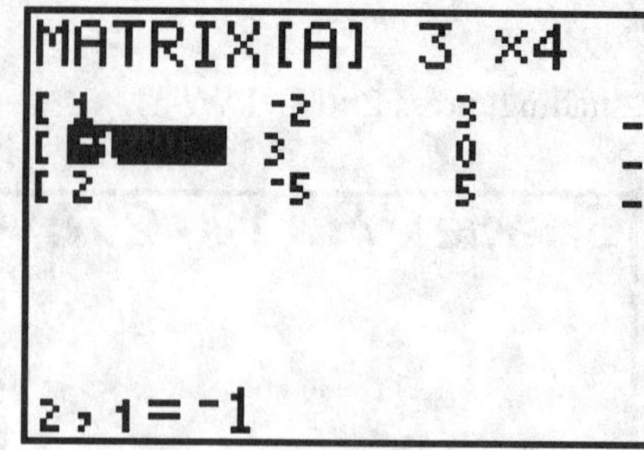

Figure 3.54: Editing a matrix

You may now change the dimensions of matrix [A] to 3×4 by pressing 3 ENTER 4 ENTER. Simply press ENTER or an arrow key to accept an existing dimension. The matrix shown in the window changes in size to reflect a changed dimension.

Use the arrow keys or ENTER to move the cursor to a matrix element you want to change. At the right edge of the screen in Figure 3.54, there are dashes to indicate more columns than are shown. Go to them by pressing ▶ as many times as necessary. The ordered pair at the bottom left of the screen show the cursor's current location within the matrix. The element in the second row and first column in Figure 3.54 is currently highlighted, so the ordered pair at the bottom of the window is 2 , 1. Continue to enter all the elements of matrix [A].

Leave the matrix [A] editing screen by pressing 2nd QUIT and return to the home screen.

3.4.2 Row Operations: Here are the keystrokes necessary to perform elementary row operations on a matrix. Your textbook provides more careful explanation of the elementary row operations and their uses.

To interchange the second and third rows of the matrix [A] that was defined above, press MATRX ▶ 8 MATRX 1 , 2 , 3) ENTER (see Figure 3.55). The format of this command is rowSwap(*matrix, row1, row2*).

To add row 2 and row 3 and store the results in row 3, press MATRX ▶ 9 MATRX 1 , 2 , 3) ENTER. The format of this command is row+(*matrix, row1, row2*).

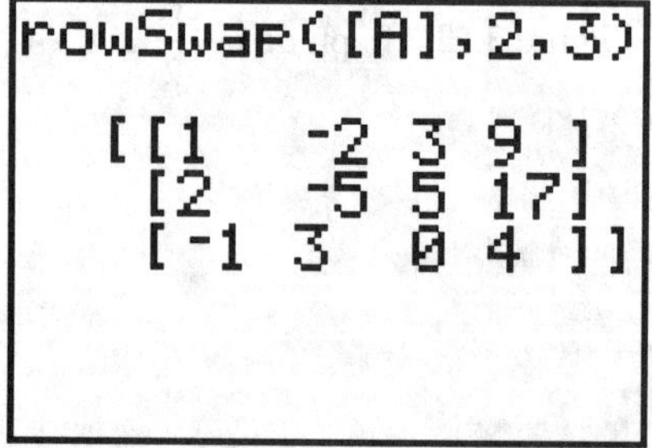

Figure 3.55: Swap rows 2 and 3

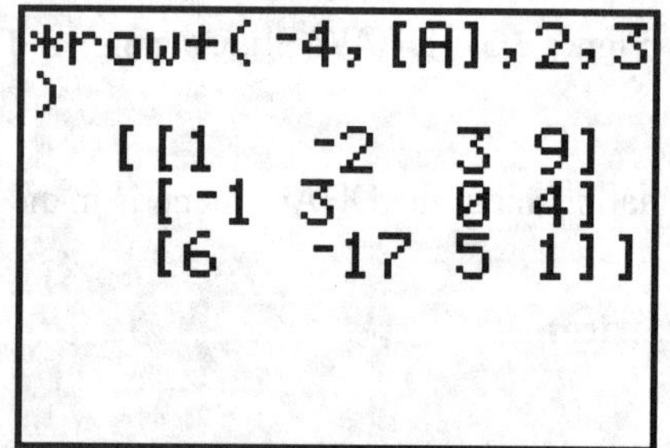

Figure 3.56: Add -4 times row 2 to row 3

To multiply row 2 by -4 and *store* the results in row 2, thereby replacing row 2 with new values, press MATRX ▶ 0 (-) 4 , MATRX 1 , 2) ENTER. The format of this command is *row(*scalar, matrix, row*).

To multiply row 2 by -4 and *add* the results to row 3, thereby replacing row 3 with new values, press MATRX ▶ ALPHA A (-) 4 , MATRX 1 , 2 , 3) ENTER (see Figure 3.56). The format of this command is *row+(*scalar, matrix, row1, row2*).

Technology Tip: It is important to remember that your TI-82 does *not* store a matrix obtained as the result of any row operations. So when you need to perform several row operations in succession, it is a good idea to store the result of each one in a temporary place. You may wish to use matrix [E] to hold such intermediate results.

For example, use elementary row operations to solve this system of linear equations: $\begin{cases} x - 2y + 3z = 9 \\ -x + 3y = -4 \\ 2x - 5y + 5z = 17 \end{cases}$.

First enter this *augmented matrix* as [A] in your TI-82: $\begin{bmatrix} 1 & -2 & 3 & 9 \\ -1 & 3 & 0 & -4 \\ 2 & -5 & 5 & 17 \end{bmatrix}$. Next store this matrix in [E] (press MATRX 1 STO▶ MATRX 5 ENTER) so you may keep the original in case you need to recall it.

Here are the row operations and their associated keystrokes. At each step, the result is stored in [E] and replaces the previous matrix [E]. The solution is shown in Figure 3.57.

Row Operation	*Keystrokes*
row+([E], 1, 2)	MATRX ▶ 9 MATRX 5 , 1 , 2) STO▶ MATRX 5 ENTER
*row+(-2, [E], 1, 3)	MATRX ▶ ALPHA A (-) 2 , MATRX 5 , 1 , 3) STO▶ MATRX 5 ENTER
row+([E], 2, 3)	MATRX ▶ 9 MATRX 5 , 2 , 3) STO▶ MATRX 5 ENTER
*row(½, [E], 3)	MATRX ▶ 0 1 ÷ 2 , MATRX 5 , 3) STO▶ MATRX 5 ENTER

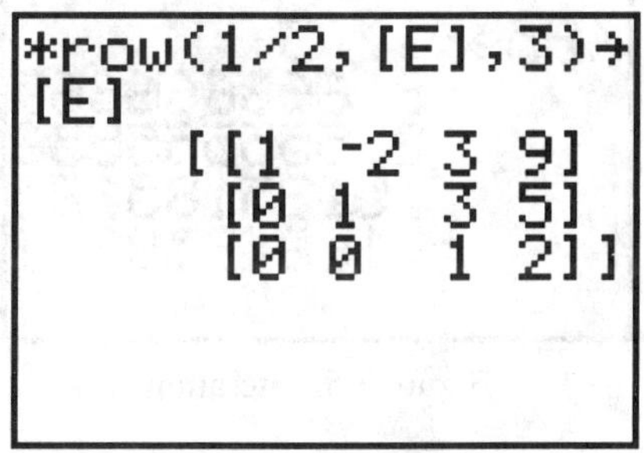

Figure 3.57: Final matrix after row operations

Thus $z = 2$, so $y = -1$ and $x = 1$.

3.4.3 Determinants: Enter this 3×3 square matrix as [A]: $\begin{bmatrix} 1 & -2 & 3 \\ -1 & 3 & 0 \\ 2 & -5 & 5 \end{bmatrix}$. To calculate its determinant,

$\begin{bmatrix} 1 & -2 & 3 \\ -1 & 3 & 0 \\ 2 & -5 & 5 \end{bmatrix}$, press MATRX ▶ 1 MATRX 1 ENTER. You should find that $\big| [A] \big| = 2$.

3.5   Additional Topics

3.5.1 Iteration: The ANS feature enables you to perform iterations to evaluate a function repeatedly. As an example, calculate $\dfrac{n-1}{3}$ for $n = 27$. Then calculate $\dfrac{n-1}{3}$ for n = the answer to the previous calculation. Continue to use each answer as n in the *next* calculation. Here are keystrokes to accomplish this iteration on the TI-82 calculator (see the results in Figure 3.58). Notice that when you use ANS in place of n in a formula, it is sufficient to press ENTER to continue an iteration.

Iteration	*Keystrokes*	*Display*
1	27 ENTER	27
2	(2nd ANS - 1) ÷ 3 ENTER	8.666666667
3	ENTER	2.555555556
4	ENTER	.5185185185
5	ENTER	-.1604938272

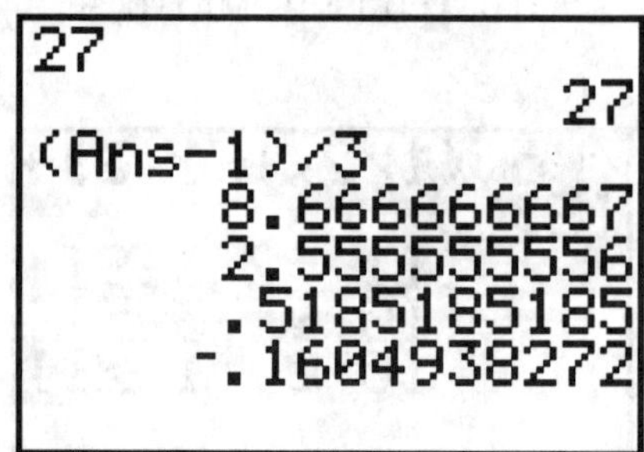

Figure 3.58: Iteration

Press ENTER several more times and see what happens with this iteration. You may wish to try it again with a different starting value.

3.5.2 Arithmetic and Geometric Sequences: Use iteration with the ANS variable to determine the n-th term of a sequence. For example, find the 18th term of an *arithmetic* sequence whose first term is 7 and whose common difference is 4. Enter the first term 7, then start the progression with the recursion formula, 2nd ANS + 4 ENTER. This yields the 2nd term, so press ENTER sixteen more times to find the 18th term. For a *geometric* sequence whose common ratio is 4, start the progression with 2nd ANS × 4 ENTER.

You can also define the sequence recursively with the TI-82 by selecting Seq in the MODE menu (see Figure 3.1). Once again, let's find the 18th term of an *arithmetic* sequence whose first term is 7 and whose common difference is 4. Press MODE ▼ ▼ ▼ ▶ ▶ ▶ ENTER 2nd QUIT. Then press Y= to edit either of the TI-82's two sequences, u_n and v_n. Make $u_n = u_{n-1} + 4$ by pressing 2nd u_{n-1} + 4. Now make $u_1 = 7$ by pressing WINDOW and setting U*n*Start = 7 and *n*Start = 1 (because the first term is u_1 where $n = 1$). Press 2nd QUIT to leave this menu and return to the home screen. To find the 18th term of this sequence, calculate u_{18} by pressing 2nd Y-VARS 4 1 (18) ENTER (see Figure 3.59).

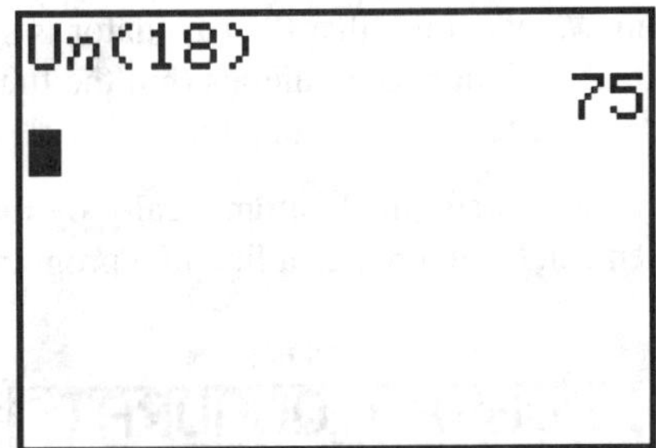

Figure 3.59: Sequence mode

Of course, you could use the *explicit* formula for the *n*-th term of an arithmetic sequence, $t_n = a + (n-1)d$. First enter values for the variables a, d, and n, then evaluate the formula by pressing ALPHA A + (ALPHA N - 1) ALPHA D ENTER. For a geometric sequence whose *n*-th term is given by $t_n = a \cdot r^{n-1}$, enter values for the variables a, r, and n, then evaluate the formula by pressing ALPHA A ALPHA R ^ (ALPHA N - 1) ENTER.

To use the explicit formula in Seq MODE, make $u_n = 7 + (n-1) \cdot 4$ by pressing Y= and then 7 + (2nd n - 1) × 4. Once more, calculate u_{18} by pressing 2nd Y-VARS 4 1 (18) ENTER.

There are more instructions for using sequence mode in the TI-82 manual.

3.5.3 Permutations and Combinations: To calculate the number of *permutations* of 12 objects taken 7 at a time, $_{12}P_7$, press 12 MATH ◀ 2 7 ENTER. Thus $_{12}P_7 = 3,991,680$, as shown in Figure 3.60.

For the number of *combinations* of 12 objects taken 7 at a time, $_{12}C_7$, press 12 MATH ◀ 3 7 ENTER. So $_{12}C_7 = 792$.

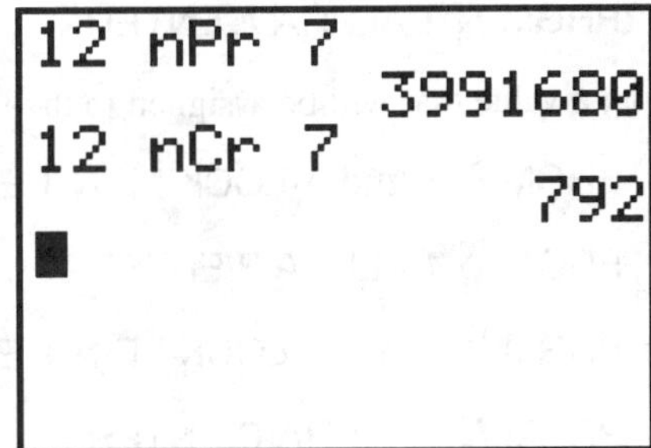

Figure 3.60: $_{12}P_7$ and $_{12}C_7$

3.6   Programming

3.6.1 Entering a Program: The TI-82 is a programmable calculator that can store sequences of commands for later replay. Here's an example to show you how to enter a useful program that solves quadratic equations by the quadratic formula.

Press PRGM to access the programming menu. The TI-82 has space for many programs, each called by a name you give it. Create a new program now, so press PRGM ◀ 1.

For convenience, the cursor is a blinking **A**, indicating that the calculator is set to receive alphabetic characters. Enter a descriptive title of up to eight characters, letters or numerals (but the first character must be a letter). Name this program QUADRAT and press ENTER to go to the program editor.

In the program, each line begins with a colon : supplied automatically by the calculator. Any command you could enter directly in the TI-82's home screen can be entered as a line in a program. There are also special programming commands.

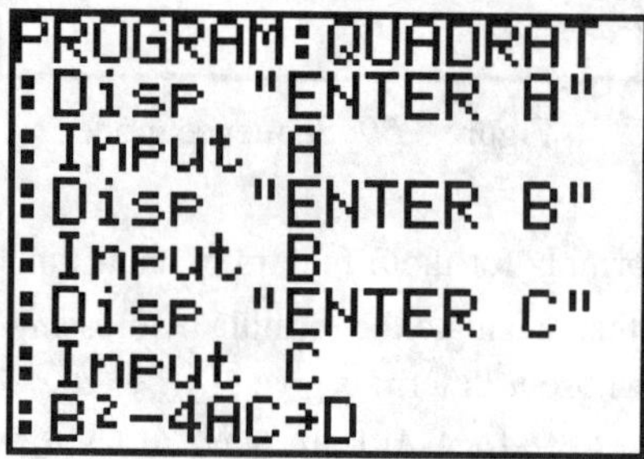

Figure 3.61: Program QUADRAT

Input the program QUADRAT by pressing the keystrokes given in the listing below. You may interrupt program input at any stage by pressing 2nd QUIT. To return later for more editing, press PRGM ▶, move the cursor down to this program's name, and press ENTER.

Program Line	*Keystrokes*
: Disp "ENTER A"	PRGM ▶ 3 2nd A-LOCK " E N T E R ⌴ A " ENTER
displays the words *Enter A* on the TI-82 screen	
: Input A	PRGM ▶ 1 ALPHA A ENTER
waits for you to input a value that will be assigned to the variable A	
: Disp "ENTER B"	PRGM ▶ 3 2nd A-LOCK " E N T E R ⌴ B " ENTER
: Input B	PRGM ▶ 1 ALPHA B ENTER
: Disp "ENTER C"	PRGM ▶ 3 2nd A-LOCK " E N T E R ⌴ C " ENTER
: Input C	PRGM ▶ 1 ALPHA C ENTER
: B^2-4AC $\rightarrow$ D	ALPHA B x² - 4 ALPHA A ALPHA C STO▶ ALPHA D ENTER
calculates the discriminant and stores its value as D	

: If D>0   PRGM 1 ALPHA D 2nd TEST 3 0 ENTER

tests to see if the discriminant is positive

: Then   PRGM 2 ENTER

in case the discriminant is positive, continues on to the next line;
if the discriminant is not positive, jumps to the command after Else below

: Disp "TWO REAL ROOTS"   PRGM ▶ 3 2nd A-LOCK " T W O ␣ R E A L ␣ R O O T S " ENTER

: (-B+√D)/(2A) → M   ((-) ALPHA B + 2nd √ ALPHA D) ÷ (2 ALPHA A)
STO ▶ ALPHA M ENTER

calculates one root and stores it as M

: Disp M   PRGM ▶ 3 ALPHA M ENTER

displays one root

: (-B-√D)/(2A) → N   ((-) ALPHA B - 2nd √ ALPHA D) ÷ (2 ALPHA A)
STO ▶ ALPHA N ENTER

: Disp N   PRGM ▶ 3 ALPHA N ENTER

: Else   PRGM 3 ENTER

continues from here if the discriminant is not positive

: If D=0   PRGM 1 ALPHA D 2nd TEST 1 0 ENTER

tests to see if the discriminant is zero

: Then   PRGM 2 ENTER

in case the discriminant is zero, continues on to the next line;
if the discriminant is not zero, jumps to the command after Else below

: Disp "DOUBLE ROOT"   PRGM ▶ 3 2nd A-LOCK " D O U B L E ␣ R O O T " ENTER

displays a message in case there is a double root

: -B/(2A) → M   (-) ALPHA B ÷ (2 ALPHA A) STO ▶ ALPHA M ENTER

the quadratic formula reduces to $\dfrac{-b}{2a}$ when $D = 0$

: Disp M   PRGM ▶ 3 ALPHA M ENTER

: Else   PRGM 3 ENTER

continues from here if the discriminant is not zero

: Disp "COMPLEX ROOTS"   PRGM ▶ 3 2nd A-LOCK " C O M P L E X ␣ R O O T S " ENTER

displays a message in case the roots are complex numbers

: Disp "REAL PART"   PRGM ▶ 3 2nd A-LOCK " R E A L ␣ P A R T " ENTER

| : -B/(2A) → R | (-) ALPHA B ÷ (2 ALPHA A) STO▶ ALPHA R ENTER |

calculates the real part $\dfrac{-b}{2a}$ of the complex roots

| : Disp R | PRGM ▶ 3 ALPHA R ENTER |

| : Disp "IMAGINARY PART" | PRGM ▶ 3 2nd A-LOCK " I M A G I N A R Y ⌴ P A R T " ENTER |

| : √-D/(2A) → I | 2nd √ (-) ALPHA D ÷ (2 ALPHA A) STO▶ ALPHA I ENTER |

calculates the imaginary part $\dfrac{\sqrt{-D}}{2a}$ of the complex roots;

since $D < 0$, we must use $-D$ as the radicand

| : Disp I | PRGM ▶ 3 ALPHA I ENTER |

| : End | PRGM 7 ENTER |

marks the end of an If-Then-Else group of commands

| : End | PRGM 7 |

When you have finished, press 2nd QUIT to leave the program editor.

You may remove a program from memory by pressing 2nd MEM 2 *[Delete...]* 6 *[Prgm...]*. Then move the cursor to the program's name and press ENTER to delete the entire program.

3.6.2 *Running a Program:*

To run the program just entered, press PRGM and the number or letter that it was named, then ENTER. If you have forgotten its name, use the arrow keys to move through the program listing to find its description QUADRAT, then press ENTER to select this program and ENTER again to run it.

The program has been written to prompt you for values of the coefficients a, b, and c in a quadratic equation $ax^2 + bx + c = 0$. Input a value, then press ENTER to continue the program.

If you need to interrupt a program during execution, press ON.

The instruction manual for your TI-82 gives detailed information about programming. Refer to it to learn more about programming and how to use other features of your calculator.

Chapter 4

Texas Instruments TI-85
Advanced Scientific Calculator

4.1 Getting started with the TI-85

4.1.1 Basics: Press the ON key to begin using your TI-85 calculator. If you need to adjust the display contrast, first press 2nd, then press and hold ▲ (the *up* arrow key) to increase the contrast or ▼ (the *down* arrow key) to decrease the contrast. As you press and hold ▲ or ▼, an integer between 0 (lightest) and 9 (darkest) appears in the upper right corner of the display. When you have finished with the calculator, turn it off to conserve battery power by pressing 2nd and then OFF.

Check the TI-85's settings by pressing 2nd MODE. If necessary, use the arrow keys to move the blinking cursor to a setting you want to change. Press ENTER to select a new setting. To start with, select the options along the left side of the MODE menu as illustrated in Figure 4.1: normal display, floating decimals, radian measure, rectangular coordinates, function graphs, decimal number system, rectangular vectors, and differentiation type. Details on alternative options will be given later in this guide. For now, leave the MODE menu by pressing EXIT or 2nd QUIT or CLEAR.

Figure 4.1: MODE menu

Figure 4.2: Home screen

4.1.2 Editing: One advantage of the TI-85 is that up to 8 lines are visible at one time, so you can *see* a long calculation. For example, type this sum (see Figure 4.2):

$$1 + 2 + 3 + 4 + 5 + 6 + 7 + 8 + 9 + 10 + 11 + 12 + 13 + 14 + 15 + 16 + 17 + 18 + 19 + 20$$

Then press ENTER to see the answer, too.

Often we do not notice a mistake until we see how unreasonable an answer is. The TI-85 permits you to re-display an entire calculation, edit it easily, then execute the *corrected* calculation.

Suppose you had typed 12 + 34 + 56 as in Figure 4.2 but had *not* yet pressed ENTER, when you realize that 34 should have been 74. Simply press ◀ (the *left* arrow key) as many times as necessary to move the blinking cursor left to 3, then type 7 to write over it. On the other hand, if 34 should have been 384, move the cursor back to 4, press 2nd INS (the cursor changes to a blinking underline) and then type 8 (inserts at the cursor position and other characters are pushed to the right). If the 34 should have been 3 only, move the cursor to 4 and press DEL to delete it.

While you are editing an expression, pressing the *up* (or *down*) arrow key causes the cursor to jump quickly to the *left* (or *right*) end of the expression.

Even if you had pressed ENTER, you may still edit the previous expression. Press 2nd and then ENTRY to *recall* the last expression that was entered. Now you can change it.

Technology Tip: When you need to evaluate a formula for different values of a variable, use the editing feature to simplify the process. For example, suppose you want to find the balance in an investment account if there is now $5000 in the account and interest is compounded annually at the rate of 8.5%. The formula for the balance is $P\left(1+\frac{r}{n}\right)^{nt}$, where P = principal, r = rate of interest (expressed as a decimal), n = number of times interest is com-

pounded each year, and t = number of years. In our example, this becomes $5000(1+.085)^t$. Here are the keystrokes for finding the balance after $t = 3, 5,$ and 10 years.

Years	Keystrokes	Balance
3	5000 (1 + .085) ^ 3 ENTER	$6386.45
5	2nd ENTRY ◀ 5 ENTER	$7518.28
10	2nd ENTRY ◀ 10 ENTER	$11,304.92

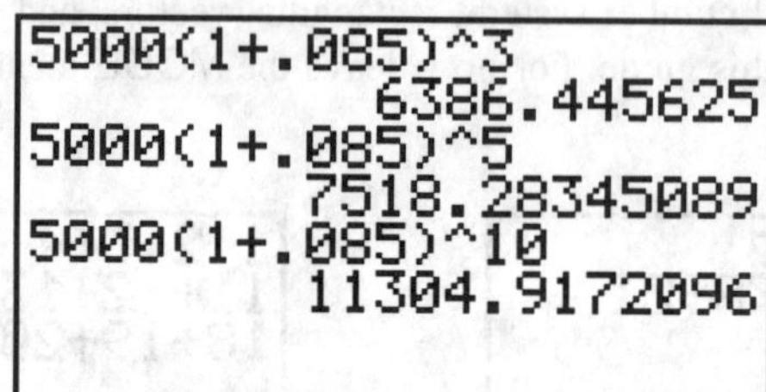

Figure 4.3: Editing expressions

Then to find the balance from the same initial investment but after 5 years when the annual interest rate is 7.5%, press these keys to change the last calculation above: 2nd ENTRY ◀ DEL ◀ 5 ◀ ◀ ◀ ◀ ◀ 7 ENTER.

4.1.3 Key Functions: Most keys on the TI-85 offer access to more than one function, just as the keys on a computer keyboard can produce more than one letter ("g" and "G") or even quite different characters ("5" and "%"). The primary function of a key is indicated on the key itself, and you access that function by a simple press on the key.

To access the *second* function indicated to the *left* above a key, first press 2nd (the cursor changes to a blinking ↑) and *then* press the key. For example, to calculate $\sqrt{25}$, press 2nd √ 25 ENTER.

When you want to use a capital letter or other character printed to the *right* above a key, first press ALPHA (the cursor changes to a blinking **A**) and then the key. For example, to use the letter K in a formula, press ALPHA K. If you need several letters in a row, press ALPHA twice in succession, which is like pressing Caps Lock on a computer keyboard, and then press all the letters you want. Remember to press ALPHA when you are finished and want to restore keys to their primary functions. To type lowercase letters, press 2nd alpha (the cursor changes to a blinking **a**). To lock in lowercase letters, press 2nd alpha 2nd alpha or 2nd alpha ALPHA. To unlock from lowercase, press ALPHA ALPHA (you'll see the cursor change from blinking **a** to blinking **A** and then to the standard blinking rectangle).

4.1.4 Order of Operations: The TI-85 performs calculations according to the standard algebraic rules. Working outwards from inner parentheses, calculations are performed from left to right. Powers and roots are evaluated first, followed by multiplications and divisions, and then additions and subtractions.

Note that the TI-85 distinguishes between *subtraction* and the *negative sign*. If you wish to enter a negative number, it is necessary to use the (-) key. For example, you would evaluate $-5-(4\cdot-3)$ by pressing (-) 5 - (4 × (-) 3) ENTER to get 7.

Enter these expressions to practice using your TI-85.

Expression	Keystrokes	Display
$7 - 5 \cdot 3$	7 - 5 × 3 ENTER	-8
$(7 - 5) \cdot 3$	(7 - 5) × 3 ENTER	6
$120 - 10^2$	120 - 10 x² ENTER	20
$(120 - 10)^2$	(120 - 10) x² ENTER	12100
$\dfrac{24}{2^3}$	24 ÷ 2 ^ 3 ENTER	3
$\left(\dfrac{24}{2}\right)^3$	(24 ÷ 2) ^ 3 ENTER	1728
$(7 - -5) \cdot -3$	(7 - (-) 5) × (-) 3 ENTER	-36

4.1.5 Algebraic Expressions and Memory: Your calculator can evaluate expressions such as $\dfrac{N(N+1)}{2}$ *after* you have entered a value for N. Suppose you want $N = 200$. Press 200 STO ▸ N ENTER to store the value 200 in memory location N. (The STO ▸ key prepares the TI-85 for an alphabetical entry, so it is *not* necessary to press ALPHA also.) Whenever you use N in an expression, the calculator will substitute the value 200 until you make a change by storing *another* number in N. Next enter the expression $\dfrac{N(N+1)}{2}$ by typing ALPHA N (ALPHA N + 1) ÷ 2 ENTER. For $N = 200$, you will find that $\dfrac{N(N+1)}{2} = 20100$.

The contents of any memory location may be revealed by typing just its letter name and then ENTER. And the TI-85 retains memorized values even when it is turned off, so long as its batteries are good.

A variable name in the TI-85 can be a single letter, or a string of up to eight characters that begins with a letter followed by other letters, numerals, and various symbols. Variable names are case sensitive, which means that length and Length and LENGTH may represent *different* quantities.

Because variable names may be more than one character in length, multiplication between variables must always be *expressed*. So for the product *ab*, you *must* enter 2nd alpha A × 2nd alpha B *with* the multiplication key. With a *numerical* coefficient, however, the multiplication does *not* need to be expressed; hence for *4ab* you may enter 4 2nd alpha A × 2nd alpha B.

4.1.6 Repeated Operations with ANS: The result of your *last* calculation is always stored in memory location ANS and replaces any previous result. This makes it easy to use the answer from one computation in another computation. For example, press 30 + 15 ENTER so that 45 is the last result displayed. Then press 2nd ANS ÷ 9 ENTER and get 5 because $\frac{45}{9} = 5$.

With a function like division, you press the ÷ key *after* you enter an argument. For such functions, whenever you would start a new calculation with the previous answer followed by pressing the function key, you may press just the function key. So instead of 2nd ANS ÷ 9 in the previous example, you could have pressed simply ÷ 9 to achieve the same result. This technique also works for these functions: + - × x² ^ x⁻¹.

Here is a situation where this is especially useful. Suppose a person makes $5.85 per hour and you are asked to calculate earnings for a day, a week, and a year. Execute the given keystrokes to find the person's incomes during these periods (results are shown in Figure 4.4):

Pay period	Keystrokes	Earnings
8-hour day	5.85 × 8 ENTER	$46.80
5-day week	× 5 ENTER	$234
52-week year	× 52 ENTER	$12,168

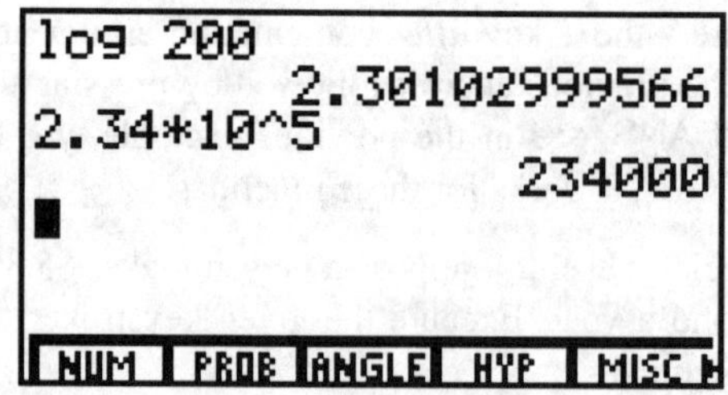

Figure 4.4: ANS variable

4.1.7 The MATH Menu: Operators and functions associated with a scientific calculator are available either immediately from the keys of the TI-85 or by 2nd keys. You have direct key access to common arithmetic operations (x^2, 2nd $\sqrt{\ }$, 2nd x^{-1}, and ^), exponential and logarithmic functions (LOG, 2nd 10^x, LN, 2nd e^x), and a famous constant (2nd π).

A significant difference between the TI-85 and many scientific calculators is that the TI-85 requires the argument of a function *after* the function, as you would see a formula written in your textbook. For example, on the TI-85 you calculate $\sqrt{16}$ by pressing the keys 2nd $\sqrt{\ }$ 16 in that order.

Here are keystrokes for basic mathematical operations. Try them for practice on your TI-85.

Expression	Keystrokes	Display
$\sqrt{3^2 + 4^2}$	2nd $\sqrt{\ }$ (3 x^2 + 4 x^2) ENTER	5
$2\frac{1}{3}$	2 + 3 2nd x^{-1} ENTER	2.33333333333
$\log 200$	LOG 200 ENTER	2.30102999566
$2.34 \cdot 10^5$	2.34 × 2nd 10^x 5 ENTER or 2.34 × 10 ^ 5 ENTER	234000

Additional mathematical operations and functions are available from the MATH menu (Figure 4.5). Press 2nd MATH to see the various options that are listed across the bottom of the screen. These options are activated by pressing corresponding menu keys, F1 through F5.

Figure 4.5: Basic MATH menu

TI-85 Advanced Scientific Calculator

For example, F1 brings up the NUM menu of numerical functions. You will learn in your mathematics textbook how to apply many of them. Note that the basic MATH menu items have moved up a line; these options are now available by pressing 2nd M1 through 2nd M5. As an example, determine $|-5|$ by pressing 2nd MATH F1 and then F5 (-) 5 ENTER (see Figure 4.6).

Next calculate $\sqrt[3]{7}$ by pressing 2nd MATH F5 (when the MATH NUM menu is displayed, as in Figure 4.6; press just 2nd M5) to access the MISC menu of miscellaneous mathematical functions. The arrow at the right end of this menu indicates there are more items that you can access. You may press the MORE key repeatedly to move down the row of options and back again. To calculate $\sqrt[3]{7}$, press 2nd MATH F5 MORE 3 F4 $[\sqrt[x]{\ }]$ 7 ENTER to see 1.9129 (Figure 4.7). To leave the MATH menu or any other menu and take no further action, press EXIT a couple of times.

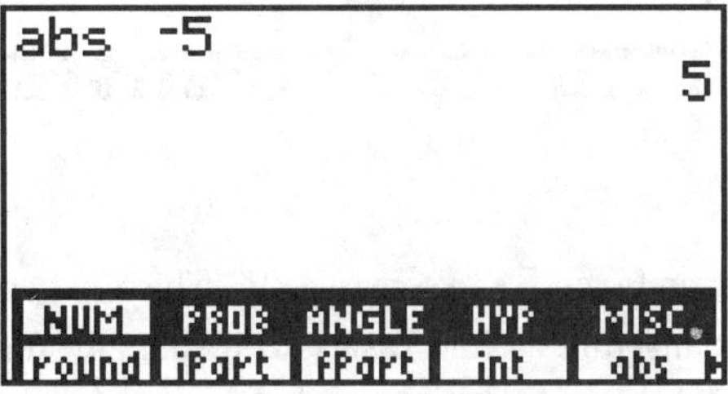

Figure 4.6: MATH NUM menu

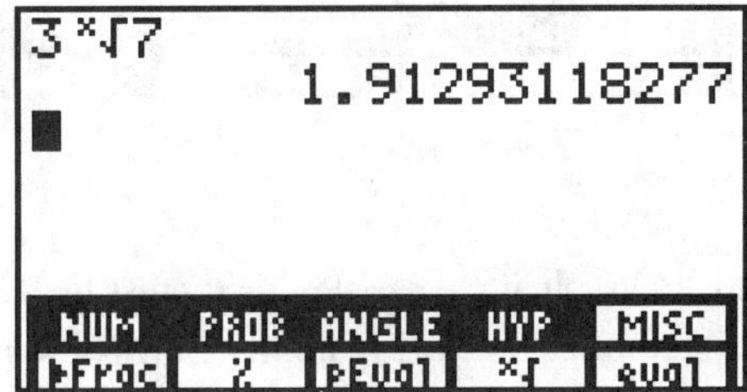

Figure 4.7: MATH MISC menu

The *factorial* of a non-negative integer is the *product* of *all* the integers from 1 up to the given integer. The symbol for factorial is the exclamation point. So 4! (pronounced *four factorial*) is $1\cdot2\cdot3\cdot4 = 24$. You will learn more about applications of factorials in your textbook, but for now use the TI-85 to calculate 4! Press these keystrokes: 2nd MATH F2 *[PROB]* 4 F1 *[!]* ENTER.

4.2   Functions and Graphs

4.2.1 Evaluating Functions: Suppose you receive a monthly salary of $1975 plus a commission of 10% of sales. Let x = your sales in dollars; then your wages W in dollars are given by the equation $W = 1975 + .10x$. If your January sales were $2230 and your February sales were $1865, what was your income during those months?

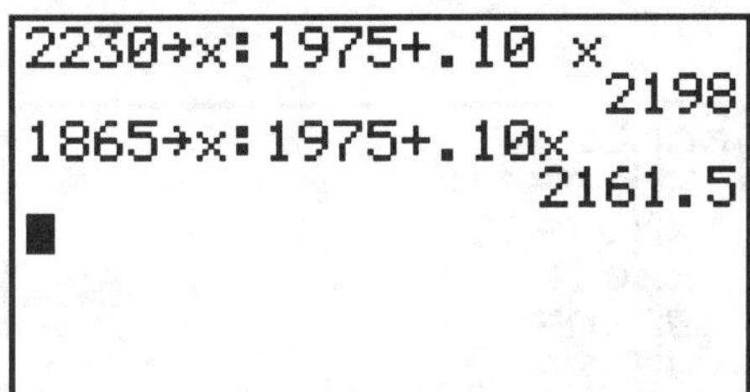

Figure 4.8: Evaluating a function

Here's how to use your TI-85 to perform this task. First press EXIT and CLEAR as necessary to get a blank home screen. Then set $x = 2230$ by pressing 2230 STO ▶ x-VAR. (The x-VAR key makes it easy to produce a lower case x for a variable name without having to use the 2nd alpha key.) Then press ALPHA to leave alphabetic entry and 2nd : to allow another expression to be entered on the same command line. Finally, enter the expression $1975 + .10x$ by pressing these keys: 1975 + .10 x-VAR. Now press ENTER to calculate the answer (Figure 4.8).

It is not necessary to repeat all these steps to find the February wages. Simply press 2nd ENTRY to recall the entire previous line and change 2230 to 1865.

4.2.2 Functions in a Graph Window: On the TI-85, once you have entered a function, you can easily generate its graph. The ability to draw a graph contributes substantially to our ability to solve problems.

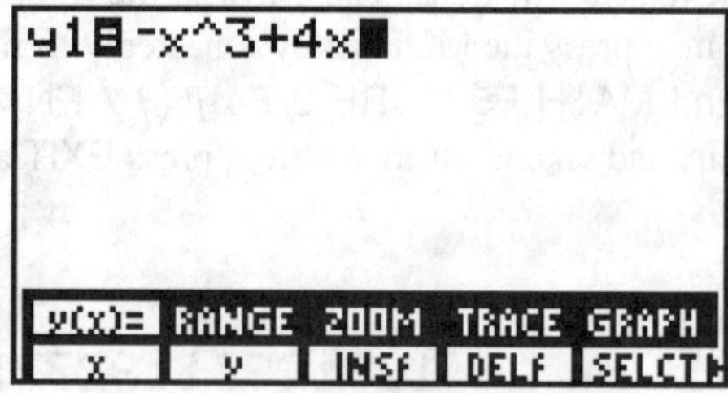

Figure 4.9: y(x)= screen

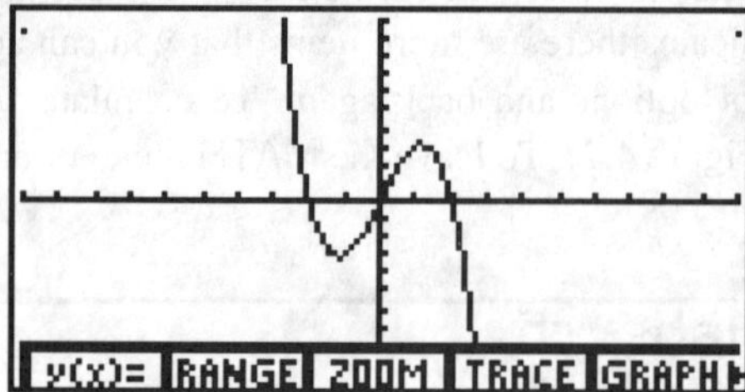

Figure 4.10: Graph of $y = -x^3 + 4x$

Here is how to graph $y = -x^3 + 4x$. First press the GRAPH key and then F1 to select y(x)=. This give you access to the function editing screen (Figure 4.9). Press F4 *[DELf]* as many times as necessary to delete any functions that may be there already. Then, with the cursor on the top line to the right of y1=, press (-) F1 ^ 3 + 4 F1 to enter the function. As you see, the TI-85 uses lower-case letters for its graphing variables, just like your mathematics textbook. Note that pressing F1 in this menu is the same as pressing either x-VAR or 2nd alpha X. Now press 2nd M5 *[GRAPH]* and the TI-85 changes to a window with the graph of $y = -x^3 + 4x$ (Figure 4.10).

While the TI-85 is calculating coordinates for a plot, it displays a busy indicator at the top right of the graph window.

Your graph window may look like the one in Figure 4.10 or it may be different. Since the graph of $y = -x^3 + 4x$ extends infinitely far left and right and also infinitely far up and down, the TI-85 can display only a piece of the actual graph. This displayed rectangular part is called a *viewing rectangle*. You can easily change the viewing rectangle to enhance your investigation of a graph.

The viewing rectangle in Figure 4.10 shows the part of the graph that extends horizontally from -10 to 10 and vertically from -10 to 10. Press F2 *[RANGE]* to see information about your viewing rectangle. Figure 4.11 shows the RANGE screen that corresponds to the viewing rectangle in Figure 4.10. This is the *standard* viewing rectangle for the TI-85.

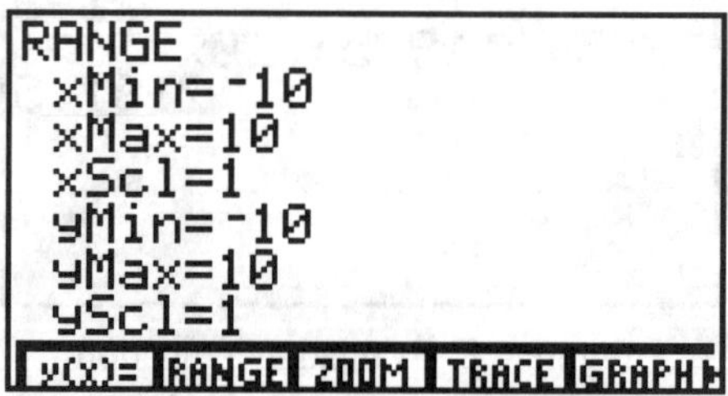

Figure 4.11: Standard RANGE

The variables xMin and xMax are the minimum and maximum *x*-values of the viewing rectangle; yMin and yMax are its minimum and maximum *y*-values.

xScl and yScl set the spacing between tick marks on the axes.

Use the arrow keys ▲ and ▼ to move up and down from one line to another in this list; pressing the ENTER key will move down the list. Press CLEAR to delete the current value and then enter a new value. You may also edit the entry as you would edit an expression. Remember that a minimum *must* be less than the corresponding maximum or the TI-85 will issue an error message. Also, remember to use the (-) key, not - (which is subtraction), when you want to enter a negative value. Figures 4.10-11, 4.12-13, and 4.14-15 show different RANGE screens and the corresponding viewing rectangle for each one.

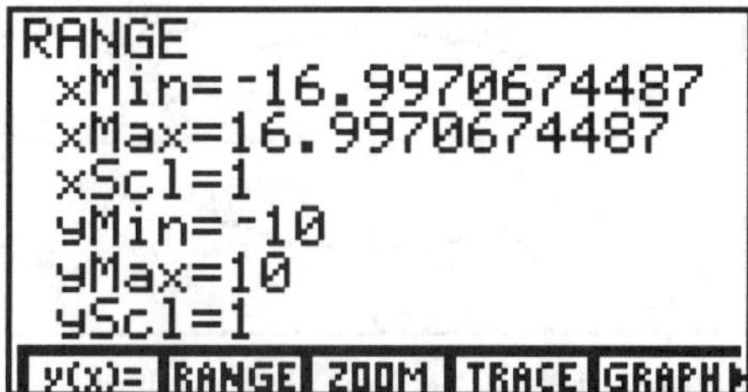

Figure 4.12: Square window

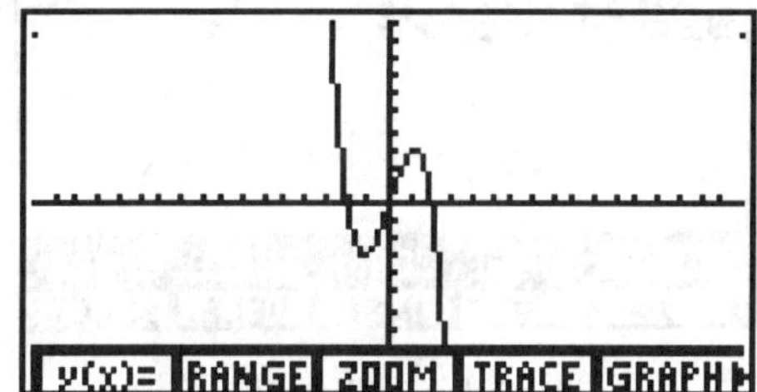

Figure 4.13: Graph of $y = -x^3 + 4x$

To set the range quickly to standard values (see Figure 4.11), press F3 F4 *[ZOOM ZSTD]*

To set the viewing rectangle quickly to a "square" window (Figure 4.12), in which the horizontal and vertical axes have the same scale, press F3 MORE F2 *[ZOOM ZSQR]* in the GRAPH menu. More information about square windows is presented later in Section 4.2.3.

Sometimes you may wish to display grid points corresponding to tick marks on the axes. This and other graph format options may be changed by pressing GRAPH MORE F3 (Figure 4.16). Use arrow keys to move the blinking cursor to GridOn, then press ENTER and EXIT. Figure 4.17 shows the same graph as in Figure 4.15 but with the grid turned on. In general, you'll want the grid turned *off*, so do that now by pressing GRAPH MORE F3 again, use the arrow keys to move the blinking cursor to GridOff, and press ENTER EXIT.

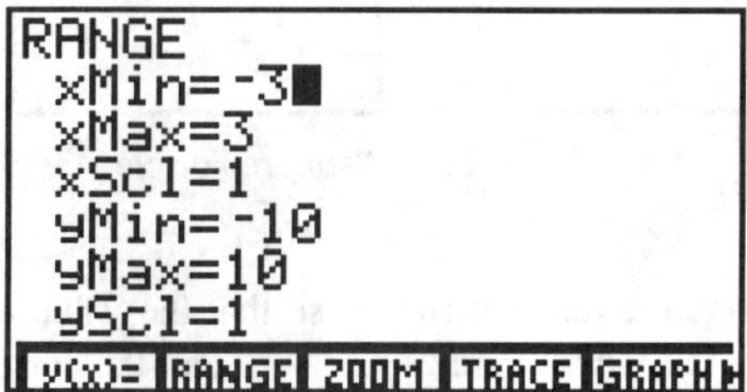

Figure 4.14: Custom window

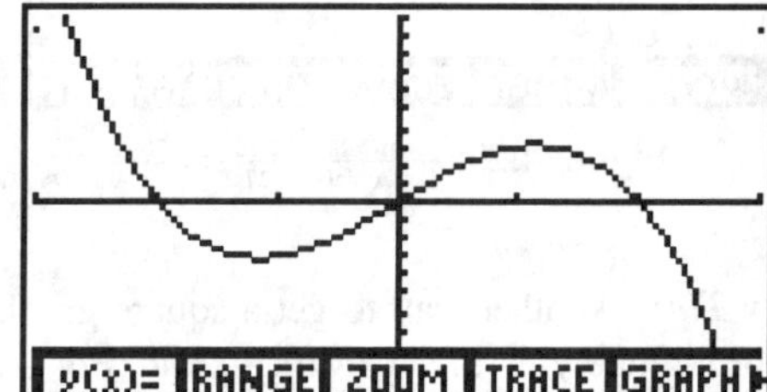

Figure 4.15: Graph of $y = -x^3 + 4x$

Figure 4.16: GRAPH FORMT menu

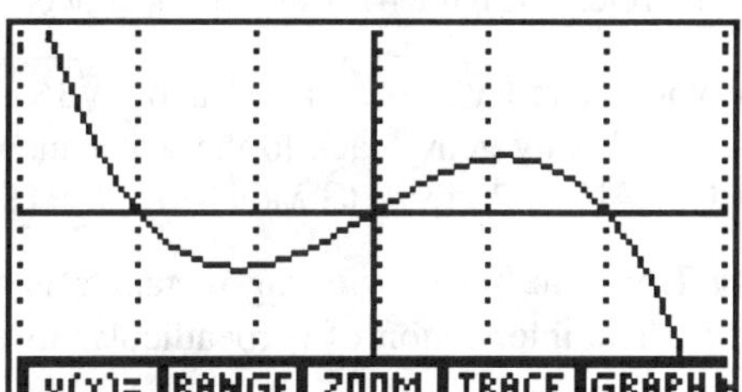

Figure 4.17: Grid on

4.2.3 Graphing a Circle: Here is a useful technique for graphs that are not functions, but that can be "split" into a top part and a bottom part, or into multiple parts. Suppose you wish to graph the circle whose equation is $x^2 + y^2 = 36$. First solve for y and get an equation for the top semicircle, $y = \sqrt{36 - x^2}$, and for the bottom semicircle, $y = -\sqrt{36 - x^2}$. Then graph the two semicircles simultaneously.

Figure 4.18: Two semicircles

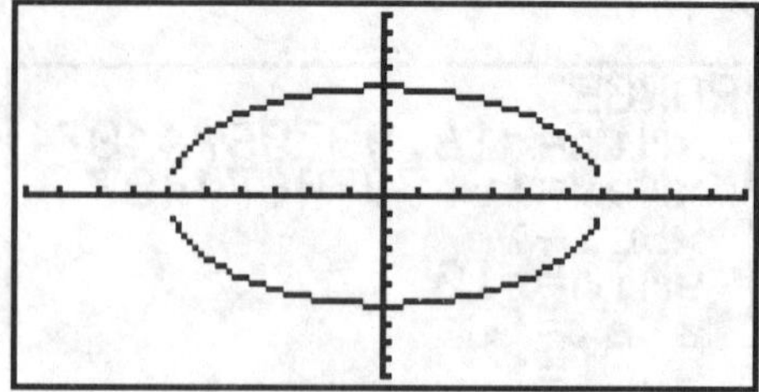

Figure 4.19: Circle's graph - standard view

The keystrokes to draw this circle's graph follow. Enter $\sqrt{36 - x^2}$ as y1 and $-\sqrt{36 - x^2}$ as y2 (see Figure 4.18) by pressing GRAPH F1 CLEAR 2nd $\sqrt{}$ (36 - F1 x²) ENTER (-) 2nd $\sqrt{}$ (36 - F1 x²). Then press 2nd M5 to draw them both.

If your range were set to the standard viewing rectangle, your graph would look like Figure 4.19. Now this does *not* look like a circle, because the units along the axes are not the same. This is where the square viewing rectangle is important. Press F3 MORE F2 and see a graph that appears more circular.

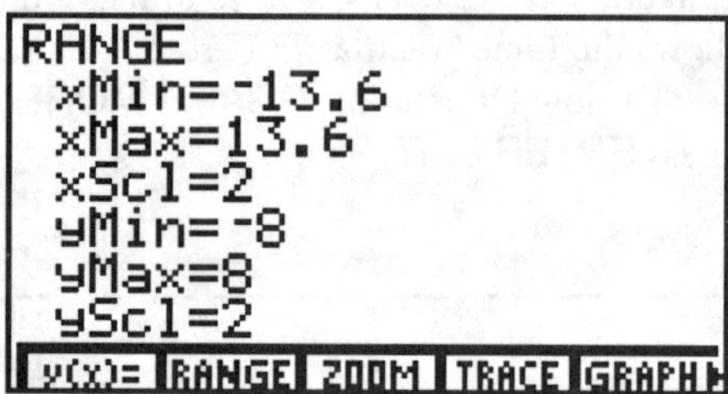

Figure 4.20: $\frac{\text{vertical}}{\text{horizontal}} = \frac{16}{27.2} = \frac{10}{17}$

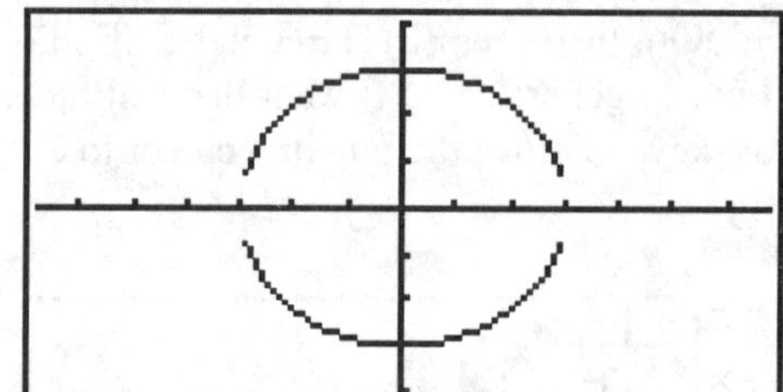

Figure 4.21: A "square" circle

Technology Tip: Another way to get a square graph is to change the range variables so that the value of yMax - yMin is approximately $\frac{10}{17}$ times xMax - xMin. For example, see the RANGE in Figure 4.20 and the corresponding graph in Figure 4.21. The method works because the dimensions of the TI-85's display are such that the ratio of vertical to horizontal is approximately $\frac{10}{17}$.

The two semicircles in Figure 4.21 do not meet because of an idiosyncrasy in the way the TI-85 plots a graph.

Back when you entered $\sqrt{36 - x^2}$ as y1 and $-\sqrt{36 - x^2}$ as y2, you could have entered -y1 for y2 and saved some keystrokes. Try this by going back to the y(x)= menu and pressing the arrow key to move the cursor down to y2. Then press CLEAR (-) 2nd VARS MORE F3 ENTER. The graph should be just as it was before.

Technology Tip: The square viewing rectangle is also important when you want to judge whether two lines are perpendicular. The intersection of perpendicular lines will always *look* like a right angle in a square viewing rectangle.

TI-85 Advanced Scientific Calculator

4.2.4 TRACE: Graph $y = -x^3 + 4x$ in the standard viewing rectangle. Press any of the arrow keys ◄ ▼ ◄ ► and see the cursor move from the center of the viewing rectangle. The coordinates of the cursor's location are displayed at the bottom of the screen, as in Figure 4.22, in floating decimal format. This cursor is called a *free-moving cursor* because it can move from dot to dot *anywhere* in the graph window.

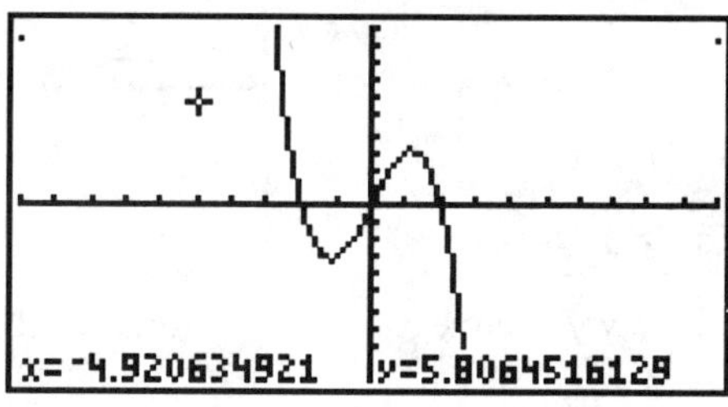

Figure 4.22: Free-moving cursor

Remove the free-moving cursor and its coordinates from the window by pressing **ENTER**, **CLEAR**, or **GRAPH** (this also restores the GRAPH menu line). An advantage of pressing **ENTER** or **CLEAR** to remove the free-moving cursor is that, if you press an arrow key once again, the cursor will reappear at the same point you left it.

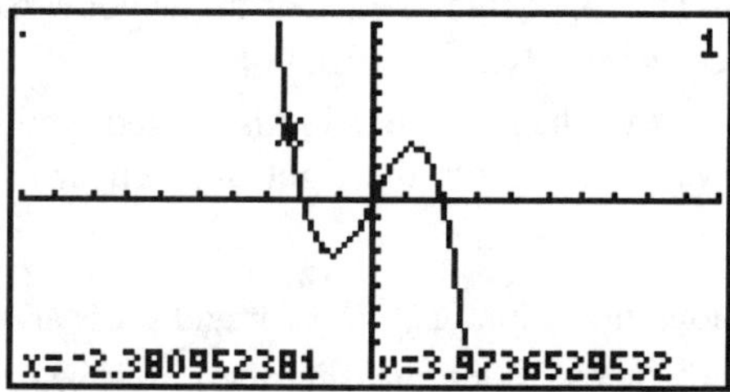

Figure 4.23: Trace on $y = -x^3 + 4x$

Press **F4** *[TRACE]* to enable the left ◄ and right ► arrow keys to move the cursor along the function. The cursor is no longer free-moving, but is now constrained to the function. The coordinates that are displayed belong to points on the function's graph, so the y-coordinate is the calculated value of the function at the corresponding x-coordinate.

Now plot a second function, $y = -.25x$, along with $y = -x^3 + 4x$. Press **GRAPH F1** for the y(x)= menu and enter $-.25x$ for **y2**, then press **2nd M5** to see their graphs (Figure 4.25).

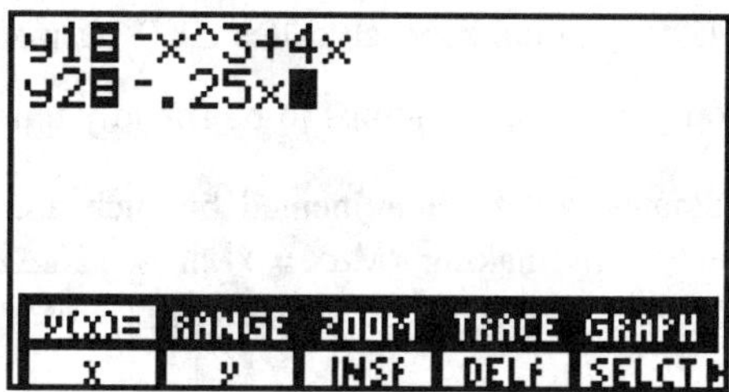

Figure 4.24: Two functions

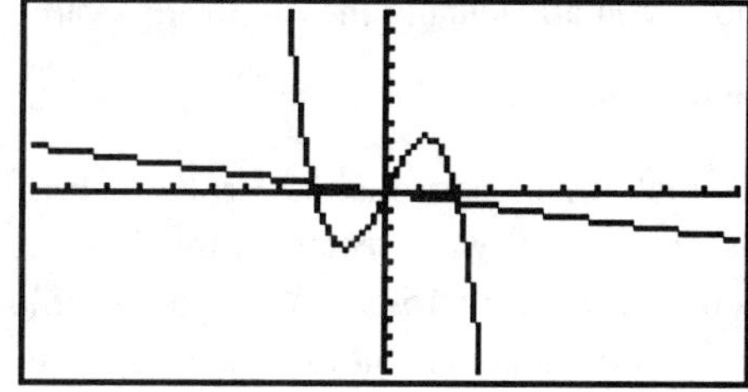

Figure 4.25: $y = -x^3 + 4x$ and $y = -.25x$

Note in Figure 4.24 that the equal signs next to **y1** and **y2** are *both* highlighted. This means *both* functions will be graphed. In the y(x)= screen, move the cursor to **y1** and press **F5** *[SELCT]* to turn function selection *off*. The equal sign beside **y1** should no longer be highlighted (see Figure 4.26). The SELCT command operates as a toggle switch; executing it once more sets function selection *on*. Now press 2nd M5 *[GRAPH]* and see that only y2 is plotted.

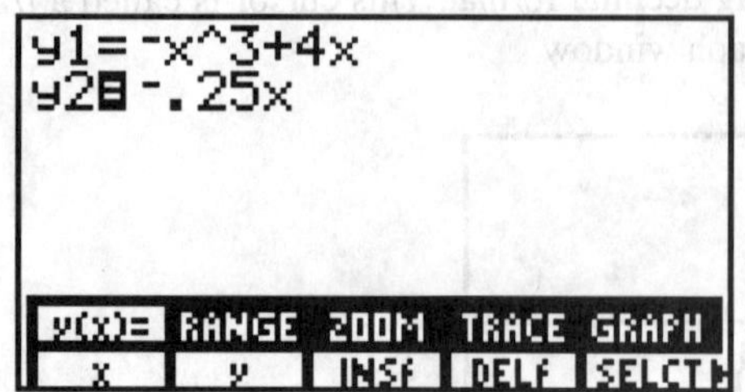

Figure 4.26: y(x)= screen with only y2 active

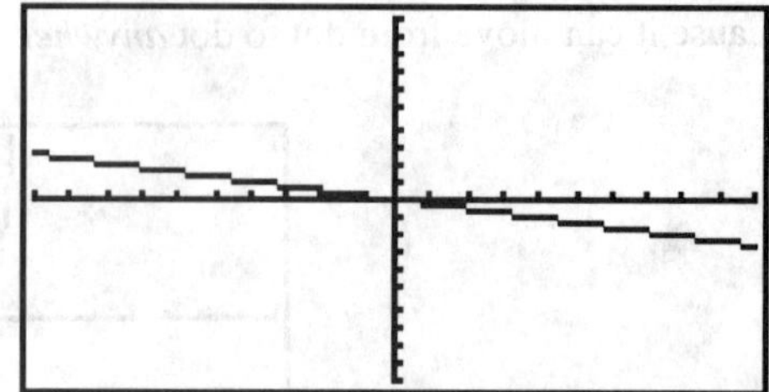

Figure 4.27: Graph of $y = -.25x$

Many different functions may be stored in the y(x)= list and any combination of them may be graphed simultaneously. You can make a function active or inactive for graphing by pressing SELCT to highlight (activate) or remove the highlight (deactivate). Go back to the y(x)= screen and do what is needed in order to graph y1 but not y2.

Now activate y2 again so that both graphs are plotted. Press GRAPH F4 *[TRACE]* and the cursor appears first on the graph of $y = -x^3 + 4x$ because it is higher up in the y(x)= list. You know that the cursor is on this function, y1, because of the numeral 1 displayed in the upper right corner of the window (see Figure 4.23). Press the up ▲ or down ▼ arrow key to move the cursor vertically to the graph of $y = -.25x$. Now the numeral 2 is displayed in the top right corner of the window. When more than one function is plotted, you can move the trace cursor vertically from one graph to another in this way. Next press the right and left arrow keys to trace along the graph of $y = -.25x$.

Technology Tip: By the way, trace along the graph of $y = -.25x$ and press and hold either ◀ or ▶. Eventually you will reach the *left* or *right* edge of the window. Keep pressing the arrow key and the TI-85 will allow you to continue the trace by panning the viewing rectangle. Check the RANGE screen to see that xMin and xMax are automatically updated.

If you trace along the graph of $y = -x^3 + 4x$, the cursor will eventually move *above* or *below* the viewing rectangle. The cursor's coordinates on the graph will still be displayed, though the cursor itself can no longer be seen.

When you are tracing along a graph, press ENTER and the window will quickly pan over so that the cursor's position on the function is centered in a new viewing rectangle. This feature is especially helpful when you trace near or beyond the edge of the current viewing rectangle.

The TI-85's display has 127 horizontal columns of pixels and 63 vertical rows. So when you trace a curve across a graph window, you are actually moving from xMin to xMax in 126 equal jumps, each called Δx. You would calculate the size of each jump to be $\Delta x = \dfrac{\text{xMax} - \text{xMin}}{126}$. Sometimes you may want the jumps to be friendly numbers like .1 or .25 so that, when you trace along the curve, the x-coordinates will be incremented by such a convenient amount. Just set your viewing rectangle for a particular increment Δx by making xMax = xMin + 126·Δx. For example, if you want xMin = -15 and Δx = .25, set xMax = -15 + 126·.25 = 16.5. Likewise, set yMax = yMin + 62·Δy if you want the vertical increment to be some special Δy.

To center your window around a particular point, say (h, k), and also have a certain Δx, set xMin = h - 63·Δx and xMax = h + 63·Δx. Likewise, make yMin = k - 31·Δy and yMax = k + 31·Δy. For example, to center a window around the origin, (0, 0), with both horizontal and vertical increments of .25, set the range so that xMin = 0 - 63·.25 = -15.75, xMax = 0 + 63·.25 = 15.75, yMin = 0 - 31·.25 = -7.75, and yMax = 0 + 31·.25 = 7.75.

TI-85 Advanced Scientific Calculator

See the benefit by first plotting $y = x^2 + 2x + 1$ in a standard graphing window. Trace near its y-intercept, which is (0, 1), and move towards its x-intercept, which is (-1, 0). Then change to a viewing rectangle that extends from -6.3 to 6.3 horizontally and from -3.1 to 3.1 vertically (center at the origin, Δx and Δy both .1), and trace again from the y-intercept. The TI-85 makes it easy to get this particular viewing rectangle: press GRAPH F3 MORE F4 *[ZOOM ZDECM]*.

4.2.5 ZOOM: Plot again the two graphs, for $y = -x^3 + 4x$ and for $y = -.25x$. There appears to be an intersection near $x = 2$. The TI-85 provides several ways to enlarge the view around this point. You can change the viewing rectangle directly by pressing RANGE and editing the values of xMin, xMax, yMin, and yMax. Figure 4.29 shows a new viewing rectangle for the range displayed in Figure 4.28. Trace has been turned on and the coordinates are displayed for a point on $y = -x^3 + 4x$ that is close to the intersection.

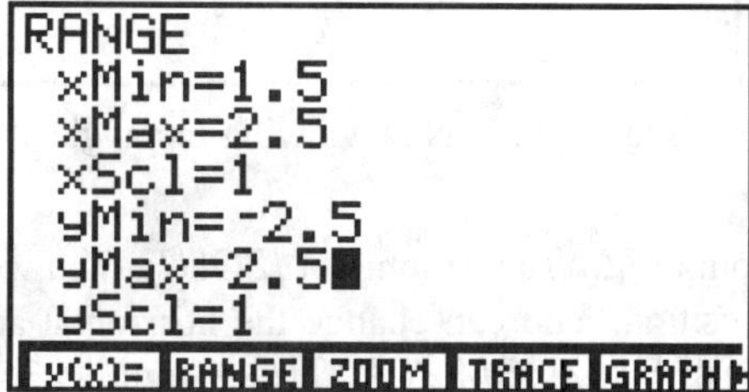

Figure 4.28: New RANGE

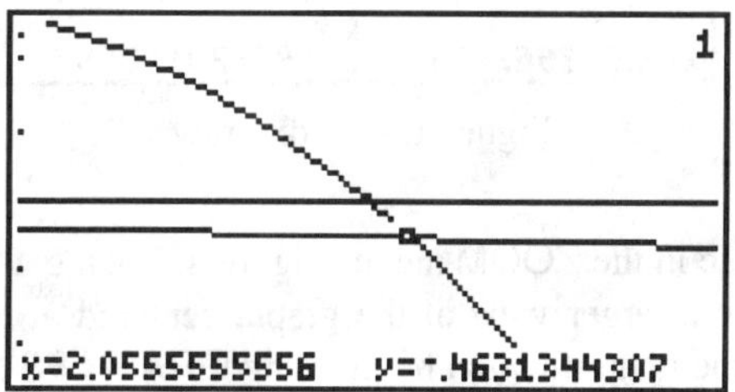

Figure 4.29: Closer view

A more efficient method for enlarging the view is to draw a new viewing rectangle with the cursor. Start again with a graph of the two functions $y = -x^3 + 4x$ and $y = -.25x$ in a standard viewing rectangle (press GRAPH F3 F4 for the standard window, from -10 to 10 along both axes).

First of all, imagine a small rectangular box around the intersection point, near $x = 2$. Press GRAPH F3 F1 *[ZOOM BOX]* to enable drawing a box (Figure 4.30) to define a new viewing rectangle. Use the arrow keys to move the cursor, whose coordinates are displayed at the bottom of the window, to one corner of the new viewing rectangle you are imagining (Figure 4.31).

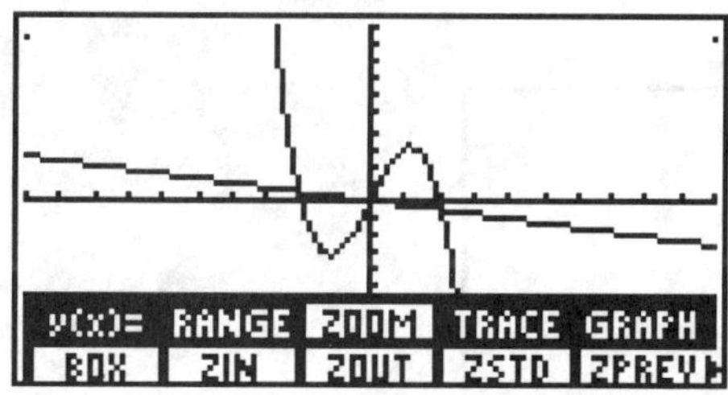

Figure 4.30: ZOOM menu

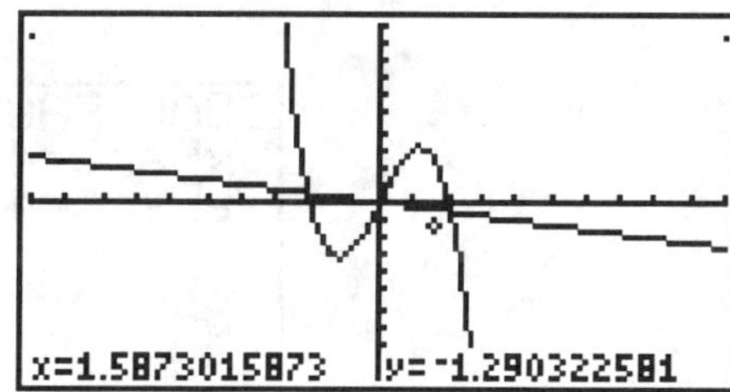

Figure 4.31: One corner selected

Press ENTER to fix the corner where you have moved the cursor; it changes shape and becomes a blinking square. Use the arrow keys again to move the cursor to the diagonally opposite corner of the new rectangle (Figure 4.32). If this box looks all right to you, press ENTER. The rectangular area you have enclosed will now enlarge to fill the graph window (Figure 4.33).

You may cancel the zoom any time *before* you press this last ENTER. Just press EXIT or GRAPH to interrupt the zoom and return to the current graph window. Even if you did execute the zoom, you may still return to the previous viewing rectangle by pressing F5 *[ZPREV]* in the ZOOM menu.

You can also gain a quick magnification of the graph around the cursor's location. Return once more to the standard range for the graph of the two functions $y = -x^3 + 4x$ and $y = -.25x$. Start the zoom by pressing GRAPH F3 F2 *[ZOOM ZIN]*; next use the arrow keys to move the cursor as close as you can to the point of intersection near $x = 2$ (see Figure 4.34). Then press ENTER and the calculator draws a magnified graph, centered at the cursor's position (Figure 4.35). The range variables are changed to reflect this new viewing rectangle. Look in the RANGE menu to check.

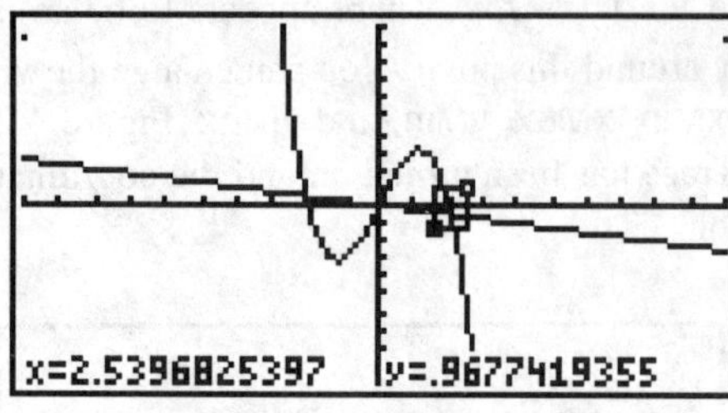

Figure 4.32: Box drawn

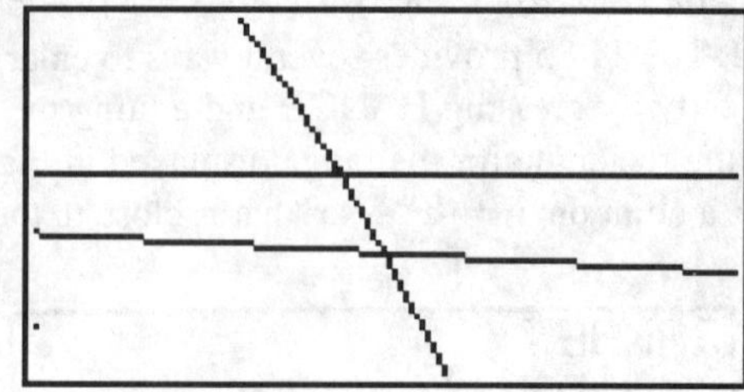

Figure 4.33: New viewing rectangle

As you see in the ZOOM menu (Figure 4.30), the TI-85 can zoom in *[ZIN]* and zoom out *[ZOUT]*. You would zoom out to see a larger view of the graph, centered at the cursor position. You can change the horizontal and vertical scale of the magnification by pressing GRAPH F3 MORE MORE F1 *[ZOOM ZFACT]* (see Figure 4.36) and editing xFact and yFact, the horizontal and vertical magnification factors.

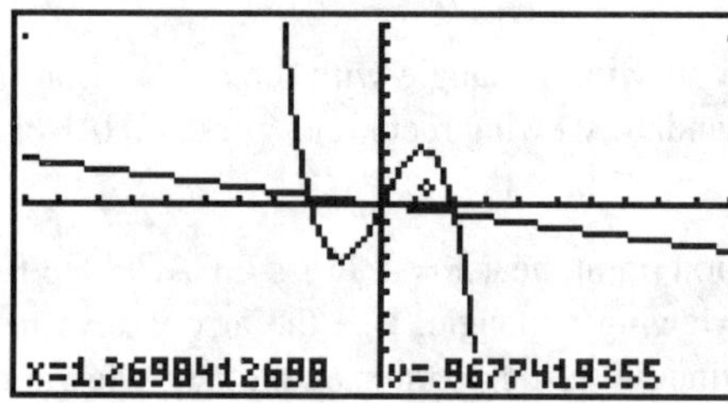

Figure 4.34: Before a zoom in

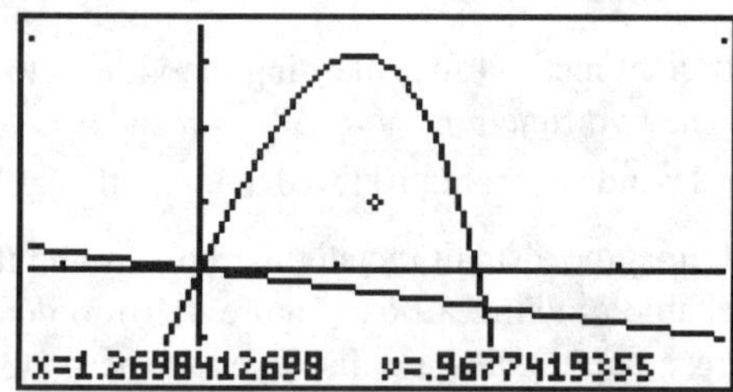

Figure 4.35: After a zoom in

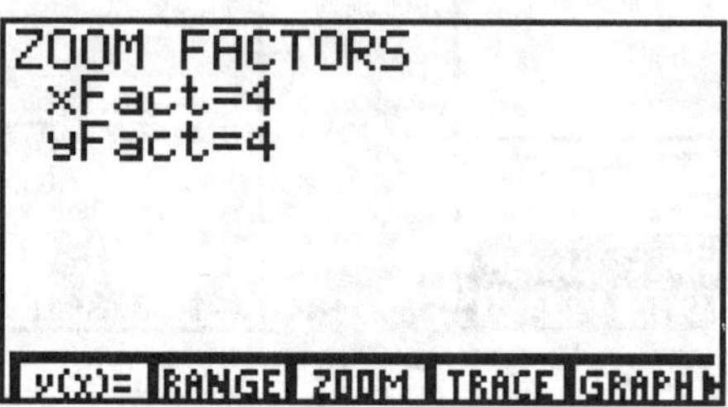

Figure 4.36: Set zoom factors

The default zoom factor is 4 in both directions. It is not necessary for xFact and yFact to be equal. Sometimes, you may prefer to zoom in one direction only, so the other factor should be set to 1. Press GRAPH or EXIT to leave the ZOOM FACTORS menu.

Technology Tip: If you should zoom in too much and lose the curve, zoom back to the standard viewing rectangle and start over.

TI-85 Advanced Scientific Calculator

4.3.1 Intercepts and Intersections: Tracing and zooming are also used to locate an *x*-intercept of a graph, where a curve crosses the *x*-axis. For example, the graph of $y = x^3 - 8x$ crosses the *x*-axis three times (see Figure 4.37). After tracing over to the *x*-intercept point that is furthest to the left, zoom in (Figure 4.38). Continue this process until you have located all three intercepts with as much accuracy as you need. The three *x*-intercepts of $y = x^3 - 8x$ are approximately -2.828, 0, and 2.828.

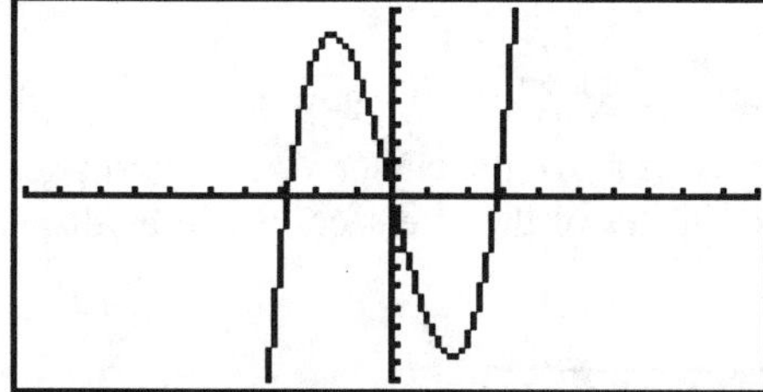

Figure 4.37: Graph of $y = x^3 - 8x$

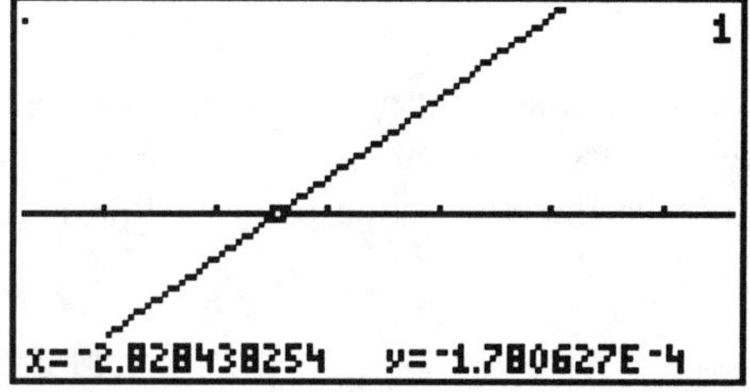

Figure 4.38: An *x*-intercept of $y = x^3 - 8x$

Technology Tip: As you zoom in, you may also wish to change the spacing between tick marks on the *x*-axis so that the viewing rectangle shows scale marks near the intercept point. Then the accuracy of your approximation will be such that the error is less than the distance between two tick marks. Change the *x*-scale on the TI-85 from the GRAPH F2 *[RANGE]* menu. Move the cursor down to xScl and enter an appropriate value.

The *x*-intercept of a function's graph is a *root* of the equation $f(x) = 0$. And the TI-85 automates the search for roots. Press GRAPH MORE F1 for the GRAPH MATH menu (Figure 4.39) and then press F3 *[ROOT]*. Trace the cursor along the graph to a point near a root and press ENTER (Figure 4.40).

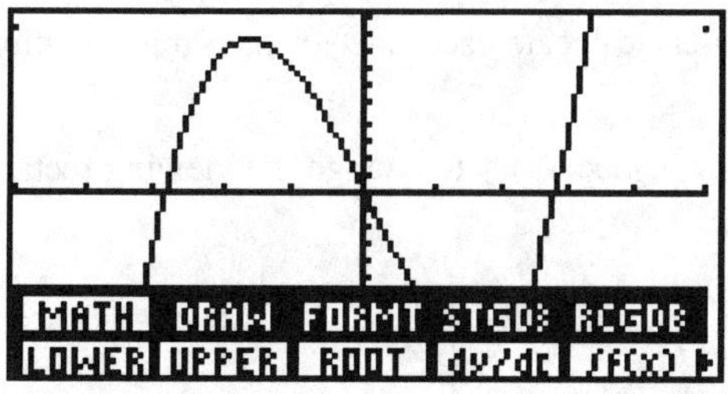

Figure 4.39: GRAPH MATH menu

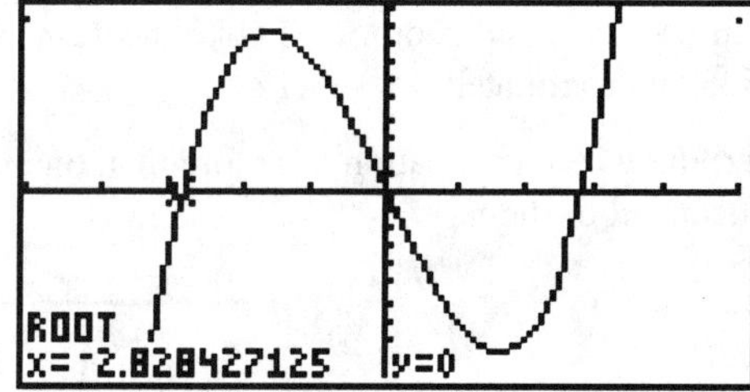

Figure 4.40: Finding a root of $y = x^3 - 8x$

TRACE and ZOOM are especially important for locating the intersection points of two graphs, say the graphs of $y = -x^3 + 4x$ and $y = -.25x$. Trace along one of the graphs until you arrive close to an intersection point. Then press ▲ or ▼ to jump to the other graph. Notice that the *x*-coordinate does not change, but the *y*-coordinate is likely to be different (see Figures 4.41 and 4.42).

When the two *y*-coordinates are as close as they can get, you have come as close as you now can to the point of intersection. So zoom in around the intersection point, then trace again until the two *y*-coordinates are as close as possible. Continue this process until you have located the point of intersection with as much accuracy as necessary.

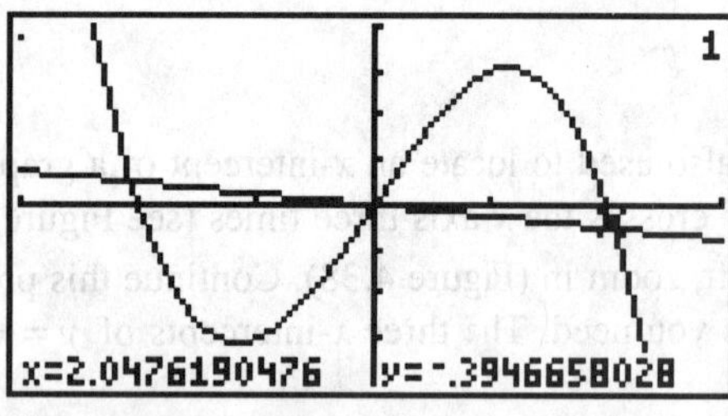
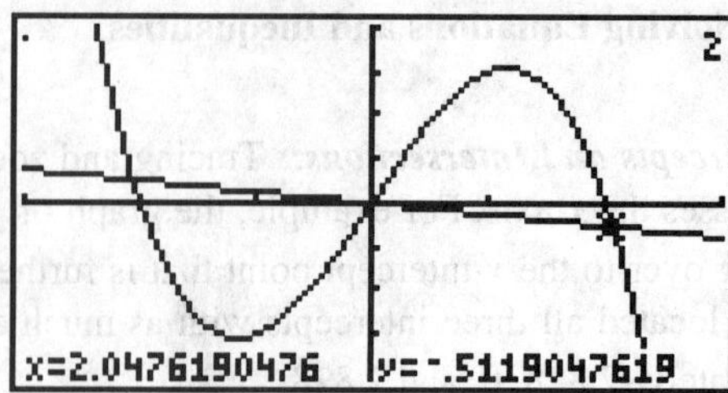

Figure 4.41: Trace on $y = -x^3 + 4x$ Figure 4.42: Trace on $y = -.25x$

You can also find the point of intersection of two graphs by pressing GRAPH MORE F1 MORE F5 *[ISECT]*. First move the cursor vertically to one graph and press ENTER. Next move the cursor vertically to select the other graph, trace near the intersection point, and press ENTER. Coordinates of the intersection will be displayed at the bottom of the window.

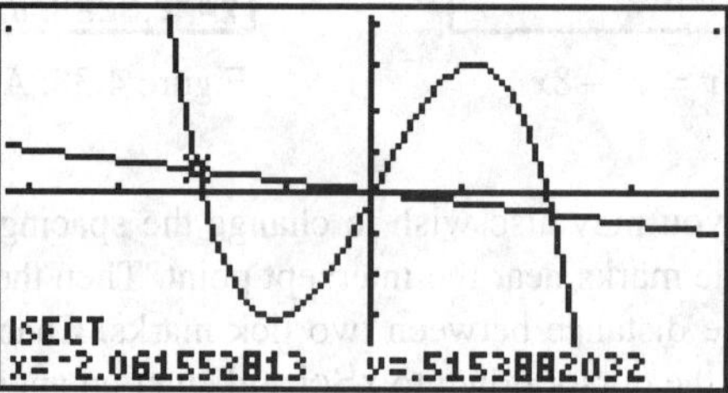

Figure 4.43: An intersection of $y = -x^3 + 4x$ and $y = -.25x$

4.3.2 Solving Equations by Graphing: Suppose you need to solve the equation $24x^3 - 36x + 17 = 0$. First graph $y = 24x^3 - 36x + 17$ in a window large enough to exhibit *all* its x-intercepts, corresponding to all the equation's roots. Then use trace and zoom, or invoke the TI-85's root finder, to locate each one. In fact, this equation has just one solution, approximately $x = -1.414$.

Remember that when an equation has more than one root, it may be necessary to change the viewing rectangle a few times to locate all of them.

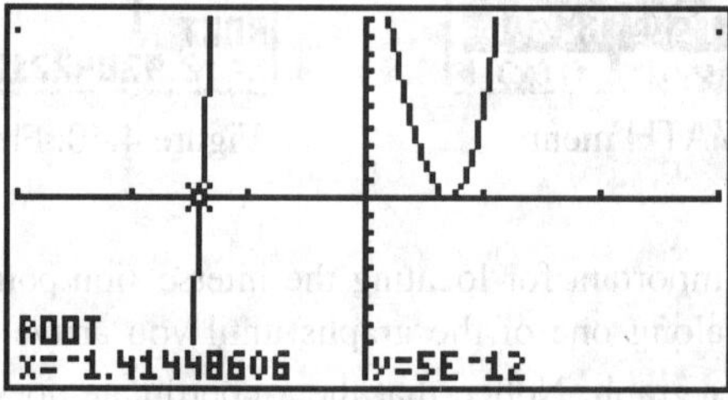

Figure 4.44: Root of $y = 24x^3 - 36x + 17$

Technology Tip: To solve an equation like $24x^3 + 17 = 36x$, you may first transform it into standard form, $24x^3 - 36x + 17 = 0$, and proceed as above to search for its x-intercepts. However, you may also graph the *two* functions $y = 24x^3 + 17$ and $y = 36x$, then zoom and trace to locate their point of intersection.

                                                           TI-85 Advanced Scientific Calculator

4.3.3 Solving Systems by Graphing: The solutions to a system of equations correspond to the points of intersection of their graphs (Figure 4.45). For example, to solve the system $y = x^2 - 3x - 4$ and $y = x^3 + 3x^2 - 2x - 1$, first graph them together. Then zoom and trace, or use the ISECT command from the GRAPH MATH menu, to locate their point of intersection, approximately (-2.17, 7.25).

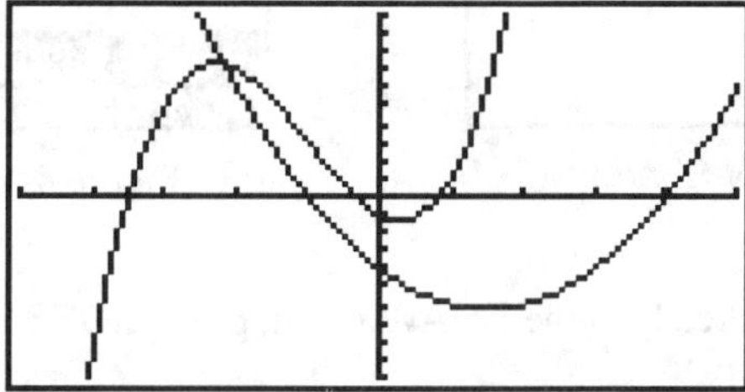

Figure 4.45: Solving a system of equations

You must judge whether the two current y-coordinates are sufficiently close for $x = -2.17$ or whether you should continue to zoom and trace to improve the approximation.

The solutions of the system of two equations $y = x^3 + 3x^2 - 2x - 1$ and $y = x^2 - 3x - 4$ correspond to the solutions of the single equation $x^3 + 3x^2 - 2x - 1 = x^2 - 3x - 4$, which simplifies to $x^3 + 2x^2 + x + 3 = 0$. So you may also graph $y = x^3 + 2x^2 + x + 3$ and find its x-intercepts to solve the system.

4.3.4 Solving Inequalities by Graphing: Consider the inequality $1 - \dfrac{3x}{2} \geq x - 4$. To solve it with your TI-85, graph the two functions $y = 1 - \dfrac{3x}{2}$ and $y = x - 4$ (Figure 4.46). First locate their point of intersection, at $x = 2$. The inequality is true when the graph of $y = 1 - \dfrac{3x}{2}$ lies *above* the graph of $y = x - 4$, and that occurs for $x < 2$. So the solution is the half-line $x \leq 2$, or $(-\infty, 2]$.

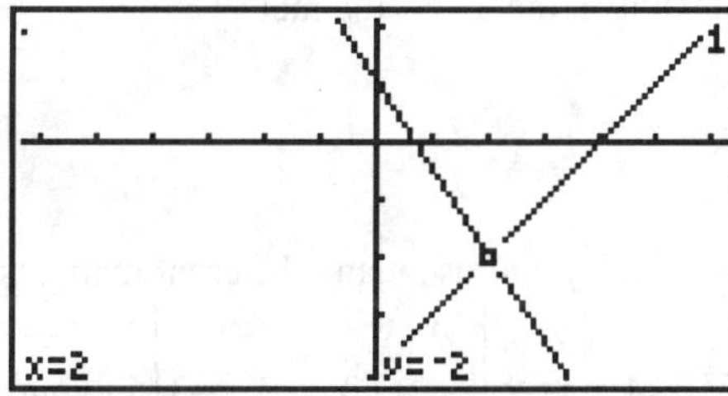

Figure 4.46: Solving $1 - \dfrac{3x}{2} \geq x - 4$

The TI-85 is capable of shading the region above or below a graph or between two graphs. For example, to graph $y \geq x^2 - 1$, first enter the function $y = x^2 - 1$ as y1 in the GRAPH y(x)= screen. Then press GRAPH MORE F2 *[DRAW]* F1 *[Shade]* 2nd VARS MORE F3 *[EQU]*, move the cursor to y1, and press ENTER , 100) (see Figure 4.47) and again ENTER. These keystrokes instruct the TI-85 to shade the region *above* $y = x^2 - 1$ and *below* $y =$ 100 (chosen because this is a sufficiently large y-value). The result is shown in Figure 4.48.

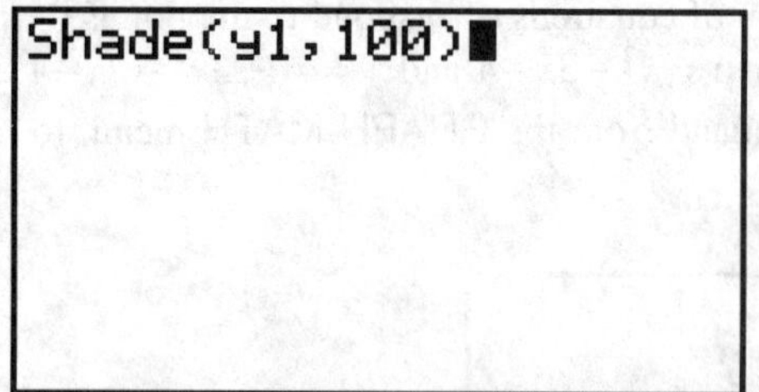

Figure 4.47: DRAW Shade

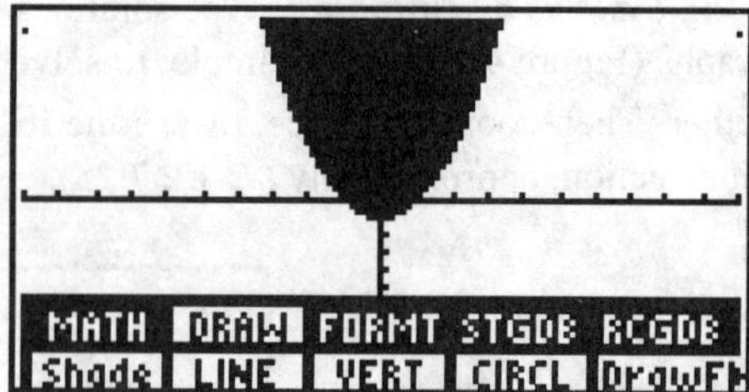

Figure 4.48: Graph of $y \geq x^2 - 1$

To clear the shading, when you are already in the DRAW menu, press MORE F5 *[CLDRW]*.

Now use shading to solve the previous inequality, $1 - \dfrac{3x}{2} \geq x - 4$. The function whose graph forms the lower boundary is named *first* in the SHADE command. To enter this in your TI-85 (see Figure 4.49), press these keys: GRAPH MORE F2 F1 x-VAR - 4 , 1 - 3 x-VAR ÷ 2) ENTER. The shading (see Figure 4.50) extends left from $x = 2$, hence the solution to $1 - \dfrac{3x}{2} \geq x - 4$ is the half-line $x \leq 2$, or $(-\infty, 2]$.

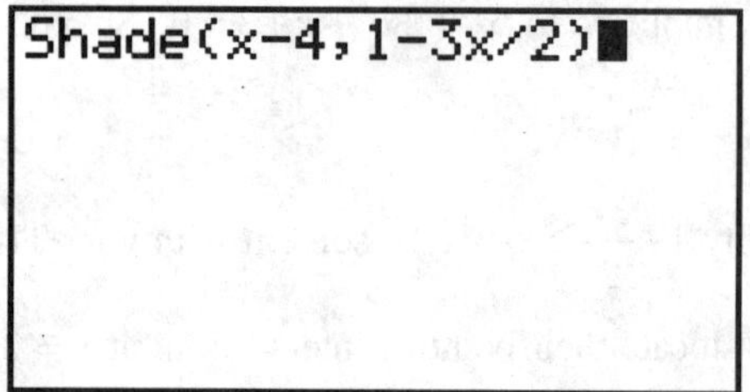

Figure 4.49: DRAW Shade command

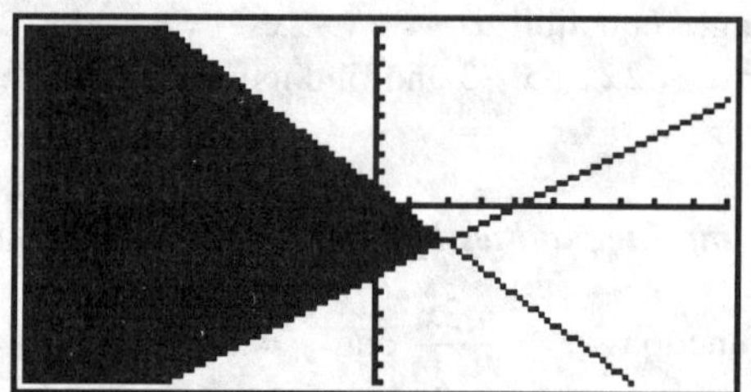

Figure 4.50: Graph of $1 - \dfrac{3x}{2} \geq x - 4$

More information about the DRAW menu is in the TI-85 manual.

4.4 Matrices

4.4.1 Making a Matrix: The TI-85 can display and use many different matrices, each with up to 255 rows and up to 255 columns! Here's how to create this 3×4 matrix $\begin{bmatrix} 1 & -4 & 3 & 5 \\ -1 & 3 & -1 & -3 \\ 2 & 0 & -4 & 6 \end{bmatrix}$ in your calculator.

Press 2nd MATRX F2 *[EDIT]* to see the matrix edit menu (Figure 4.51). You must first name the matrix; let's name this matrix *A* (the TI-85 is already set for alphabetic entry) and press ENTER to continue.

You may now change the dimensions of matrix *A* to 3×4 by pressing 3 ENTER 4 ENTER. Simply press ENTER or the *down* arrow key to accept an existing dimension. Next enter 1 in the first row and first column of the matrix, then press ENTER to move horizontally across this row to the second column. Continue to enter the top row of elements. Press ENTER after the last element of the first row has been entered to move to the second row. You may use the up and down arrow keys to move vertically through the columns of the matrix.

TI-85 Advanced Scientific Calculator

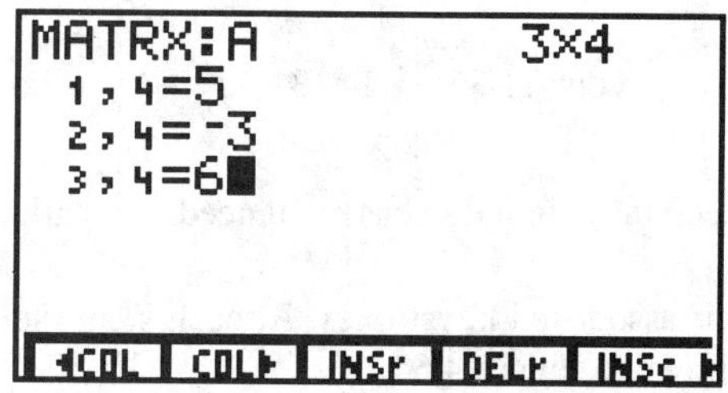

Figure 4.51: MATRX EDIT menu

Leave the matrix *A* editing screen by pressing EXIT or 2nd QUIT and return to the home screen.

4.4.2 Row Operations: Here are the keystrokes necessary to perform elementary row operations on a mtrix. Your textbook provides more careful explanation of the elementary row operations and their uses.

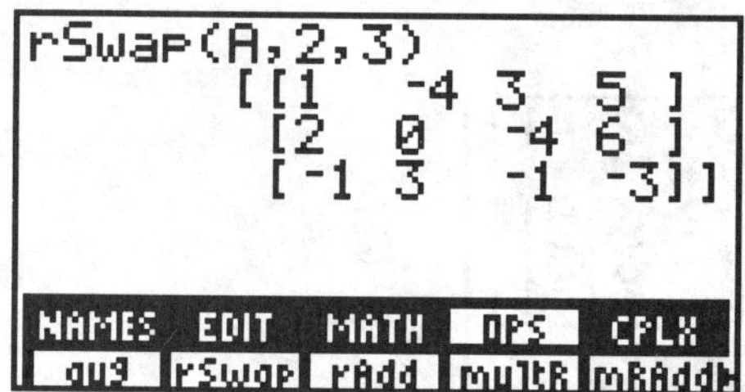

Figure 4.52: Swap rows 2 and 3

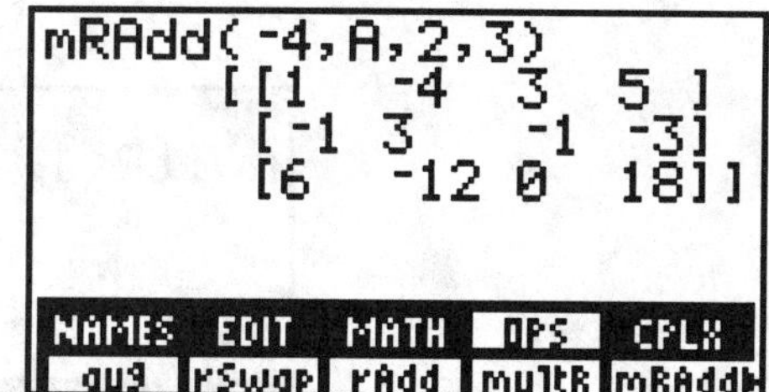

Figure 4.53: Add -4 times row 2 to row 3

To interchange the second and third rows of the matrix *A* that was defined above, press these keys: 2nd MATRX F4 *[OPS]* MORE F2 *[rSwap]* ALPHA A , 2 , 3) ENTER (see Figure 4.52). The format of this command is rSwap(*matrix, row1, row2*).

To add row 2 and row 3 and store the results in row 3, press 2nd MATRX F4 MORE F3 ALPHA A , 2 , 3) ENTER. The format of this command is rAdd(*matrix, row1, row2*).

To multiply row 2 by -4 and *store* the results in row 2, thereby replacing row 2 with new values, press 2nd MATRX F4 MORE F4 (-) 4 , ALPHA A , 2) ENTER. The format of this command is multR(*scalar, matrix, row*).

To multiply row 2 by -4 and *add* the results to row 3, thereby replacing row 3 with new values, press 2nd MATRX F4 MORE F5 (-) 4 , ALPHA A , 2 , 3) ENTER (see Figure 4.53). The format of this command is mRAdd(*scalar, matrix, row1, row2*).

Technology Tip: It is important to remember that your TI-85 does *not automatically* store a matrix obtained as the result of any row operations. So when you need to perform several row operations in succession, it is a good idea to store the result of each one in a temporary place.

For example, use elementary row operations to solve this system of linear equations: $\begin{cases} x - 2y + 3z = 9 \\ -x + 3y = -4 \\ 2x - 5y + 5z = 17 \end{cases}$.

First enter this *augmented matrix* as A in your TI-85: $\begin{bmatrix} 1 & -2 & 3 & 9 \\ -1 & 3 & 0 & -4 \\ 2 & -5 & 5 & 17 \end{bmatrix}$. Next store this matrix in C (press ALPHA A STO ► C ENTER) so you may keep the original in case you need to recall it.

Here are the row operations and their associated keystrokes. At each step, the result is stored in C and replaces the previous matrix C. The solution is shown in Figure 4.54.

Row Operation	*Keystrokes*
rAdd(C, 1, 2)	2nd MATRX F4 MORE F3 ALPHA C , 1 , 2) STO ► C ENTER
mRAdd(-2, C, 1, 3)	F5 (-) 2 , ALPHA C , 1 , 3) STO ► C ENTER
rAdd(C, 2, 3)	F3 ALPHA C , 2 , 3) STO ► C ENTER
multR(½, C, 3)	F4 1 ÷ 2 , ALPHA C , 3) STO ► C ENTER

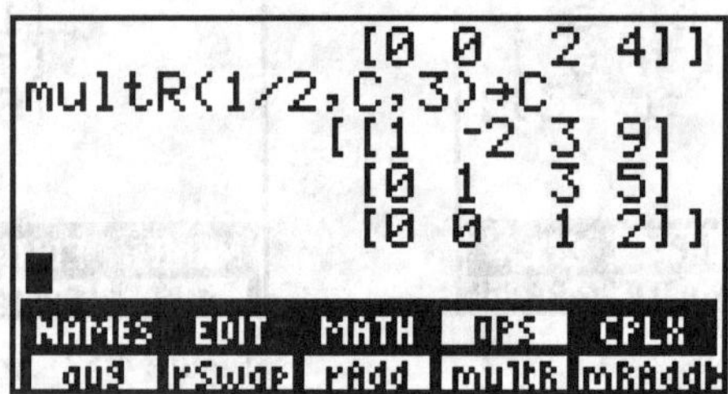

Figure 4.54: Final matrix after row operations

Thus $z = 2$, so $y = -1$ and $x = 1$.

4.4.3 Determinants: Enter this 3×3 square matrix as A: $\begin{bmatrix} 1 & -2 & 3 \\ -1 & 3 & 0 \\ 2 & -5 & 5 \end{bmatrix}$. To calculate its determinant, press 2nd MATRX F3 F1 ALPHA A ENTER. You should find that $|A| = 2$.

4.5 Additional Topics

4.5.1 Iteration: The ANS feature enables you to perform iterations to evaluate a function repeatedly. As an example, calculate $\dfrac{n-1}{3}$ for $n = 27$. Then calculate $\dfrac{n-1}{3}$ for $n =$ the answer to the previous calculation. Continue to use each answer as n in the *next* calculation. Here are keystrokes to accomplish this iteration on the TI-85 (see the results in Figure 4.55). Notice that when you use ANS in place of n in a formula, it is sufficient to press ENTER to continue an iteration.

Iteration	*Keystrokes*	*Display*
1	27 ENTER	27
2	(2nd ANS - 1) ÷ 3 ENTER	8.66666666667

TI-85 Advanced Scientific Calculator

3	ENTER	2.55555555556
4	ENTER	.518518518519
5	ENTER	-.16049382716

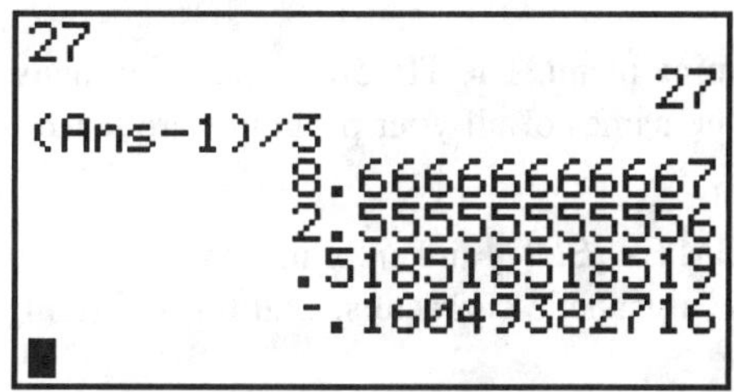

Figure 4.55: Iteration

Press ENTER several more times and see what happens with this iteration. You may wish to try it again with a different starting value.

4.5.2 Arithmetic and Geometric Sequences: Use iteration with the ANS variable to determine the n-th term of a sequence. For example, find the 18th term of an *arithmetic* sequence whose first term is 7 and whose common difference is 4. Enter the first term 7, then start the progression with the recursion formula, 2nd ANS + 4 ENTER. This yields the 2nd term, so press ENTER sixteen more times to find the 18th term. For a *geometric* sequence whose common ratio is 4, start the progression with 2nd ANS × 4 ENTER.

Of course, you could also use the *explicit* formula for the n-th term of an arithmetic sequence, $t_n = a + (n-1)d$. First enter values for the variables a, d, and n, then evaluate the formula by pressing 2nd alpha a + (2nd alpha n - 1) 2nd alpha d ENTER. For a geometric sequence whose n-th term is given by $t_n = a \cdot r^{n-1}$, enter values for the variables a, r, and n, then evaluate the formula by pressing 2nd alpha a 2nd alpha r ^ (2nd alpha n - 1) ENTER.

4.5.3 Permutations and Combinations: To calculate the number of *permutations* of 12 objects taken 7 at a time, $_{12}P_7$, press 2nd MATH F2 12 F2 7 ENTER. Then $_{12}P_7 = 3,991,680$, as shown in Figure 4.56.

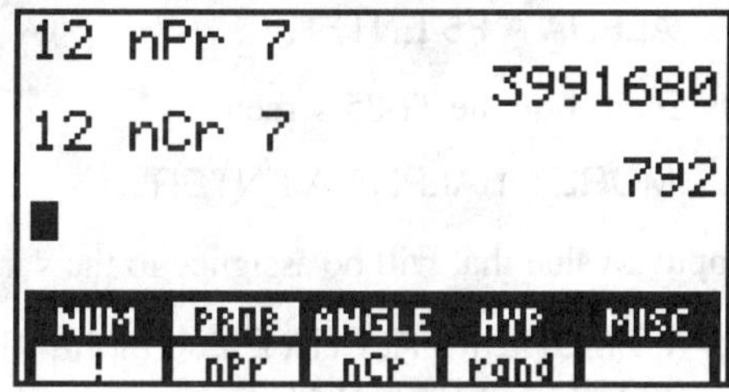

Figure 4.56: $_{12}P_7$ and $_{12}C_7$

For the number of *combinations* of 12 objects taken 7 at a time, $_{12}C_7$, press 2nd MATH F2 12 F3 7 ENTER. So $_{12}C_7 = 792$.

4.6   Programming

4.6.1 Entering a Program: The TI-85 is a programmable calculator that can store sequences of commands for later replay. Here's an example to show you how to enter a useful program that solves quadratic equations by the quadratic formula.

Press PRGM to access the programming menu. The TI-85 has space for many programs, each identified by a name that is up to eight characters long. The names of all your programs are listed alphabetically in the PRGM NAMES menu.

To create a new program, press PRGM F2 *[EDIT]* and enter its name. The cursor is now a blinking **A**, indicating the calculator is set to receive upper case alphabetic characters. Call this program QUADRAT and press ENTER when you have finished.

Within the program itself, each line begins with a colon **:** supplied automatically by the calculator after you press ENTER. Any command you could enter directly in the TI-85's home screen can be entered as a line in a program. There are also special programming commands.

Note that the TI-85 calculator checks for program errors as it *runs* a program, not while you enter or edit it.

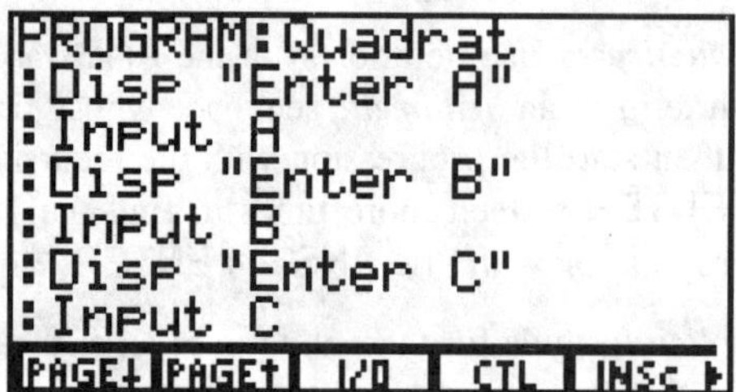

Figure 4.57: Program QUADRAT

Enter the program QUADRAT by pressing the keystrokes given in the listing below.

Program Line	Keystrokes
: Disp "Enter A"	F3 F3 MORE F5 ALPHA E 2nd alpha ALPHA N T E R ␣ ALPHA A F5 ENTER

displays the words *Enter A* on the TI-85 screen

: Input A	MORE F1 ALPHA A ENTER

waits for you to input a value that will be assigned to the variable A

: Disp "Enter B"	F3 MORE F5 ALPHA E 2nd alpha ALPHA N T E R ␣ ALPHA B F5 ENTER
: Input B	MORE F1 ALPHA B ENTER
: Disp "Enter C"	F3 MORE F5 ALPHA E 2nd alpha ALPHA N T E R ␣ ALPHA C F5 ENTER
: Input C	MORE F1 ALPHA C ENTER
: ClLCD	MORE F3 ENTER

clears the calculator's display

: B²-4AC → D   ALPHA B x² - 4 ALPHA A × ALPHA C STO▸ D ENTER

    calculates the discriminant and stores its value as D

: If D>0   EXIT F4 F1 ALPHA D 2nd TEST F3 0 ENTER

    tests to see if the discriminant is positive

: Then   EXIT F2 ENTER

    in case the discriminant is positive, continues on to the next line;
    if the discriminant is not positive, jumps to the command after **Else** below

: Disp "Two real roots"   EXIT F3 F3 MORE F5 ALPHA T 2nd alpha ALPHA W O ␣
       R E A L ␣ R O O T S F5 ENTER

: (-B+√D)/(2A) → M   ((-) ALPHA B + 2nd √ ALPHA D) ÷ (2 ALPHA A)
       STO▸ M ENTER

    calculates one root and stores it as M

: Disp M   MORE F3 ALPHA M ENTER

    displays one root

: (-B-√D)/(2A) → N   ((-) ALPHA B − 2nd √ ALPHA D) ÷ (2 ALPHA A)
       STO▸ N ENTER

: Disp N   F3 ALPHA N ENTER

: Else   EXIT F4 F3 ENTER

    continues from here if the discriminant is not positive

: If D==0   F1 ALPHA D 2nd TEST F1 0 ENTER

    tests to see if the discriminant is zero

: Then   EXIT F2 ENTER

    in case the discriminant is zero, continues on to the next line;
    if the discriminant is not zero, jumps to the command after **Else** below

: Disp "Double root"   EXIT F3 F3 MORE F5 ALPHA D 2nd alpha ALPHA O U B L E ␣
       R O O T F5 ENTER

    displays a message in case there is a double root

: -B/(2A) → M   (-) ALPHA B ÷ (2 ALPHA A) STO▸ M ENTER

    the quadratic formula reduces to $\dfrac{-b}{2a}$ when $D = 0$

: Disp M   MORE F3 ALPHA M ENTER

: Else   EXIT F4 F3 ENTER

    continues from here if the discriminant is not zero

: Disp "Complex roots"   EXIT F3 F3 MORE F5 ALPHA C 2nd alpha ALPHA O M P L E X ␣
       R O O T S F5 ENTER

    displays a message in case the roots are complex numbers

: Disp "Real part"	MORE F3 MORE F5 ALPHA R 2nd alpha ALPHA E A L ⊔ P A R T F5 ENTER
: -B/(2A) → R	(-) ALPHA B ÷ (2 ALPHA A) STO▸ R ENTER

calculates the real part $\dfrac{-b}{2a}$ of the complex roots

: Disp R	MORE F3 ALPHA R ENTER
: Disp "Imaginary part"	F3 MORE F5 ALPHA I 2nd alpha ALPHA M A G I N A R Y ⊔ P A R T F5 ENTER
: √-D/(2A) → I	2nd √ (-) ALPHA D ÷ (2 ALPHA A) STO▸ I ENTER

calculates the imaginary part $\dfrac{\sqrt{-D}}{2a}$ of the complex roots;

since $D < 0$, we must use $-D$ as the radicand

: Disp I	MORE F3 ALPHA I ENTER
: End	EXIT F4 F5 ENTER

marks the end of an If-Then-Else group of commands

: End	F5

When you have finished, press 2nd QUIT to leave the program editor.

You may remove a program from memory by pressing 2nd MEM F2 *[DELET]* MORE F5 *[PRGM]*. Then move the cursor to the program's name and press ENTER to delete the entire program.

4.6.2 *Running a Program:* To run the program just entered, press PRGM F1 *[NAMES]* and look for QUADRAT. The names of programs are listed alphabetically; press MORE to advance through the listing. Press the function key below *[QUADR]* to select this program, then press ENTER.

The program has been written to prompt you for values of the coefficients a, b, and c in a quadratic equation $ax^2 + bx + c = 0$. Input a value, then press ENTER to continue the program.

If you need to interrupt a program during execution, press ON.

The instruction manual for your TI-85 gives detailed information about programming. Refer to it to learn more about programming and how to use other features of your calculator.

TI-85 Advanced Scientific Calculator

Chapter 5

Casio fx-7700GE and fx-9700GE Power Graphic Calculators

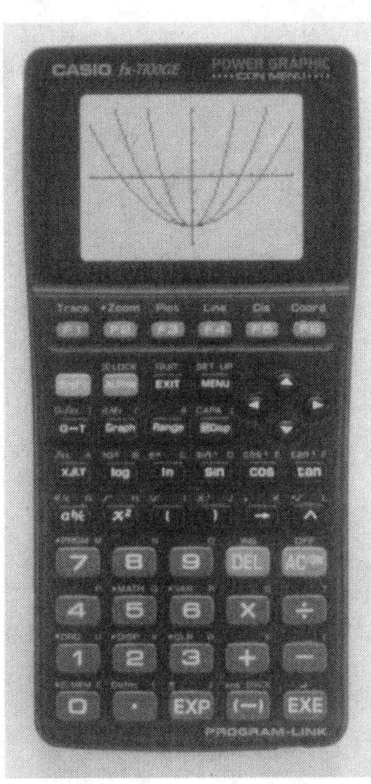 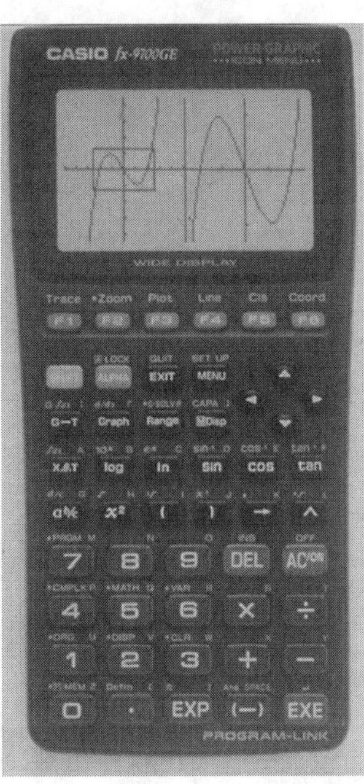

Note: The Casio 9700GE has a wider screen than the 7700GE model and displays more significant digits. Illustrations in this chapter are provided only for the Casio 9700GE whenever the mathematical difference between the two displays is not significant. Likewise, when menu names are only slightly different (for example, RECT on the Casio 9700GE and REC on the 7700GE), we use the Casio 9700GE's names. And, for simplicity, we shall refer to the "Casio 9700/7700GE" whenever the *same* sequence of keystrokes works on *both* calculator models.

5.1.1 Basics: Press the AC/ON key to begin using your Casio 9700/7700GE calculator. If you need to adjust the display contrast, first press MENU, then use the arrow keys [right ▶, left ◀, up ▲, or down ▼] to move to the CONT icon and press EXE. Next press ▶ (the *right* arrow key) to increase the contrast or ◀ (the *left* arrow key) to decrease the contrast (see Figure 5.2). Press MENU once again to return to the main menu. When you have finished with the calculator, turn it off to conserve battery power by pressing SHIFT and then OFF.

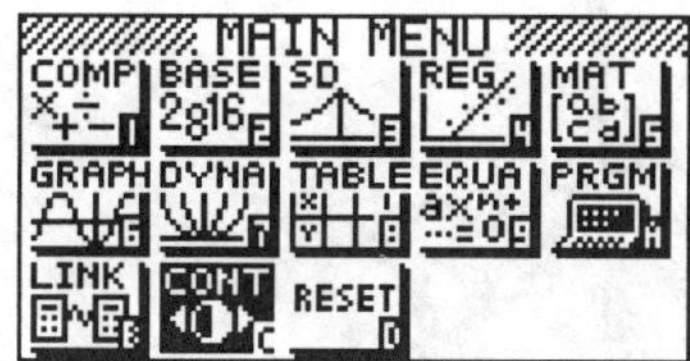

Figure 5.1a: Casio fx-9700GE
MAIN MENU

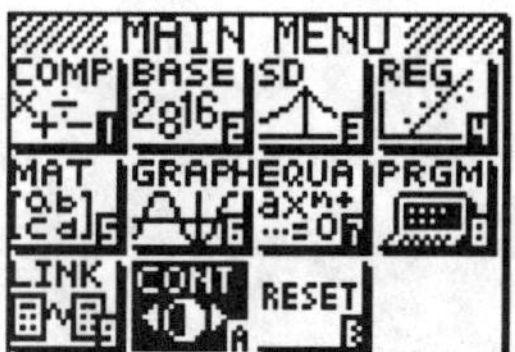

Figure 5.1b: Casio fx-7700GE
MAIN MENU

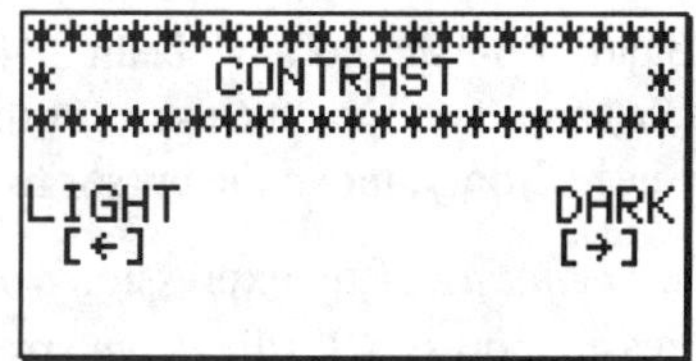

Figure 5.2: CONTRAST

Technology Tip: You can jump quickly to the CONTRAST screen by pressing MENU C *[CONT]* on the Casio fx-9700GE or MENU A *[CONT]* on the Casio fx-7700GE.

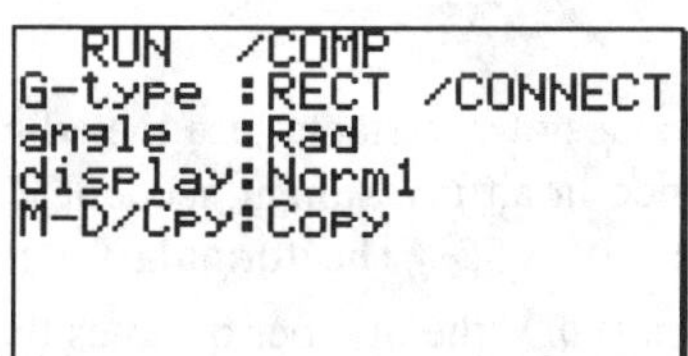

Figure 5.3a: Casio fx-9700GE
settings

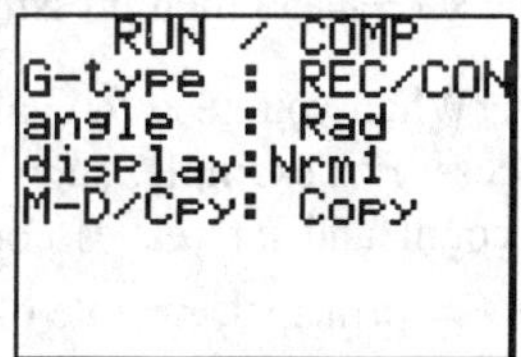

Figure 5.3b: Casio fx-7700GE
settings

Check the Casio 9700/7700GE's settings by pressing MENU 1 *[COMP]* for standard computations. To start with, here are the keystrokes to configure your calculator to conform with the instructions in this guide: first press SHIFT SET-UP F1 for rectangular coordinates, next press ▼ (the *down* arrow key), then press F1 for connected graphs. If you now press ▼ F1 once again, you will configure the ⓂDisp key so that whenever you press and hold it down, the current settings will be displayed. (This is a *different* configuration from what is shown in Figure 5.3.) Details on other options will be given later in this guide. For now, remove any menu that remains by pressing EXIT and AC/ON until the screen is clear.

5.1.2 Editing: One advantage of the Casio 9700/7700GE is that up to seven lines are visible at one time, so you can *see* a long calculation. For example, first press MENU 1 and then type this sum (see Figure 5.4):

$$1 + 2 + 3 + 4 + 5 + 6 + 7 + 8 + 9 + 10 + 11 + 12 + 13 + 14 + 15 + 16 + 17 + 18 + 19 + 20$$

Then press EXE to see the answer, too.

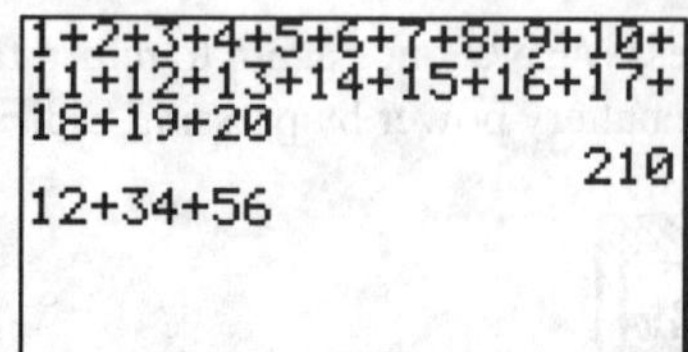

Figure 5.4: Home screen

Often we do not notice a mistake until we see how unreasonable an answer is. The Casio 9700/7700GE permits you to re-display an entire calculation, edit it easily, then execute the *corrected* calculation.

Suppose you had typed 12 + 34 + 56 as in Figure 5.4 but had *not* yet pressed EXE, when you realize that 34 should have been 74. Simply press ◀ (the *left* arrow key) as many times as necessary to move the blinking cursor left to 3, then type 7 to write over it. On the other hand, if 34 should have been 384, move the cursor back to 4, press SHIFT INS (the cursor changes to a blinking frame) and then type 8 (inserts at the cursor position and other characters are pushed to the right). If the 34 should have been 3 only, move the cursor to 4 and press DEL to delete it.

Technology Tip: To move quickly to the *beginning* of an expression you are currently editing, press ▲ (the *up* arrow key); to jump to the *end* of that expression, press ▼ (the *down* arrow key).

Even if you had pressed EXE, you may still edit the previous expression. Press the *left* or *right* arrow key to *redisplay* the last expression that was entered. Now you can change it. If you press ◀, the cursor will start at the *end* of the previous expression; if you press ▶, the cursor will appear at the *beginning*. Even if you have already pressed some keys since the last EXE, but *not* EXE again, you can still recall the previous expression by first pressing AC/ON to clear the screen and then pressing ◀ or ▶.

Technology Tip: When you need to evaluate a formula for different values of a variable, use the editing feature to simplify the process. For example, suppose you want to find the balance in an investment account if there is now $5000 in the account and interest is compounded annually at the rate of 8.5%. The formula for the balance is $P\left(1+\frac{r}{n}\right)^{nt}$, where P = principal, r = rate of interest (expressed as a decimal), n = the number of times that the interest is compounded each year, and t = the number of years. In our example, this becomes $5000(1+.085)^{t}$. Here are the keystrokes for finding the balance after $t = 3$, 5, and 10 years.

Years	*Keystrokes*	*Balance*
3	5000 (1 + .085) ^ 3 EXE	$6386.45
5	◀ ◀ 5 EXE	$7518.28
10	◀ ◀ 10 EXE	$11,304.92

                                        Casio fx-9700GE and fx-7700GE Power Graphic Calculators

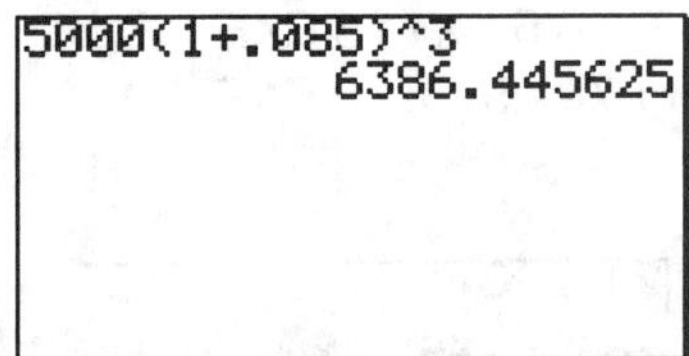

Figure 5.5: Editing expressions

Then to find the balance from the same initial investment but after 5 years when the annual interest rate is 7.5%, press these keys to change the last calculation above: ◄ ◄ DEL ◄ 5 ◄ ◄ ◄ ◄ ◄ 7 EXE.

5.1.3 Key Functions: Most keys on the Casio 9700/7700GE offer access to more than one function, just as the keys on a computer keyboard can produce more than one letter ("g" and "G") or even quite different characters ("5" and "%"). The primary function of a key is indicated on the key itself, and you access that function by a simple press on the key.

To access the *second* function indicated in yellow letters to the *left* above a key, first press the yellow SHIFT key (the cursor changes to a blinking S and a menu appears at the bottom of the screen) and *then* press the key. For example, to calculate $\sqrt{25}$, press SHIFT √ 25 EXE.

When you want to use a letter or other character printed in red letters to the *right* above a key, first press the red ALPHA key (the cursor changes to a blinking A and a menu appears at the bottom of the screen) and then the key. For example, to use the letter K in a formula, press ALPHA K. If you need several letters in a row, press SHIFT A-LOCK, which is like CAPS LOCK on a computer keyboard, and then press all the letters you want. Remember to press ALPHA when you are finished and want to restore the keys to their primary functions.

5.1.4 Order of Operations: The Casio 9700/7700GE performs calculations according to the standard algebraic rules. Working outwards from inner parentheses, calculations are performed from left to right. Powers and roots are evaluated first, followed by multiplications and divisions, and then additions and subtractions.

Technology Tip: In many contexts, the Casio 9700/7700GE does not distinguish between *subtraction* and the *negative sign*. To enter a negative number, you may generally use either the (-) key or the – key. The one exception is when you are *starting* a new calculation; see Section 5.1.6 for an explanation. It is, however, a good habit to use the (-) key whenever you need an *opposite* and to use the – key when you want a *subtraction*.

Enter these expressions to practice using your Casio 9700/7700GE. Press MENU 1 first if it is necessary to put the calculator in computation mode.

Expression	*Keystrokes*	*Display*
$7-5\cdot3$	7 - 5 × 3 EXE	-8
$(7-5)\cdot3$	(7 - 5) × 3 EXE	6
$120-10^2$	120 - 10 x² EXE	20
$(120-10)^2$	(120 - 10) x² EXE	12100
$\dfrac{24}{2^3}$	24 ÷ 2 ^ 3 EXE	3
$\left(\dfrac{24}{2}\right)^3$	(24 ÷ 2) ^ 3 EXE	1728

$$(7 - -5) \cdot -3 \qquad (7 - (\text{-}) 5) \times (\text{-}) 3 \text{ EXE} \qquad -36$$
$$\text{or } (7 - - 5) \times - 3 \text{ EXE}$$

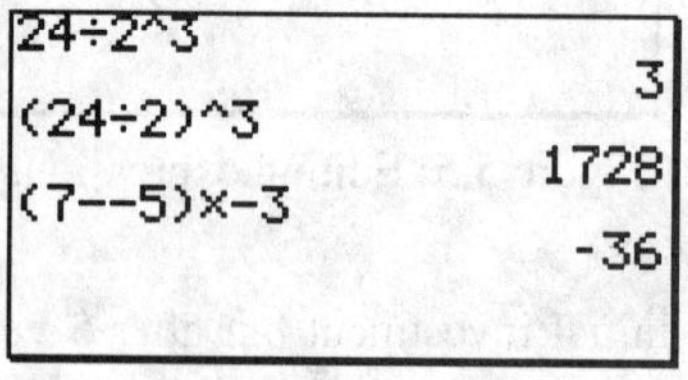

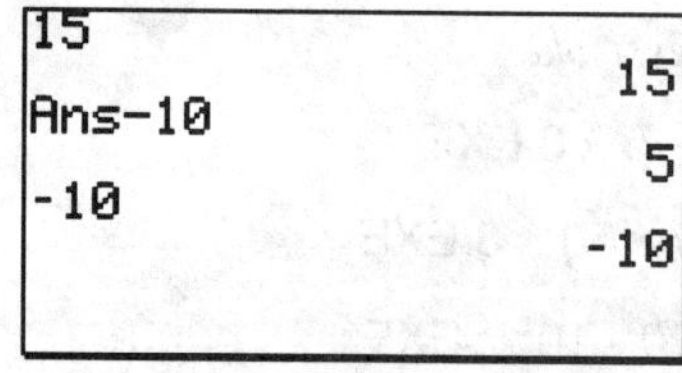

Figure 5.6: Order of operations

5.1.5 Algebraic Expressions and Memory: Your calculator can evaluate expressions such as $\dfrac{N(N+1)}{2}$ *after* you have entered a value for N. Suppose you want $N = 200$. Press $200 \rightarrow$ ALPHA N EXE to store the value 200 in memory location N. Whenever you use N in an expression, the calculator will substitute the value 200 until you make a change by storing *another* number in N. Next enter the expression $\dfrac{N(N+1)}{2}$ by typing ALPHA N (ALPHA N + 1) $\div$ 2 EXE. For $N = 200$, you will find that $\dfrac{N(N+1)}{2} = 20100$.

The contents of any memory location may be revealed by typing just its letter name and then EXE. And the Casio 9700/7700GE retains memorized values even when it is turned off, so long as its batteries are good.

5.1.6 Repeated Operations with Ans: The result of your *last* calculation is always stored in memory location Ans and replaces any previous result. This makes it easy to use the answer from one computation in another computation. For example, press 30 + 15 EXE so that 45 is the last result displayed. Then press SHIFT Ans $\div$ 9 EXE and get 5 because $\frac{45}{9} = 5$.

With a function like division, you press the $\div$ key *after* you enter an argument. For such functions, whenever you would start a new calculation with the previous answer followed by pressing the function key, you may press just the function key. So instead of SHIFT Ans $\div$ 9 in the previous example, you could have pressed simply $\div$ 9 to achieve the same result. This technique also works for these functions: $+$, $-$, $\times$, x^2, $\wedge$, and SHIFT $x^{\text{-}1}$.

Technology Tip: The *negative sign* (-) key and the *subtraction* $-$ key operate differently when pressed at the *start* of a new calculation. Try these keystrokes to see the difference: press 15 EXE, then $-$ 10 EXE, and finally (-) 10 EXE.

Figure 5.7: $-$ and (-)

Here is a situation where Ans is especially useful. Suppose a person makes \$5.85 per hour and you are asked to calculate earnings for a day, a week, and a year. Execute the given keystrokes to find the person's incomes during these periods (results are shown in Figure 5.8):

Pay period	Keystrokes	Earnings
8-hour day	5.85 × 8 EXE	$46.80
5-day week	SHIFT Ans × 5 EXE	$234
52-week year	× 52 EXE	$12,168

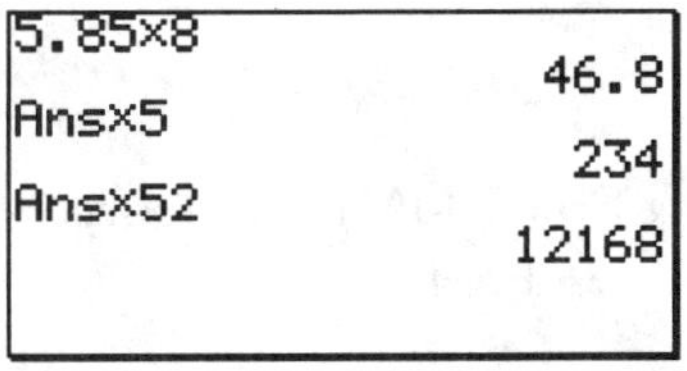

```
5.85×8
            46.8
Ans×5
             234
Ans×52
           12168
```

Figure 5.8: Ans

5.1.7 The MATH Menu: Operators and functions associated with a scientific calculator are available either immediately from the keys of the Casio 9700/7700GE or by SHIFT keys. You have direct key access to common arithmetic operations (x^2, SHIFT $\sqrt{\ }$, SHIFT x^{-1}, ^), exponential and logarithmic functions (log, SHIFT 10^x, ln, SHIFT e^x), and a famous constant (SHIFT π).

A significant difference between the Casio 9700/7700GE and many scientific calculators is that the Casio 9700/7700GE requires the argument of a function *after* the function, as you would see a formula written in your textbook. For example, on the Casio 9700/7700GE you calculate $\sqrt{16}$ by pressing the keys $\sqrt{\ }$ 16 in that order.

The Casio 9700/7700GE has a special fraction key $a^b\!/_c$ for entering fractions and mixed numbers. To enter a fraction such as $\frac{2}{5}$, press 2 $a^b\!/_c$ 5 EXE. To enter a mixed number like $2\frac{3}{4}$, press 2 $a^b\!/_c$ 3 $a^b\!/_c$ 4 EXE. Press $a^b\!/_c$ to toggle between the mixed number and its decimal equivalent; press SHIFT $^d\!/_c$ and see $2\frac{3}{4}$ as an improper fraction, $\frac{11}{4}$.

Here are keystrokes for basic mathematical operations. Try them for practice on your Casio 9700/7700GE.

Expression	Keystrokes	Display
$\sqrt{3^2 + 4^2}$	SHIFT $\sqrt{\ }$ (3 x^2 + 4 x^2) EXE	5
$2\frac{1}{3}$	2 $a^b\!/_c$ 1 $a^b\!/_c$ 3 EXE $a^b\!/_c$	2.33333333333
$\log 200$	log 200 EXE	2.30102999566
$2.34 \cdot 10^5$	2.34 × SHIFT 10^x 5 EXE	234000

Additional mathematical operations and functions are available from the MATH menu. Press SHIFT MATH to see the categories of mathematical functions. They are listed across the bottom of the Casio 9700/7700GE screen and correspond to the six function keys, F1 to F6. You will learn in your mathematics textbook how to apply many of them.

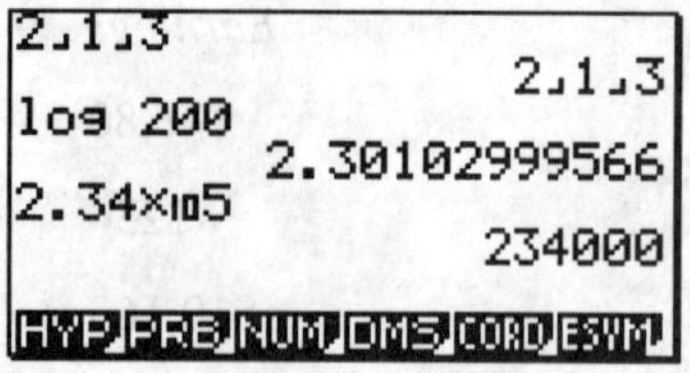

Figure 5.9a: Casio fx-9700GE
MATH menu

Figure 5.9b: Casio fx-7700GE
MATH menu

As an example, calculate $|-5|$ by pressing SHIFT MATH F3 (for access to numerical functions) and then F1 - 5 EXE. To clear any menu from the screen, press EXIT.

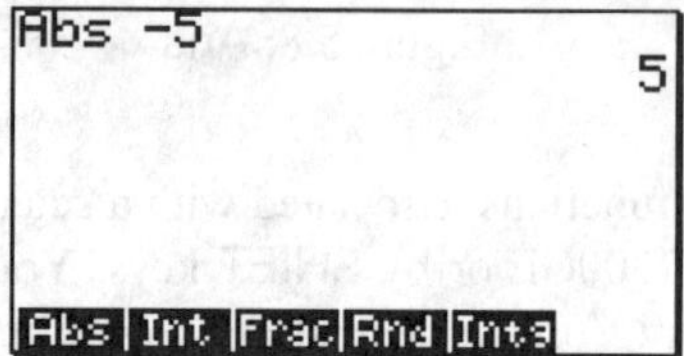

Figure 5.10: MATH NUM menu

The *factorial* of a non-negative integer is the *product* of *all* the integers from 1 up to the given integer. The symbol for factorial is the exclamation point. So 4! (pronounced *four factorial*) is $1 \cdot 2 \cdot 3 \cdot 4 = 24$. You will learn more about applications of factorials in your textbook, but for now use the Casio 9700/7700GE to calculate 4! Press these keystrokes: 4 SHIFT MATH F2 F1 EXE.

5.2 Functions and Graphs

5.2.1 Evaluating Functions: Suppose you receive a monthly salary of \$1975 plus a commission of 10% of sales. Let x = your sales in dollars; then your wages W in dollars are given by the equation $W = 1975 + .10x$. If your January sales were \$2230 and your February sales were \$1865, what was your income during those months?

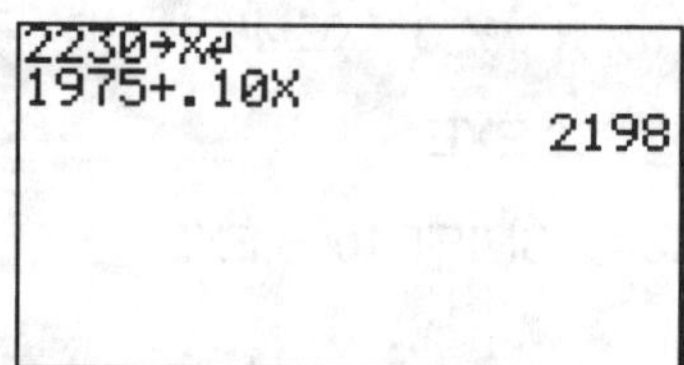

Figure 5.11: Evaluating a function

Here's how to use your Casio 9700/7700GE to perform this task. First press MENU 1 AC/ON to get a blank home screen in COMP mode. Next set $x = 2230$ by pressing 2230 → X,θ,T. (The X,θ,T key lets you enter a variable x without having to use the ALPHA key.) Then press SHIFT ⏎ to allow another expression to be input on a single command line. Finally, enter the expression $1975 + .10x$ by pressing these keys: 1975 + .10 X,θ,T. Now press EXE to calculate the answer (Figure 5.11).

It is not necessary to repeat all these steps to find the February wages. Simply press ▶ to recall the entire previous line, change 2230 to 1865, and press EXE.

   Casio fx-9700GE and fx-7700GE Power Graphic Calculators

The Casio fx-9700GE also has a **TABLE** mode for evaluating functions. [This feature is *not* available on the Casio fx-7700GE.] Press **MENU 8 F1** *[FUNC]* for a function table.

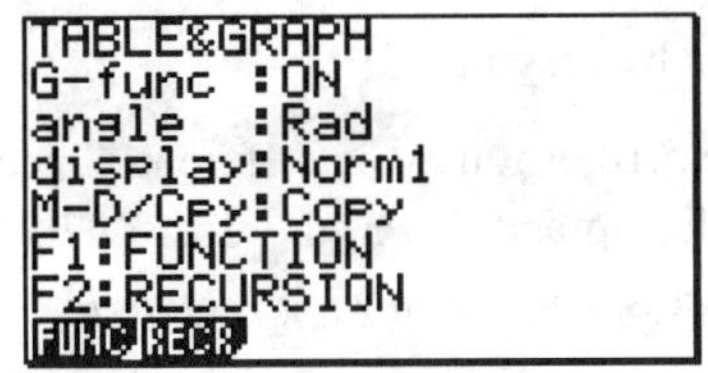

Figure 5.12: TABLE&GRAPH menu

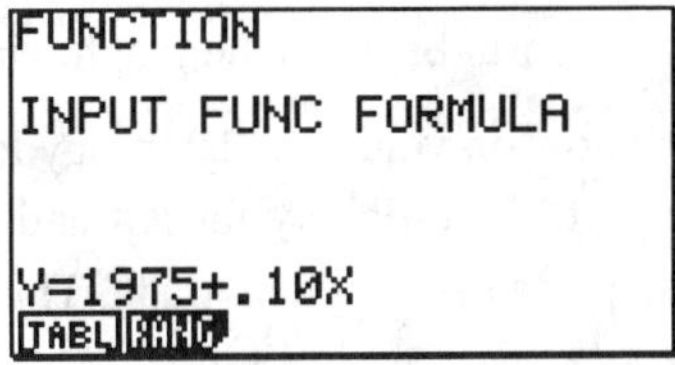

Figure 5.13: FUNCTION menu

Enter the expression $1975 + .10x$ as before (Figure 5.13). Press **F2** *[RANG]* and set the table's range as shown in Figure 5.14. Then x will start at 2230 and also end at 2230, in increments (*pitch*) of 1. The effect is a table with just one row (Figure 5.15), which you see after pressing **F1** *[TABL]*.

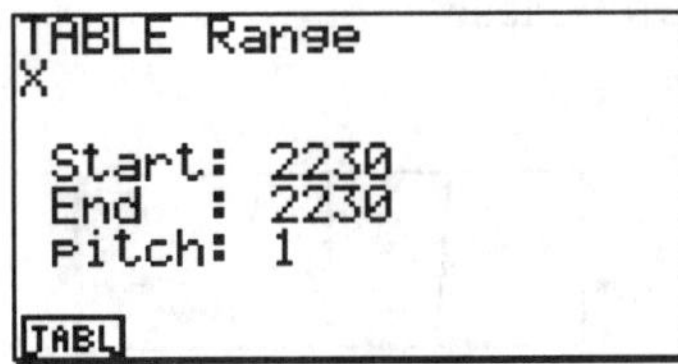

Figure 5.14: TABLE Range

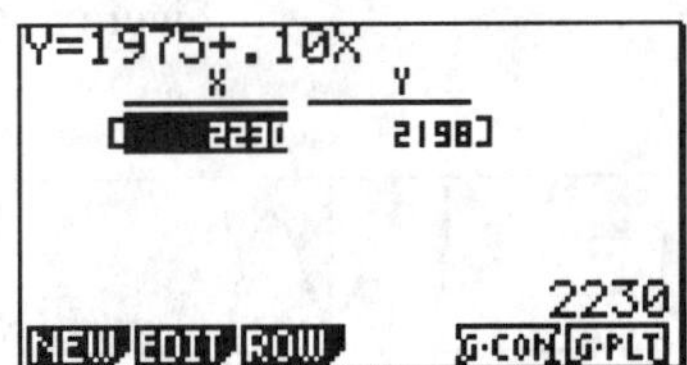

Figure 5.15: TABLE

While viewing the table, with the highlight in the x-column, press **1865 EXE**. The y-value is automatically updated to February's wages. Or add another row to the table below the cursor location by pressing **F3** *[ROW]* **F3** *[ADD]* and changing the x-value in the new row to 1865 (Figure 5.16).

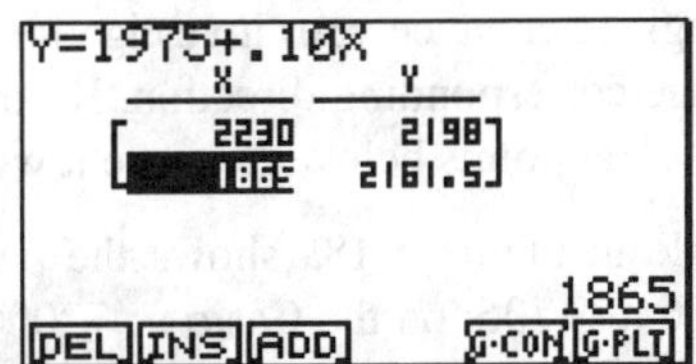

Figure 5.16: Evaluating a function in a table

Technology Tip: The Casio 9700/7700GE does not require multiplication to be expressed between variables, so xxx means x^3. It is often easier to press two or three x's together than to search for the square key or the powers key. Of course, expressed multiplication is also not required between a constant and a variable. Hence to enter $2x^3 + 3x^2 - 4x + 5$ in the Casio 9700/7700GE, you might save keystrokes and press just these keys: 2 X,θ,T X,θ,T X,θ,T + 3 X,θ,T X,θ,T - 4 X,θ,T + 5.

5.2.2 Functions in a Graph Window: On the Casio 9700/7700GE, you can easily generate the graph of a function. The ability to draw a graph contributes substantially to our ability to solve problems.

For example, here is the Casio 9700/7700GE's quick way to graph $y = -x^3 + 4x$. In **COMP** mode (**MENU 1**), press **Graph** and then - X,θ,T ^ 3 + 4 X,θ,T to enter the function (as in Figure 5.17). Now press **EXE** and the Casio 9700/7700GE changes to a window with the graph of $y = -x^3 + 4x$.

While the Casio 9700/7700GE is busy calculating coordinates for a plot, it displays a solid square at the top right of the graph window. When you see this indicator, even though the screen does not change, you know that the calculator is working.

Switch back and forth between the graph window and the home screen by pressing G↔T.

The graph window on your calculator may look like the one in Figure 5.18 or it may be different. Since the graph of $y = -x^3 + 4x$ extends infinitely far left and right and also infinitely far up and down, the Casio 9700/7700GE can display only a piece of the actual graph. This displayed rectangular part is called a *viewing rectangle*.

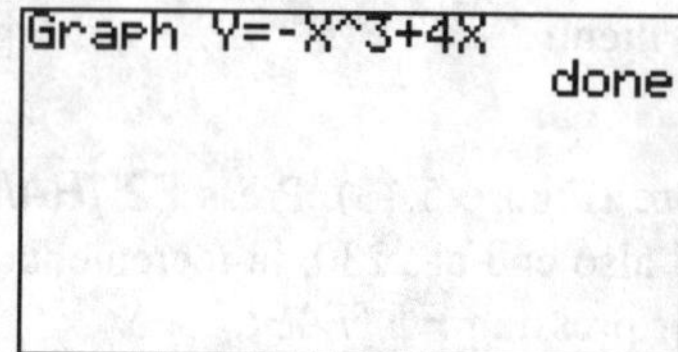

Figure 5.17: Graph command in COMP mode

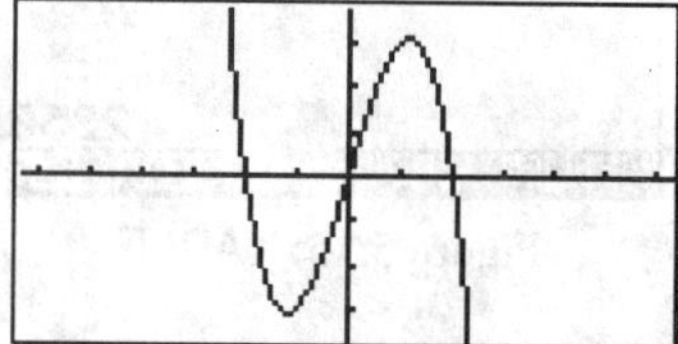

Figure 5.18a: Casio fx-9700GE
graph of $y = -x^3 + 4x$

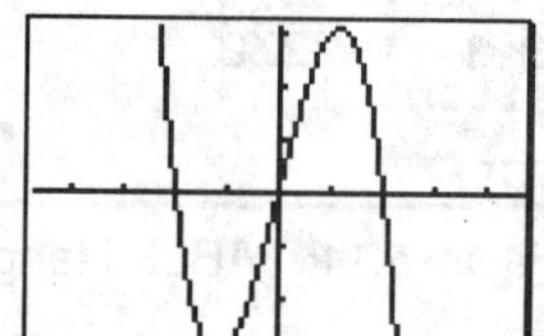

Figure 5.18b: Casio fx-7700GE
graph of $y = -x^3 + 4x$

You can easily change the viewing rectangle to enhance your investigation of a graph. For example, press any of the arrow keys to pan the graph window in the corresponding direction. If you press the down arrow, for example, the window will pan down so that you may look at points below the current window.

The Casio fx-9700GE's viewing rectangle in Figure 5.18a shows the part of the graph that extends horizontally from -6.3 to 6.3 and vertically from -3.706 to 3.706; on the Casio fx-7700GE, the rectangle in Figure 5.18b extends horizontally from -4.7 to 4.7 and vertically from -3.1 to 3.1. Press RANGE to see information about your viewing rectangle. Figure 5.19a shows the RANGE screen that corresponds to the Casio fx-9700GE viewing rectangle in Figure 5.18a; the RANGE screen for the Casio fx-7700GE viewing rectangle in Figure 5.18b is in Figure 5.19b. This is the *standard* viewing rectangle for your calculator.

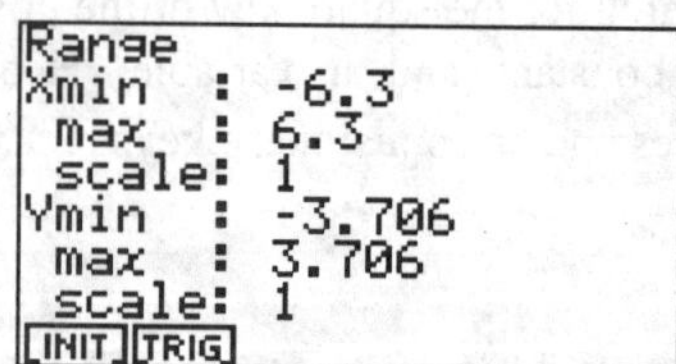

Figure 5.19a: Casio fx-9700GE
standard RANGE

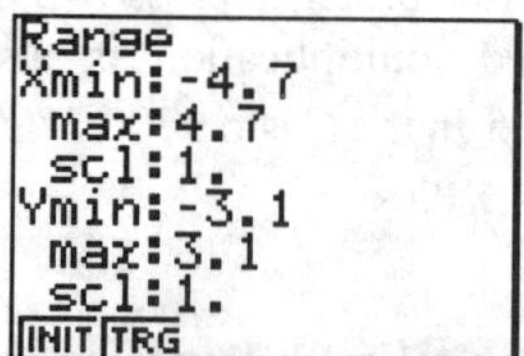

Figure 5.19b: Casio fx-7700GE
standard RANGE

The variables Xmin and Xmax are the minimum and maximum *x*-values of the viewing rectangle; Ymin and Ymax are its minimum and maximum *y*-values.

Casio fx-9700GE and fx-7700GE Power Graphic Calculators

Xscale and Yscale set the spacing between tick marks on the axes.

Use the arrow keys ▲ and ▼ to move up and down from one line to another in this list; pressing the EXE key will move down the list. Enter a new value to over-write a previous value. You may also edit the entry as you would edit an expression. To leave the RANGE menu, press the RANGE key once or twice more. Finally, press EXE to redraw the graph. The following figures show different RANGE screens and the corresponding viewing rectangle for each one.

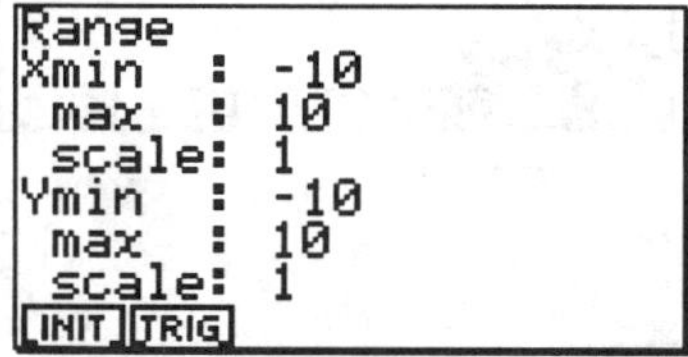

Figure 5.20: -10 to 10 in both directions

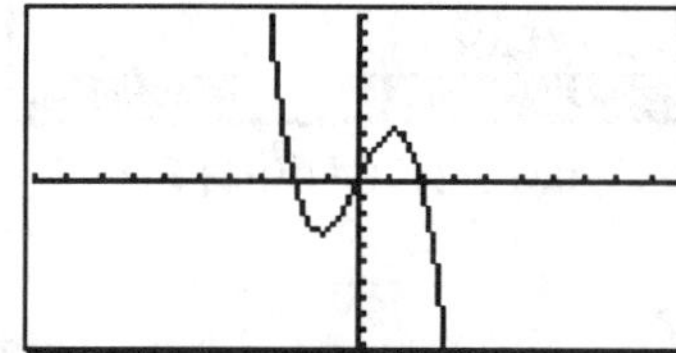

Figure 5.21: Graph of $y = -x^3 + 4x$

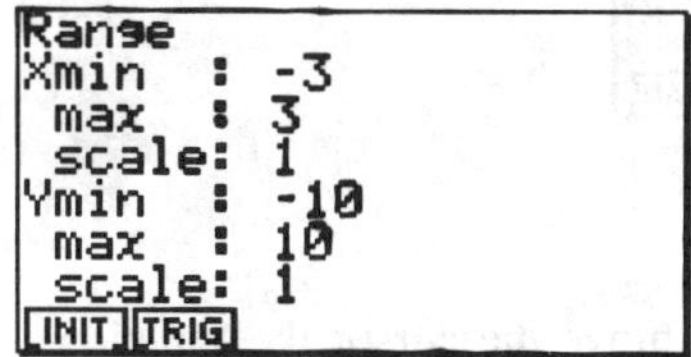

Figure 5.22: **Custom window**

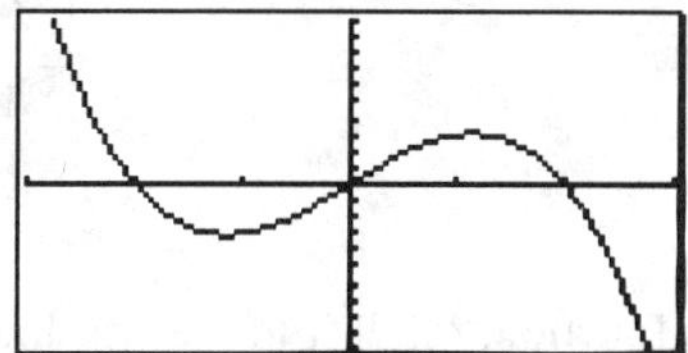

Figure 5.23: Graph of $y = -x^3 + 4x$

To initialize the viewing rectangle quickly to standard values (see Figure 5.19), press **RANGE F1** *[INIT]* **RANGE RANGE**. Then press **EXE** to redraw the graph.

As you pan over the graph by pressing the arrow keys, the RANGE dimensions are updated automatically. More information about windows is presented later, in Section 5.2.3.

Technology Tip: Clear any graphs in COMP mode by pressing F5 when the Casio 9700/7700GE is showing the graph screen or SHIFT F5 when it is displaying the home screen. The Cls command now appears in the home screen; press **EXE** to implement it.

Another way to clear the graph window is to press **RANGE**, re-enter the *current* value for Xmin (or make any "change" in any range value), then press **RANGE RANGE** to exit. This method *keeps* the graph command as the *current* command, so you may edit it as necessary. Also, the Casio 9700/7700GE keeps a graph "active" for zooming and tracing in COMP mode only if the graphing instruction is the *last* command executed.

If you're going to use a function later, or if you need to perform some calculations before returning to its graph, save it in the Casio 9700/7700GE's FUNCTION MEMORY. Six different functions, expressions, or commands can be stored here. Press SHIFT ⊟-MEM and then F5 for a listing of current contents of function memory. To *store* a function or command, enter it first in the home screen, but do *not* press EXE. Press SHIFT ⊟-MEM F1 and then an integer from 1 to 6, corresponding to a function memory location. To *recall* a function or command from mem… to the home screen, press SHIFT ⊟-MEM F2 and the integer corresponding to the function you want.

Technology Tip: It's a good idea to reserve at least one function memory location, say f_1, for temporary storage of functions, and use the remaining locations for longer-term storage.

If you plan to do more extensive investigation of functions, use the calculator's graphic function memory. Here you may store up to 20 different functions in rectangular, polar, and parametric form, and also inequalities. For example, let's graph $y = -x^3 + 4x$ once again, this time in GRAPH mode. Press MENU 6 and enter $-x^3 + 4x$ as before (see

Figure 5.24). Then store this as function Y1 by pressing F1 *[STO]*, move the cursor if necessary to Y1, and press F6 *[SET]*. Next press F6 *[DRAW]* to see the graph (same as Figure 5.18 if your calculator is using its standard range).

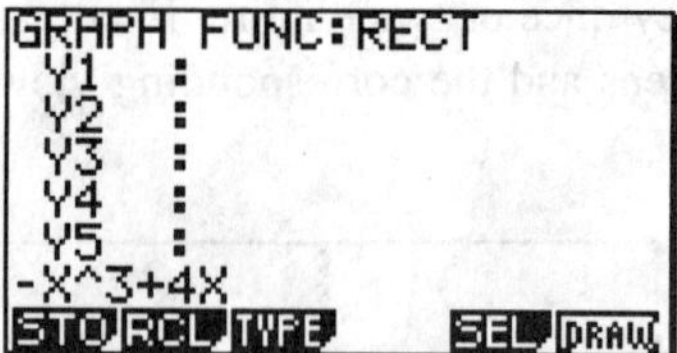

Figure 5.24: GRAPH FUNC

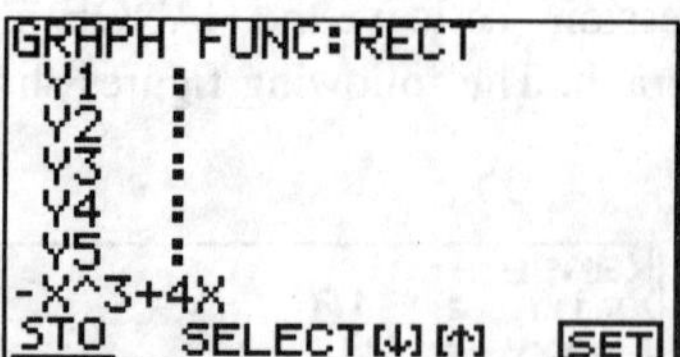

Figure 5.25: Storing an expression

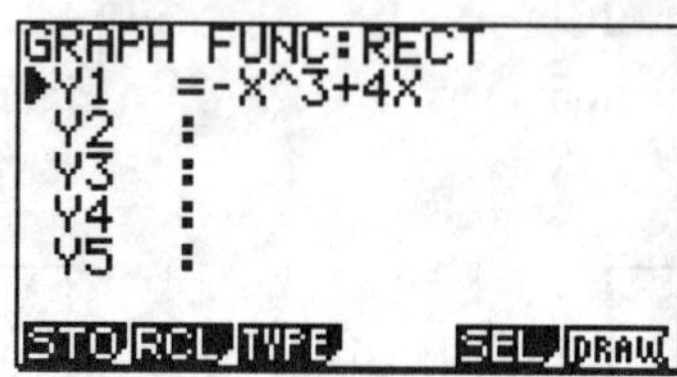

Figure 5.26: $Y1 = -x^3 + 4x$

To change a function, recall it to the edit line by pressing F2 *[RCL]*, move the cursor the function you want, and press F6 *[SET]*.

Delete a function by storing nothing in its place. First press AC/ON to clear the edit line and F1 *[STO]*, then move the cursor the function you want to remove and press F6 *[SET]*.

Change the range in GRAPH mode just as you did in COMP mode, by pressing the RANGE key.

Technology Tip: Redraw graphs in GRAPH mode by pressing G↔T to switch between the Casio 9700/7700GE's GRAPH FUNC screen and its graph screen. Then press F6 *[DRAW]* to clear the graph screen and plot the functions again.

5.2.3 Graphing a Circle: Here is a useful technique for graphs that are not functions, but that can be "split" into a top part and a bottom part, or into multiple parts. Suppose you wish to graph the circle whose equation is $x^2 + y^2 = 36$. First solve for y and get an equation for the top semicircle, $y = \sqrt{36 - x^2}$, and for the bottom semicircle, $y = -\sqrt{36 - x^2}$. Then graph the two semicircles simultaneously.

The keystrokes to draw this circle's graph in COMP mode (MENU 1) follow. Store $\sqrt{36 - x^2}$ as f_1 by pressing SHIFT √ (36 - X,θ,T x²) SHIFT ⊟-MEM F1 1. Then press AC/ON GRAPH SHIFT ⊟-MEM F2 *[RCL]* 1 SHIFT ↵ GRAPH - F2 *[RCL]* 1 EXE to draw both halves of the circle.

Figure 5.27: Two semicircles in COMP mode

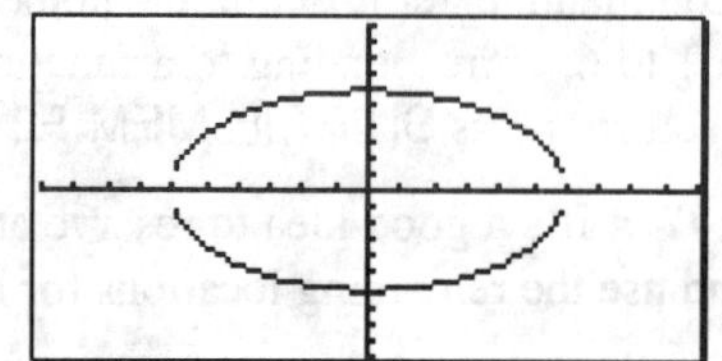

Figure 5.28: Circle's graph - one view

Casio fx-9700GE and fx-7700GE Power Graphic Calculators

To plot the circle in GRAPH mode (MENU 6), store $\sqrt{36-x^2}$ as Y1 and store $-\sqrt{36-x^2}$ as Y2. Or you may store -Y1 as Y2 by pressing these Casio fx-9700GE keystrokes: - SHIFT VAR F3 *[GRPH]* F1 *[Y]* 1; for the Casio fx-7700GE, the keystrokes are - SHIFT VAR F1 *[GRP]* F1 *[Y]* 1. The VAR menu (displayed along the bottom of the screen in Figure 5.29) enables you to recall graphic functions and other information from memory.

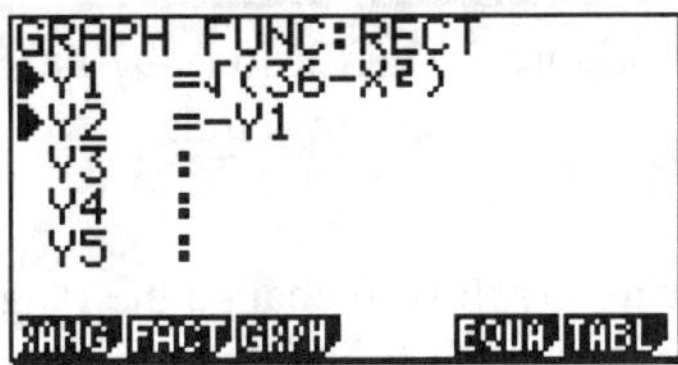

Figure 5.29a: Casio fx-9700GE
GRAPH mode

Figure 5.29b: Casio fx-7700GE
GRAPH mode

If your range were set to a viewing rectangle extending from -10 to 10 in both directions, your graph would look like Figure 5.28. Now this does *not* look like a circle, because the units along the axes are not the same. You need what is called a "square" viewing rectangle.

The Casio calculator's standard viewing rectangle is square, but too small to display a circle of radius 6. So double the dimensions of the Casio fx-9700GE's standard window and change it to extend horizontally from -12.6 to 12.6 and vertically from -7.412 to 7.412; on the Casio fx-7700GE, change it to extend horizontally from -9.4 to 9.4 and vertically from -6.2 to 6.2.

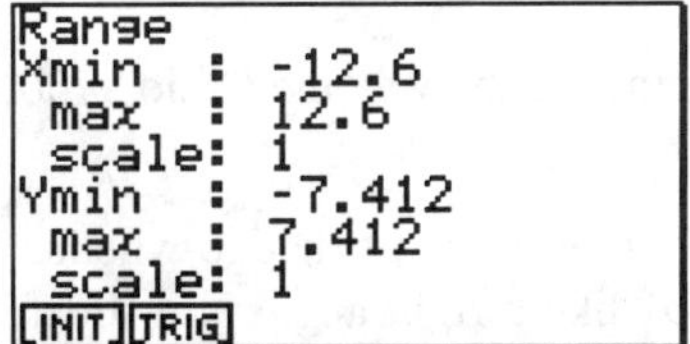

Figure 5.30a: Casio fx-9700GE
twice standard range

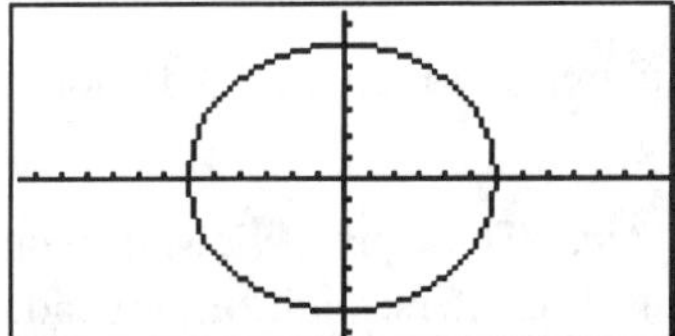

Figure 5.31a: Casio fx-9700GE
better circle

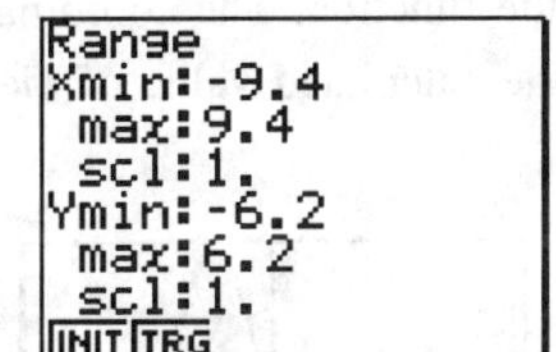

Figure 5.30b: Casio fx-7700GE
twice standard range

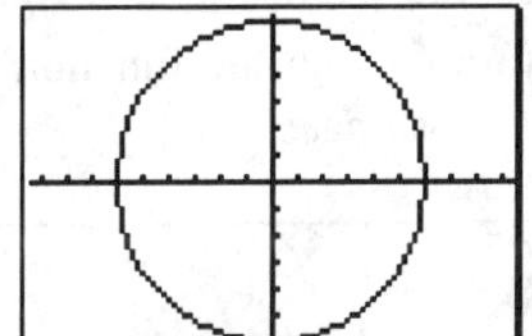

Figure 5.31b: Casio fx-7700GE
better circle

Technology Tip for the Casio fx-9700GE: Another way to get a square graph is to change the range variables so that the value of Ymax - Ymin is $\frac{3}{5}$ times Xmax - Xmin. For example, see the RANGE in Figure 5.32a and the corresponding graph in Figure 5.33a. The method works because the dimensions of the Casio fx-9700GE's display are such that the ratio of vertical to horizontal is approximately $\frac{3}{5}$.

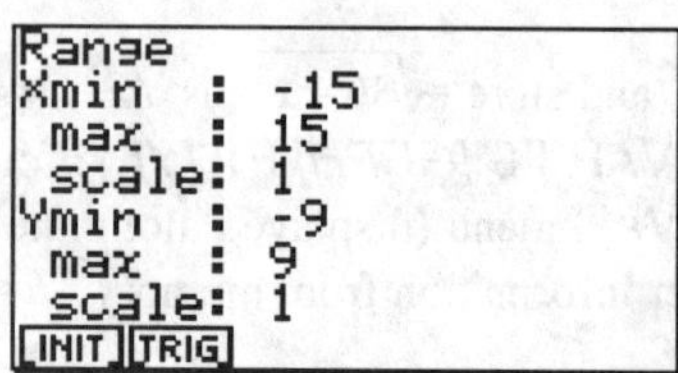

Figure 5.32a: Casio fx-9700GE

$$\frac{\text{vertical}}{\text{horizontal}} = \frac{18}{30} = \frac{3}{5}$$

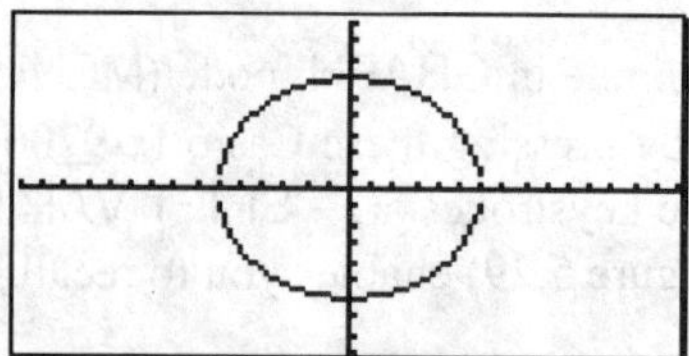

Figure 5.33a: Casio fx-9700GE
"square" circle

Technology Tip for the Casio fx-7700GE: Another way to get a square graph is to change the range variables so that the value of Ymax - Ymin is $\frac{2}{3}$ times Xmax - Xmin. For example, see the RANGE in Figure 5.32b and the corresponding graph in Figure 5.33b. The method works because the dimensions of the Casio 9700/7700GE's display are such that the ratio of vertical to horizontal is approximately $\frac{2}{3}$.

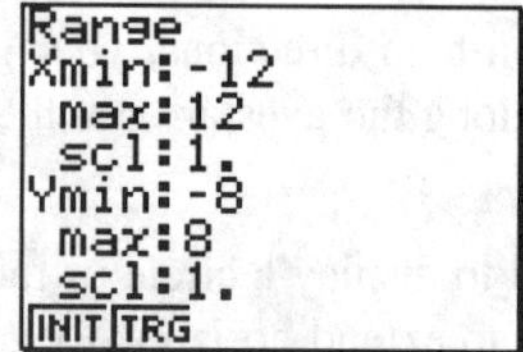

Figure 5.32b: Casio fx-7700GE

$$\frac{\text{vertical}}{\text{horizontal}} = \frac{16}{24} = \frac{2}{3}$$

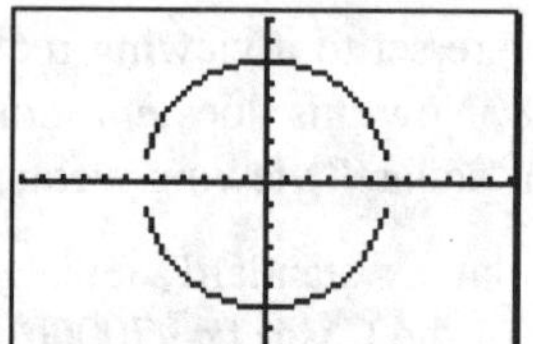

Figure 5.33b: Casio fx-7700GE
"square" circle

The two semicircles in Figure 5.33 do not meet because of an idiosyncrasy in the way the Casio 9700/7700GE plots a graph.

Technology Tip: The square viewing rectangle is also important when you want to judge whether two lines are perpendicular. The intersection of perpendicular lines will always *look* like a right angle in a square viewing rectangle.

5.2.4 TRACE: Graph $y = -x^3 + 4x$ in the standard viewing rectangle. When the graph window is displayed, press F1 *[Trace]* to enable the left ◄ and right ► arrow keys to trace along the function. The coordinates that are displayed belong to points on the function's graph, so the y-coordinate is the calculated value of the function at the corresponding x-coordinate.

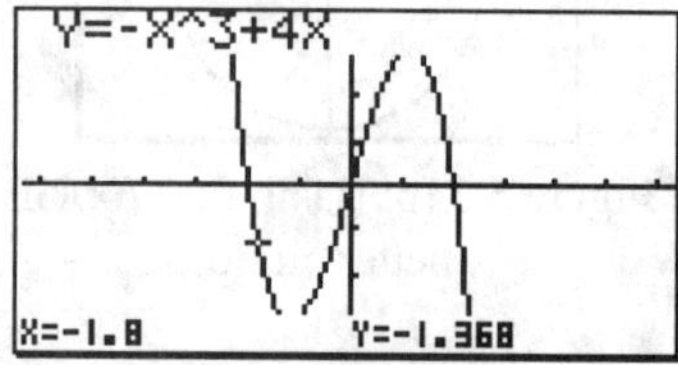

Figure 5.34a: Casio fx-9700GE
Trace

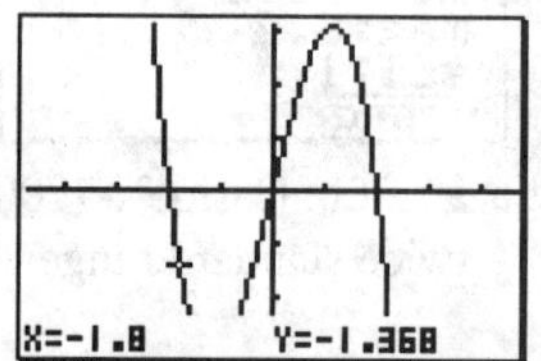

Figure 5.34b: Casio fx-7700GE
Trace

To see more decimal places in the coordinates of the points that are traced, press F6 to cycle among the x-coordinate alone, the y-coordinate alone, and both coordinates.

Casio fx-9700GE and fx-7700GE Power Graphic Calculators

Now plot a second function, $y = -.25x$, along with $y = -x^3 + 4x$. In COMP mode, first press the keys to graph $y = -x^3 + 4x$ but don't press EXE yet. Add the second graph command to this by pressing SHIFT ⏎ GRAPH and the keys for $-.25x$ (Figure 5.35). Finally, press EXE to draw both functions.

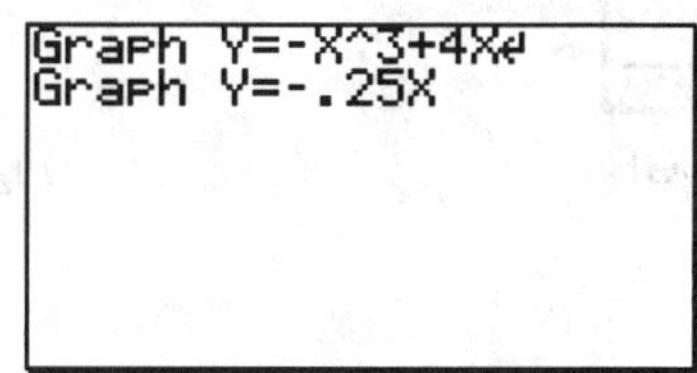

Figure 5.35: Two functions in COMP mode

In GRAPH mode, store $-.25x$ as Y2 (Figure 5.36). Then press F6 *[DRAW]* to draw both functions.

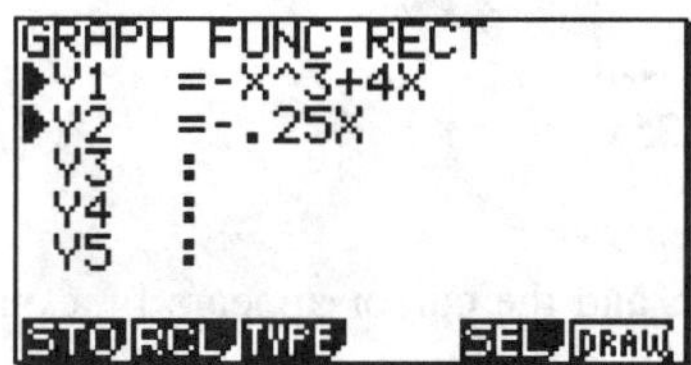

Figure 5.36a: Casio fx-9700GE
two functions in GRAPH mode

Figure 5.36b: Casio fx-7700GE
two functions in GRAPH mode

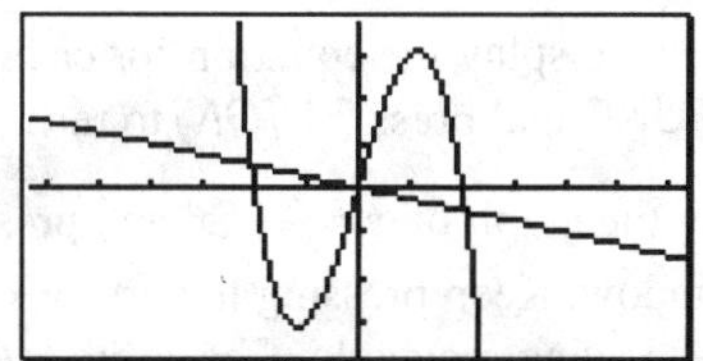

Figure 5.37: $y = -x^3 + 4x$ and $y = -.25x$

Note in Figure 5.36a that there are filled arrows next to *both* Y1 and Y2. This means *both* functions will be graphed on your Casio fx-9700GE. In the GRAPH FUNC window, press F5 *[SEL]*, move the cursor next to Y1, and press F2 *[CAN]*. There should no longer be an arrow here (see Figure 5.38a). Now press EXIT F6 and see that only Y2 is plotted (Figure 5.39).

Note in Figure 5.36b that the equal signs next to Y1 and Y2 are *both* highlighted. This means *both* functions will be graphed on your Casio fx-7700GE. In the GRAPH FUNC window, press F5 *[SEL]*, move the cursor next to Y1, and press F2 *[CAN]*. This equal sign should no longer be highlighted (see Figure 5.38b). Now press EXIT F6 and see that only Y2 is plotted (Figure 5.39).

Many different functions may be stored in the GRAPH FUNC list and any combination of them may be graphed simultaneously. You can make a function active or inactive for graphing by pressing F1 *[SET]* or F2 *[CAN]* to set the highlight (activate) or remove the highlight (deactivate). Go back and do what is needed in order to graph Y1 but not Y2.

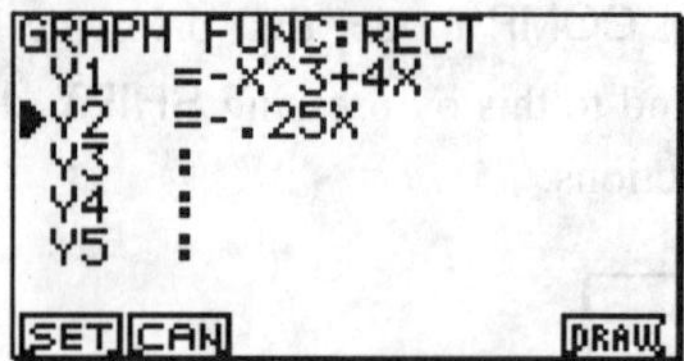

Figure 5.38a: Casio fx-9700GE
only Y2 active

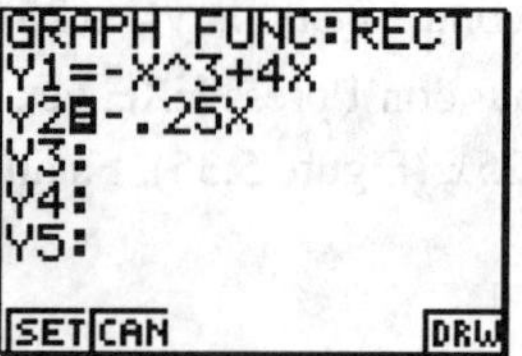

Figure 5.38b: Casio fx-7700GE
only Y2 active

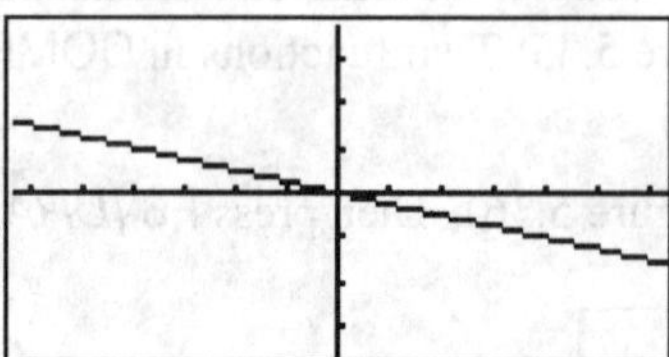

Figure 5.39: Graph of $y = -.25x$

Now activate Y2 again so that both graphs are plotted. Press **TRACE** and the cursor appears first on the graph of $y = -x^3 + 4x$ because it is higher up in the GRAPH FUNC list. Press the up ▲ or down ▼ arrow key to move the cursor vertically to the graph of $y = -.25x$. Next press the right and left arrow keys to trace along the graph of $y = -.25x$. When more than one function is plotted, you can move the trace cursor vertically from one graph to another in this way.

Technology Tip: The Casio fx-9700GE can display the equation for each function as it is plotted or traced. In SET UP, move the cursor down to GRAPH FUNC and press F1 *[ON]* to turn the display on or F2 *[OFF]* to turn it off.

Technology Tip: By the way, trace along the graph of $y = -.25x$ and press and hold either ◀ or ▶. Eventually you will reach the left or right edge of the window. Keep pressing the arrow key and the Casio 9700/7700GE will allow you to continue the trace by panning the viewing rectangle. Check the RANGE screen to see that Xmin and Xmax are automatically updated.

The Casio fx-9700GE's display has 127 horizontal columns of pixels and 63 vertical rows. So when you trace a curve across a graph window, you are actually moving from Xmin to Xmax in 126 equal jumps, each called Δx. You would calculate the size of each jump to be $\Delta x = \dfrac{\text{Xmax} - \text{Xmin}}{126}$. Sometimes you may want the jumps to be friendly numbers like .1 or .25 so that, when you trace along the curve, the x-coordinates will be incremented by such a convenient amount. Just set your viewing rectangle for a particular increment Δx by making Xmax = Xmin + 126·Δx. For example, if you want Xmin = -5 and Δx = .3, set Xmax = -5 + 126·.3 = 38.3. Likewise, set Ymax = Ymin + 62·Δy if you want the vertical increment to be some special Δy.

On the Casio fx-9700GE, to center your window around a particular point, say (h, k), and also have a certain Δx, set Xmin = h - 63·Δx and Xmax = h + 63·Δx. Likewise, make Ymin = k - 31·Δy and Ymax = k + 31·Δy. For example, to center a window around the origin, (0, 0), with both horizontal and vertical increments of .25, set the range so that Xmin = 0 - 63·.25 = -15.75, Xmax = 0 + 63·.25 = 15.75, Ymin = 0 - 31·.25 = -7.75, and Ymax = 0 + 31·.25 = 7.75

The Casio fx-7700GE's display has 95 horizontal columns of pixels and 63 vertical rows. So when you trace a curve across a graph window, you are actually moving from Xmin to Xmax in 94 equal jumps, each called Δx. You would calculate the size of each jump to be $\Delta x = \dfrac{\text{Xmax} - \text{Xmin}}{94}$. Sometimes you may want the jumps to be friendly numbers like .1 or .25 so that, when you trace along the curve, the x-coordinates will be incremented by such a convenient

                    Casio fx-9700GE and fx-7700GE Power Graphic Calculators

amount. Just set your viewing rectangle for a particular increment Δx by making $\mathsf{Xmax} = \mathsf{Xmin} + 94 \cdot \Delta x$. For example, if you want $\mathsf{Xmin} = -5$ and $\Delta x = .3$, set $\mathsf{Xmax} = -5 + 94 \cdot .3 = 23.2$. Likewise, set $\mathsf{Ymax} = \mathsf{Ymin} + 62 \cdot \Delta y$ if you want the vertical increment to be some special Δy.

On the Casio fx-7700GE, to center your window around a particular point, say (h, k), and also have a certain Δx, set $\mathsf{Xmin} = \mathsf{h} - 47 \cdot \Delta x$ and $\mathsf{Xmax} = \mathsf{h} + 47 \cdot \Delta x$. Likewise, make $\mathsf{Ymin} = \mathsf{k} - 31 \cdot \Delta y$ and $\mathsf{Ymax} = \mathsf{k} + 31 \cdot \Delta y$. For example, to center a window around the origin, (0, 0), with both horizontal and vertical increments of .25, set the range so that $\mathsf{Xmin} = 0 - 47 \cdot .25 = -11.75$, $\mathsf{Xmax} = 0 + 47 \cdot .25 = 11.75$, $\mathsf{Ymin} = 0 - 31 \cdot .25 = -7.75$, and $\mathsf{Ymax} = 0 + 31 \cdot .25 = 7.75$.

The Casio fx-7700GE's standard window is already a friendly viewing rectangle, centered at the origin (0, 0) with $\Delta x = \Delta y = 0.1$. The Casio fx-9700GE's standard window is a square window, centered at the origin with $\Delta x = 0.1$.

See the benefit by first plotting $y = x^2 + 2x + 1$ in a window that extends from -10 to 10 in both directions. Trace near its y-intercept, which is (0, 1), and move towards its x-intercept, which is (-1, 0). Then initialize the range to the standard window and trace again near the intercepts.

5.2.5 ZOOM: Plot again the two graphs, for $y = -x^3 + 4x$ and for $y = -.25x$. There appears to be an intersection near $x = 2$. The Casio 9700/7700GE provides several ways to enlarge the view around this point. You can change the viewing rectangle directly by pressing RANGE and editing the values of Xmin, Xmax, Ymin, and Ymax. Figure 5.40 shows a new viewing rectangle for the range extending from 1.5 to 2.5 horizontally and from -2.5 to 2.5 vertically.

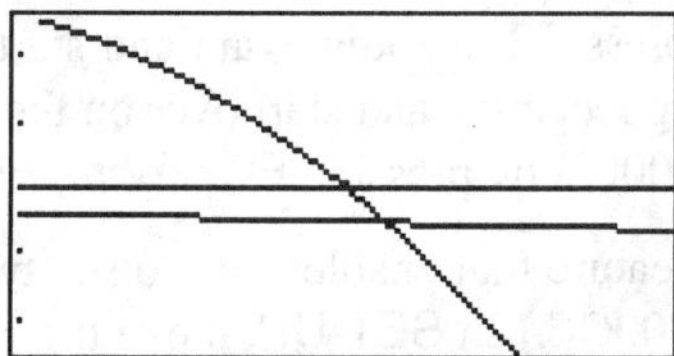

Figure 5.40: Closer view

Trace along the graphs until coordinates of a point that is close to the intersection are displayed.

A more efficient method for enlarging the view is to draw a new viewing rectangle with the cursor. Start again with a graph of the two functions $y = -x^3 + 4x$ and $y = -.25x$ in a standard viewing rectangle.

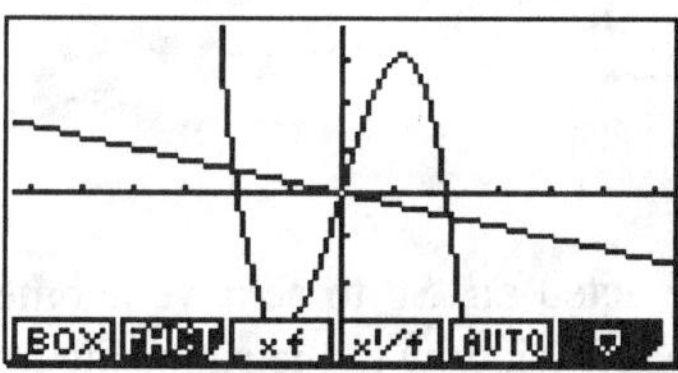

Figure 5.41a: Casio fx-9700GE
Zoom menu

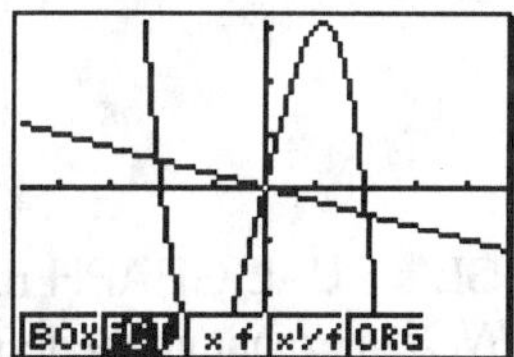

Figure 5.41b: Casio fx-7700GE
Zoom menu

Now imagine a small rectangular box around the intersection point, near $x = 2$. Press $\mathsf{F2}$ *[Zoom]* $\mathsf{F1}$ *[BOX]* to draw a box to define this new viewing rectangle. Use the arrow keys to move the cursor, which is now free-moving and whose coordinates are displayed at the bottom of the window, to one corner of the new viewing rectangle you imagine (Figure 5.42).

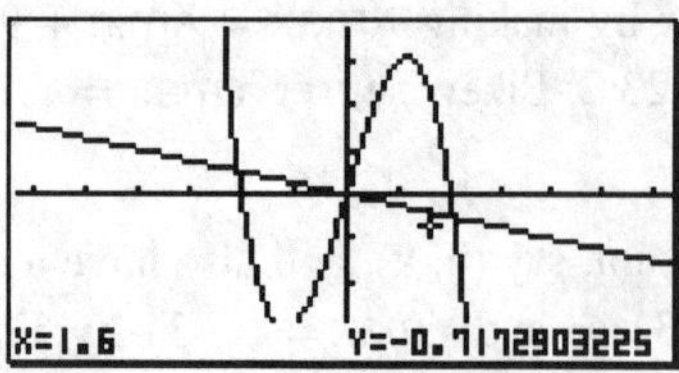

Figure 5.42: One corner selected

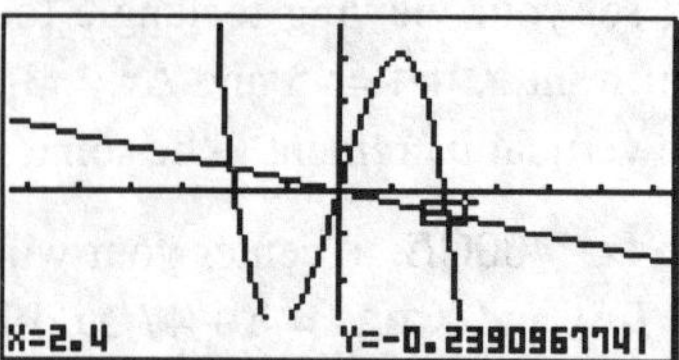

Figure 5.43: Box drawn

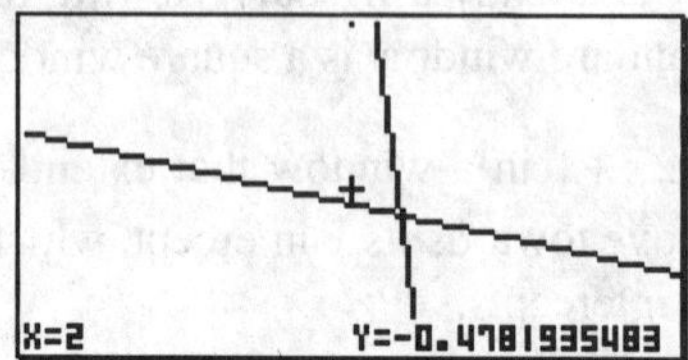

Figure 5.44: New viewing rectangle

Press **EXE** to fix the corner where you have moved the cursor. Use the arrow keys again to move the cursor to the diagonally opposite corner of the new rectangle (Figure 5.43). If this box looks all right to you, press **EXE**. The rectangular area you have enclosed will now enlarge to fill the graph window (Figure 5.44).

You may cancel the zoom any time *before* you press this last **EXE**. Press another function key such as **F1** to cancel the zoom and initiate a trace instead, or press **F2** to zoom again and start over. Even if you did execute the zoom, you may still return to the original viewing rectangle and start over on the Casio fx-9700GE by pressing **F2** *[Zoom]* **F6** *[●]* **F1** *[ORG]* and on the Casio fx-7700GE by pressing **F2** *[Zoom]* **F5** *[ORG]*.

The Casio fx-9700GE has a split screen feature that enables you to see two views of a graph simultaneously. [This feature is *not* available on the Casio fx-7700GE.] In **SET UP**, move the cursor down to **DUAL GRAPH** and toggle it on. Now when you zoom, the left window displays the original graph and the right window displays the result of the zoom (see Figure 5.45).

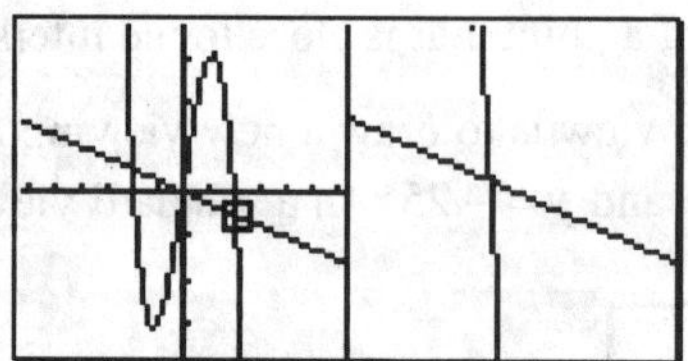
Figure 5.45: DUAL GRAPH

In Casio fx-9700GE's **DUAL GRAPH** mode, only the left side can be acted on. So to achieve another zoom, first press **F6 F2** *[CHNG]* to exchange the left and right windows. Copy the left window to the right side by pressing **F6 F1** *[COPY]*. When you press **RANGE**, you will find *two* ranges that can be changed independently. The **F6** key toggles between the left side range and the right side range.

Technology Tip: Use the **G↔T** key to toggle the Casio fx-9700GE from dual graph to full-screen left side to full-screen right side to **GRAPH FUNC** screen.

The Casio 9700/7700GE can quickly magnify a graph around the cursor's location. Return once more to the standard range for the graph of the two functions $y = -x^3 + 4x$ and $y = -.25x$. Trace along the graphs to move the cursor as close as you can to the point of intersection near $x = 2$ (see Figure 5.46). Then press **F2 F3** *[×f]* and the calculator draws a magnified graph, centered at the cursor's position (Figure 5.47). The range values are changed to reflect this new viewing rectangle. Look in the RANGE menu to check.

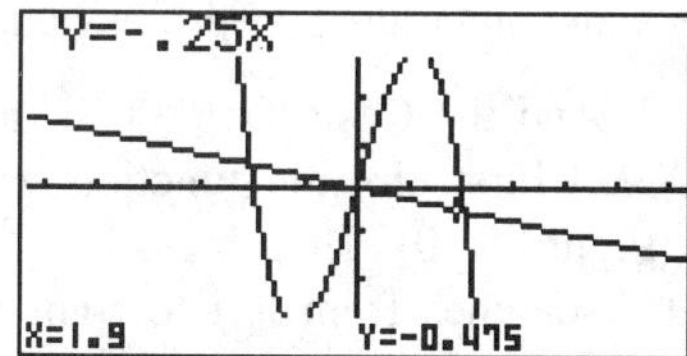

Figure 5.46: Before a zoom in

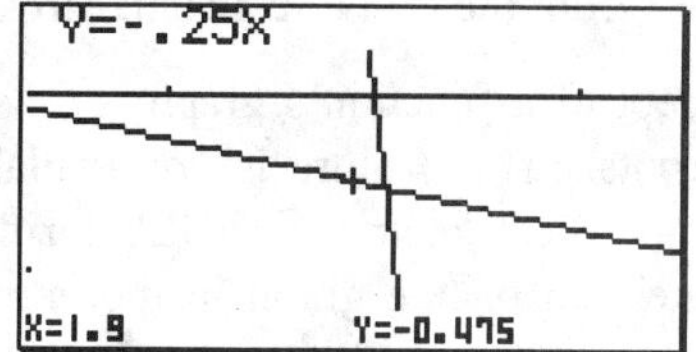

Figure 5.47: After a zoom in

As you see in the Zoom menu (press F2), the Casio 9700/7700GE can zoom in (press F2 F3 [×f]) or zoom out (press F2 F4 [×1/f]). Zoom out to see a larger view of the graph, centered at the cursor position. You can change the horizontal and vertical scale of the magnification by pressing F2 F2 and editing Xfact and Yfact, the horizontal and vertical magnification factors.

Technology Tip: An advantage of zooming in from the default viewing rectangle is that subsequent windows will also be square. Likewise, if you zoom in from a friendly viewing rectangle, the zoomed windows will also be friendly.

The default zoom factor is 2 in both directions (press F1 *[INIT]* in the Zoom Factor menu). It is not necessary for Xfact and Yfact to be equal. Sometimes, you may prefer to zoom in one direction only, so the other factor should be set to 1. Press EXIT to leave the Zoom Factor menu.

Technology Tip: If you should zoom in too much and lose the curve, zoom back to the original viewing rectangle and start over. Or use the arrow keys to pan over if you think the curve is not too far away. You can also just initialize the range to the Casio 9700/7700GE's standard window.

Technology Tip: The Casio fx-9700GE can automatically select the necessary *vertical* range for a function. For auto scaling, press F2 *[Zoom]* F5 *[AUTO]*. Take care, because sometimes when you are graphing two functions together, the calculator will auto scale for one function in such a way that the other function will no longer be visible. For example, plot the two functions $y = -x^3 + 4x$ and $y = -.25x$ in the Casio fx-9700GE's standard viewing rectangle, then auto scale and trace along both functions.

5.3   Solving Equations and Inequalities

5.3.1 Intercepts and Intersections: Tracing and zooming are also used to locate an x-intercept of a graph, where a curve crosses the x-axis. For example, the graph of $y = x^3 - 8x$ crosses the x-axis three times (see Figure 5.48). After tracing over to the x-intercept point that is furthest to the left, zoom in (Figure 5.49). Continue this process until you have located all three intercepts with as much accuracy as you need. The three x-intercepts of $y = x^3 - 8x$ are approximately -2.828, 0, and 2.828.

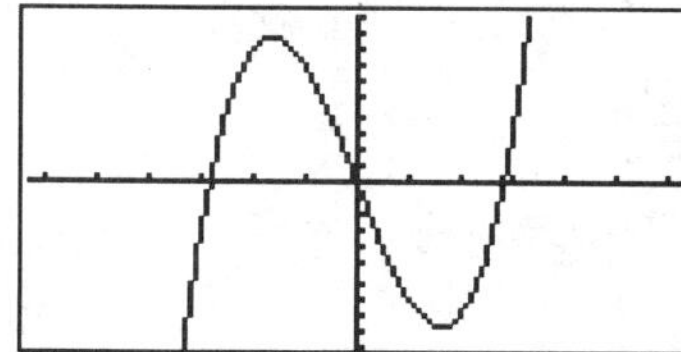

Figure 5.48: Graph of $y = x^3 - 8x$

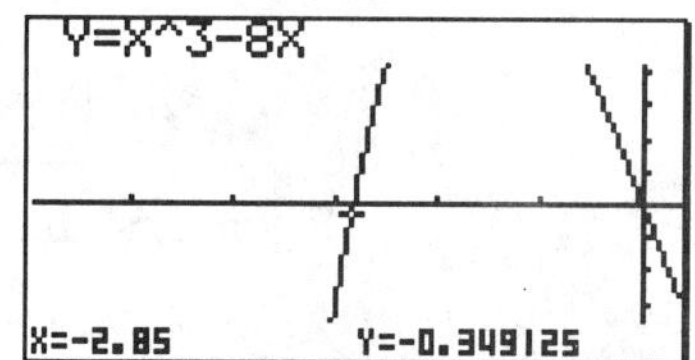

Figure 5.49: Near an x-intercept of $y = x^3 - 8x$

Technology Tip: As you zoom in, you may also wish to change the spacing between tick marks on the *x*-axis so that the viewing rectangle shows scale marks near the intercept point. Then the accuracy of your approximation will be such that the error is less than the distance between two tick marks. Change the *x*-scale on the Casio 9700/7700GE from the RANGE menu. Move the cursor down to Xscale and enter an appropriate value.

The *x*-intercept of a function's graph is a *root* of the equation $f(x) = 0$. And the Casio fx-9700GE automates the search for roots. [This feature is *not* available on the Casio fx-7700GE.] First plot the function in graph mode (MENU 6) and press SHIFT G-SOLV for the graphical solver menu (Figure 5.50). Then press F1 *[ROOT]* to locate an *x*-intercept on the graph in the current window. The calculator searches from left to right to find an *x*-intercept in the current window; press ▶ to continue the search for the *next x*-intercept.

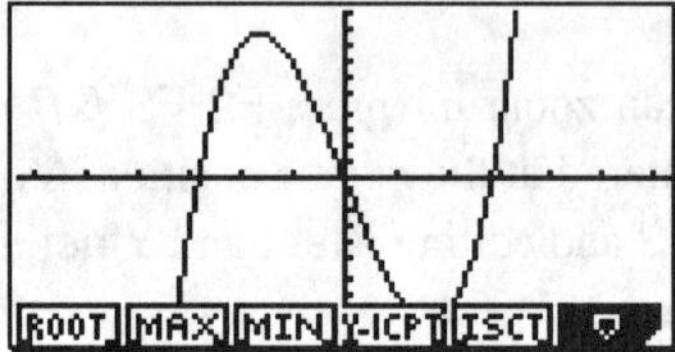

Figure 5.50: G-SOLV menu

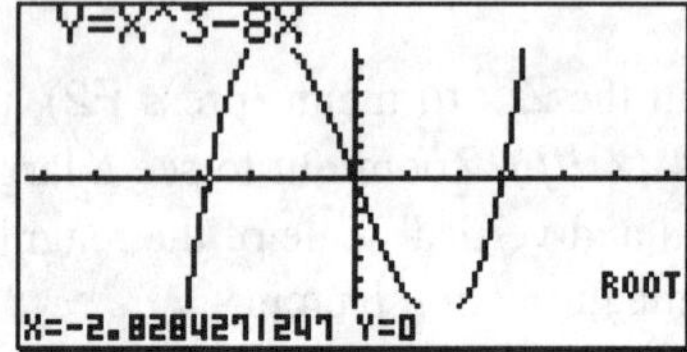

Figure 5.51: A root of $y = x^3 - 8x$

TRACE and ZOOM are especially important for locating the intersection points of two graphs, say the graphs of $y = -x^3 + 4x$ and $y = -.25x$. Trace along one of the graphs until you arrive close to an intersection point. Then press ▲ or ▼ to jump to the other graph. Notice that the *x*-coordinate does not change, but the *y*-coordinate is likely to be different (see Figures 5.52 and 5.53).

When the two *y*-coordinates are as close as they can get, you have come as close as you now can to the point of intersection. So zoom in around the intersection point, then trace again until the two *y*-coordinates are as close as possible. Continue this process until you have located the point of intersection with as much accuracy as necessary.

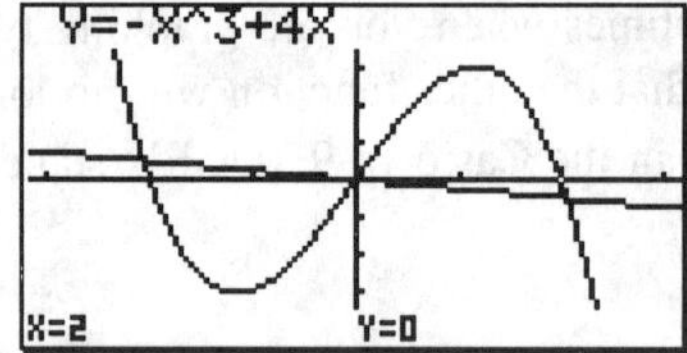

Figure 5.52: Trace on $y = -x^3 + 4x$

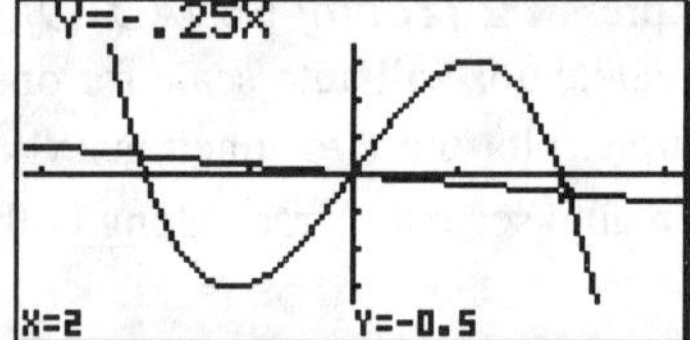

Figure 5.53: Trace on $y = -.25x$

Technology Tip: Press F6 a couple of times to display only the *y*-coordinate. Then while tracing towards an intersection, it's easier to see where the *y*-coordinates are closest.

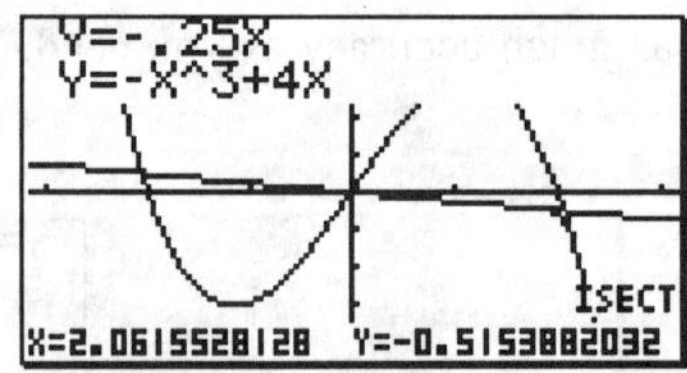

Figure 5.54: Intersection of $y = -x^3 + 4x$ and $y = -.25x$

Automate the Casio fx-9700GE's search for points of intersection by pressing SHIFT G-SOLV F5 *[ISCT]*. [This feature is *not* available on the Casio fx-7700GE.] If more than two functions are being plotted, the calculator will

   Casio fx-9700GE and fx-7700GE Power Graphic Calculators

ask you to specify the two whose intersection you seek. The calculator searches from left to right to find an intersection point in the current window; press $\blacktriangleright$ to continue the search for the *next* intersection point.

5.3.2 Solving Equations by Graphing: Suppose you need to solve the equation $24x^3 - 36x + 17 = 0$. First graph $y = 24x^3 - 36x + 17$ in a window large enough to exhibit *all* its x-intercepts, corresponding to all the equation's roots. Then use trace and zoom, or the Casio fx-<u>9700</u>GE's graphical solver, to locate each one. In fact, this equation has just one solution, approximately $x = -1.414$.

Remember that when an equation has more than one root, it may be necessary to change the viewing rectangle a few times to locate all of them.

Technology Tip: To solve an equation like $24x^3 + 17 = 36x$, you may first transform it into standard form, $24x^3 - 36x + 17 = 0$, and proceed as above. However, you may also graph the *two* functions $y = 24x^3 + 17$ and $y = 36x$, then zoom and trace to locate their point of intersection.

5.3.3 Solving Systems by Graphing: The solutions to a system of equations correspond to the points of intersection of their graphs (Figure 5.55). For example, to solve the system $y = x^2 - 3x - 4$ and $y = x^3 + 3x^2 - 2x - 1$, first graph them together. Then zoom and trace, or the Casio fx-<u>9700</u>GE's graphical solver, to locate their point of intersection, approximately (-2.17, 7.25).

You must judge whether the two current y-coordinates are sufficiently close for $x = -2.17$ or whether you should continue to zoom and trace to improve the approximation.

The solutions of the system of two equations $y = x^3 + 3x^2 - 2x - 1$ and $y = x^2 - 3x - 4$ correspond to the solutions of the single equation $x^3 + 3x^2 - 2x - 1 = x^2 - 3x - 4$, which simplifies to $x^3 + 2x^2 + x + 3 = 0$. So you may also graph $y = x^3 + 2x^2 + x + 3$ and find its x-intercepts to solve the system.

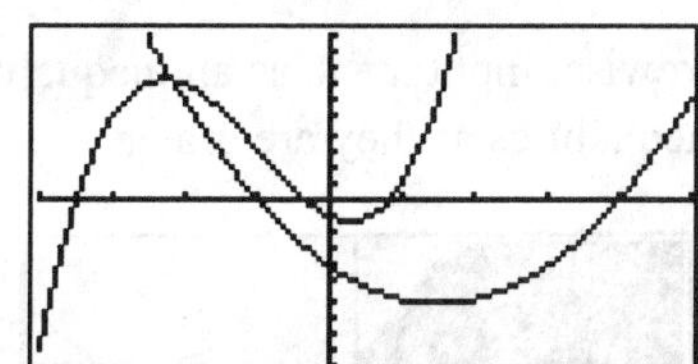

Figure 5.55: Solving a system of equations

5.3.4 Solving Inequalities by Graphing: Consider the inequality $1 - \dfrac{3x}{2} \geq x - 4$. To solve it with your Casio 9700/7700GE, graph the two functions $y = 1 - \dfrac{3x}{2}$ and $y = x - 4$ (Figure 5.56). First locate their point of intersection, at $x = 2$. The inequality is true when the graph of $y = 1 - \dfrac{3x}{2}$ lies *above* the graph of $y = x - 4$, and that occurs for $x < 2$. So the solution is the half-line $x \leq 2$, or $(-\infty, 2]$.

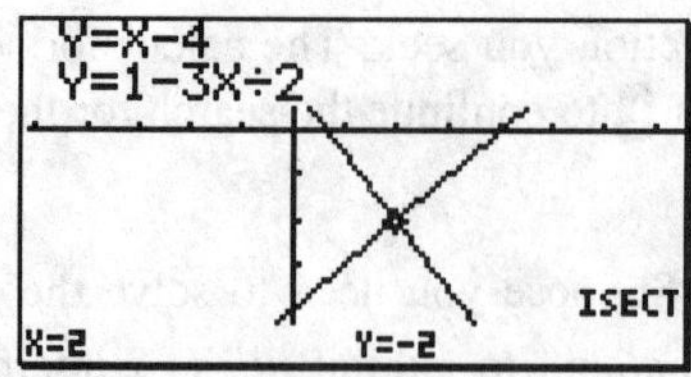

Figure 5.56: Solving $1 - \dfrac{3x}{2} \geq x - 4$

The Casio 9700/7700GE is capable of graphing inequalities of the form $y \leq x$, $y < x$, $y \geq x$, or $y > x$. For example, to graph $y \geq x^2 - 1$ in GRAPH mode, press F3 *[TYPE]* F4 *[INEQ]*. Input $x^2 - 1$. Now when you press F1 *[STO]* to store this expression, several inequality options appear (see Figure 5.57); we need F3 *[Y≥]*.

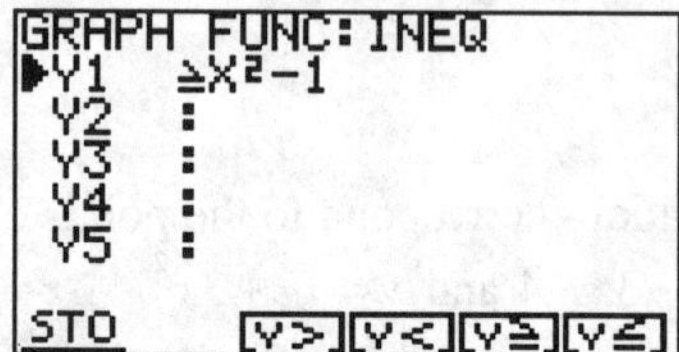

Figure 5.57: Inequality options

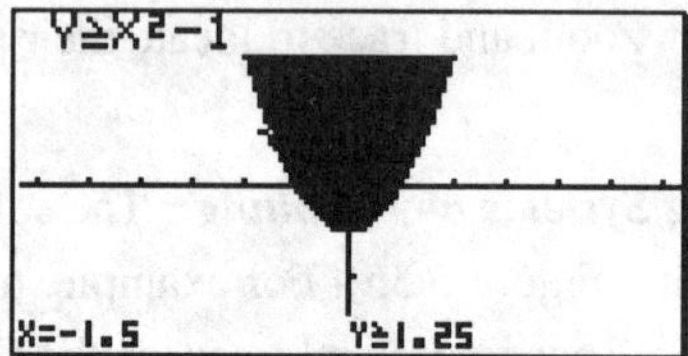

Figure 5.58: Graph of $y \geq x^2 - 1$

Next press F1 to trace along the boundaries of the inequality. Notice that the Casio 9700/7700GE displays coordinates appropriately as inequalities. Zooming is also available for inequality graphs.

Solve a system of inequalities, such as $1 - \dfrac{3x}{2} \geq y$ and $y > x - 4$, by plotting the two inequality graphs simultaneously. First, clear the graph window and reset the range to a convenient window. Input $1 - \dfrac{3x}{2}$ as an inequality type and store it as Y1 by pressing F6 *[Y≤]*; likewise, input $x - 4$ as an inequality type and store it as Y2 by pressing F4 *[Y>]*. After you press F6, watch the two inequalities as they are drawn.

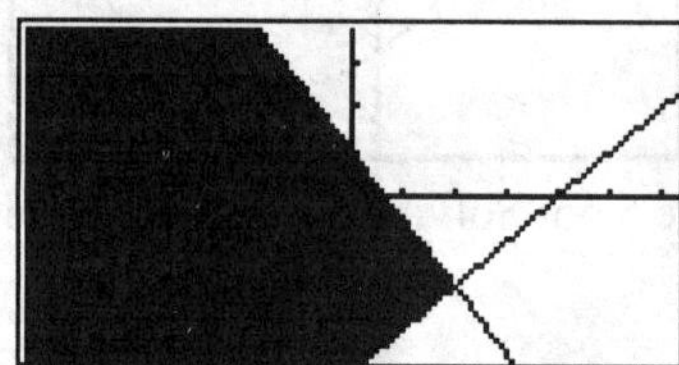

Figure 5.59: Graphs of $1 - \dfrac{3x}{2} \geq y$ and $y > x - 4$

Technology Tip: Since you can change the mode of the Casio 9700/7700GE at any time, you can graph inequalities and equations together at the same time. Simply change to inequality type before entering an inequality; then change to rectangular type before entering an equation.

5.4   Matrices

5.4.1 Making a Matrix: The Casio fx-9700GE can display and use 26 different matrices, each named by a letter of the alphabet. The Casio fx-7700GE can work with 5 different matrices. Here's how to create this 3×4 matrix $\begin{bmatrix} 1 & -4 & 3 & 5 \\ -1 & 3 & -1 & -3 \\ 2 & 0 & -4 & 6 \end{bmatrix}$ in your calculator.

Press MENU 5, then F4 for the Matrix List. Move the cursor to Mat A and press F2 3 EXE 4 EXE to enter its dimensions of 3 rows and 4 columns. Return to the Matrix List by pressing EXIT once, then press F1 to edit matrix A.

Figure 5.60: Matrix List

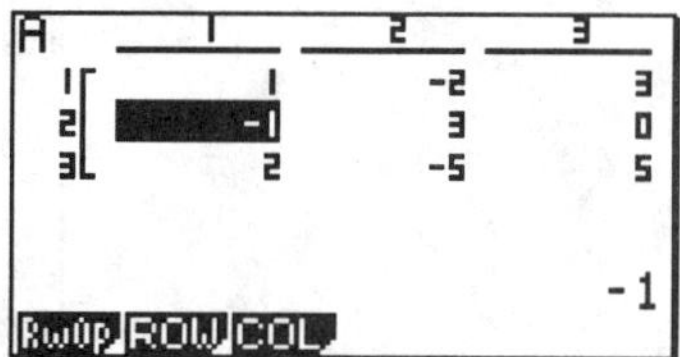

Figure 5.61: Editing a matrix

Use the arrow keys or press EXE repeatedly to move the cursor to a matrix element you want to change. If you press EXE, you will move right across a row and then back to the first column of the next row. The element in the second row and first column in Figure 5.61 is highlighted, so that element's current value is displayed at the bottom right corner of the screen. Continue to enter all the elements of matrix A; press EXE after inputing each value.

When you are finished, leave matrix A's editing screen by pressing EXIT once to return to the Matrix List.

5.4.2 Row Operations: Here are the keystrokes necessary to perform elementary row operations on a matrix. Your textbook provides more careful explanation of the elementary row operations and their uses.

Return, if necessary, to matrix A's editing screen (Figure 5.62). Press F1 and follow the Casio 9700/7700GE's prompts through the various row operations (Figure 5.62).

To interchange the second and third rows of the matrix A that was defined above, press F1 *[Swap]* 2 EXE 3 EXE (see Figure 5.63). The format of this command is Swap *row1* EXE *row2* EXE.

To add row 2 and row 3 and store the results in row 3, press F4 *[Rw+]* 2 EXE 3 EXE. The format of this command is Rw+ *row1* EXE *row2* EXE.

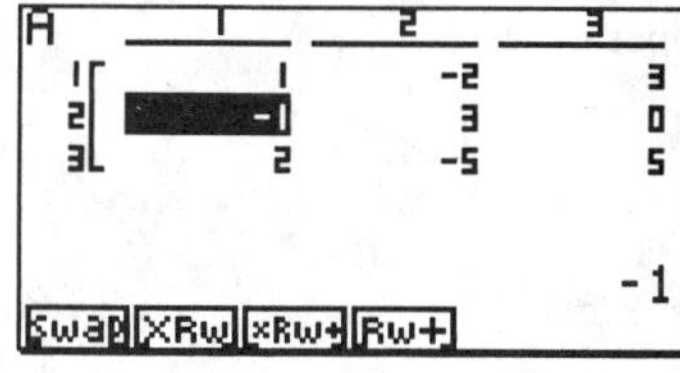

Figure 5.62: Row operations

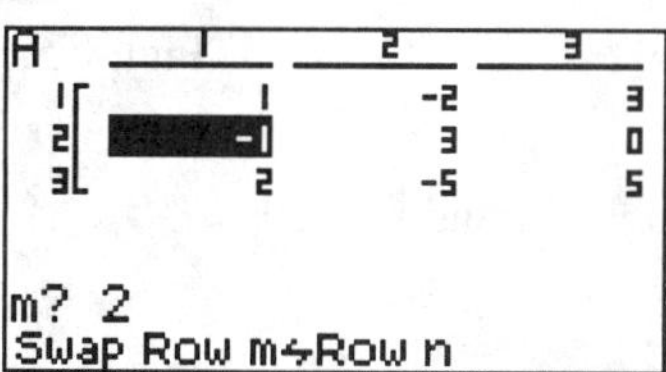

Figure 5.63: Swap rows 2 and 3

To multiply row 2 by -4 and *store* the results in row 2, thereby replacing row 2 with new values, press F2 *[×Rw]* (-) 4 EXE 2 EXE. The format of this command is ×Rw *scalar* EXE *row* EXE.

To multiply row 2 by -4 and *add* the results to row 3, thereby replacing row 3 with new values, press F3 *[×Rw+]* (-) 4 EXE 2 EXE 3 EXE. The format of this command is ×Rw+ *scalar* EXE *row1* EXE *row2* EXE.

For example, use elementary row operations to solve this system of linear equations: $\begin{cases} x-2y+3z=9 \\ -x+3y=-4 \\ 2x-5y+5z=17 \end{cases}$.

First enter this *augmented matrix* as A in your Casio 9700/7700GE: $\begin{bmatrix} 1 & -2 & 3 & 9 \\ -1 & 3 & 0 & -4 \\ 2 & -5 & 5 & 17 \end{bmatrix}$. Next store this matrix in E

(press EXIT a couple of times to go back to the matrix home screen, then F1 *[Mat]* ALPHA A $\rightarrow$ F1 *[Mat]* ALPHA E EXE, as in Figure 5.64) so you may keep the original in case you need to recall it.

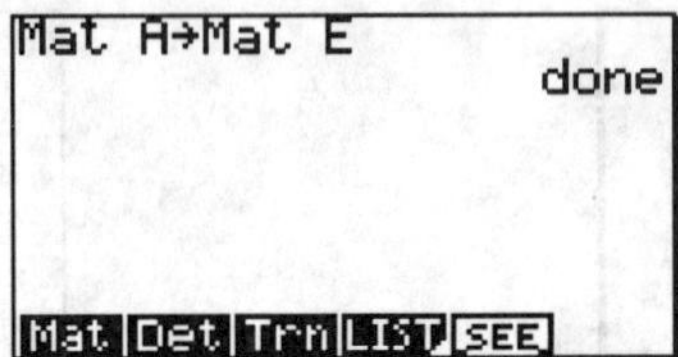

Figure 5.64: Storing a matrix

Here are the row operations and their associated keystrokes. At each step, the result is stored in E and replaces the previous matrix E. The solution is shown in Figure 5.61.

Row Operation	Keystrokes
add row 1 to row 2	F4 *[Rw+]* 1 EXE 2 EXE
add -2 times row 1 to row 3	F3 *[×Rw+]* (-) 2 EXE 1 EXE 3 EXE
add row 2 to row 3	F4 *[Rw+]* 2 EXE 3 EXE
mult row 3 by ½	F2 *[×Rw]* 1 $a^b/_c$ 2 EXE 3 EXE

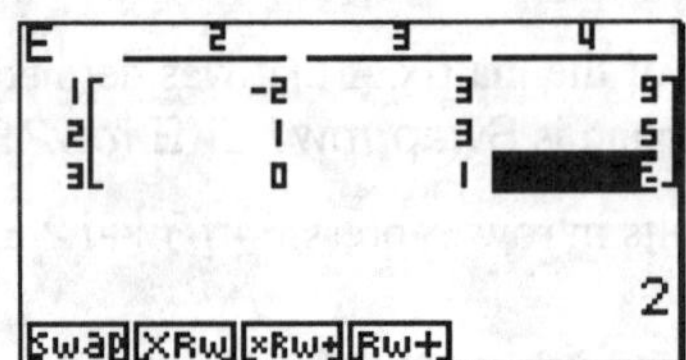

Figure 5.65: Final matrix after row operations

Thus $z = 2$, so $y = -1$ and $x = 1$.

5.4.3 Determinants: Enter this 3×3 square matrix as A: $\begin{bmatrix} 1 & -2 & 3 \\ -1 & 3 & 0 \\ 2 & -5 & 5 \end{bmatrix}$. To calculate its determinant, $\begin{vmatrix} 1 & -2 & 3 \\ -1 & 3 & 0 \\ 2 & -5 & 5 \end{vmatrix}$,

go to the matrix home screen and press F2 *[Det]* F1 *[Mat]* ALPHA A EXE. You should find that $|A| = 2$.

　　Casio fx-9700GE and fx-7700GE Power Graphic Calculators

5.5.1 *Iteration:* The Ans feature enables you to perform iterations to evaluate a function repeatedly. As an example, calculate $\dfrac{n-1}{3}$ for $n = 27$. Then calculate $\dfrac{n-1}{3}$ for n = the answer to the previous calculation. Continue to use each answer as n in the *next* calculation. Here are keystrokes to accomplish this iteration on the Casio 9700/7700GE calculator (see the results in Figure 5.66). Notice that when you use Ans in place of n in a formula, it is sufficient to press EXE to continue an iteration.

Iteration	*Keystrokes*	*Display*
1	27 EXE	27
2	(SHIFT Ans - 1) ÷ 3 EXE	8.66666666667
3	EXE	2.55555555556
4	EXE	0.518518518519
5	EXE	-0.16049382716

Press EXE several more times and see what happens with this iteration. You may wish to try it again with a different starting value.

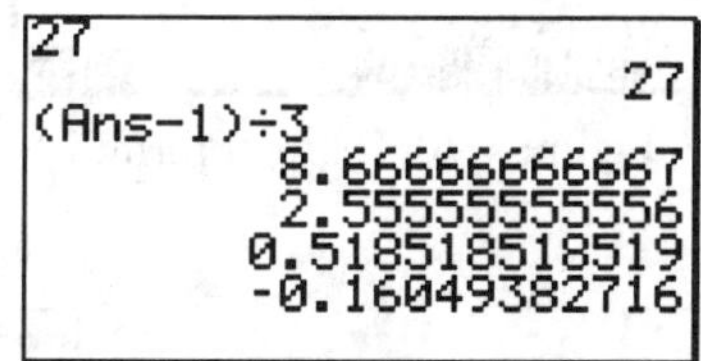

Figure 5.66: Iteration

5.5.2 *Arithmetic and Geometric Sequences:* Use iteration with the Ans variable to determine the n-th term of a sequence. For example, find the 18th term of an *arithmetic* sequence whose first term is 7 and whose common difference is 4. Enter the first term 7, then start the progression with the recursion formula, SHIFT Ans + 4 EXE. This yields the 2nd term, so press EXE sixteen more times to find the 18th term. For a *geometric* sequence whose common ratio is 4, start the progression with SHIFT Ans × 4 EXE.

You can also define the sequence recursively with the Casio fx-9700GE (this feature is not available on the Casio fx-7700GE) by selecting MENU 8 *[TABLE]* F2 *[RECR]* (see Figure 5.67). Next press F6 *[TYPE]* F2 *[an+1]* to select the recursion type. Once again, let's find the 18th term of an *arithmetic* sequence whose first term is 7 and whose common difference is 4. Input the recursion formula $a_{n+1} = a_n + 4$ by pressing F4 *[an]* + 4. Now make $a_1 = 7$ (because the first term is a_1 where $n = 1$) and display a table that contains the 16th term a_{16} to the 20th term a_{20} by pressing F2 *[RANG]* F6 *[a1]* 16 EXE 20 EXE 7 F1 *[TABL]* (see Figures 5.68 and 5.69).

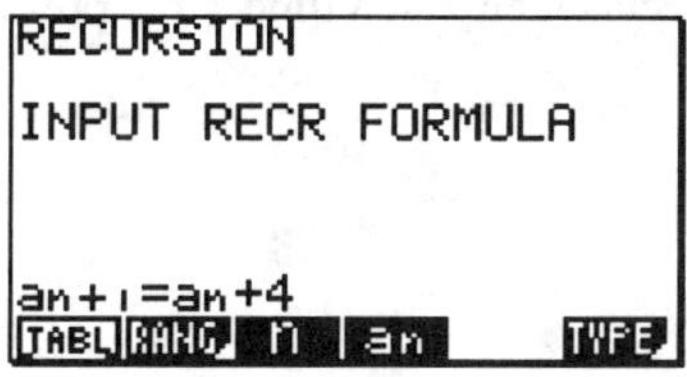

Figure 5.67: Recursion formula

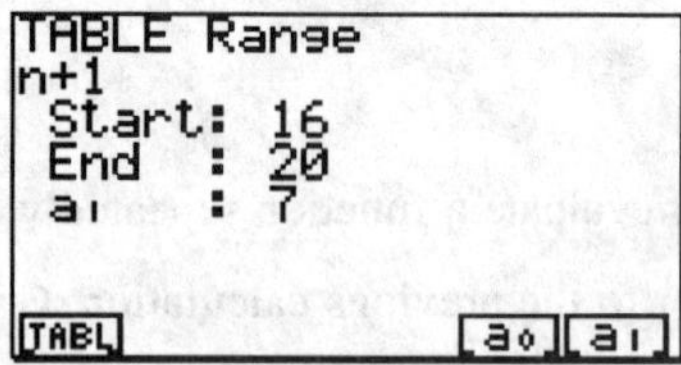
Figure 5.68: TABLE Range

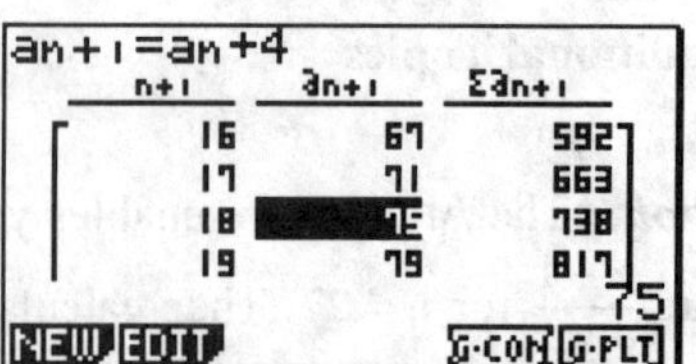
Figure 5.69: $a_{18} = 75$

Of course, you could also use the *explicit* formula for the n-th term of an arithmetic sequence, $t_n = a + (n-1)d$. First enter values for the variables a, d, and n, then evaluate the formula by pressing ALPHA A + (ALPHA N - 1) ALPHA D EXE. For a geometric sequence whose n-th term is given by $t_n = a \cdot r^{n-1}$, enter values for the variables a, r, and n, then evaluate the formula by pressing ALPHA A ALPHA R ^ (ALPHA N - 1) EXE.

To use the explicit formula in a Casio fx-9700GE recursion table, make $a_n = 7 + (n-1) \cdot 4$ by pressing MENU 8 *[TABLE]* F2 *[RECR]* F6 *[TYPE]* F1 *[an]* 7 + (F3 *[n]* - 1) × 4. Once more, calculate a_{18} by pressing F2 *[RANG]* 18 EXE 18 F1 *[TABL]*.

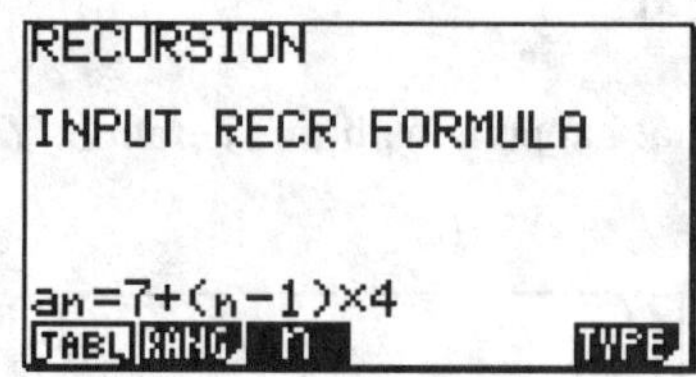
Figure 5.70: Explicit formula

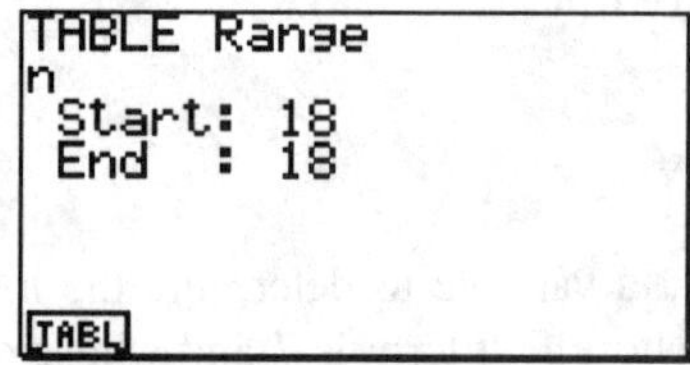
Figure 5.71: TABLE Range

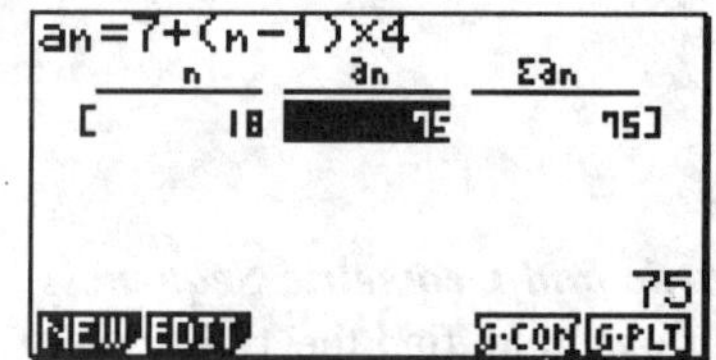
Figure 5.72: $a_{18} = 75$

Technology Tip: A table whose starting and ending range values are the same has just one entry. So to display a single n-th term in a series, set both the starting and ending range values to n.

There are more instructions for using table recursion mode in the Casio fx-9700GE manual.

5.5.3 Permutations and Combinations:

To calculate the number of *permutations* of 12 objects taken 7 at a time, $_{12}P_7$, press 12 SHIFT MATH F2 *[PRB]* F2 *[nPr]* 7 EXE. Thus $_{12}P_7 = 3{,}991{,}680$, as shown in Figure 5.73.

For the number of *combinations* of 12 objects taken 7 at a time, $_{12}C_7$, press 12 SHIFT MATH F2 *[PRB]* F3 *[nCr]* 7 EXE. So $_{12}C_7 = 792$.

Casio fx-9700GE and fx-7700GE Power Graphic Calculators

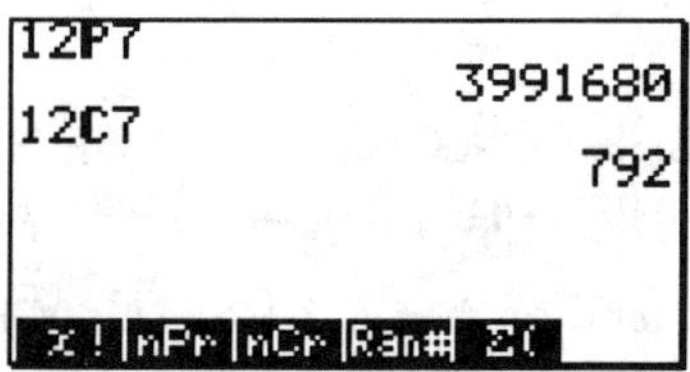

Figure 5.73: $_{12}P_7$ and $_{12}C_7$

5.6   Programming

5.3.1 Entering a Program: The Casio 9700/7700GE is a programmable calculator that can store sequences of commands for later replay. Here's an example to show you how to enter a useful program that solves quadratic equations by the quadratic formula.

Press MENU A *[PRGM]* F1 *[PRGM]* on your Casio fx-9700GE, to write a program; on the Casio fx-7700GE, press MENU 8 *[PRGM]*. You start with the program list. The Casio 9700/7700GE has space for up to 38 programs, each named by a number or letter. If a program location is not used, the word *empty* appears to the right of its name in the list. Press the up or down arrow keys to move the cursor to an empty program area; you may also press the key corresponding to a program's name and jump directly there. For example, to go to program 5, press 5; to edit program B, press ALPHA B.

Figure 5.74a: Casio fx-9700GE
program list

Figure 5.74b: Casio fx-7700GE
program list

When the cursor is blinking next to the program area you've chosen, press EXE to write a new program in that area or to edit a program that is already there.

Now enter a descriptive title, so press SHIFT ⓐ-LOCK and name this program QUADRATIC. Press ALPHA to cancel the alpha lock. Then press EXE to begin writing the actual program. If you do not enter a title, the first line of the program appears in the program list.

Any command you could enter directly in the Casio 9700/7700GE's home screen can be entered as a line in a program. There are also special programming commands.

Technology Tip: Each time you press EXE while writing a program, the Casio 9700/7700GE *automatically* inserts the ↵ character at the end of the previous line. For simplicity, since this happens every time you press EXE, the ↵ character is not shown in the program listing below.

Enter the program QUADRATIC by pressing the given keystrokes.

Program Line	*Keystrokes*

"ENTER A"? → A   SHIFT A-LOCK F2 E N T E R SPACE A F2
                     SHIFT PRGM F4 → ALPHA A EXE

displays the words *Enter A* on the Casio 9700/7700GE screen and
waits for you to input a value that will be assigned to the variable A

"ENTER B"? → B   SHIFT A-LOCK F2 E N T E R SPACE B F2
                     SHIFT PRGM F4 → ALPHA B EXE

"ENTER C"? → C   SHIFT A-LOCK F2 E N T E R SPACE C F2
                     SHIFT PRGM F4 → ALPHA C EXE

B^2-4AC → D   ALPHA B x^2 − 4 ALPHA A ALPHA C → ALPHA D EXE

calculates the discriminant and stores its value as D

D<0 ⇒ Goto 1   ALPHA D F2 F4 0 EXIT F1 F1 F2 1 EXE

tests to see if the discriminant is negative;

in case the discriminant is negative, jumps to the line Lbl 1 below;
if the discriminant is not negative, continues on to the next line

D=0 ⇒ Goto 2   ALPHA D EXIT F2 F1 0 EXIT F1 F1 F2 2 EXE

tests to see if the discriminant is zero;

in case the discriminant is zero, jumps to the line Lbl 2 below;
if the discriminant is not zero, continues on to the next line

"TWO REAL ROOTS"   SHIFT A-LOCK F2 T W O SPACE R E A L SPACE
                     R O O T S F2 ALPHA EXE

(-B+√D)/(2A) → M : M◢   ((-) ALPHA B + SHIFT √ ALPHA D) ÷ (2 ALPHA A)
                        → ALPHA M EXIT F6 ALPHA M F5

calculates one root and stores it as M, then displays it and pauses

(-B-√D)/(2A) → N : N   ((-) ALPHA B − SHIFT √ ALPHA D) ÷ (2 ALPHA A)
                       → ALPHA N F6 ALPHA N EXE

Goto 3   F1 F2 3 EXE

jumps to *end* of program

Lbl 1   F3 1 EXE

jumping point for the Goto command above

"COMPLEX ROOTS"   SHIFT A-LOCK F2 C O M P L E X SPACE R O O T S F2 EXE

displays a message in case the roots are complex numbers

"REAL PART"   F2 R E A L SPACE P A R T F2 ALPHA EXE

-B/(2A) → R : R◢   (-) ALPHA B ÷ (2 ALPHA A) → ALPHA R EXIT F6 ALPHA R F5

calculates and displays the real part $\dfrac{-b}{2a}$ of the complex roots

"IMAGINARY PART"   SHIFT Ⓐ-LOCK F2 I M A G I N A R Y SPACE P A R T
                    F2 ALPHA EXE

√-D/(2A) → I : I   SHIFT √ (-) ALPHA D ÷ (2 ALPHA A) → ALPHA I F6 ALPHA I EXE

    calculates and displays the imaginary part $\dfrac{\sqrt{-D}}{2a}$ of the complex roots;
    since $D < 0$, we must use $-D$ as the radicand

Goto 3   F1 F2 3 EXE

Lbl 2   F3 2 EXE

"DOUBLE ROOT"   SHIFT Ⓐ-LOCK F2 D O U B L E SPACE R O O T F2 ALPHA EXE

    displays a message in case there is a double root

-B/(2A) → M : M   (-) ALPHA B ÷ (2 ALPHA A) → ALPHA M EXIT F6 ALPHA M EXE

    the quadratic formula reduces to $\dfrac{-b}{2a}$ when $D = 0$

Lbl 3   F1 F3 3

When you have finished, press **MENU** to leave the program editor and move on.

Here, for the Casio fx-9700GE, is an alternate version of the program **QUADRATIC** that also find roots of quadratic equations while taking advantage of that calculator's ability to work with complex numbers.

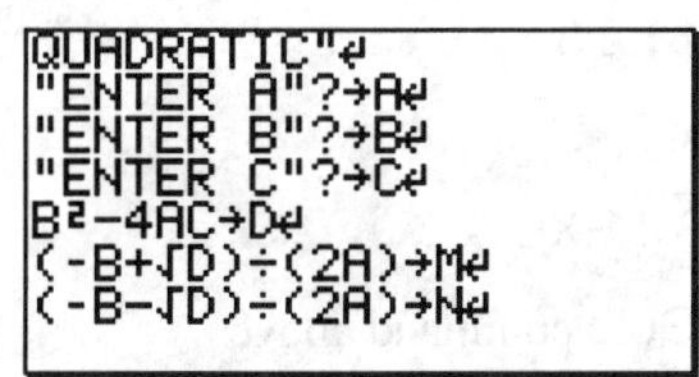

Figure 5.75: Program **QUADRATIC**

Program Line   *Keystrokes*

"ENTER A"? → A   SHIFT Ⓐ-LOCK F2 E N T E R SPACE A F2
                        SHIFT PRGM F4 → ALPHA A EXE

    displays the words *Enter A* on the Casio 9700GE screen and
    waits for you to input a value that will be assigned to the variable A

"ENTER B"? → B   SHIFT Ⓐ-LOCK F2 E N T E R SPACE B F2
                        SHIFT PRGM F4 → ALPHA B EXE

"ENTER C"? → C   SHIFT Ⓐ-LOCK F2 E N T E R SPACE C F2
                        SHIFT PRGM F4 → ALPHA C EXE

B²-4AC → D   ALPHA B x² − 4 ALPHA A ALPHA C → ALPHA D EXE

    calculates the discriminant and stores its value as D

(-B+√D)/(2A) → M   ((-) ALPHA B + SHIFT √ ALPHA D) ÷ (2 ALPHA A)
                       → ALPHA M EXE

   calculates one root and stores it as M

(-B-√D)/(2A) → N   ((-) ALPHA B – SHIFT √ ALPHA D) ÷ (2 ALPHA A)
                       → ALPHA N EXE

D<0 ⇒ Goto 1   ALPHA D F2 F4 0 EXIT F1 F1 F2 1 EXE

   tests to see if the discriminant is negative;

   in case the discriminant is negative, jumps to the line Lbl 1 below;
   if the discriminant is not negative, continues on to the next line

D=0 ⇒ Goto 2   ALPHA D EXIT F2 F1 0 EXIT F1 F1 F2 2 EXE

   tests to see if the discriminant is zero;

   in case the discriminant is zero, jumps to the line Lbl 2 below;
   if the discriminant is not zero, continues on to the next line

"TWO REAL ROOTS"   SHIFT Ⓐ-LOCK F2 T W O SPACE R E A L SPACE
                       R O O T S F2 ALPHA EXE

M◢   ALPHA M EXIT F5

   displays one root and pauses

N   ALPHA N EXE

Goto 3   F1 F2 3 EXE

   jumps to *end* of program

Lbl 1   F3 1 EXE

   jumping point for the Goto command above

"COMPLEX ROOTS"   SHIFT Ⓐ-LOCK F2 C O M P L E X SPACE R O O T S
                       F2 ALPHA EXE

   displays a message in case the roots are complex numbers

M◢   ALPHA M EXIT F5

N   ALPHA N EXE

Goto 3   F1 F2 3 EXE

Lbl 2   F3 2 EXE

"DOUBLE ROOT"   SHIFT Ⓐ-LOCK F2 D O U B L E SPACE R O O T F2 ALPHA EXE

   displays a message in case there is a double root

M   ALPHA M EXE

   displays one root and pauses

Lbl 3   F1 F3 3

                                                    Casio fx-9700GE and fx-7700GE Power Graphic Calculators

If you want to clear a program, enter the program editor again. Move to the program you want to delete, and when the cursor is blinking next to its name, press F2 to remove it from the calculator's memory.

5.3.2 Running a Program: To run the program you have entered, press MENU 1 SHIFT PRGM F3 and then the number or letter that it was named; finally, press EXE to run it. If you have forgotten its name, you must go back to the program editor to find the program, then press F1 to run it.

The program has been written to prompt you for values of the coefficients a, b, and c in a quadratic equation $ax^2 + bx + c = 0$. Input a value, then press EXE to continue the program.

If you need to interrupt a program during execution, press AC/ON.

The instruction manual for your Casio 9700/7700GE gives detailed information about programming. Refer to it to learn more about programming and how to use other features of your calculator.

Chapter 6

Casio CFX-9800G
Color Power Graphic Calculator

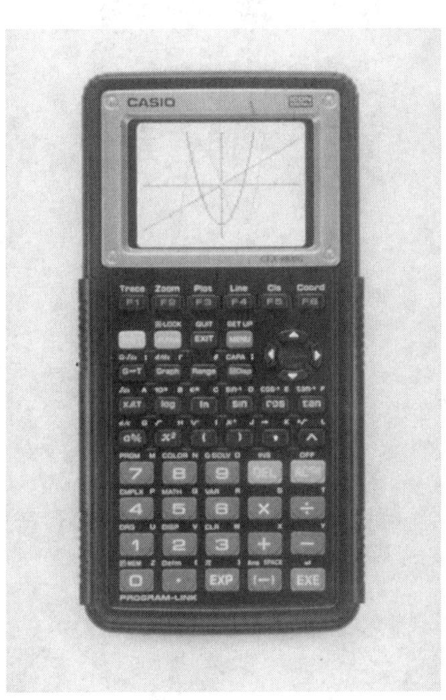

6.1 Getting started with the Casio CFX-9800G

6.1.1 Basics: Press the AC/ON key to begin using your Casio 9800 calculator. If you need to adjust the display contrast, first press MENU, then use the arrow keys [right ▶, left ◀, up ▲, or down ▼] to move to the OPTION icon in the lower right corner of the MAIN MENU and press EXE twice. Next press ▶ (the *right* arrow key) to increase the contrast or ◀ (the *left* arrow key) to decrease the contrast (see Figure 6.2). Press MENU once again to return to the main menu. When you have finished with the calculator, turn it off to conserve battery power by pressing SHIFT and then OFF.

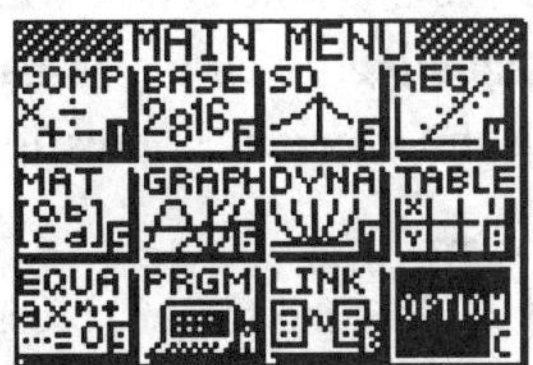

Figure 6.1: MAIN MENU

Figure 6.2: CONTRAST

Technology Tip: You can jump quickly to the OPTION screen by pressing MENU C *[OPTION]*.

Figure 6.3: COMP settings

Check the Casio 9800's settings by pressing MENU 1 *[COMP]* for standard computations. To start with, here are the keystrokes to configure your calculator to conform with the instructions in this guide: first press SHIFT SET-UP F1 for rectangular coordinates and F5 for connected graphs. Next press ▼ ▼ (the *down* arrow key two times), and press F3 for normal display (if display changes to Norm2 instead of Norm1, just press F3 another time). If you now press ▼ F1 once again, you will configure the Ⓜ Disp key so that whenever you press and hold it down, the current settings will be displayed. (This is a *different* configuration from what is shown in Figure 6.3.) Details on other options will be given later in this guide. For now, remove any menu that remains by pressing EXIT and AC/ON until the screen is clear.

6.1.2 Editing: One advantage of the Casio 9800 is that up to seven lines are visible at one time, so you can *see* a long calculation. For example, first press MENU 1 and then type this sum (see Figure 6.4):

$$1 + 2 + 3 + 4 + 5 + 6 + 7 + 8 + 9 + 10 + 11 + 12 + 13 + 14 + 15 + 16 + 17 + 18 + 19 + 20$$

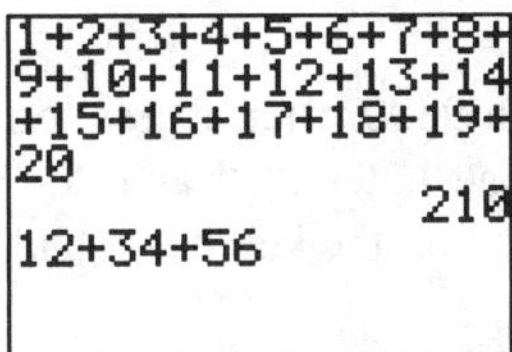

Figure 6.4: Home screen

Then press EXE to see the answer, too.

Suppose you had typed 12 + 34 + 56 as in Figure 6.4 but had *not* yet pressed EXE, when you realize that 34 should have been 74. Simply press ◀ (the *left* arrow key) as many times as necessary to move the blinking cursor left to 3, then type 7 to write over it. On the other hand, if 34 should have been 384, move the cursor back to 4, press SHIFT INS (the cursor changes to a blinking frame) and then type 8 (inserts at the cursor position and other characters are pushed to the right). If the 34 should have been 3 only, move the cursor to 4 and press DEL to delete it.

Even if you had pressed EXE, you may still edit the previous expression. Press the *left* or *right* arrow key to *redisplay* the last expression that was entered. Now you can change it. If you press ◀, the cursor will start at the *end* of the previous expression; if you press ▶, the cursor will appear at the *beginning*. Even if you have already pressed some keys since the last EXE, but *not* EXE again, you can still recall the previous expression by first pressing AC/ON to clear the screen and then pressing ◀ or ▶.

In fact, the Casio 9800 retains many prior entries. After pressing AC/ON to clear the screen, press ▲ repeatedly to cycle back through previous expressions. If you pass by an expression that you want, just press ▼ as many times as necessary to cycle forward.

Technology Tip: When you need to evaluate a formula for different values of a variable, use the editing feature to simplify the process. For example, suppose you want to find the balance in an investment account if there is now $5000 in the account and interest is compounded annually at the rate of 8.5%. The formula for the balance is $P\left(1+\frac{r}{n}\right)^{nt}$, where P = principal, r = rate of interest (expressed as a decimal), n = the number of times that the interest is compounded each year, and t = the number of years. In our example, this becomes $5000(1+.085)^t$. Here are the keystrokes for finding the balance after $t = 3$, 5, and 10 years.

Years	*Keystrokes*	*Balance*
3	5000 (1 + .085) ^ 3 EXE	$6386.45
5	◀ ◀ 5 EXE	$7518.28
10	◀ ◀ 10 EXE	$11,304.92

Figure 6.5: Editing expressions

Then to find the balance from the same initial investment but after 5 years when the annual interest rate is 7.5%, press these keys to change the last calculation above: ◀ ◀ DEL ◀ 5 ◀ ◀ ◀ ◀ 7 EXE.

6.1.3 Key Functions: Most keys on the Casio 9800 offer access to more than one function, just as the keys on a computer keyboard can produce more than one letter ("g" and "G") or even quite different characters ("5" and "%"). The primary function of a key is indicated on the key itself, and you access that function by a simple press on the key.

Casio CFX-9800G Color Power Graphic Calculator

To access the *second* function indicated in yellow letters to the *left* above a key, first press the yellow SHIFT key (the cursor changes to a blinking **s** and a menu appears at the bottom of the screen) and *then* press the key. For example, to calculate $\sqrt{25}$, press SHIFT √ 25 EXE.

When you want to use a letter or other character printed in red letters to the *right* above a key, first press the red ALPHA key (the cursor changes to a blinking **A** and a menu appears at the bottom of the screen) and then the key. For example, to use the letter K in a formula, press ALPHA K. If you need several letters in a row, press SHIFT Ⓐ-LOCK, which is like CAPS LOCK on a computer keyboard, and then press all the letters you want. Remember to press ALPHA when you are finished and want to restore the keys to their primary functions.

6.1.4 Order of Operations: The Casio 9800 performs calculations according to the standard algebraic rules. Working outwards from inner parentheses, calculations are performed from left to right. Powers and roots are evaluated first, followed by multiplications and divisions, and then additions and subtractions.

Technology Tip: In many contexts, the Casio 9800 does not distinguish between *subtraction* and the *negative sign*. To enter a negative number, you may generally use either the (-) key or the – key. The one exception is when you are *starting* a new calculation; see Section 6.1.6 for an explanation. It is, however, a good habit to use the (-) key whenever you need an *opposite* and to use the – key when you want a *subtraction*.

Enter these expressions to practice using your Casio 9800. Press MENU 1 first if it is necessary to put the calculator in computation mode.

Expression	Keystrokes	Display
$7 - 5 \cdot 3$	7 - 5 × 3 EXE	-8
$(7 - 5) \cdot 3$	(7 - 5) × 3 EXE	6
$120 - 10^2$	120 - 10 x² EXE	20
$(120 - 10)^2$	(120 - 10) x² EXE	12100
$\dfrac{24}{2^3}$	24 ÷ 2 ^ 3 EXE	3
$\left(\dfrac{24}{2}\right)^3$	(24 ÷ 2) ^ 3 EXE	1728
$(7 - -5) \cdot -3$	(7 - (-) 5) × (-) 3 EXE or (7 - - 5) × - 3 EXE	-36

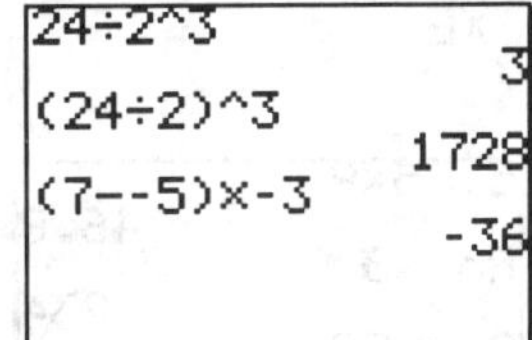

Figure 6.6: Order of operations

6.1.5 Algebraic Expressions and Memory: Your calculator can evaluate expressions such as $\dfrac{N(N+1)}{2}$ *after* you have entered a value for N. Suppose you want $N = 200$. Press 200 SHIFT → ALPHA N EXE to store the value 200 in memory location N. Whenever you use N in an expression, the calculator will substitute the value 200 until you make a change by storing *another* number in N. Next enter the expression $\dfrac{N(N+1)}{2}$ by typing ALPHA N (ALPHA N + 1) ÷ 2 EXE. For $N = 200$, you will find that $\dfrac{N(N+1)}{2} = 20100$.

The contents of any memory location may be revealed by typing just its letter name and then EXE. And the Casio 9800 retains memorized values even when it is turned off, so long as its batteries are good.

6.1.6 Repeated Operations with Ans: The result of your *last* calculation is always stored in memory location Ans and replaces any previous result. This makes it easy to use the answer from one computation in another computation. For example, press 30 + 15 EXE so that 45 is the last result displayed. Then press SHIFT Ans ÷ 9 EXE and get 5 because $\frac{45}{9} = 5$.

With a function like division, you press the ÷ key *after* you enter an argument. For such functions, whenever you would start a new calculation with the previous answer followed by pressing the function key, you may press just the function key. So instead of SHIFT Ans ÷ 9 in the previous example, you could have pressed simply ÷ 9 to achieve the same result. This technique also works for these functions: +, −, ×, x^2, ^, and SHIFT x^{-1}.

Technology Tip: The *negative sign* (-) key and the *subtraction* − key operate differently when pressed at the *start* of a new calculation. Try these keystrokes to see the difference: press 15 EXE, then − 10 EXE, and finally (-) 10 EXE.

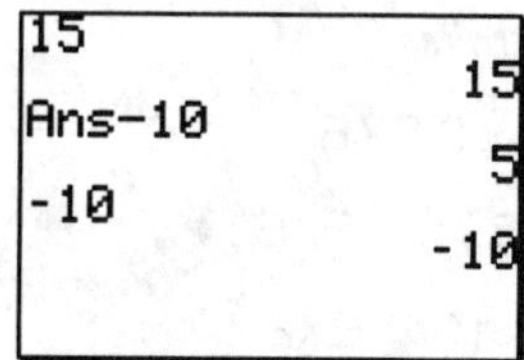

Figure 6.7: − and (-)

Here is a situation where Ans is especially useful. Suppose a person makes \$5.85 per hour and you are asked to calculate earnings for a day, a week, and a year. Execute the given keystrokes to find the person's incomes during these periods (results are shown in Figure 6.8):

Pay period	*Keystrokes*	*Earnings*
8-hour day	5.85 × 8 EXE	\$46.80
5-day week	SHIFT Ans × 5 EXE	\$234
52-week year	× 52 EXE	\$12,168

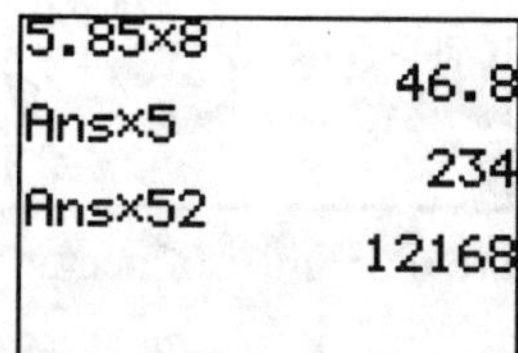

Figure 6.8: Ans

Casio CFX-9800G Color Power Graphic Calculator

6.1.7 The MATH Menu: Operators and functions associated with a scientific calculator are available either immediately from the keys of the Casio 9800 or by SHIFT keys. You have direct key access to common arithmetic operations (x^2, SHIFT $\sqrt{}$, SHIFT x^{-1}, ^), exponential and logarithmic functions (log, SHIFT 10^x, ln, SHIFT e^x), and a famous constant (SHIFT π).

A significant difference between the Casio 9800 and many scientific calculators is that the Casio 9800 requires the argument of a function *after* the function, as you would see a formula written in your textbook. For example, on the Casio 9800 you calculate $\sqrt{16}$ by pressing the keys $\sqrt{}$ 16 in that order.

The Casio 9800 has a special fraction key $a\!b\!/\!c$ for entering fractions and mixed numbers. To enter a fraction such as $\frac{2}{5}$, press 2 $a\!b\!/\!c$ 5 EXE. To enter a mixed number like $2\frac{3}{4}$, press 2 $a\!b\!/\!c$ 3 $a\!b\!/\!c$ 4 EXE. Press $a\!b\!/\!c$ to toggle between the mixed number and its decimal equivalent; press SHIFT $\frac{d}{c}$ and see $2\frac{3}{4}$ as an improper fraction, $\frac{11}{4}$.

Here are keystrokes for basic mathematical operations. Try them for practice on your Casio 9800.

Expression	Keystrokes	Display
$\sqrt{3^2 + 4^2}$	SHIFT $\sqrt{}$ (3 x^2 + 4 x^2) EXE	5
$2\frac{1}{3}$	2 $a\!b\!/\!c$ 1 $a\!b\!/\!c$ 3 EXE $a\!b\!/\!c$	2.33333333333
$\log 200$	log 200 EXE	2.30102999566
$2.34 \cdot 10^5$	2.34 × SHIFT 10^x 5 EXE	234000

Additional mathematical operations and functions are available from the MATH menu. Press SHIFT MATH to see the categories of mathematical functions. They are listed across the bottom of the Casio 9800 screen and correspond to the six function keys, F1 to F6. You will learn in your mathematics textbook how to apply many of them.

Figure 6.9: MATH menu

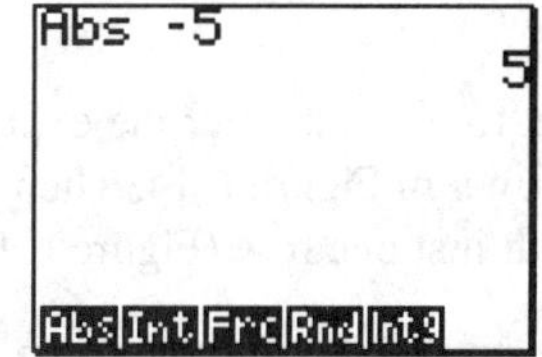

Figure 6.10: MATH NUM menu

As an example, calculate $|{-5}|$ by pressing SHIFT MATH F3 (for access to numerical functions) and then F1 - 5 EXE. To clear any menu from the screen, press EXIT.

The *factorial* of a non-negative integer is the *product* of *all* the integers from 1 up to the given integer. The symbol for factorial is the exclamation point. So 4! (pronounced *four factorial*) is $1\cdot2\cdot3\cdot4 = 24$. You will learn more about applications of factorials in your textbook, but for now use the Casio 9800 to calculate 4! Press these keystrokes: 4 SHIFT MATH F2 F1 EXE.

6.2   Functions and Graphs

6.2.1 Evaluating Functions: Suppose you receive a monthly salary of \$1975 plus a commission of 10% of sales. Let x = your sales in dollars; then your wages W in dollars are given by the equation $W = 1975 + .10x$. If your January sales were \$2230 and your February sales were \$1865, what was your income during those months?

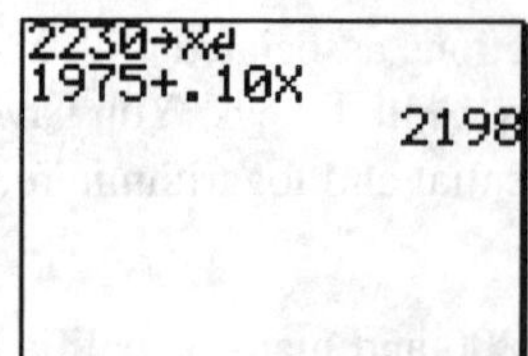

Figure 6.11: Evaluating a function

Here's how to use your Casio 9800 to perform this task. First press MENU 1 AC/ON to get a blank home screen in COMP mode. Next set $x = 2230$ by pressing 2230 SHIFT → X,θ,T. (The X,θ,T key lets you enter a variable x without having to use the ALPHA key.) Then press SHIFT ↵ to allow another expression to be input on a single command line. Finally, enter the expression $1975 + .10x$ by pressing these keys: 1975 + .10 X,θ,T. Now press EXE to calculate the answer (Figure 6.11).

It is not necessary to repeat all these steps to find the February wages. Simply press ▶ to recall the entire previous line, change 2230 to 1865, and press EXE.

The Casio 9800 also has a TABLE mode for evaluating functions. Press MENU 8 F1 *[FUNC]* for a range function table.

Figure 6.12: TABLE&GRAPH menu

Figure 6.13: RANGE FUNCTION menu

Move the highlight to Y1 and enter the expression $1975 + .10x$ as before (Figure 6.13). Press F5 *[RNG]* and set the table's range as shown in Figure 6.14. Then x will start at 2230 and also end at 2230, in increments (*pitch*) of 1. The effect is a table with just one row (Figure 6.15), which you see after pressing EXIT F6 *[TBL]*.

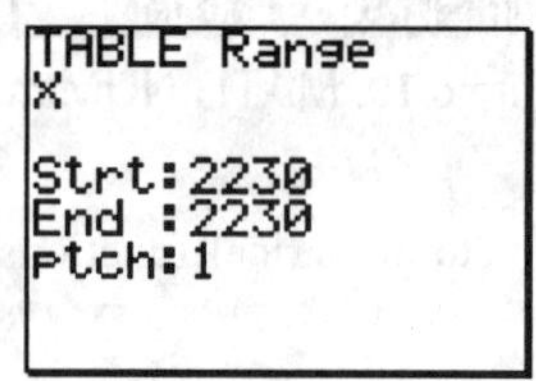

Figure 6.14: TABLE Range

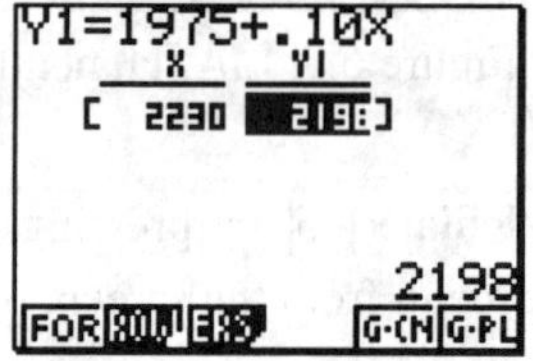

Figure 6.15: TABLE

While viewing the table, with the highlight in the x-column, press 1865 EXE. The y-value is automatically updated to February's wages. Or add another row to the table below the cursor location by pressing F2 *[ROW]* F3 *[ADD]* and changing the x-value in the new row to 1865 (Figure 6.16).

Figure 6.16: Evaluating a function in a table

Technology Tip: The Casio 9800 does not require multiplication to be expressed between variables, so *xxx* means x^3. It is often easier to press two or three *x*'s together than to search for the square key or the powers key. Of course, expressed multiplication is also not required between a constant and a variable. Hence to enter $2x^3 + 3x^2 - 4x + 5$ in the Casio 9800, you might save keystrokes and press just these keys: 2 X,θ,T X,θ,T X,θ,T + 3 X,θ,T X,θ,T - 4 X,θ,T + 5.

6.2.2 Functions in a Graph Window: On the Casio 9800, you can easily generate the graph of a function. The ability to draw a graph contributes substantially to our ability to solve problems.

For example, here is the Casio 9800's quick way to graph $y = -x^3 + 4x$. In COMP mode (MENU 1), press Graph and then (-) X,θ,T ^ 3 + 4 X,θ,T to enter the function (as in Figure 6.17). Now press EXE and the Casio 9800 changes to a window with the graph of $y = -x^3 + 4x$.

While the Casio 9800 is busy calculating coordinates for a plot, it displays a solid square at the top right of the graph window. When you see this indicator, even though the screen does not change, you know that the calculator is working.

Switch back and forth between the graph window and the home screen by pressing G↔T.

The graph window on your calculator may look like the one in Figure 6.18 or it may be different. Since the graph of $y = -x^3 + 4x$ extends infinitely far left and right and also infinitely far up and down, the Casio 9800 can display only a piece of the actual graph. This displayed rectangular part is called a *viewing rectangle*.

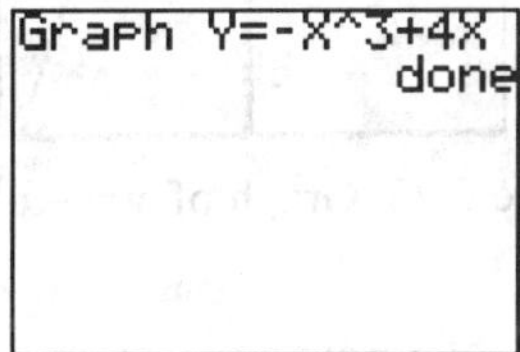

Figure 6.17: Graph command in COMP mode

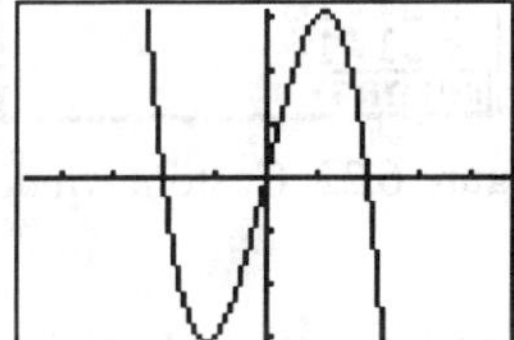

Figure 6.18: Graph of $y = -x^3 + 4x$

You can easily change the viewing rectangle to enhance your investigation of a graph. For example, press any of the arrow keys to pan the graph window in the corresponding direction. If you press the down arrow, for example, the window will pan down so that you may look at points below the current window.

The Casio 9800's viewing rectangle in Figure 6.18 shows the part of the graph that extends horizontally from -4.7 to 4.7 and vertically from -3.1 to 3.1. Press Range to see information about your viewing rectangle. Figure 6.19 shows the Range screen that corresponds to the Casio 9800 viewing rectangle in Figure 6.18. This is the *standard* viewing rectangle for your calculator.

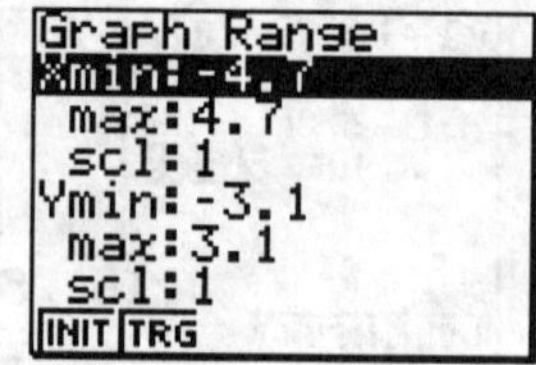

Figure 6.19: Standard Range

The variables Xmin and Xmax are the minimum and maximum *x*-values of the viewing rectangle; Ymin and Ymax are its minimum and maximum *y*-values.

Xscl and Yscl set the spacing between tick marks on the axes.

Use the arrow keys ▲ and ▼ to move up and down from one line to another in this list; pressing the EXE key will move down the list. Enter a new value to over-write a previous value. You may also edit the entry as you would edit an expression. To leave the Range menu, press the Range key once or twice more. Finally, press EXE to re-draw the graph. The following figures show different Range screens and the corresponding viewing rectangle for each one.

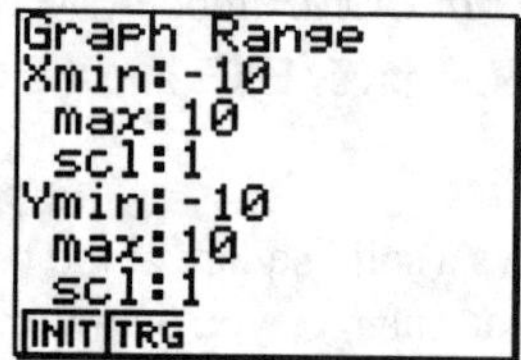

Figure 6.20: -10 to 10 in both directions

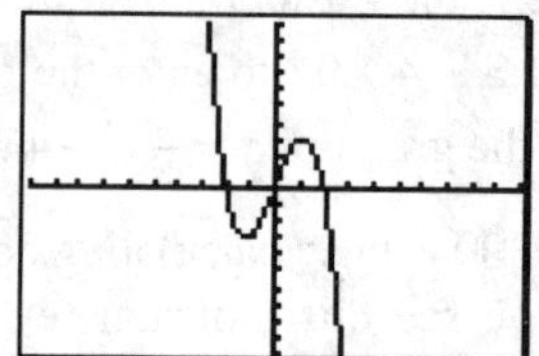

Figure 6.21: Graph of $y = -x^3 + 4x$

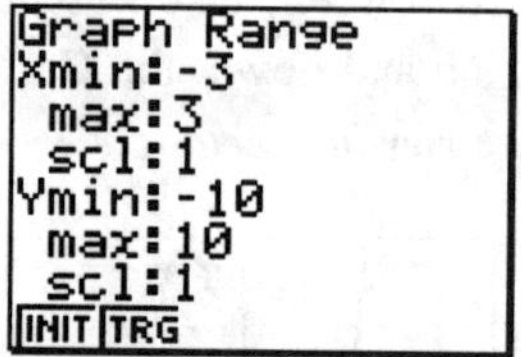

Figure 6.22: Custom window

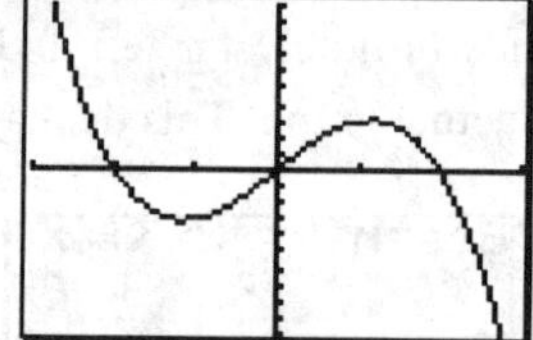

Figure 6.23: Graph of $y = -x^3 + 4x$

To initialize the viewing rectangle quickly to standard values (see Figure 6.19), press Range F1 *[INIT]* Range Range. Then press EXE to redraw the graph.

As you pan over the graph by pressing the arrow keys, the Range dimensions are updated automatically. More information about windows is presented later, in Section 6.2.3.

Technology Tip: Clear any graphs in COMP mode by pressing F5 when the Casio 9800 is showing the graph screen or SHIFT F5 when it is displaying the home screen. The Cls command now appears in the home screen; press EXE to implement it.

Another way to clear the graph window is to press Range, re-enter the *current* value for Xmin (or make any "change" in any range value), then press Range Range to exit. This method *keeps* the graph command as the *current* command, so you may edit it as necessary. Also, the Casio 9800 keeps a graph "active" for zooming and tracing in COMP mode only if the graphing instruction is the *last* command executed.

Casio CFX-9800G Color Power Graphic Calculator

If you're going to use a function later, or if you need to perform some calculations before returning to its graph, save it in the Casio 9800's FUNCTION MEMORY. Six different functions, expressions, or commands can be stored here. Press SHIFT ⊞-MEM and then F4 *[SEE]* for a listing of current contents of function memory. To *store* a function or command, enter it first in the home screen, but do *not* press EXE. Press SHIFT ⊞-MEM F1 and then some function key from F1 to F6, corresponding to a function memory location. To *recall* a function or command from memory to the home screen, press SHIFT ⊞-MEM F2 and the key corresponding to the function you want.

Technology Tip: It's a good idea to reserve at least one function memory location, say f_1, for temporary storage of functions, and use the remaining locations for longer-term storage.

If you plan to do more extensive investigation of functions, use the calculator's graph function memory. Here you may store up to 30 different functions in rectangular, polar, or parametric form, and also inequalities. For example, let's graph $y = -x^3 + 4x$ once again, this time in GRAPH mode. Press MENU 6, move the highlight if necessary to Y1, and enter $-x^3 + 4x$ as before (see Figure 6.24). Then store this as function Y1 by pressing EXE. Next press F6 *[DRW]* to see the graph (same as Figure 6.18 if your calculator is using its standard range).

Figure 6.24: $Y1 = -x^3 + 4x$

To change a function, recall it to the edit line by moving the highlight to the function you want and pressing F1 *[EDIT]*.

Delete a function by moving the highlight over it and pressing F2 *[DEL]*; the calculator asks you to confirm a deletion by pressing F1.

Change the range in GRAPH mode just as you did in COMP mode, by pressing the Range key.

Technology Tip: Redraw graphs in GRAPH mode by pressing G↔T to switch between the Casio 9800's graph screen and its GRAPH FUNC listing. Then press F6 *[DRW]* to clear the previous graph screen and plot the functions again.

6.2.3 Graphing a Circle: Here is a useful technique for graphs that are not functions, but that can be "split" into a top part and a bottom part, or into multiple parts. Suppose you wish to graph the circle whose equation is $x^2 + y^2 = 36$. First solve for y and get an equation for the top semicircle, $y = \sqrt{36 - x^2}$, and for the bottom semicircle, $y = -\sqrt{36 - x^2}$. Then graph the two semicircles simultaneously.

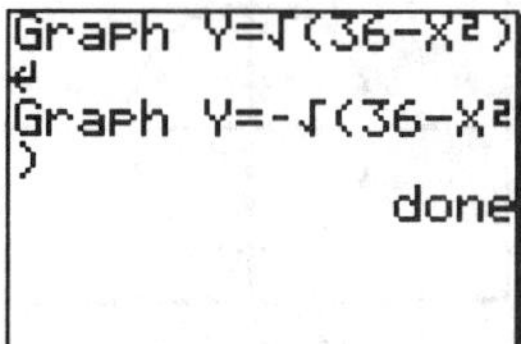

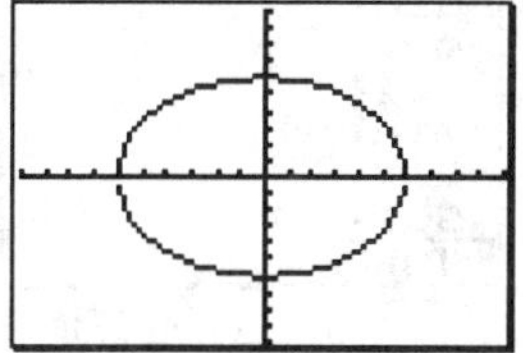

Figure 6.25: Two semicircles in COMP mode   Figure 6.26: Circle's graph - one view

The keystrokes to draw this circle's graph in COMP mode (MENU 1) follow. Store $\sqrt{36-x^2}$ as f_1 by pressing SHIFT √ (36 - x,θ,T x²) SHIFT ⊟-MEM F1 F1. Set the Graph Range to extend from -10 to 10 in both directions. Then press AC/ON GRAPH SHIFT ⊟-MEM F2 *[RCL]* F1 SHIFT ⏎ GRAPH (-) F2 *[RCL]* F1 EXE to draw both halves of the circle.

To plot the circle in GRAPH mode (MENU 6), store $\sqrt{36-x^2}$ as Y1 and store $-\sqrt{36-x^2}$ as Y2. Or you may store -Y1 as Y2 by pressing these Casio 9800 keystrokes: (-) SHIFT VAR F3 *[GPH]* F1 *[Y]* 1 EXE. The VAR menu (displayed along the bottom of the screen in Figure 6.27) enables you to recall graphic functions and other information from memory.

Figure 6.27: GRAPH mode

If your range were set to a viewing rectangle extending from -10 to 10 in both directions, your graph would look like Figure 6.26. Now this does *not* look like a circle, because the units along the axes are not the same. You need what is called a "square" viewing rectangle.

The Casio calculator's standard viewing rectangle *is* square, but too small to display a circle of radius 6. So double the dimensions of the Casio 9800's standard window and change it to extend horizontally from -9.4 to 9.4 and vertically from -6.2 to 6.2.

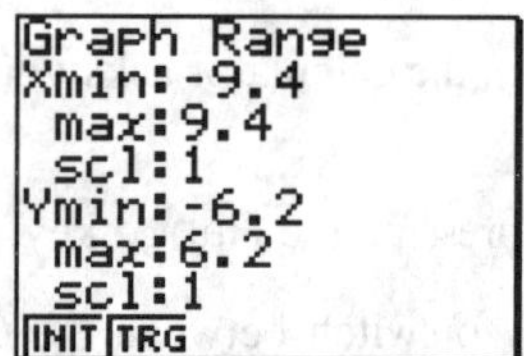

Figure 6.28: Twice standard range

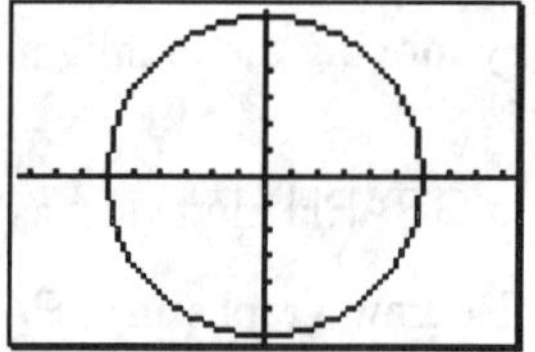

Figure 6.29: Better circle

Technology Tip: Another way to get a square graph is to change the range variables so that the value of Ymax - Ymin is $\frac{2}{3}$ times Xmax - Xmin. For example, see the Range in Figure 6.30 and the corresponding graph in Figure 6.31. The method works because the dimensions of the Casio 9800's display are such that the ratio of vertical to horizontal is approximately $\frac{2}{3}$.

Figure 6.30: $\frac{\text{vertical}}{\text{horizontal}} = \frac{16}{24} = \frac{2}{3}$

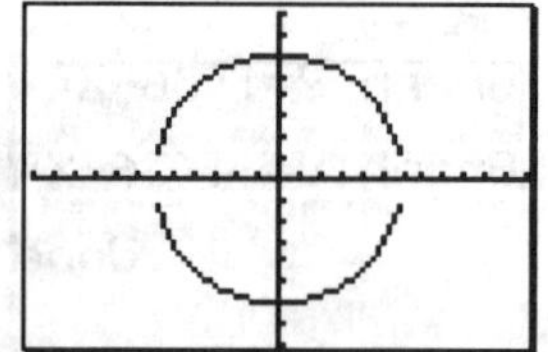

Figure 6.31: "Square" circle

The two semicircles in Figure 6.31 do not meet because of an idiosyncrasy in the way the Casio 9800 plots a graph.

Technology Tip: The square viewing rectangle is also important when you want to judge whether two lines are perpendicular. The intersection of perpendicular lines will always *look* like a right angle in a square viewing rectangle.

6.2.4 TRACE: Graph $y = -x^3 + 4x$ in the standard viewing rectangle. When the graph window is displayed, press F1 *[Trace]* to enable the left ◀ and right ▶ arrow keys to trace along the function. The coordinates that are displayed belong to points on the function's graph, so the *y*-coordinate is the calculated value of the function at the corresponding *x*-coordinate.

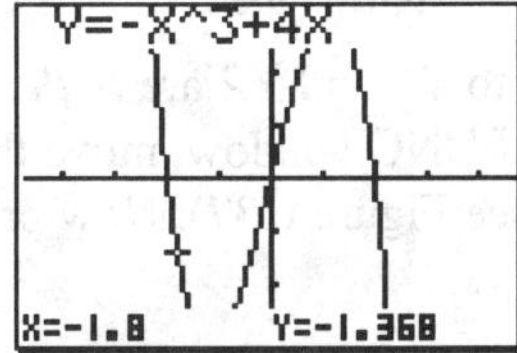

Figure 6.32: Trace

To see more decimal places in the coordinates of the points that are traced, press F6 to cycle among the *x*-coordinate alone, the *y*-coordinate alone, and both coordinates.

Now plot a second function, $y = -.25x$, along with $y = -x^3 + 4x$. In COMP mode, first press the keys to graph $y = -x^3 + 4x$ but don't press EXE yet. Add the second graph command to this by pressing SHIFT ↵ GRAPH and the keys for $-.25x$ (Figure 6.33). Finally, press EXE to draw both functions.

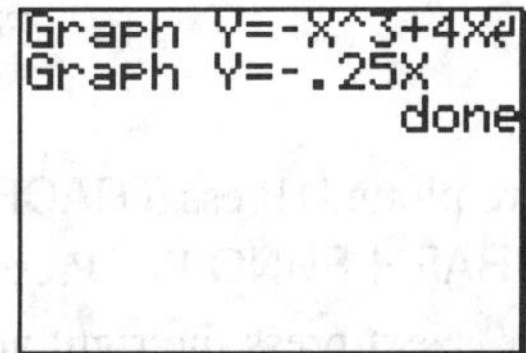

Figure 6.33: Two functions in COMP mode

In GRAPH mode, store $-.25x$ as Y2 (Figure 6.34). Then press F6 *[DRW]* to draw both functions.

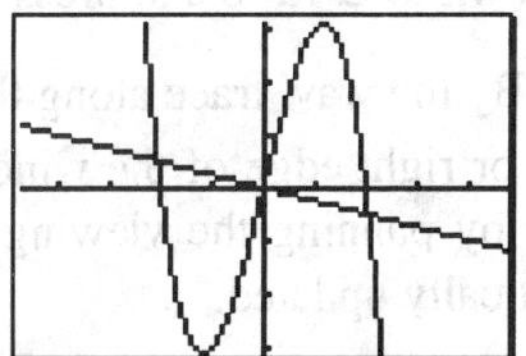

Figure 6.34: Two functions in GRAPH mode   Figure 6.35: $y = -x^3 + 4x$ and $y = -.25x$

Technology Tip: The Casio 9800 can display a graph in one of three colors: blue, orange, or green. So when you are plotting more than one function, it's helpful to color their graphs distinctly. In the GRAPH FUNC window, move the highlight to a function and press F4 *[COLR]*, then select F1 *[BLU]* for blue, F2 *[ORN]* for orange, or F3 *[GRN]* for green. Notice that each function's formula is colored to match its graph. Press EXIT to leave the color menu.

Figure 6.36: Color choices

Technology Tip: Since the Casio 9800 always draws axes in green, you may wish to color graphs in blue and orange for contrast. Also, the trace cursor will be orange only.

Note in Figure 6.36 that the equal signs next to Y1 and Y2 are *both* highlighted. This means *both* functions will be graphed on your Casio 9800. In the GRAPH FUNC window, move the cursor next to Y1, and press F5 *[SEL]*. This equal sign should no longer be highlighted (see Figure 6.37). Now press F6 and see that only Y2 is plotted (Figure 6.38).

Many different functions may be stored in the GRAPH FUNC list and any combination of them may be graphed simultaneously. You can make a function active or inactive for graphing by pressing F5 *[SEL]* to set the highlight (activate) or remove the highlight (deactivate). Go back and do what is needed in order to graph Y1 but not Y2.

Figure 6.37: Only Y2 active

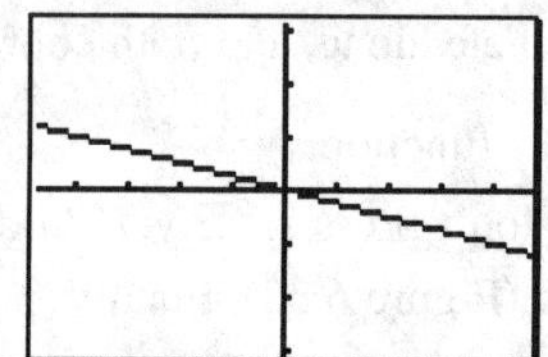

Figure 6.38: Graph of $y = -.25x$

Now activate Y2 again so that both graphs are plotted. Press TRACE and the cursor appears first on the graph of $y = -x^3 + 4x$ because it is higher up in the GRAPH FUNC list. Press the up ▲ or down ▼ arrow key to move the cursor vertically to the graph of $y = -.25x$. Next press the right and left arrow keys to trace along the graph of $y = -.25x$. When more than one function is plotted, you can move the trace cursor vertically from one graph to another in this way.

Technology Tip: The Casio 9800 can display the equation for each function as it is plotted or traced. In SET UP, move the cursor down to G-func and press F1 *[ON]* to turn the display on or F2 *[OFF]* to turn it off.

Technology Tip: By the way, trace along the graph of $y = -.25x$ and press and hold either ◀ or ▶. Eventually you will reach the left or right edge of the window. Keep pressing the arrow key and the Casio 9800 will allow you to continue the trace by panning the viewing rectangle left or right. Check the Range screen to see that Xmin and Xmax are automatically updated.

The Casio 9800's display has 95 horizontal columns of pixels and 63 vertical rows. So when you trace a curve across a graph window, you are actually moving from Xmin to Xmax in 94 equal jumps, each called Δx. You would calculate the size of each jump to be $\Delta x = \dfrac{\text{Xmax} - \text{Xmin}}{94}$. Sometimes you may want the jumps to be friendly numbers like .1 or .25 so that, when you trace along the curve, the x-coordinates will be incremented by such a convenient amount. Just set your viewing rectangle for a particular increment Δx by making Xmax = Xmin + 94·Δx. For example, if you want Xmin = -5 and Δx = .3, set Xmax = -5 + 94·.3 = 23.2. Likewise, set Ymax = Ymin + 62·Δy if you want the vertical increment to be some special Δy.

To center your window around a particular point, say (h, k), and also have a certain Δx, set Xmin = h - 47·Δx and Xmax = h + 47·Δx. Likewise, make Ymin = k - 31·Δy and Ymax = k + 31·Δy. For example, to center a window around the origin, (0, 0), with both horizontal and vertical increments of .25, set the range so that Xmin = 0 - 47·.25 = -11.75, Xmax = 0 + 47·.25 = 11.75, Ymin = 0 - 31·.25 = -7.75, and Ymax = 0 + 31·.25 = 7.75.

The Casio 9800's standard window is already a friendly viewing rectangle, centered at the origin (0, 0) with $\Delta x = \Delta y$ = 0.1.

See the benefit by first plotting $y = x^2 + 2x + 1$ in a window that extends from -10 to 10 in both directions. Trace near its y-intercept, which is (0, 1), and move towards its x-intercept, which is (-1, 0). Then initialize the range to the standard window and trace again near the intercepts.

6.2.5 ZOOM: Plot again the two graphs, for $y = -x^3 + 4x$ and for $y = -.25x$. There appears to be an intersection near $x = 2$. The Casio 9800 provides several ways to enlarge the view around this point. You can change the viewing rectangle directly by pressing Range and editing the values of Xmin, Xmax, Ymin, and Ymax. Figure 6.39 shows a new viewing rectangle for the range extending from 1.5 to 2.5 horizontally and from -2.5 to 2.5 vertically.

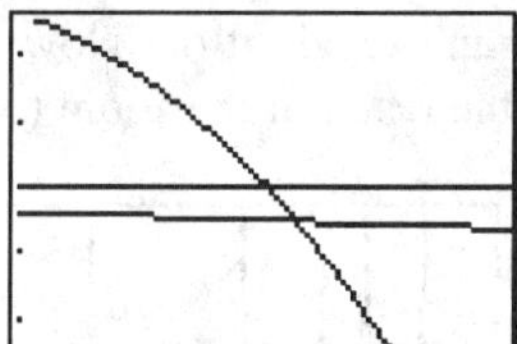

Figure 6.39: Closer view

Trace along the graphs until coordinates of a point that is close to the intersection are displayed.

A more efficient method for enlarging the view is to draw a new viewing rectangle with the cursor. Start again with a graph of the two functions $y = -x^3 + 4x$ and $y = -.25x$ in a standard viewing rectangle.

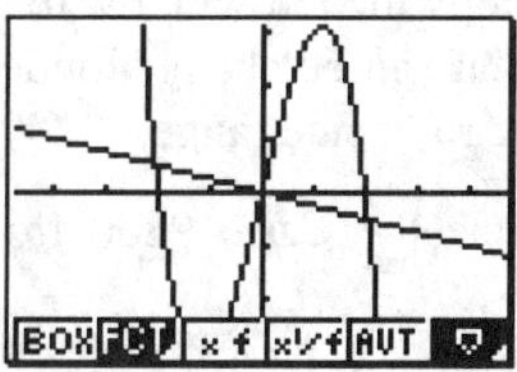

Figure 6.40: Zoom menu

Now imagine a small rectangular box around the intersection point, near $x = 2$. Press F2 *[Zoom]* F1 *[BOX]* to draw a box to define this new viewing rectangle. Use the arrow keys to move the cursor, which is now free-moving and whose coordinates are displayed at the bottom of the window, to one corner of the new viewing rectangle you imagine (Figure 6.41).

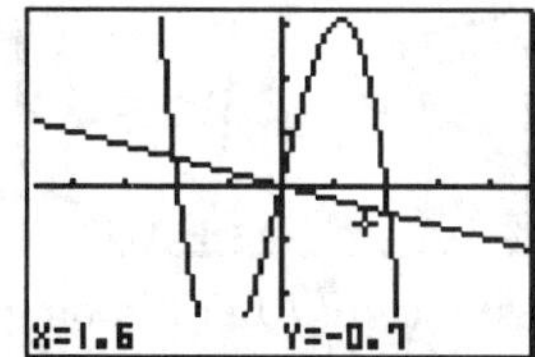

Figure 6.41: One corner selected

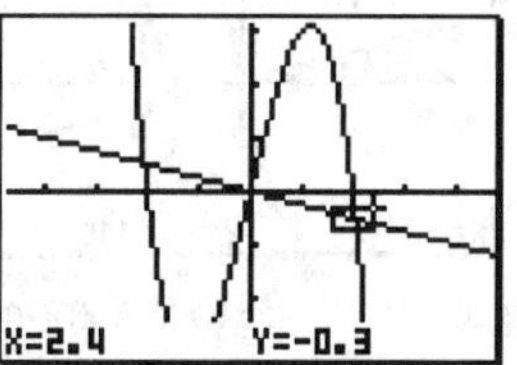

Figure 6.42: Box drawn

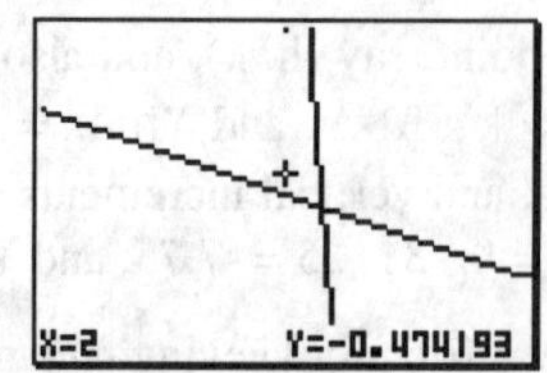

Figure 6.43: New viewing rectangle

Press **EXE** to fix the corner where you have moved the cursor. Use the arrow keys again to move the cursor to the diagonally opposite corner of the new rectangle (Figure 6.42). If this box looks all right to you, press **EXE**. The rectangular area you have enclosed will now enlarge to fill the graph window (Figure 6.43).

You may cancel the zoom any time *before* you press this last **EXE**. Press another function key such as **F1** to cancel the zoom and initiate a trace instead, or press **F2** to zoom again and start over. Even if you did execute the zoom, you may still return to the original viewing rectangle and start over on the Casio 9800 by pressing **F2** *[Zoom]* **F6** *[●]* **F1** *[ORG]*.

The Casio 9800 has a split screen feature that enables you to see two views of a graph simultaneously. Press **SHIFT SET UP**, move the cursor down to **Dual-G**, and toggle it on. Now when you zoom, the left window displays the original graph and the right window displays the result of the zoom (see Figure 6.44).

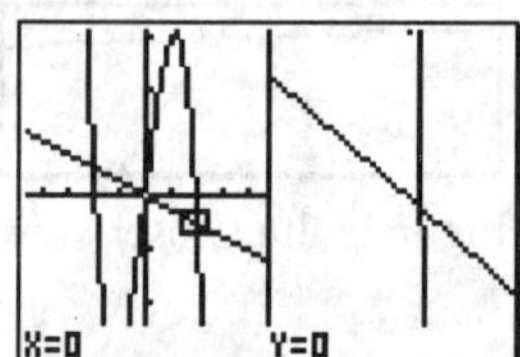

Figure 6.44: DUAL GRAPH

In Dual Graph mode, only the left side can be acted on. So to achieve another zoom, first press **F6 F2** *[CHG]* to exchange the left and right windows. Or just copy the left window to the right side by pressing **F6 F1** *[COP]*. When you press **Range**, you will find *two* ranges that can be changed independently. While in the **Range** menu, the **F6** key toggles between the left side range and the right side range.

Technology Tip: Use the G↔T key to cycle the Casio 9800 from dual graph to full-screen/left side to full-screen/right side to **GRAPH FUNC** screen.

The Casio 9800 can quickly magnify a graph around the cursor's location. Return once more to the standard range for the graph of the two functions $y = -x^3 + 4x$ and $y = -.25x$. Trace along the graphs to move the cursor as close as you can to the point of intersection near $x = 2$ (see Figure 6.45). Then press **F2** *[Zoom]* **F3** *[×f]* and the calculator draws a magnified graph, centered at the cursor's position (Figure 6.46). The range values are changed to reflect this new viewing rectangle. Look in the **Range** menu to check.

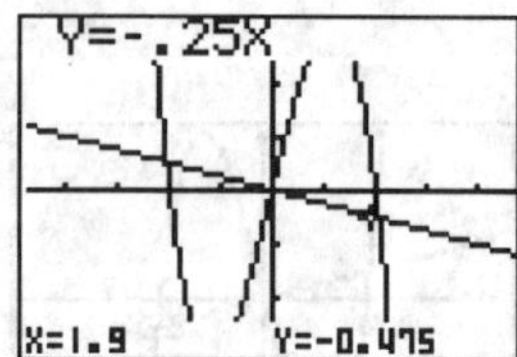

Figure 6.45: Before a zoom in

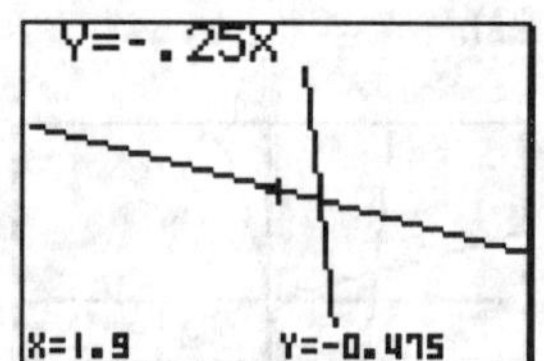

Figure 6.46: After a zoom in

As you see in the Zoom menu (press F2), the Casio 9800 can zoom in (press F2 F3 *[×f]*) or zoom out (press F2 F4 *[×1/f]*). Zoom out to see a larger view of the graph, centered at the cursor position. You can change the horizontal and vertical scale of the magnification by pressing F2 F2 *[FCT]* and editing Xfct and Yfct, the horizontal and vertical magnification factors.

Technology Tip: An advantage of zooming in from the default viewing rectangle is that subsequent windows will also be square. Likewise, if you zoom in from a friendly viewing rectangle, the zoomed windows will also be friendly.

The default zoom factor is 2 in both directions (press F1 *[INIT]* in the Factor menu). And it is not necessary for Xfct and Yfct to be equal. Sometimes, you may prefer to zoom only in one direction, so the other factor should be set to 1. As usual, press EXIT to leave the Factor menu.

Technology Tip: If you should zoom in too much and lose the curve, zoom back to the original viewing rectangle and start over. Or use the arrow keys to pan over if you think the curve is not too far away. You can also just initialize the range to the Casio 9800's standard window.

Technology Tip: The Casio 9800 can automatically select the necessary *vertical* range for a function. For auto scaling, press F2 *[Zoom]* F5 *[AUT]*. Take care, because sometimes when you are graphing two functions together, the calculator will auto scale for one function in such a way that the other function will no longer be visible. For example, plot the two functions $y = -x^3 + 4x$ and $y = -.25x$ in the Casio 9800's standard viewing rectangle, then auto scale and trace along both functions.

6.3   Solving Equations and Inequalities

6.3.1 Intercepts and Intersections: Tracing and zooming are also used to locate an x-intercept of a graph, where a curve crosses the x-axis. For example, the graph of $y = x^3 - 8x$ crosses the x-axis three times (see Figure 6.47). After tracing over to the x-intercept point that is furthest to the left, zoom in (Figure 6.48). Continue this process until you have located all three intercepts with as much accuracy as you need. The three x-intercepts of $y = x^3 - 8x$ are approximately -2.828, 0, and 2.828.

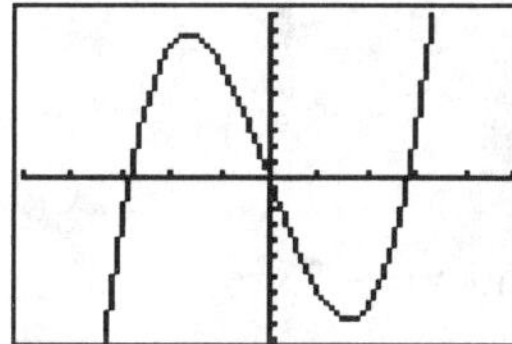
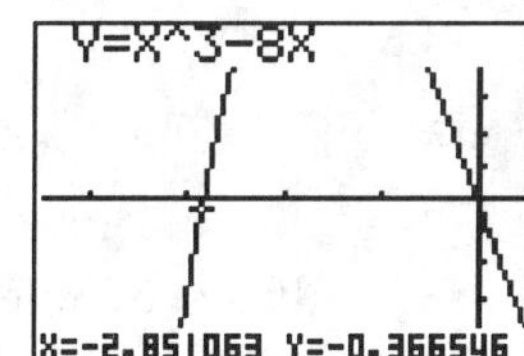

Figure 6.47: Graph of $y = x^3 - 8x$ Figure 6.48: Near an x-intercept of $y = x^3 - 8x$

Technology Tip: As you zoom in, you may also wish to change the spacing between tick marks on the x-axis so that the viewing rectangle shows scale marks near the intercept point. Then the accuracy of your approximation will be such that the error is less than the distance between two tick marks. Change the x-scale on the Casio 9800 from the Range menu. Move the cursor down to Xscl and enter an appropriate value.

The x-intercept of a function's graph is a *root* of the equation $f(x) = 0$. And the Casio 9800 automates the search for roots. First plot the function in graph mode (MENU 6) and press SHIFT G-SOLV for the graphical solver menu (Figure 6.49). Then press F1 *[RT]* to locate an x-intercept visible in the current window. The calculator searches from left to right to find an x-intercept in the current window; press ▶ to continue the search for the *next* x-intercept.

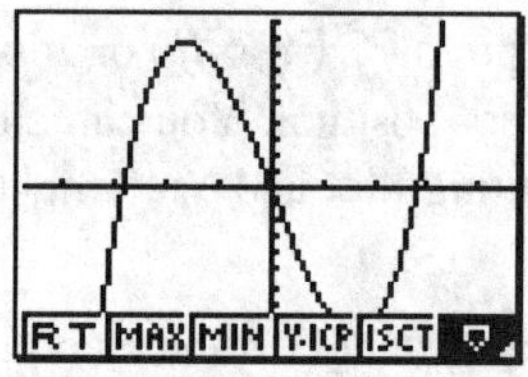

Figure 6.49: G-SOLV menu

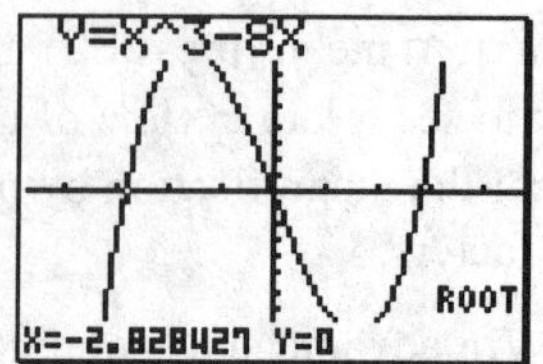

Figure 6.50: A root of $y = x^3 - 8x$

TRACE and ZOOM are especially important for locating the intersection points of two graphs, say the graphs of $y = -x^3 + 4x$ and $y = -.25x$. Trace along one of the graphs until you arrive close to an intersection point. Then press ▲ or ▼ to jump to the other graph. Notice that the x-coordinate does not change, but the y-coordinate is likely to be different (see Figures 6.51 and 6.52).

When the two y-coordinates are as close as they can get, you have come as close as you now can to the point of intersection. So zoom in around the intersection point, then trace again until the two y-coordinates are as close as possible. Continue this process until you have located the point of intersection with as much accuracy as necessary.

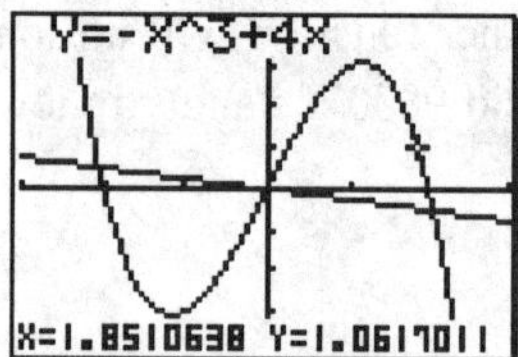

Figure 6.51: Trace on $y = -x^3 + 4x$

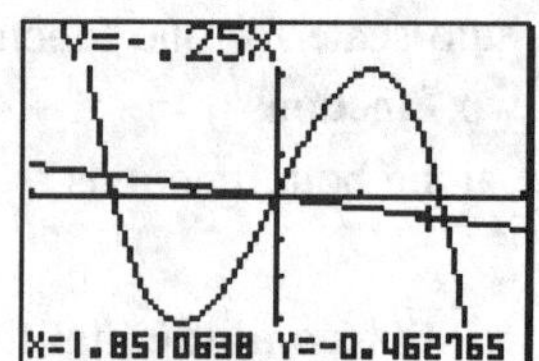

Figure 6.52: Trace on $y = -.25x$

Technology Tip: Press F6 a couple of times to display only the y-coordinate. Then while tracing towards an intersection, it's easier to see where the y-coordinates are closest.

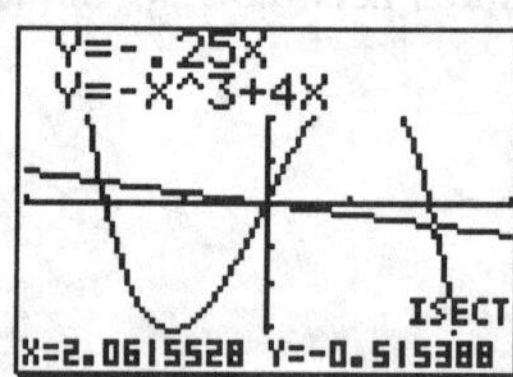

Figure 6.53: Intersection of $y = -x^3 + 4x$ and $y = -.25x$

Automate the Casio 9800's search for points of intersection by pressing SHIFT G-SOLV F5 *[ISCT]*. If more than two functions are being plotted, the calculator will ask you to specify the two whose intersection you seek. The calculator searches from left to right to find an intersection point in the current window; press ▶ to continue the search for the *next* intersection point.

6.3.2 Solving Equations by Graphing: Suppose you need to solve the equation $24x^3 - 36x + 17 = 0$. First graph $y = 24x^3 - 36x + 17$ in a window large enough to exhibit *all* its x-intercepts, corresponding to all the equation's roots. Then use trace and zoom, or the Casio 9800's graphical solver, to locate each one. In fact, this equation has just one solution, approximately $x = -1.414$.

Remember that when an equation has more than one root, it may be necessary to change the viewing rectangle a few times to locate all of them.

Casio CFX-9800G Color Power Graphic Calculator

Technology Tip: To solve an equation like $24x^3 + 17 = 36x$, you may first transform it into standard form, $24x^3 - 36x + 17 = 0$, and proceed as above. However, you may also graph the *two* functions $y = 24x^3 + 17$ and $y = 36x$, then zoom and trace to locate their point of intersection.

6.3.3 Solving Systems by Graphing: The solutions to a system of equations correspond to the points of intersection of their graphs (Figure 6.54). For example, to solve the system $y = x^2 - 3x - 4$ and $y = x^3 + 3x^2 - 2x - 1$, first graph them together. Then zoom and trace, or the Casio 9800's graphical solver, to locate their point of intersection, approximately (-2.17, 7.25).

You must judge whether the two current y-coordinates are sufficiently close for $x = -2.17$ or whether you should continue to zoom and trace to improve the approximation.

The solutions of the system of two equations $y = x^3 + 3x^2 - 2x - 1$ and $y = x^2 - 3x - 4$ correspond to the solutions of the single equation $x^3 + 3x^2 - 2x - 1 = x^2 - 3x - 4$, which simplifies to $x^3 + 2x^2 + x + 3 = 0$. So you may also graph $y = x^3 + 2x^2 + x + 3$ and find its x-intercepts to solve the system.

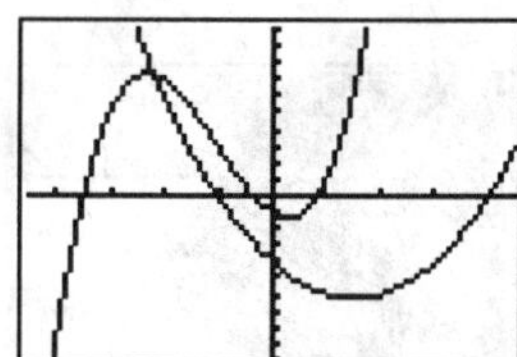

Figure 6.54: Solving a system of equations

6.3.4 Solving Inequalities by Graphing: Consider the inequality $1 - \dfrac{3x}{2} \geq x - 4$. To solve it with your Casio 9800, graph the two functions $y = 1 - \dfrac{3x}{2}$ and $y = x - 4$ (Figure 6.55). First locate their point of intersection, at $x = 2$. The inequality is true when the graph of $y = 1 - \dfrac{3x}{2}$ lies *above* the graph of $y = x - 4$, and that occurs for $x < 2$. So the solution is the half-line $x \leq 2$, or $(-\infty, 2]$.

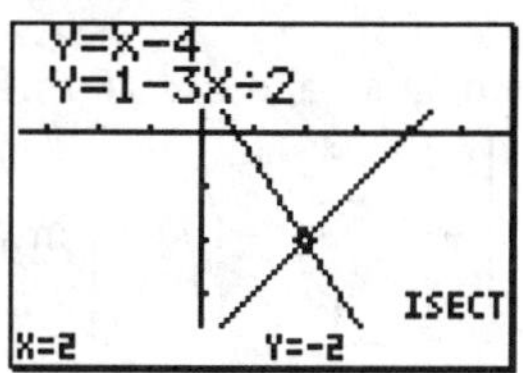

Figure 6.55: Solving $1 - \dfrac{3x}{2} \geq x - 4$

The Casio 9800 is capable of graphing inequalities of the form $y \leq x$, $y < x$, $y \geq x$, or $y > x$. For example, to plot $y \geq x^2 - 1$ in GRAPH mode, press F3 *[TYP]* F4 *[INQ]* and input $x^2 - 1$. Now several inequality options appear (see Figure 6.56); we need F3 *[Y≥]*. Then press EXE to enter this inequality and F6 to draw its graph.

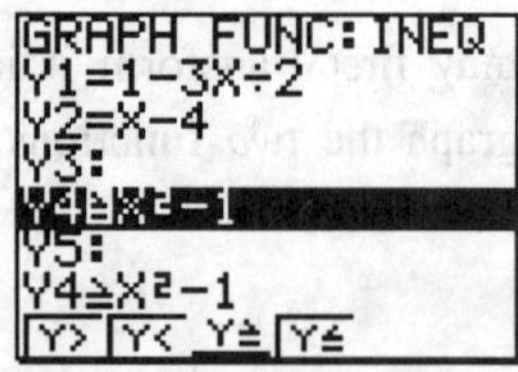

Figure 6.56: Inequality options

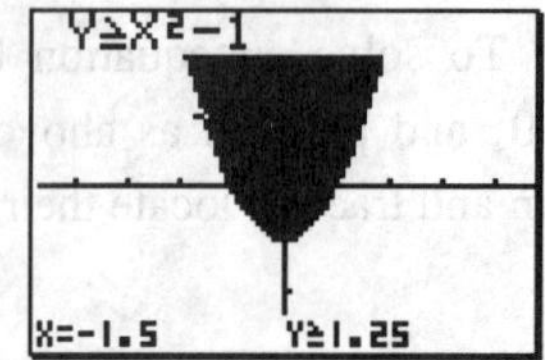

Figure 6.57: Graph of $y \geq x^2 - 1$

Next press **F1** to trace along the boundaries of the inequality. Notice that the Casio 9800 displays coordinates appropriately as inequalities. Zooming is also available for inequality graphs.

Solve a system of inequalities, such as $1 - \dfrac{3x}{2} \geq y$ and $y > x - 4$, by plotting the two inequality graphs simultaneously. First, clear the graph window and reset the range to a convenient window. Input $1 - \dfrac{3x}{2}$ as an inequality type and store it as **Y1** by pressing **F4** *[Y≤]*; likewise, input $x - 4$ as an inequality type and store it as **Y2** by pressing **F1** *[Y>]*. After you press **F6**, watch the two inequalities as they are drawn.

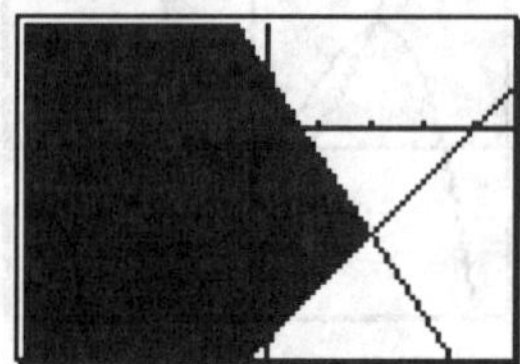

Figure 6.58: Graphs of $1 - \dfrac{3x}{2} \geq y$ and $y > x - 4$

Technology Tip: Since you can change the mode of the Casio 9800 at any time, you can graph inequalities and equations together at the same time. Simply change to inequality type before entering an inequality; then change to rectangular type before entering an equation.

6.4   Matrices

6.4.1 Making a Matrix: The Casio 9800 can display and use 26 different matrices, each named by a letter of the alphabet. Here's how to create this 3×4 matrix $\begin{bmatrix} 1 & -4 & 3 & 5 \\ -1 & 3 & -1 & -3 \\ 2 & 0 & -4 & 6 \end{bmatrix}$ in your calculator.

Press **MENU 5**, then **F4** *[EDIT]* for the **MATRIX** list. Move the cursor to **Mat A** and press **F2** *[Det]* 3 **EXE** 4 **EXE** to enter its dimensions of 3 rows and 4 columns. Return to the **MATRIX** list by pressing **EXIT** once, then press **F1** to edit matrix A.

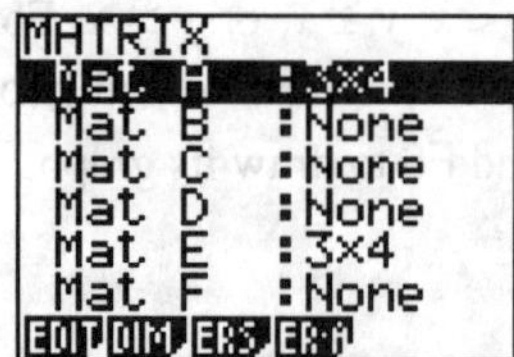

Figure 6.59: MATRIX list

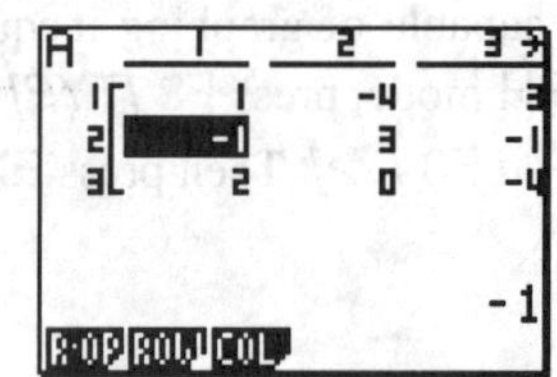

Figure 6.60: Editing a matrix

Casio CFX-9800G Color Power Graphic Calculator

Use the arrow keys or press EXE repeatedly to move the cursor to a matrix element you want to change. If you press EXE, you will move right across a row and then back to the first column of the next row. The element in the second row and first column in Figure 6.60 is highlighted, so that element's current value is displayed at the bottom right corner of the screen. Continue to enter all the elements of matrix A; press EXE after inputing each value.

When you are finished, leave matrix A's editing screen by pressing EXIT once to return to the MATRIX list.

6.4.2 Row Operations: Here are the keystrokes necessary to perform elementary row operations on a matrix. Your textbook provides more careful explanation of the elementary row operations and their uses.

Return, if necessary, to matrix A's editing screen (Figure 6.60). Press F1 *[R-OP]* and follow the Casio 9800's prompts through the various row operations (Figure 6.61).

To interchange the second and third rows of the matrix A that was defined above, press F1 *[RSw]* 2 EXE 3 EXE (see Figure 6.62). The format of this command is F1 *row1* EXE *row2* EXE.

To add row 2 and row 3 and store the results in row 3, press F4 *[R+]* 2 EXE 3 EXE. The format of this command is F4 *row1* EXE *row2* EXE.

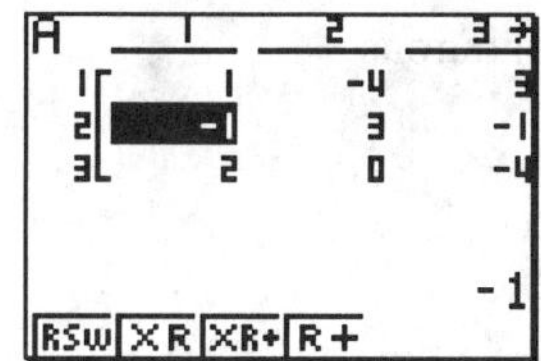

Figure 6.61: Row operations

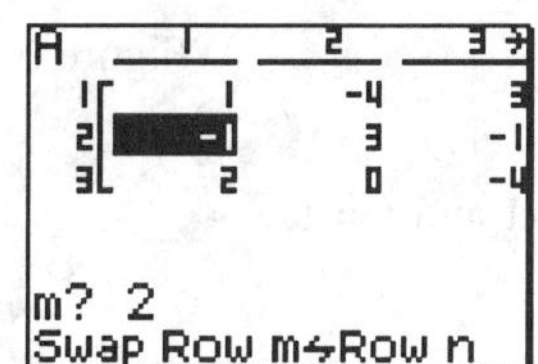

Figure 6.62: Swap rows 2 and 3

To multiply row 2 by -4 and *store* the results in row 2, thereby replacing row 2 with new values, press F2 *[×R]* (-) 4 EXE 2 EXE. The format of this command is F2 *scalar* EXE *row* EXE.

To multiply row 2 by -4 and *add* the results to row 3, thereby replacing row 3 with new values, press F3 *[×R+]* (-) 4 EXE 2 EXE 3 EXE. The format of this command is F3 *scalar* EXE *row1* EXE *row2* EXE.

For example, use elementary row operations to solve this system of linear equations: $\begin{cases} x - 2y + 3z = 9 \\ -x + 3y = -4 \\ 2x - 5y + 5z = 17 \end{cases}$.

First enter this *augmented matrix* as A in your Casio 9800: $\begin{bmatrix} 1 & -2 & 3 & 9 \\ -1 & 3 & 0 & -4 \\ 2 & -5 & 5 & 17 \end{bmatrix}$. Next store this matrix in E (press

EXIT a couple of times to go back to the matrix home screen, then F1 *[Mat]* ALPHA A SHIFT → F1 *[Mat]* ALPHA E EXE, as in Figure 6.63) so you may keep the original in case you need to recall it.

Figure 6.63: Storing a matrix

Here are the row operations and their associated keystrokes. At each step, the result is stored in E and replaces the previous matrix E. The solution is shown in Figure 6.64.

Row Operation	Keystrokes
add row 1 to row 2	F4 *[R+]* 1 EXE 2 EXE
add -2 times row 1 to row 3	F3 *[×R+]* (-) 2 EXE 1 EXE 3 EXE
add row 2 to row 3	F4 *[R+]* 2 EXE 3 EXE
mult row 3 by ½	F2 *[×R]* 1 $a^b/_c$ 2 EXE 3 EXE

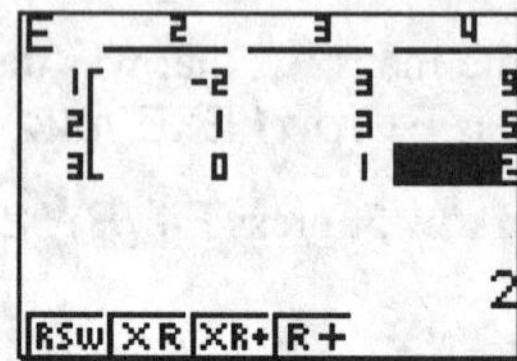

Figure 6.64: Final matrix after row operations

Thus $z = 2$, so $y = -1$ and $x = 1$.

6.4.3 Determinants: Enter this 3×3 square matrix as A: $\begin{bmatrix} 1 & -2 & 3 \\ -1 & 3 & 0 \\ 2 & -5 & 5 \end{bmatrix}$. To calculate its determinant, $\begin{vmatrix} 1 & -2 & 3 \\ -1 & 3 & 0 \\ 2 & -5 & 5 \end{vmatrix}$,

go to the matrix home screen and press F2 *[Det]* F1 *[Mat]* ALPHA A EXE. You should find that $|A| = 2$.

6.5   Additional Topics

6.5.1 Iteration: The Ans feature enables you to perform iterations to evaluate a function repeatedly. As an example, calculate $\dfrac{n-1}{3}$ for $n = 27$. Then calculate $\dfrac{n-1}{3}$ for n = the answer to the previous calculation. Continue to use each answer as n in the *next* calculation. Here are keystrokes to accomplish this iteration on the Casio 9800 calculator (see the results in Figure 6.65). Notice that when you use Ans in place of n in a formula, it is sufficient to press EXE to continue an iteration.

Iteration	Keystrokes	Display
1	27 EXE	27
2	(SHIFT Ans - 1) ÷ 3 EXE	8.66666666667
3	EXE	2.55555555556
4	EXE	0.518518518519
5	EXE	-0.16049382716

Press EXE several more times and see what happens with this iteration. You may wish to try it again with a different starting value.

                    Casio CFX-9800G Color Power Graphic Calculator

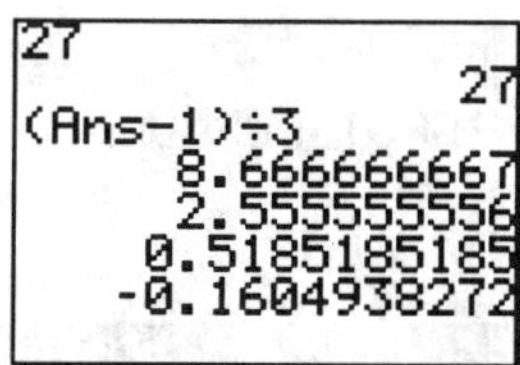

Figure 6.65: Iteration

6.5.2 Arithmetic and Geometric Sequences: Use iteration with the Ans variable to determine the n-th term of a sequence. For example, find the 18th term of an *arithmetic* sequence whose first term is 7 and whose common difference is 4. Enter the first term 7, then start the progression with the recursion formula, SHIFT Ans + 4 EXE. This yields the 2nd term, so press EXE sixteen more times to find the 18th term. For a *geometric* sequence whose common ratio is 4, start the progression with SHIFT Ans × 4 EXE.

You can also define the sequence recursively with the Casio 9800 by selecting MENU 8 *[TABLE]* F3 *[REC]* (see Figure 6.66). Next press F4 *[TYP]* F2 *[an+1]* to select the recursion type. Once again, let's find the 18th term of an *arithmetic* sequence whose first term is 7 and whose common difference is 4. Input the recursion formula $a_{n+1} = a_n + 4$ by pressing F2 *[an]* + 4 EXE. Now make $a_1 = 7$ (because the first term is a_1 where $n = 1$) and display a table that contains the 16th term a_{16} to the 20th term a_{20} by pressing F5 *[RNG]* F2 *[a1]* 16 EXE 20 EXE 7 EXIT F6 *[TBL]* (see Figures 6.67 and 6.68).

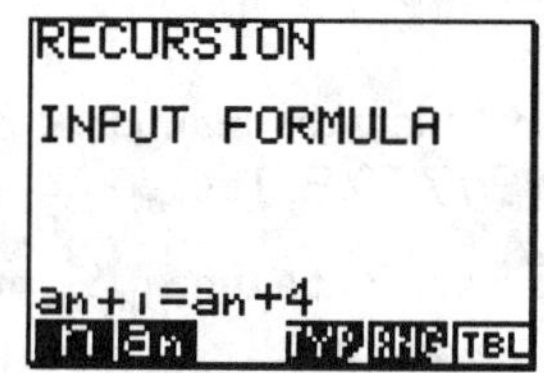

Figure 6.66: Recursion formula

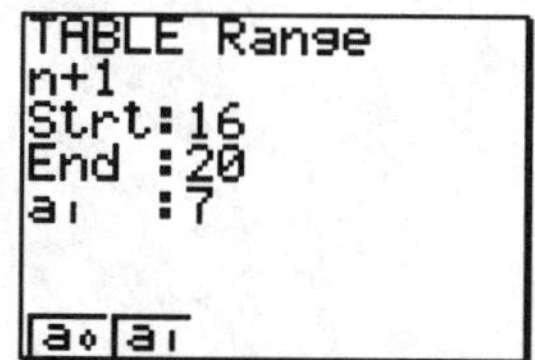

Figure 6.67: TABLE Range

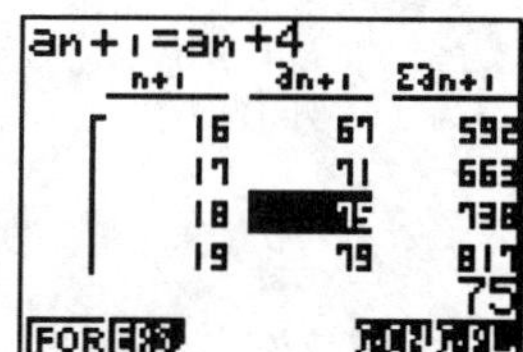

Figure 6.68: $a_{18} = 75$

Of course, you could also use the *explicit* formula for the n-th term of an arithmetic sequence, $t_n = a + (n-1)d$. First enter values for the variables a, d, and n, then evaluate the formula by pressing ALPHA A + (ALPHA N - 1) ALPHA D EXE. For a geometric sequence whose n-th term is given by $t_n = a \cdot r^{n-1}$, enter values for the variables a, r, and n, then evaluate the formula by pressing ALPHA A ALPHA R ^ (ALPHA N - 1) EXE.

To use the explicit formula in a Casio 9800 recursion table, make $a_n = 7 + (n-1) \cdot 4$ by pressing MENU 8 *[TABLE]* F3 *[REC]* F4 *[TYP]* F1 *[an]* 7 + (F1 *[n]* - 1) × 4. Once more, calculate a_{18} by pressing F5 *[RNG]* 18 EXE 18 EXIT F6 *[TBL]*.

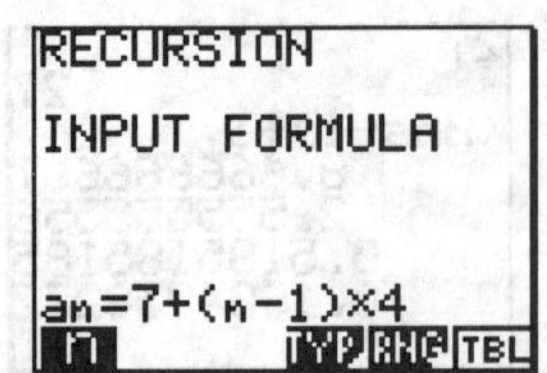

Figure 6.69: Explicit formula

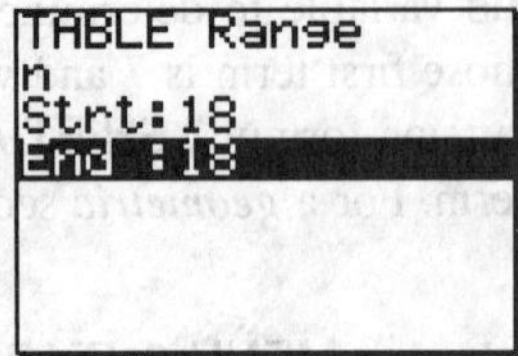

Figure 6.70: TABLE Range

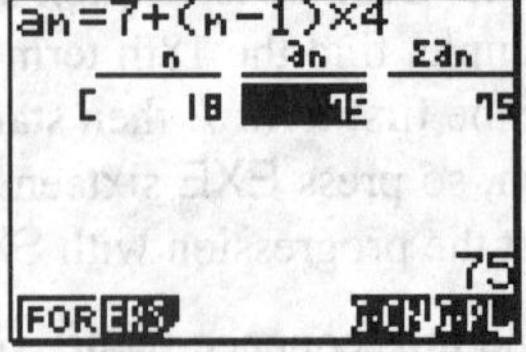

Figure 6.71: $a_{18} = 75$

Technology Tip: A table whose starting and ending range values are the same has just one entry. So to display a single n-th term in a series, set both the starting and ending range values to n.

There are more instructions for using table recursion mode in the Casio 9800 manual.

6.5.3 *Permutations and Combinations:* To calculate the number of *permutations* of 12 objects taken 7 at a time, $_{12}P_7$, press 12 SHIFT MATH F2 *[PRB]* F2 *[nPr]* 7 EXE. Thus $_{12}P_7 = 3,991,680$, as shown in Figure 6.72.

For the number of *combinations* of 12 objects taken 7 at a time, $_{12}C_7$, press 12 SHIFT MATH F2 *[PRB]* F3 *[nCr]* 7 EXE. So $_{12}C_7 = 792$.

Figure 6.72: $_{12}P_7$ and $_{12}C_7$

6.6 Programming

6.3.1 *Entering a Program:* The Casio 9800 is a programmable calculator that can store sequences of commands for later replay. Here's an example to show you how to enter a useful program that solves quadratic equations by the quadratic formula.

Press MENU A *[PRGM]* F1 *[PRG]* to write a program. The Casio 9800 has space for up to 38 programs, each named by a number or letter. If a program location is not used, the word *empty* appears to the right of its name in the list. Press the up or down arrow keys to move the cursor to an empty program area; you may also press the key corresponding to a program's name and jump directly there. For example, to go to program 5, press 5; to edit program B, press ALPHA B.

    Casio CFX-9800G Color Power Graphic Calculator

Figure 6.73: Program list

When the cursor is blinking next to the program area you've chosen, press **EXE** to write a new program in that area or to edit a program that is already there.

Now enter a descriptive title, so press **SHIFT** **Ⓐ-LOCK** and name this program **QUADRATIC**. Press **ALPHA** to cancel the alpha lock. Then press **EXE** to begin writing the actual program. If you do not enter a title, the first line of the program appears in the program list.

Any command you could enter directly in the Casio 9800's home screen can be entered as a line in a program. There are also special programming commands.

Technology Tip: Each time you press **EXE** while writing a program, the Casio 9800 *automatically* inserts the ↵ character at the end of the previous line. For simplicity, since this happens every time you press **EXE**, the ↵ character is not shown in the program listing below.

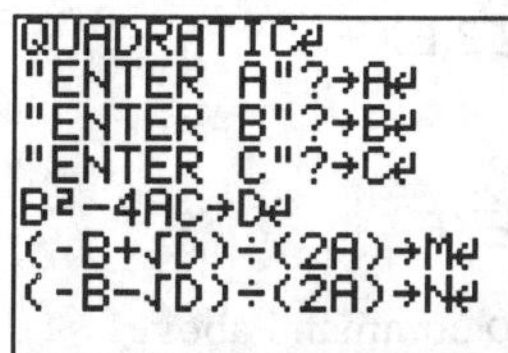

Figure 6.74: Program **QUADRATIC**

Enter the program **QUADRATIC** by pressing the given keystrokes.

Program Line	*Keystrokes*
"ENTER A"? → A	**SHIFT** **Ⓐ-LOCK** **F2** E N T E R **SPACE** A **F2** **SHIFT** **PRGM** **F4** **SHIFT** **→** **ALPHA** A **EXE**

    displays the words *Enter A* on the Casio 9700GE screen and
    waits for you to input a value that will be assigned to the variable A

"ENTER B"? → B	**SHIFT** **Ⓐ-LOCK** **F2** E N T E R **SPACE** B **F2** **SHIFT** **PRGM** **F4** **SHIFT** **→** **ALPHA** B **EXE**
"ENTER C"? → C	**SHIFT** **Ⓐ-LOCK** **F2** E N T E R **SPACE** C **F2** **SHIFT** **PRGM** **F4** **SHIFT** **→** **ALPHA** C **EXE**
B^2-4AC → D	**ALPHA** B x^2 – 4 **ALPHA** A **ALPHA** C **SHIFT** **→** **ALPHA** D **EXE**

    calculates the discriminant and stores its value as D

(-B+√D)/(2A) → M	((-) **ALPHA** B + **SHIFT** √ **ALPHA** D) ÷ (2 **ALPHA** A) **SHIFT** **→** **ALPHA** M **EXE**

    calculates one root and stores it as M

(-B-√D)/(2A) → N	((-) ALPHA B − SHIFT √ ALPHA D) ÷ (2 ALPHA A) SHIFT → ALPHA N EXE

D<0 ⇒ Goto 1	ALPHA D F2 F4 0 EXIT F1 F1 F2 1 EXE

tests to see if the discriminant is negative;

in case the discriminant is negative, jumps to the line Lbl 1 below;
if the discriminant is not negative, continues on to the next line

D=0 ⇒ Goto 2	ALPHA D EXIT F2 F1 0 EXIT F1 F1 F2 2 EXE

tests to see if the discriminant is zero;

in case the discriminant is zero, jumps to the line Lbl 2 below;
if the discriminant is not zero, continues on to the next line

"TWO REAL ROOTS"	SHIFT A-LOCK F2 T W O SPACE R E A L SPACE R O O T S F2 ALPHA EXE

M◢	ALPHA M EXIT F5

displays one root and pauses

N	ALPHA N EXE

Goto 3	F1 F2 3 EXE

jumps to *end* of program

Lbl 1	F3 1 EXE

jumping point for the Goto command above

"COMPLEX ROOTS"	SHIFT A-LOCK F2 C O M P L E X SPACE R O O T S F2 ALPHA EXE

displays a message in case the roots are complex numbers

M◢	ALPHA M EXIT F5

N	ALPHA N EXE

Goto 3	F1 F2 3 EXE

Lbl 2	F3 2 EXE

"DOUBLE ROOT"	SHIFT A-LOCK F2 D O U B L E SPACE R O O T F2 ALPHA EXE

displays a message in case there is a double root

M	ALPHA M EXE

displays one root and pauses

Lbl 3	F1 F3 3

When you have finished, press MENU to leave the program editor and move on.

If you want to clear a program, enter the program editor again. Move to the program you want to delete, and when the highlight is on its name, press F2 to remove it from the calculator's memory.

6.3.2 Running a Program: To run the program you have entered, press **MENU A**, move the highlight to the program's name, and press **F1** *[RUN]*.

The program has been written to prompt you for values of the coefficients a, b, and c in a quadratic equation $ax^2 + bx + c = 0$. Input a value, then press **EXE** to continue the program.

If you need to interrupt a program during execution, press **AC/ON**.

The instruction manual for your Casio 9800 gives detailed information about programming. Refer to it to learn more about programming and how to use other features of your calculator.

Chapter 7

Hewlett Packard HP 38G
Graphing Calculator

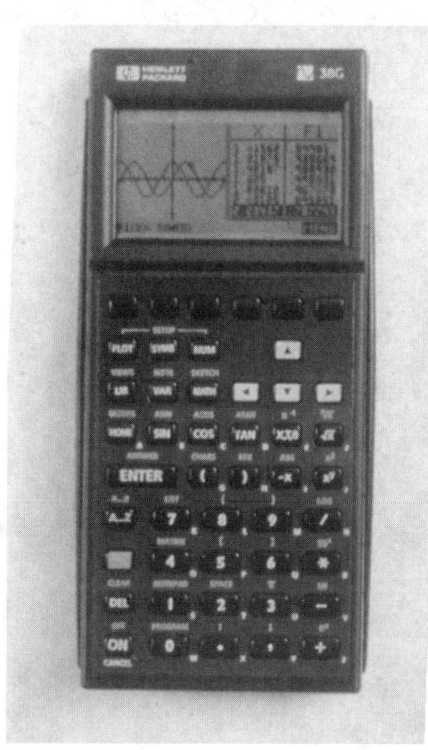

7.1   Getting started with the HP 38G

7.1.1 Basics: Press the ON key to begin using your HP 38G calculator. If you need to adjust the display contrast, first press and hold ON, then press + to increase the contrast or press − to decrease the contrast.

> Midway between the ON key and the ENTER key is a turquoise key that functions like the SHIFT key on a computer keyboard. We use the symbol ◘ for this turquoise shift key. After you press ◘, the symbol ↵ appears at the top left corner of the screen.
>
> Across the top of the HP 38G's keypad are six black keys that assume different functions in different contexts. When pressing a black key has the effect COMMAND within the current context, we use the symbol [COMMAND] to refer to that key.

When you have finished with the calculator, turn it off to conserve battery power by pressing the turquoise shift key ◘ and then OFF.

Check the HP 38G's settings by pressing ◘ MODES. If necessary, use the arrow keys to move the blinking cursor to a setting you want to change. Press [CHOOSE] to select a new setting. To start with, select these options illustrated in Figure 7.1: standard number format and dot (period) for the decimal point. Now return to the home screen by pressing HOME.

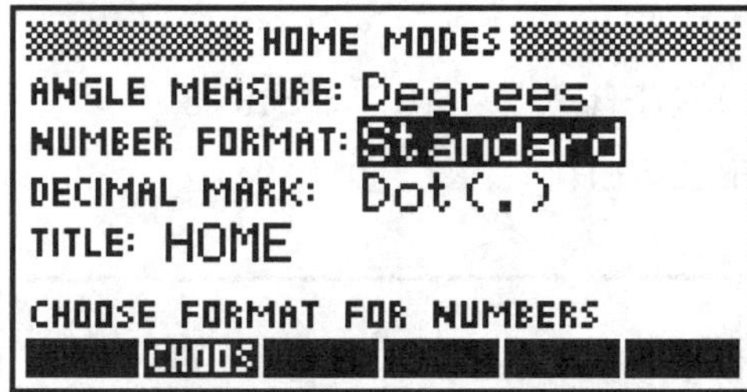

Figure 7.1: HOME MODES

Figure 7.2: Home screen

7.1.2 Editing: The HP 38G's home screen (see Figure 7.2) has labels for the six black function keys across the bottom (not every function key may be active, in which case its label is blank). Above the function key labels is the edit line, where input first appears; and above the edit line is a history area, where previous input and results are stored. For example, type this sum in the home screen: 12 + 34 + 56; then press ENTER to move this up into the history area and to calculate its value.

Often we do not notice a mistake until we see how unreasonable an answer is. The HP 38G permits you to re-display an entire calculation, edit it easily, then execute the *corrected* calculation.

Suppose you had typed 12 + 34 + 56 when you realize that 34 should have been 74. While this sum is still in the edit line, simply press ◄ (the *left* arrow key) or ► (the *right* arrow key) as many times as necessary to move the blinking cursor over the 3, then press 7 DEL. On the other hand, if 34 should have been 384, move the cursor back to 4 and type 8 (inserts at the cursor position and other characters are pushed to the right). If the 34 should have been 3 only, move the cursor to 4 and press DEL to delete it.

If you want to clear the entire edit line, press ON.

Technology Tip: To move quickly to the *beginning* of an expression you are currently editing, press ◘ ◄; to jump to the *end* of that expression, press ◘ ►.

The history area may contain many previous entries, arranged from most recent at the bottom to the oldest entry way above, even out of view. You may still edit one of these older expressions. First, press ON to clear the edit line.

Next press ▲ and ▼ as necessary to move the highlight up and down through the history list until you reach the expression you want, then press [COPY] to bring it back to the edit line. Now you can change it. When you are finished, press ENTER to evaluate this new expression.

Technology Tip: To move quickly to the *oldest* entry at the very top of the history area (which may be out of view), press ◻ ▲; to jump back down to the edit line, press ◻ ▼.

The HP 38G retains its history area even when it is turned off, so long as its batteries are good. When you want to clear the history area, press ◻ CLEAR; this clears the edit line at the same time. Since the history area takes up calculator memory, it's a good idea to clear the history area frequently.

Technology Tip: When you need to evaluate a formula for different values of a variable, use the editing feature to simplify the process. For example, suppose you want to find the balance in an investment account if there is now $5000 in the account and interest is compounded annually at the rate of 8.5%. The formula for the balance is $P\left(1+\frac{r}{n}\right)^{nt}$, where P = principal, r = rate of interest (expressed as a decimal), n = number of times interest is compounded each year, and t = number of years. In our example, this becomes $5000(1+.085)^{t}$. Here are the keystrokes for finding the balance after t = 3, 5, and 10 years.

Years	Keystrokes	Balance
3	5000 (1 + .085) x^y 3 ENTER	$6386.45
5	▲ ▲ [COPY] ◀ 5 DEL ENTER	$7518.28
10	▲ ▲ [COPY] ◀ 10 DEL ENTER	$11,304.92

Figure 7.3: Editing expressions

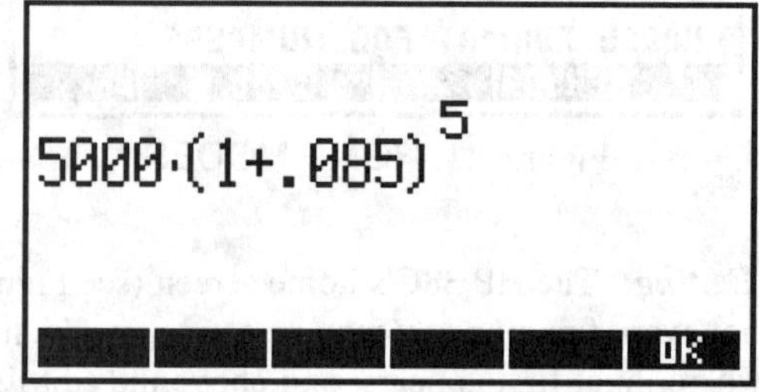

Figure 7.4: [SHOW]

Then to find the balance from the same initial investment but after 5 years when the annual interest rate is 7.5%, press these keys to change the last calculation above: ▲ ▲ [COPY] DEL DEL 5 ◀ ◀ ◀ ◀ ◀ 7 DEL ENTER.

Technology Tip: Press ▲ as many times as necessary to move the highlight up into the history area and onto one of the expressions you just entered. Then press [SHOW] for the HP 38G to display this expression in standard mathematical form, the way you see expressions in your textbook. This is especially helpful for checking your entry of a complicated formula. When you have finished examining the expression in standard form, press [OK] to return to the home screen.

7.1.3 Key Functions: Most keys on the HP 38G offer access to more than one function, just as the keys on a computer keyboard can produce more than one letter ("g" and "G") or even quite different characters ("5" and "%"). The primary function of a key is indicated on the key itself, and you access that function by a simple press on the key.

To access the *second* function indicated *above* a key, first press ◻ (the symbol ↰ appears at the top left corner of the screen) and *then* press the key. For example, to calculate 25^2, press 25 ◻ x² ENTER.

When you want to use an uppercase letter printed at the *lower right* corner of a key, first press A...Z (the symbol α appears at the top of the screen) and then the key. For example, to use the letter K in a formula, press A...Z K. If you need several letters in a row, press and hold A...Z, then press all the letters you want. For a lowercase letter, press ◻ a...z and then the letter. So press ◻ a...z K for the letter k.

7.1.4 Order of Operations: The HP 38G performs calculations according to the standard algebraic rules. Working outwards from inner parentheses, calculations are performed from left to right. Powers and roots are evaluated first, followed by multiplications and divisions, and then additions and subtractions.

Note that the HP 38G distinguishes between *subtraction* and the *negative sign*. If you wish to enter a negative number, it is necessary to use the -x key. For example, you would evaluate $-5-(4\cdot-3)$ by pressing -x 5 - (4 * -x 3) ENTER to get 7.

Technology Tip: When you enter $-5-(4\cdot-3)$ into the history list, the parentheses are not retained. The HP 38G does not display parentheses when they are not required according to the standard algebraic order of operations. Also, a final close parenthesis) before ENTER is not required; the HP 38G will supply it automatically.

Enter these expressions to practice using your HP 38G.

Expression	Keystrokes	Display
$7-5\cdot3$	7 - 5 * 3 ENTER	-8
$(7-5)\cdot3$	(7 - 5) * 3 ENTER	6
$120-10^2$	120 - 10 x² ENTER	20
$(120-10)^2$	(120 - 10) x² ENTER	12100
$\dfrac{24}{2^3}$	24 / 2 xʸ 3 ENTER	3
$\left(\dfrac{24}{2}\right)^3$	(24 / 2) xʸ 3 ENTER	1728
$(7--5)\cdot-3$	(7 - -x 5) * -x 3 ENTER	-36

7.1.5 Algebraic Expressions and Memory: Your calculator can evaluate expressions such as $\dfrac{N(N+1)}{2}$ *after* you have entered a value for N. Suppose you want $N = 200$. Press 200 [STO ▶] A...Z N ENTER to store the value 200 in memory location N. Whenever you use N in an expression, the calculator will substitute the value 200 until you make a change by storing *another* number in N. Next enter the expression $\dfrac{N(N+1)}{2}$ by typing A...Z N * (A...Z N + 1) / 2 ENTER. For $N = 200$, you will find that $\dfrac{N(N+1)}{2} = 20100$.

The contents of any memory location may be revealed by typing just its letter name and then ENTER. And the HP 38G retains memorized values even when it is turned off, so long as its batteries are good.

7.1.6 Repeated Operations with Ans: The result of your *last* calculation is always stored in memory location Ans and replaces any previous result. This makes it easy to use the answer from one computation in another computation. For example, press 30 + 15 ENTER so that 45 is the last result displayed. Then press ◻ ANSWER / 9 ENTER and get 5 because $\frac{45}{9} = 5$.

With a function like division, you press the / key *after* you enter an argument. For such functions, whenever you would start a new calculation with the previous answer followed by pressing the function key, you may press just the function key. So instead of ◘ ANSWER / 9 in the previous example, you could have pressed simply / 9 to achieve the same result. This technique also works for these functions: + - * x^y ◘ x^2 ◘ x^{-1}.

Here is a situation where this is especially useful. Suppose a person makes $5.85 per hour and you are asked to calculate earnings for a day, a week, and a year. Execute the given keystrokes to find the person's incomes during these periods (results are shown in Figure 7.5):

Pay period	Keystrokes	Earnings
8-hour day	5.85 * 8 ENTER	$46.80
5-day week	* 5 ENTER	$234
52-week year	* 52 ENTER	$12,168

Figure 7.5: Ans variable

7.1.7 The MATH Menu: Operators and functions associated with a scientific calculator are available either immediately from the keys of the HP 38G or by ◘ keys. You have direct key access to common arithmetic operations (◘ x^2, $\sqrt{x}$, ◘ x^{-1}, x^y, ◘ ABS), exponential and logarithmic functions (◘ LOG, ◘ 10^x, ◘ LN, ◘ e^x), and a famous constant (◘ π).

A significant difference between the HP 38G and many scientific calculators is that the HP 38G requires the argument of a function *after* the function, as you would see a formula written in your textbook. For example, on the HP 38G you calculate $\sqrt{16}$ by pressing the keys $\sqrt{x}$ 16 in that order.

Here are keystrokes for basic mathematical operations. Try them for practice on your HP 38G.

Expression	Keystrokes	Display
$\sqrt{3^2 + 4^2}$	$\sqrt{x}$ (3 ◘ x^2 + 4 ◘ x^2) ENTER	5
$2\frac{1}{3}$	2 + 3 ◘ x^{-1} ENTER	2.33333333333
$|-5|$	◘ ABS -x 5) ENTER	5
$\log 200$	◘ LOG 200) ENTER	2.30102999566
$2.34 \cdot 10^5$	2.34 * ◘ 10^x 5 ENTER	234000

Additional mathematical operations and functions are available from the MATH menu (Figure 7.6). Press MATH to see the various options. You will learn in your mathematics textbook how to apply many of them. To leave the MATH menu and take no other action, press [OK].

Figure 7.6: MATH menu

The *factorial* of a non-negative integer is the *product* of *all* the integers from 1 up to the given integer. The symbol for factorial is the exclamation point. So 4! (pronounced *four factorial*) is $1 \cdot 2 \cdot 3 \cdot 4 = 24$. You will learn more about applications of factorials in your textbook, but for now use the HP 38G to calculate 4! The factorial command is located in the MATH menu's Prob. sub-menu. To compute 4!, press these keystrokes: 4 MATH ▲ ▶ ▼. [OK] ENTER.

7.2   Functions and Graphs

7.2.1 Evaluating Functions: Suppose you receive a monthly salary of \$1975 plus a commission of 10% of sales. Let x = your sales in dollars; then your wages W in dollars are given by the equation $W = 1975 + .10x$. If your January sales were \$2230 and your February sales were \$1865, what was your income during those months?

Here's how to use your HP 38G to perform this task. Press the LIB key to display the APLET LIBRARY (Figure 7.7) where the calculator organizes its built-in applications. Move the highlight, if necessary, to FUNCTION and press [START] or ENTER.

You may enter as many as ten different functions here for the HP 38G to use at one time. If there is already a function F1, press ▲ as many times as necessary to move the highlight to F1 and press DEL to delete whatever was there.

Technology Tip: Press ◻ CLEAR to erase all ten functions in FUNCTION SYMBOLIC VIEW.

Technology Tip: To move quickly to the *first* function (which may be out of view), press ◻ ▲; to jump down to the *last* function, press ◻ ▼.

Enter the expression $1975 + .10x$ for F1 by pressing these keys: 1975 + .10 X,T,θ and either [OK] or ENTER. (The X,T,θ key lets you enter the variable X easily without having to use the A...Z key.) Now press HOME to return to the main calculations screen.

Technology Tip: The function key [X] in the FUNCTION SYMBOLIC VIEW, as you see in Figure 7.8, serves the same purpose as X,T,θ and A...Z X.

Figure 7.7: APLET LIBRARY

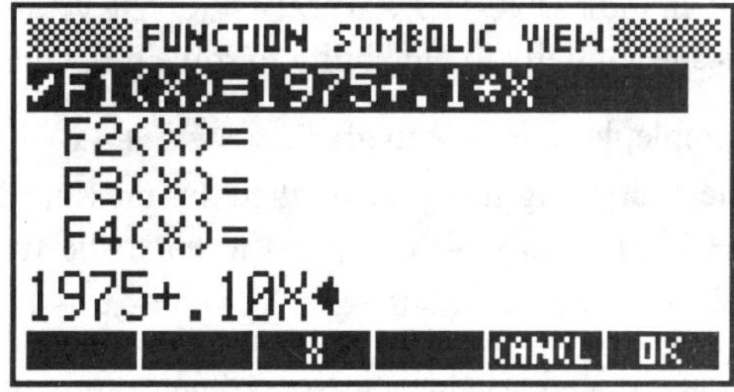
Figure 7.8: FUNCTION SYMBOLIC VIEW

Assign the value 2230 to the variable x by these keystrokes (see Figure 7.9): 2230 [STO ▶] X,T,θ. Next press ▢ : to allow another expression to be entered on the same command line. Like your textbook, the HP 38G uses standard function notation. So press the following keystrokes to evaluate F1 and find January's wages: A...Z F 1 (X,T,θ) ENTER.

Figure 7.9: Function notation

It is not necessary to repeat all these steps to find the February wages. Simply copy the entire previous input line to the edit line and change 2230 to 1865.

You may also have the HP 38G make a table of values for the function. Press ▢ NUM to set up the numerical tables. For NUMTYPE, choose Build Your Own (Figure 7.10); the other options are not important now. Then press NUM, enter 2230 for x, and press [OK] or ENTER (see Figure 7.11). Continue to enter additional values for x and the calculator automatically completes the table with corresponding values of F1.

Figure 7.10: FUNCTION NUMERIC SETUP

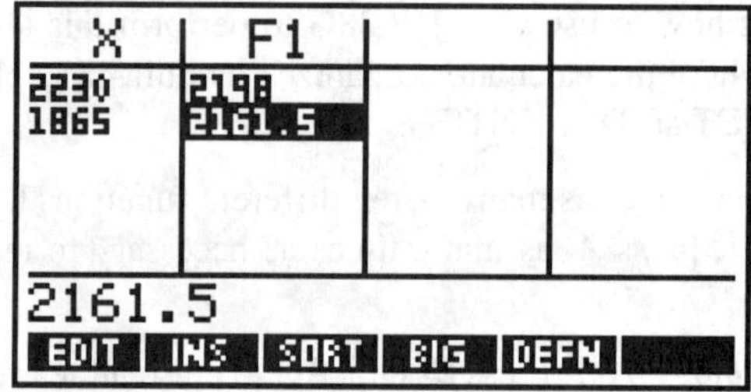

Figure 7.11: Numerical table

Technology Tip: The HP 38G does not require multiplication to be expressed between variables, so xxx means x^3. It is often easier to press two or three x's together than to search for the square key. Of course, expressed multiplication is also not required between a constant and a variable. Hence to enter $2x^3 + 3x^2 - 4x + 5$ in the HP 38G, you might save keystrokes and press just these keys: 2 X,T,θ X,T,θ X,T,θ + 3 X,T,θ X,T,θ - 4 X,T,θ + 5.

7.2.2 Functions in a Graph Window: Once you have started the HP 38G's FUNCTION aplet and entered an expression in the FUNCTION SYMBOLIC VIEW, just press PLOT to see its graph. The ability to draw a graph contributes substantially to our ability to solve problems.

For example, here is how to graph $y = -x^3 + 4x$. First press LIB, select Function, and [START]. Next press SYMB and delete anything that may be there by pressing ▢ CLEAR [YES]. Then, with the highlight on the top line F1, press -x X,T,θ x^y 3 + 4 X,T,θ [OK] to enter the function (as in Figure 7.12). Now press PLOT and the HP 38G changes to a window with the graph of $y = -x^3 + 4x$.

While the HP 38G is calculating coordinates for a plot, it displays a busy indicator at the top of the graph window.

HP 38G Graphing Calculator

Technology Tip: Tap the [MENU] key a couple of times to clear the screen of everything except the graph. Tap any function key to restore the menu options.

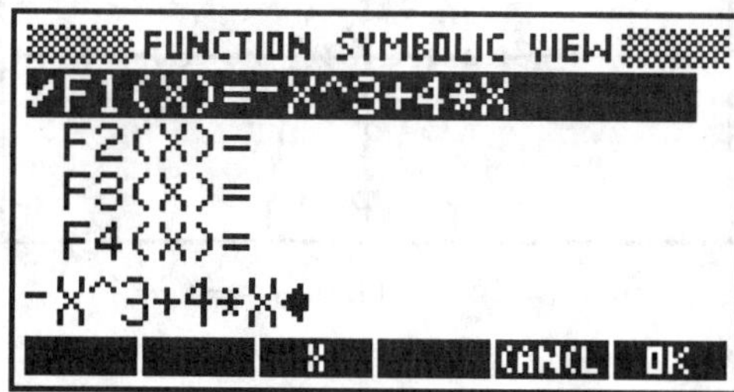

Figure 7.12: FUNCTION SYMBOLIC VIEW

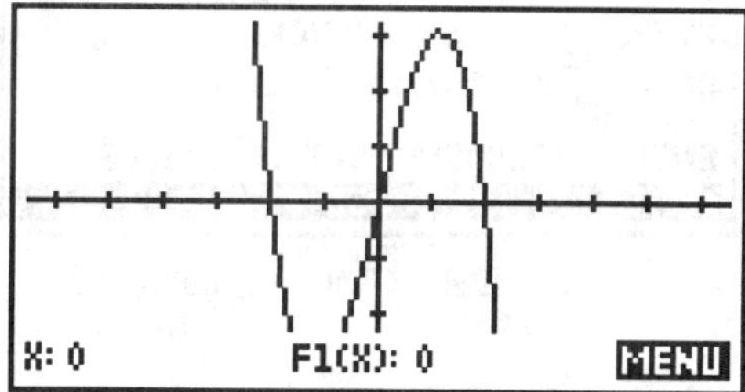

Figure 7.13: Graph of $y = -x^3 + 4x$

Your graph window may look like the one in Figure 7.13 or it may be different. Since the graph of $y = -x^3 + 4x$ extends infinitely far left and right and also infinitely far up and down, the HP 38G can display only a piece of the actual graph. This displayed rectangular part is called a *viewing rectangle*. You can easily change the viewing rectangle to enhance your investigation of a graph.

The viewing rectangle in Figure 7.13 shows the part of the graph that extends horizontally from -6.5 to 6.5 and vertically from -3.1 to 3.2. Press ◻ PLOT to see setup information about your viewing rectangle. Figure 7.14 shows the FUNCTION PLOT SETUP screen that corresponds to the viewing rectangle in Figure 7.13. This is the *standard* viewing rectangle for the HP 38G.

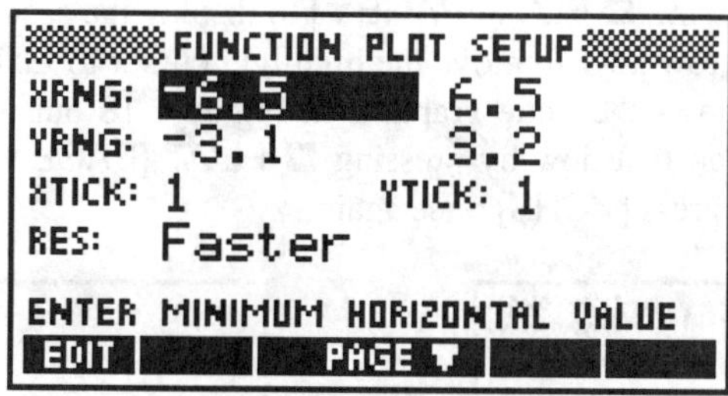

Figure 7.14: FUNCTION PLOT SETUP

Following XRNG are the minimum and maximum *x*-values of the viewing rectangle; after YRNG are its minimum and maximum *y*-values.

XTICK and YTICK set the spacing between tick marks on the axes.

Use arrow keys to move around this list; enter a new value and press ENTER or [OK] to move along to the next item. You may also press [EDIT] to edit a highlighted entry as you would edit an expression in the home screen. Remember to use the -x key, not - (which is subtraction), when you want to enter a negative value. Figures 7.13-14, 7.15-16, and 7.17-18 show different plots and the corresponding viewing rectangle for each one.

To set the range quickly to standard values (see Figure 7.14), press ◻ CLEAR when you are in FUNCTION PLOT SETUP. To set the viewing rectangle quickly to a square (Figure 7.15), press ZOOM 5. More information about square windows is presented later in Section 7.2.3.

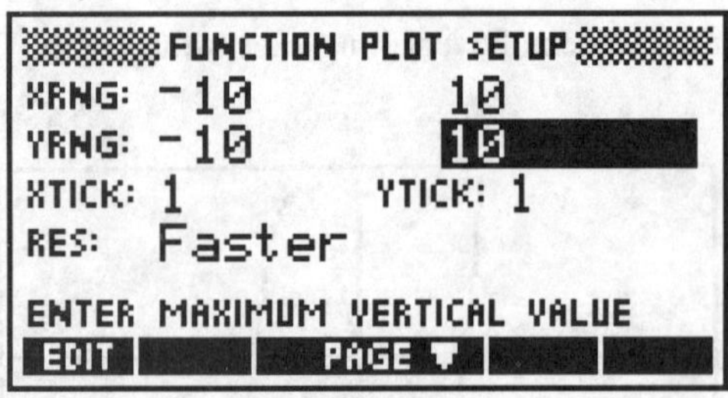

Figure 7.15: Custom window

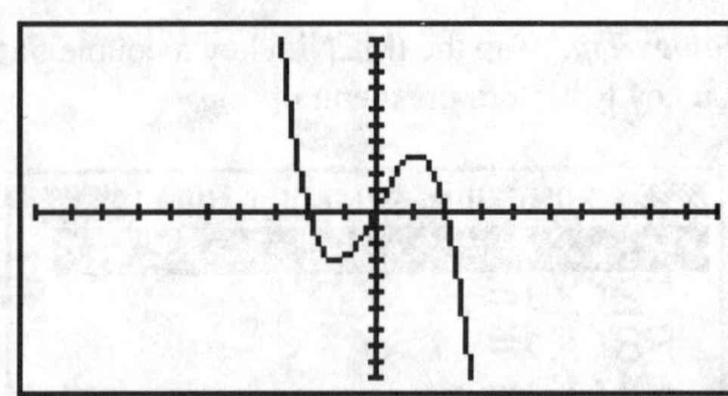

Figure 7.16: Graph of $y = -x^3 + 4x$

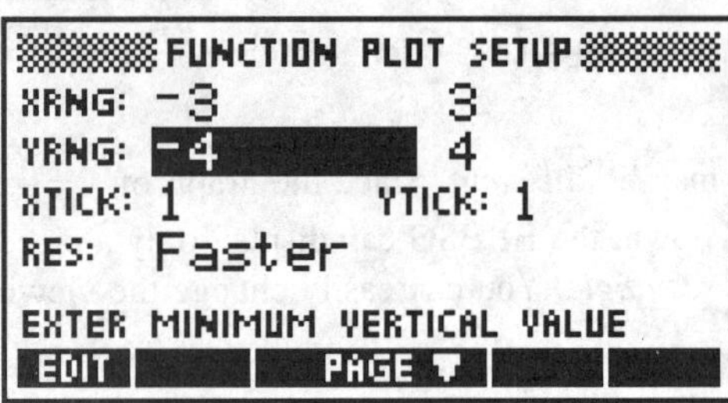

Figure 7.17: Custom window

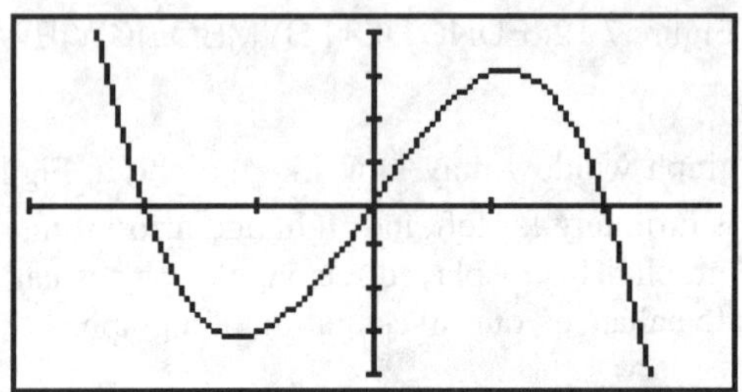

Figure 7.18: Graph of $y = -x^3 + 4x$

Sometimes you may wish to display grid points corresponding to tick marks on the axes. This and other graph format options may be changed by pressing ▣ PLOT [PAGE▼] to display the second page of the FUNCTION PLOT SETUP menu (Figure 7.19). Use arrow keys to move the highlight cursor to GRID and press [✓CHK]; then PLOT to redraw the graph. Figure 7.20 shows the same graph as in Figure 7.18 but with the grid turned on. In general, you'll want the grid turned *off*, so do that now by pressing ▣ PLOT [PAGE▼], use the arrow keys to move the highlight cursor back to GRID, and press [✓CHK] once again.

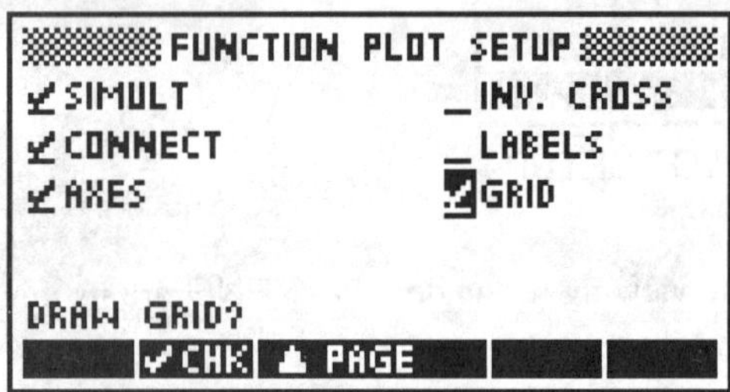

Figure 7.19: FUNCTION PLOT SETUP

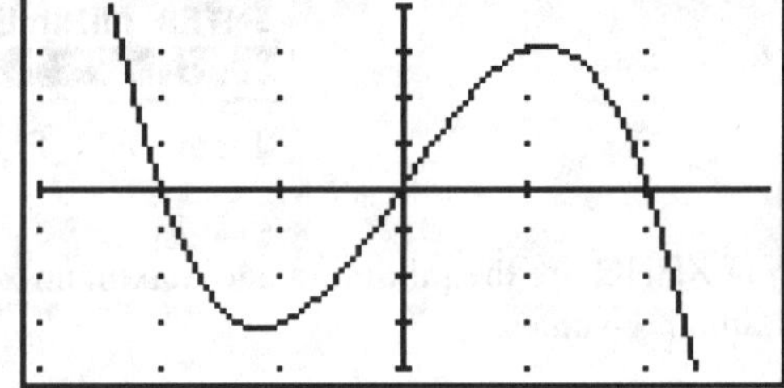

Figure 7.20: Grid turned on for $y = -x^3 + 4x$

7.2.3 Graphing a Circle: Here is a useful technique for graphs that are not functions, but that can be "split" into a top part and a bottom part, or into multiple parts. Suppose you wish to graph the circle whose equation is $x^2 + y^2 = 36$. First solve for y and get an equation for the top semicircle, $y = \sqrt{36 - x^2}$, and for the bottom semicircle, $y = -\sqrt{36 - x^2}$. Then graph the two semicircles simultaneously.

The keystrokes to draw this circle's graph, assuming you have already started the HP 38G's FUNCTION aplet, follow. Press SYMB and enter $\sqrt{36 - x^2}$ as F1 and $-\sqrt{36 - x^2}$ as F2 (see Figure 7.21) by moving the highlight to F1 and pressing ▣ CLEAR [YES] √x (36 - X,T,θ ▣ x²) ENTER -x √x (36 - X,T,θ ▣ x²) ENTER. Then press PLOT to draw them both.

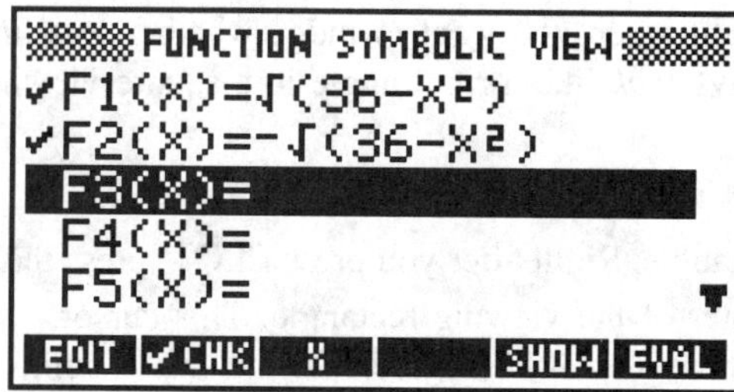

Figure 7.21: Two semicircles

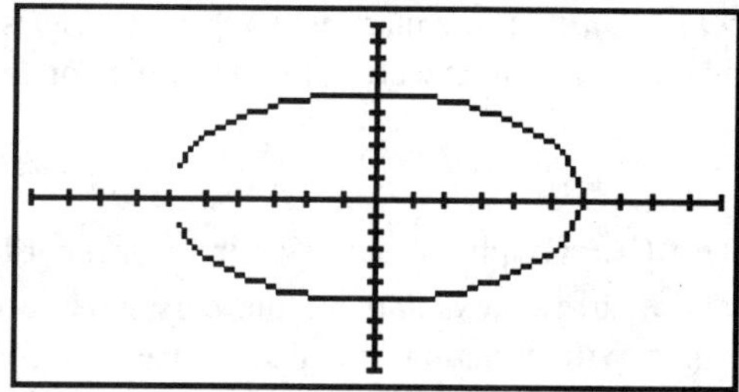

Figure 7.22: Circle's graph - one view

If your range were set to a viewing rectangle extending from -10 to 10 in both directions, your graph would look like Figure 7.22. Now this does *not* look like a circle, because the units along the axes are not the same. You need what is called a "square" viewing rectangle.

The HP 38G's standard viewing rectangle is square, but too small to display a circle of radius 6. So double the dimensions of the standard window and change it to extend horizontally from -13 to 13 and vertically from -6.2 to 6.2.

Technology Tip: Another way to get a square graph is to change the range variables so that the value of Ymax - Ymin is approximately $\frac{1}{2}$ times Xmax - Xmin. For example, see the viewing rectangle in Figure 7.23 and the corresponding graph in Figure 7.24. The method works because the dimensions of the HP 38G's display are such that the ratio of vertical to horizontal is approximately $\frac{1}{2}$.

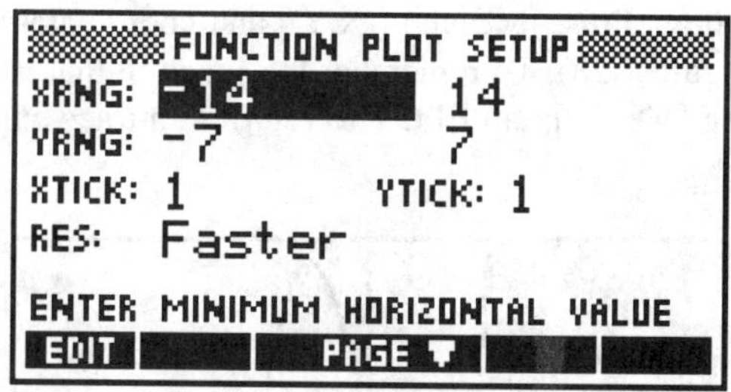

Figure 7.23: $\frac{\text{vertical}}{\text{horizontal}} = \frac{14}{28} = \frac{1}{2}$

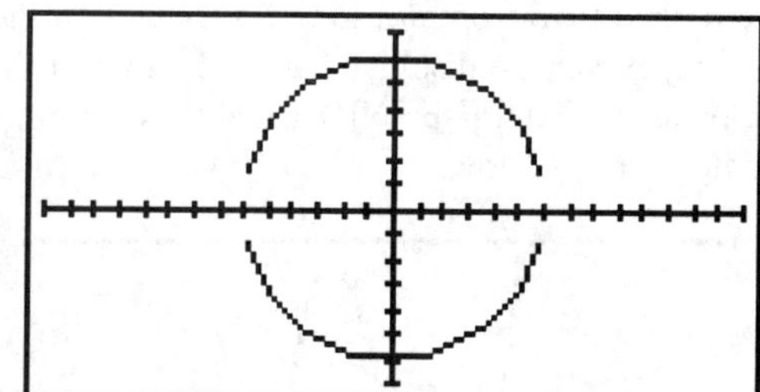

Figure 7.24: A "square" circle

The two semicircles in Figure 7.24 do not meet because of an idiosyncrasy in the way the HP 38G plots a graph.

Back when you entered $\sqrt{36 - x^2}$ as F1 and $-\sqrt{36 - x^2}$ as F2, you could have entered -F1 as F2 and saved some keystrokes. Try this by going back to the SYMB menu and pressing the arrow key to move the cursor down to F2. Then press DEL -x A...Z F 1 ([X]) ENTER. The graph should be just as it was before.

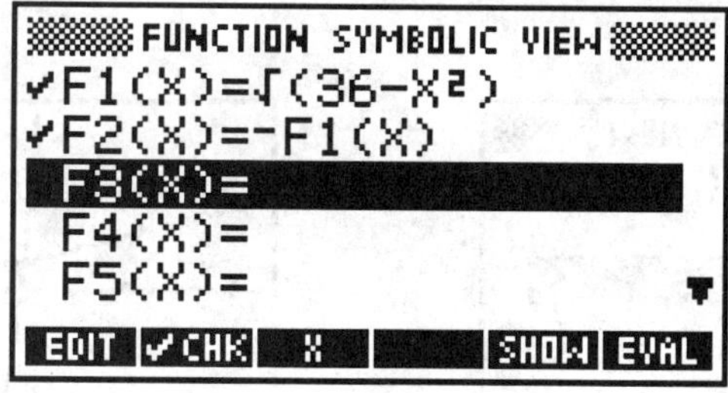

Figure 7.25: -F1 as F2

Technology Tip: The square viewing rectangle is also important when you want to judge whether two lines are perpendicular. The intersection of perpendicular lines will always *look* like a right angle in a square viewing rectangle.

7.2.4 TRACE: Graph $y = -x^3 + 4x$ in the standard viewing rectangle. Right after you press PLOT, press the left ◄ and right ► arrow keys and see the cursor move from the center of the viewing rectangle. This cursor, which is constrained to the function, is called a trace. The coordinates that are displayed (Figure 7.26) belong to points on the function's graph, so the y-coordinate is the calculated value of the function at the corresponding x-coordinate..

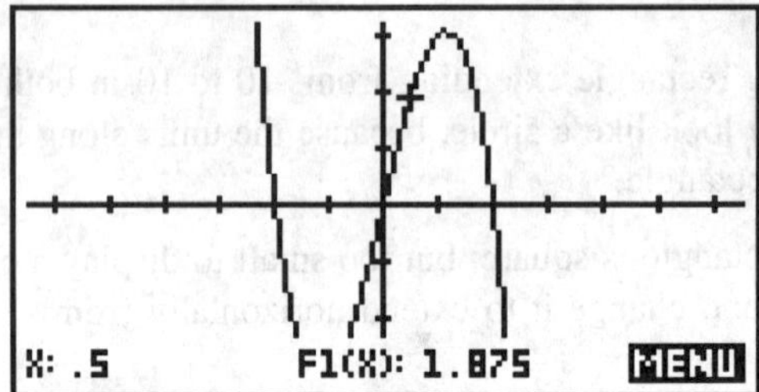

Figure 7.26: Trace on $y = -x^3 + 4x$

Press [MENU] to display various options for exploring this graph (Figure 7.27). Tap [TRACE] to toggle the trace on and off. When trace is off, use any of the arrow keys ▲ ▼ ◄ ► to move the cursor, called a *free-moving cursor* because it can move from dot to dot *anywhere* in the graph window. Press [MENU] [(X,Y)] and coordinates of the free-moving cursor are displayed at the bottom of the screen (Figure 7.28). To remember the function that is being plotted, press [MENU] [DEFN]. Cancel these options by pressing [MENU]; tap PLOT to return to a trace cursor at the middle of the window.

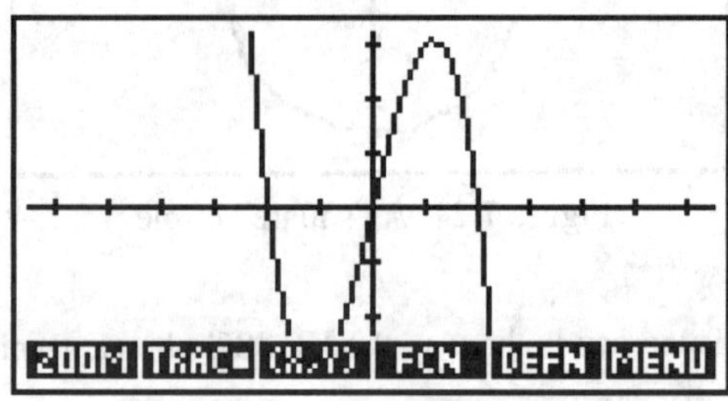

Figure 7.27: PLOT MENU

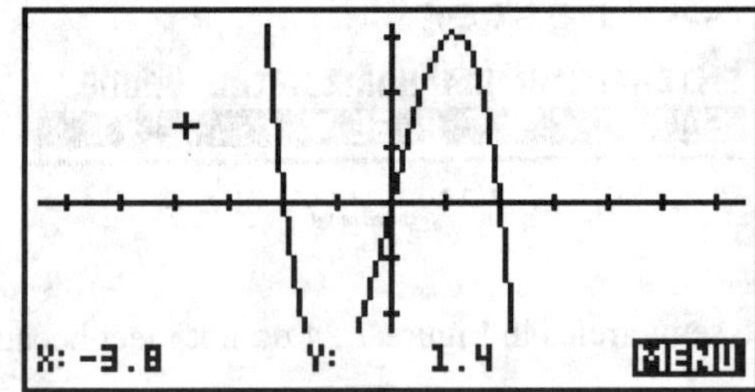

Figure 7.28: Free-moving cursor

Now plot a second function, $y = -.25x$, along with $y = -x^3 + 4x$. Press SYMB and enter $-.25x$ for F2, then press PLOT.

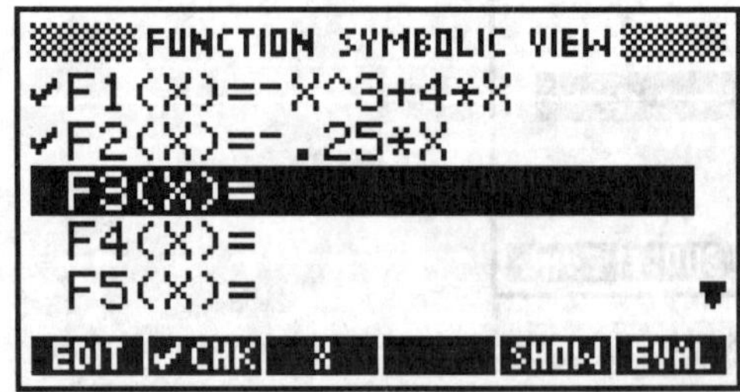

Figure 7.29: Two functions

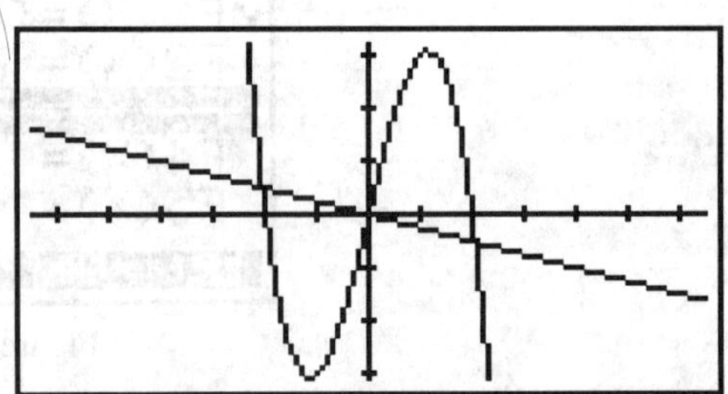

Figure 7.30: $y = -x^3 + 4x$ and $y = -.25x$

HP 38G Graphing Calculator

Note in Figure 7.29 that there are check marks to the left of *both* F1 and F2. This means *both* functions will be graphed. Press SYMB for SYMBOLIC FUNCTION VIEW, move the highlight onto F1, and press [✓CHK]. There should no longer be a check mark (see Figure 7.31). Now press PLOT and see that only F2 is plotted (Figure 7.32).

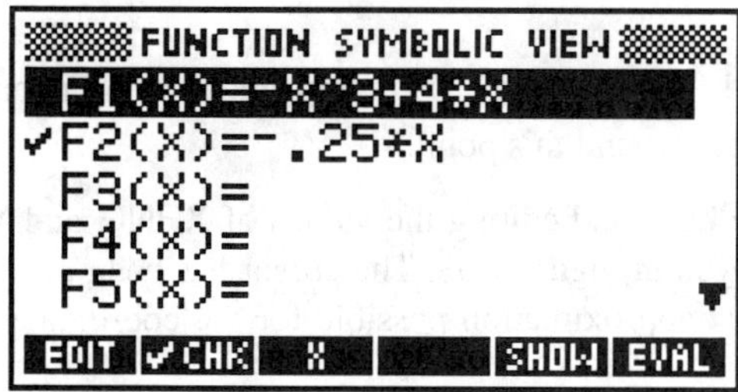

Figure 7.31: Only F2 active

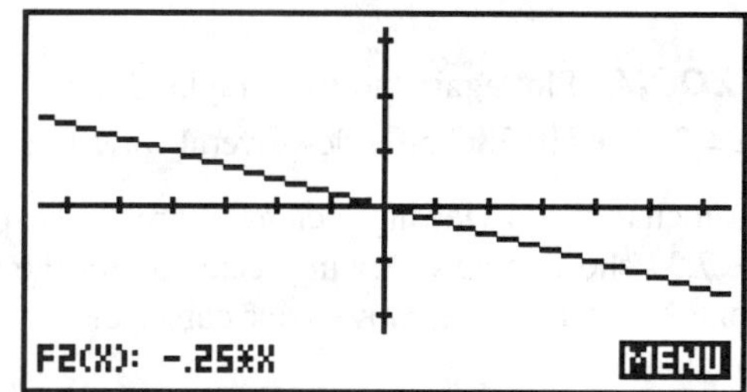

Figure 7.32: Graph of $y = -.25x$

Many different functions may be stored in the SYMBOLIC FUNCTION VIEW list and any combination of them may be graphed simultaneously. You can make a highlighted function active or inactive for graphing by pressing [✓CHK] to add a check (activate) or remove a check (deactivate). Go back to the SYMBOLIC FUNCTION VIEW and do what is needed in order to graph F1 but not F2.

Now activate F2 again so that both graphs are plotted. Press PLOT and the trace cursor appears first on the graph of $y = -x^3 + 4x$ because it is higher up in the SYMBOLIC FUNCTION VIEW list. You know that the cursor is on this function, F1, because F1(X) is displayed in the bottom of the window (see Figure 7.26). Press the up ▲ or down ▼ arrow key to move the cursor vertically to the graph of $y = -.25x$. Now F2(X) is displayed in the bottom line of the window. Next press the right and left arrow keys to trace along the graph of $y = -.25x$. When more than one function is plotted, you can move the trace cursor vertically from one graph to another in this way.

Technology Tip: By the way, trace along the graph of $y = -.25x$ and press and hold either ◄ or ►. Eventually you will reach the left or right edge of the window. Keep pressing the arrow key and the HP 38G will allow you to continue the trace by panning the viewing rectangle. Check FUNCTION PLOT SETUP (press ▢ PLOT) to see that XRNG is automatically updated.

Technology Tip: Jump quickly to the left-most point (or to the right-most point) of a function in the current view by pressing ▢ ◄ (or ▢ ►) while tracing on its graph.

The HP 38G's display has 131 horizontal columns of pixels and 64 vertical rows. So when you trace a curve across a graph window, you are actually moving from Xmin to Xmax in 130 equal jumps, each called Δx. You would calculate the size of each jump to be $\Delta x = \dfrac{Xmax - Xmin}{130}$. Sometimes you may want the jumps to be friendly numbers like .1 or .25 so that, when you trace along the curve, the x-coordinates will be incremented by such a convenient amount. Just set your viewing rectangle for a particular increment Δx by making Xmax = Xmin + 130·Δx. For example, if you want Xmin = -20 and Δx = .3, set Xmax = -20 + 130·.3 = 19. Likewise, set Ymax = Ymin + 63·Δy if you want the vertical increment to be some special Δy.

To center your window around a particular point, say (h, k), and also have a certain Δx, set Xmin = h - 65·Δx and Xmax = h + 65·Δx. Likewise, make Ymin = k - 31·Δy and Ymax = k + 32·Δy. For example, to center a window around the origin, (0, 0), with both horizontal and vertical increments of .25, set the range so that Xmin = 0 - 65·.25 = -16.25, Xmax = 0 + 65·.25 = 16.25, Ymin = 0 - 31·.25 = -7.75, and Ymax = 0 + 32·.25 = 8.

See the benefit by first plotting $y = x^2 + 2x + 1$ in a window that extends from -10 to 10 in both directions. Trace near its y-intercept, which is (0, 1), and move towards its x-intercept, which is (-1, 0). Then initialize the viewing rectangle to the standard window and trace again near the intercepts.

7.2.5 *ZOOM*: Plot again the two graphs, for $y = -x^3 + 4x$ and for $y = -.25x$. There appears to be an intersection near $x = 2$. The HP 38G provides several ways to enlarge the view around this point.

You can change the viewing rectangle directly by pressing ◻ PLOT and editing the values of XRNG and YRNG. Figure 7.34 shows a new viewing rectangle for the range displayed in Figure 7.33. The cursor has been moved near the point of intersection; move your cursor closer to get the best approximation possible for the coordinates of the intersection.

Figure 7.33: New window

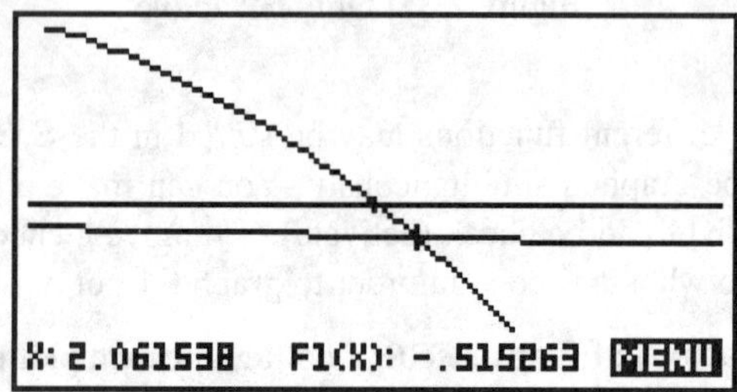

Figure 7.34: Closer view

A more efficient method for enlarging the view is to draw a new viewing rectangle with the cursor. Start again with a graph of the two functions $y = -x^3 + 4x$ and $y = -.25x$ in a standard viewing rectangle (press ◻ PLOT ◻ CLEAR for the standard window, from -6.5 to 6.5 horizontally and from -3.1 to 3.2 vertically).

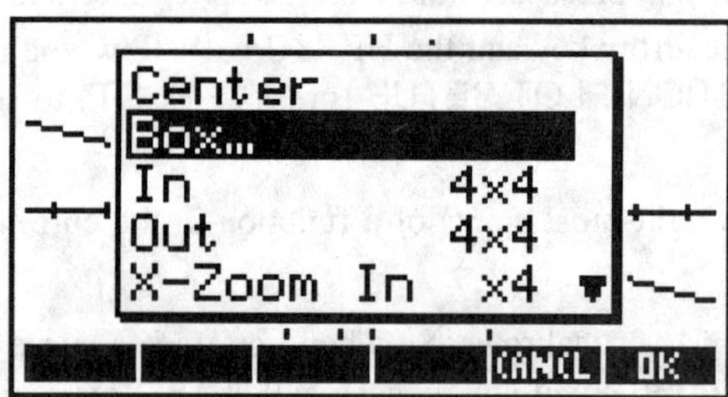

Figure 7.35: Zoom menu

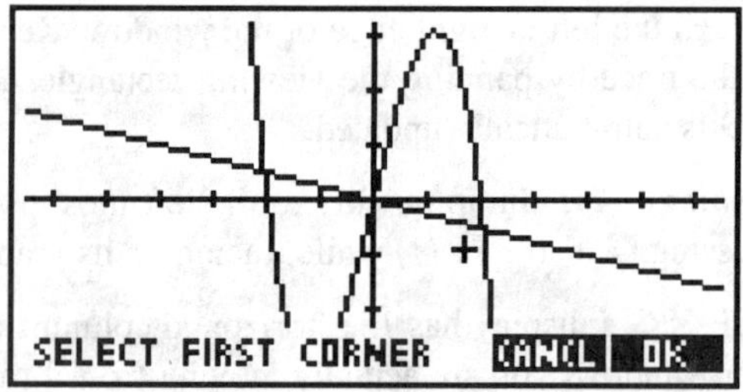

Figure 7.36: One corner selected

Now imagine a small rectangular box around the intersection point, near $x = 2$. Press [MENU] [ZOOM] ▼ [OK] (Figure 7.35) to draw a box to define this new viewing rectangle. Use the arrow keys to move the trace to one corner of the new viewing rectangle you imagine (Figure 7.36).

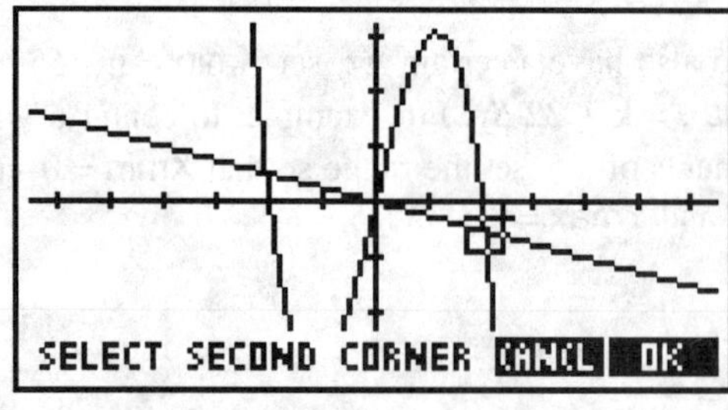

Figure 7.37: Box drawn

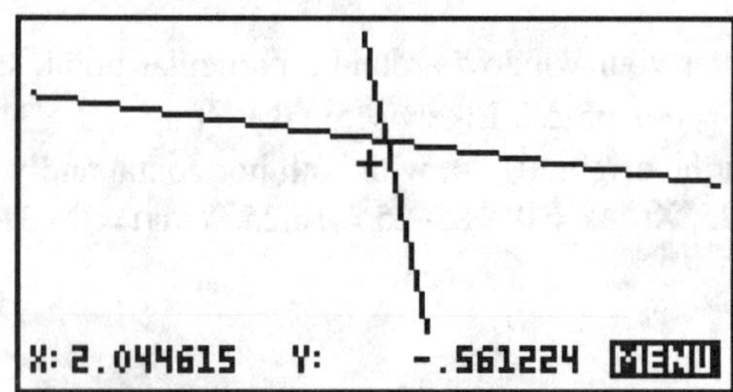

Figure 7.38: New viewing rectangle

HP 38G Graphing Calculator

Press [OK] or ENTER to fix the corner where you have moved the cursor. Use the arrow keys again to move the cursor to the diagonally opposite corner of the new rectangle (Figure 7.37). If this box looks all right to you, press [OK]. The rectangular area you have enclosed will now enlarge to fill the graph window (Figure 7.38).

You may interrupt the zoom any time *before* you press this last [OK]. Press ON and start over.

You can also gain a quick magnification of the graph around the cursor's location. Return once more to the standard window for the graph of the two functions $y = -x^3 + 4x$ and $y = -.25x$. Next use arrow keys to move the cursor as close as you can to the point of intersection near $x = 2$ (see Figure 7.39). Press [MENU] [ZOOM] ▼ ▼ [OK] and the calculator draws a magnified graph, centered at the cursor's position (Figure 7.40). The range values are changed to reflect this new viewing rectangle. Look in FUNCTION PLOT SETUP to verify this.

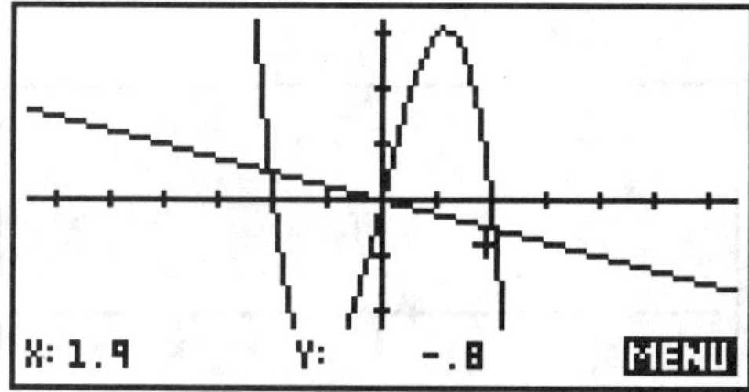

Figure 7.39: Before a zoom in

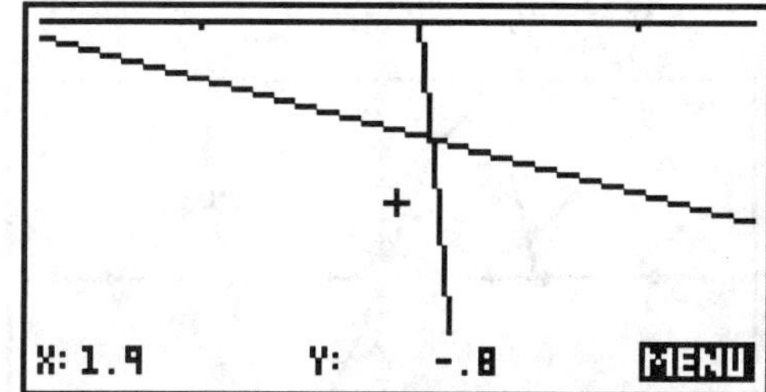

Figure 7.40: After a zoom in

As you see in the zoom menu (Figure 7.35), the HP 38G can zoom In or zoom Out. Zoom out to see a larger view of the graph, centered at the cursor position. You can change the horizontal and vertical scale of the magnification by pressing [ZOOM] and moving the highlight up or down to Set Factors... (see Figure 7.41). Press [OK] and edit XZOOM and YZOOM, the horizontal and vertical magnification factors.

The default zoom factor is 4 in both directions. It is not necessary for XZOOM and YZOOM to be equal. Sometimes, you may prefer to zoom in one direction only. In that case, choose X-Zoom In or X-Zoom Out or Y-Zoom In or Y-Zoom Out from the zoom menu. As usual, press [CANCL] to leave the ZOOM menu and take no action.

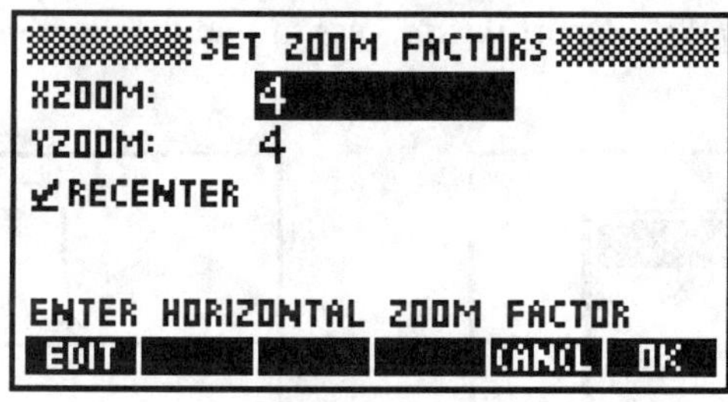

Figure 7.41: SET ZOOM FACTORS

Technology Tip: The HP 38G remembers the window it displayed before a zoom. So if you should zoom in too much and lose the curve, press [ZOOM] ▲ [OK] to Un-zoom and go back to the window before. Also, you may wish to use [ZOOM] and then the Square option to make a viewing rectangle in which the vertical scale matches the horizontal scale. This would be helpful if you want to graph the two halves of a circle, as in Section 7.2.3.

Technology Tip: The HP 38G can automatically find the necessary *vertical* range for a function. For auto scaling, press ◻ VIEWS and select Auto Scale. Take care, because sometimes when you are graphing two functions together, the calculator will auto scale for one function in such a way that the other function will no longer be visible.

For example, plot the two functions $y = -x^3 + 4x$ and $y = -.25x$ in the HP 38G's standard viewing rectangle, then auto scale and trace along both functions.

7.3   Solving Equations and Inequalities

7.3.1 Intercepts and Intersections: Tracing and zooming are also used to locate an *x*-intercept of a graph, where a curve crosses the *x*-axis. For example, the graph of $y = x^3 - 8x$ crosses the *x*-axis three times (see Figure 7.42). After tracing over to the *x*-intercept point that is furthest to the left, zoom in (Figure 7.43). Continue this process until you have located all three intercepts with as much accuracy as you need. The three *x*-intercepts of $y = x^3 - 8x$ are approximately -2.828, 0, and 2.828.

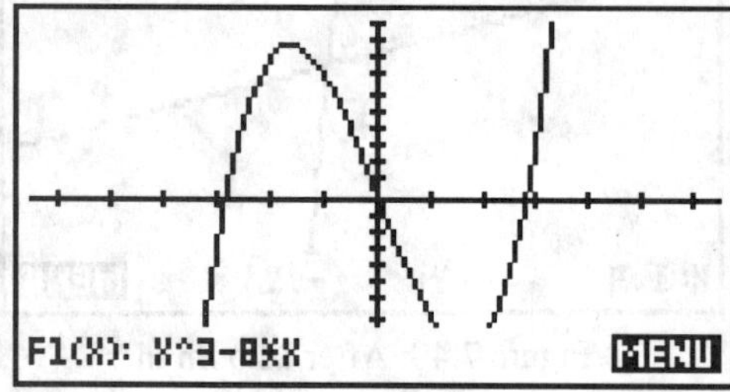

Figure 7.42: Graph of $y = x^3 - 8x$

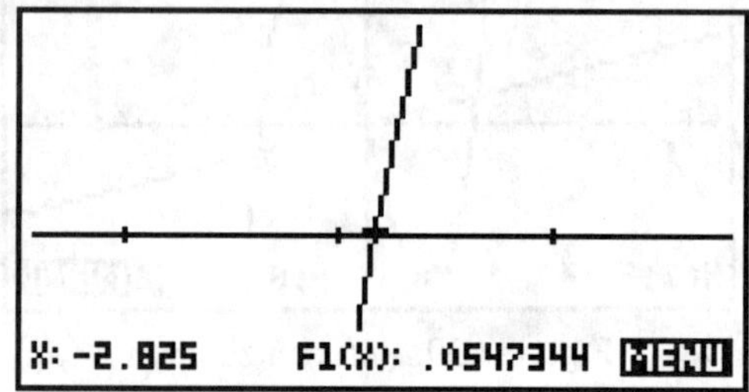

Figure 7.43: An *x*-intercept of $y = x^3 - 8x$

Technology Tip: As you zoom in, you may also wish to change the spacing between tick marks on the *x*-axis so that the viewing rectangle shows scale marks near the intercept point. Then the accuracy of your approximation will be such that the error is less than the distance between two tick marks. Change the *x*-scale on the HP 38G from the FUNCTION PLOT SETUP menu. Move the highlight down to XTICK and enter an appropriate value.

The *x*-intercept of a function's graph is a *root* of the equation $f(x) = 0$. And the HP 38G automates the search for roots. First trace along the graph to a point close to a root. Then press [MENU] [FCN] [OK] and the coordinates of a root will be displayed (see Figure 7.45). Repeat this process to find the coordinates of any other root the function may have.

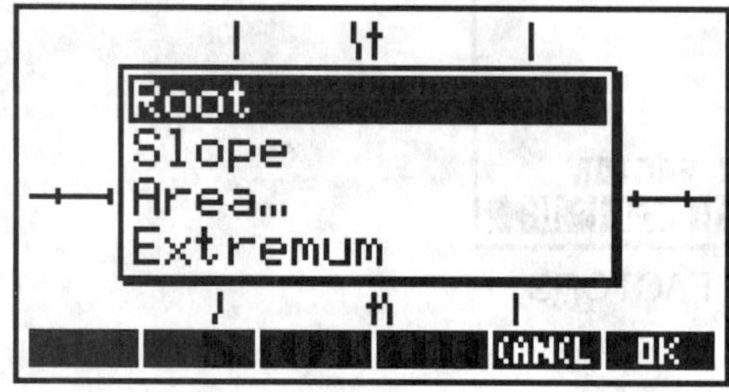

Figure 7.44: Root option

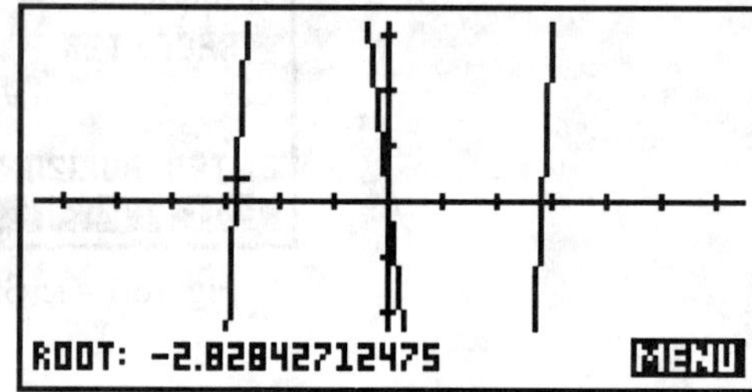

Figure 7.45: A root of $y = x^3 - 8x$

TRACE and ZOOM are especially important for locating the intersection points of two graphs, say the graphs of $y = -x^3 + 4x$ and $y = -.25x$. Trace along one of the graphs until you arrive close to an intersection point. Then press ▲ or ▼ to jump to the other graph. Notice that the *x*-coordinate does not change, but the *y*-coordinate is likely to be different (see Figures 7.46 and 7.47).

HP 38G Graphing Calculator

When the two *y*-coordinates are as close as they can get, you have come as close as you now can to the point of intersection. So zoom in around the intersection point, then trace again until the two *y*-coordinates are as close as possible. Continue this process until you have located the point of intersection with as much accuracy as necessary.

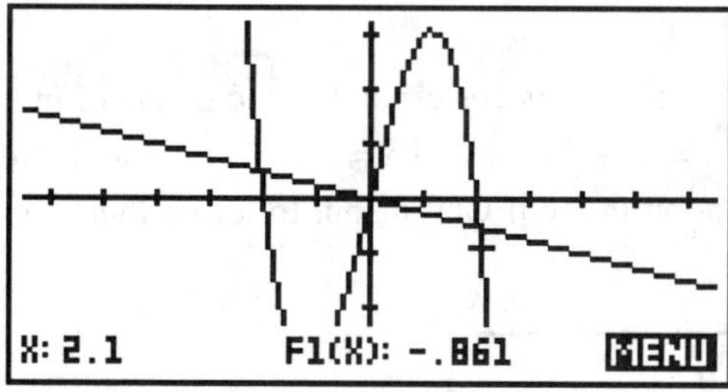

Figure 7.46: Trace on $y = -x^3 + 4x$

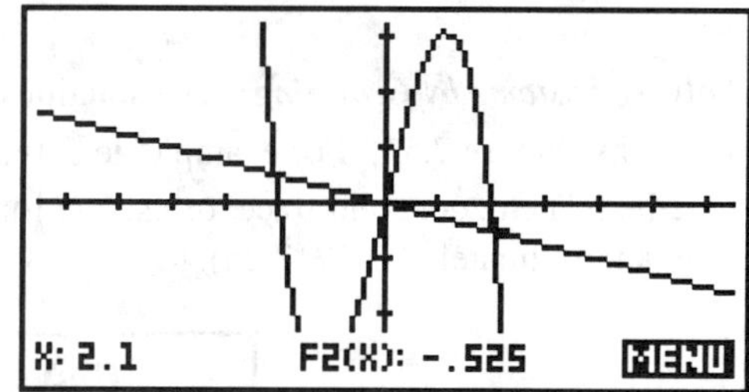

Figure 7.47: Trace on $y = -.25x$

You can also find the point of intersection of two graphs automatically. Trace along one graph near the intersection. Then press [MENU] [FCN] ▼ [OK] (see Figure 7.48). Move the highlight, if necessary, to the name of the second function (Figure 7.49) and press [OK]. Coordinates of the intersection will be displayed at the bottom of the window (Figure 7.50).

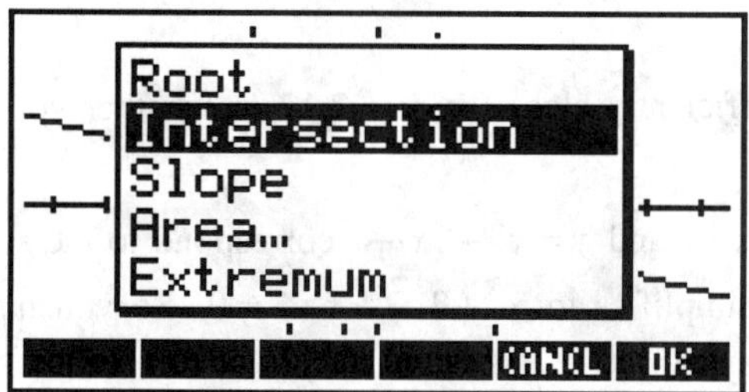

Figure 7.48: Intersection option

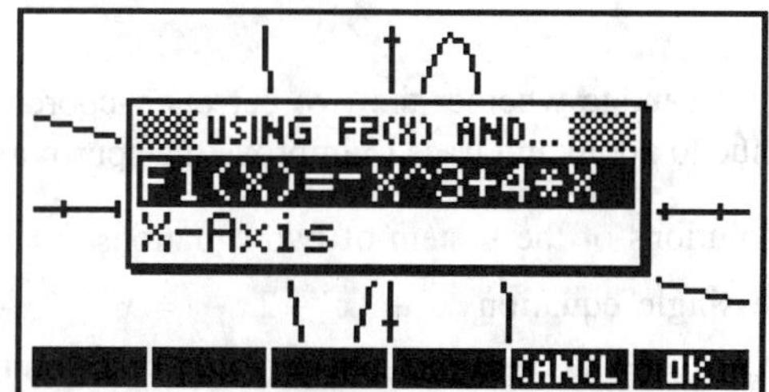

Figure 7.49: Choosing the second function

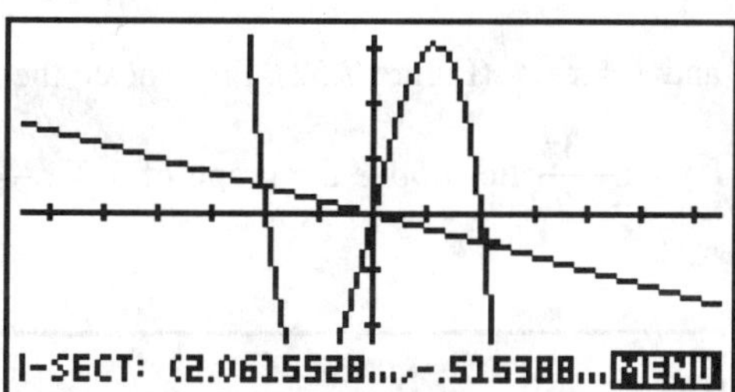

Figure 7.50: Intersection of $y = -x^3 + 4x$ and $y = -.25x$

7.3.2 Solving Equations by Graphing: Suppose you need to solve the equation $24x^3 - 36x + 17 = 0$. First graph $y = 24x^3 - 36x + 17$ in a window large enough to exhibit *all* its *x*-intercepts, corresponding to all the equation's roots. Then use trace and zoom, or the HP 38G's root finder, to locate each one. In fact, this equation has just one solution, approximately $x = -1.414$.

Remember that when an equation has more than one root, it may be necessary to change the viewing rectangle a few times to locate all of them.

Technology Tip: To solve an equation like $24x^3 + 17 = 36x$, you may first transform it into standard form, $24x^3 - 36x + 17 = 0$, and proceed as above. However, you may also graph the *two* functions $y = 24x^3 + 17$ and $y = 36x$, then zoom and trace to locate their point of intersection.

7.3.3 Solving Systems by Graphing: The solutions to a system of equations correspond to the points of intersection of their graphs (Figure 7.51). For example, to solve the system $y = x^2 - 3x - 4$ and $y = x^3 + 3x^2 - 2x - 1$, first graph them together. Then zoom and trace, or use the Intersection option in the [FCN] menu, to locate their point of intersection, approximately (-2.17, 7.25).

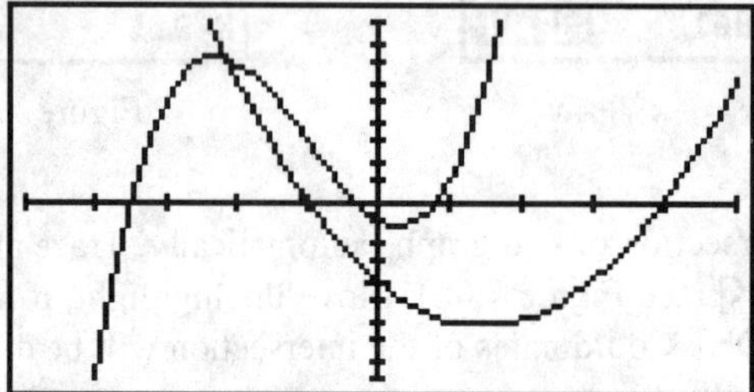

Figure 7.51: Solving a system of equations

You must judge whether the two current y-coordinates are sufficiently close for $x = $ -2.17 or whether you should continue to zoom and trace to improve the approximation.

The solutions of the system of two equations $y = x^3 + 3x^2 - 2x - 1$ and $y = x^2 - 3x - 4$ correspond to the solutions of the single equation $x^3 + 3x^2 - 2x - 1 = x^2 - 3x - 4$, which simplifies to $x^3 + 2x^2 + x + 3 = 0$. So you may also graph $y = x^3 + 2x^2 + x + 3$ and find its x-intercepts to solve the system.

7.3.4 Solving Inequalities by Graphing: Consider the inequality $1 - \dfrac{3x}{2} \geq x - 4$. To solve it with your HP 38G, graph the two functions $y = 1 - \dfrac{3x}{2}$ and $y = x - 4$ (Figure 7.52). First locate their point of intersection, at $x = 2$. The inequality is true when the graph of $y = 1 - \dfrac{3x}{2}$ lies *above* the graph of $y = x - 4$, and that occurs for $x < 2$. So the solution is the half-line $x \leq 2$, or $(-\infty, 2]$.

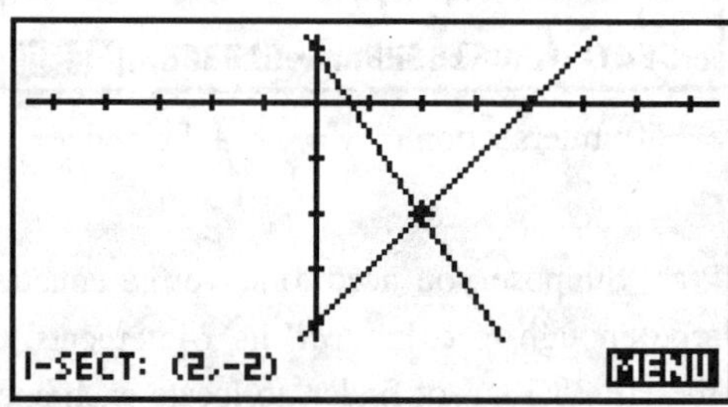

Figure 7.52: Solving $1 - \dfrac{3x}{2} \geq x - 4$

7.4   Matrices

7.4.1 Making a Matrix: The HP 38G can display and use ten different matrices. Here's how to create this 3×4 matrix $\begin{bmatrix} 1 & -4 & 3 & 5 \\ -1 & 3 & -1 & -3 \\ 2 & 0 & -4 & 6 \end{bmatrix}$ in your calculator.

Press ◻ MATRIX to see the MATRIX CATALOG (Figure 7.53).

Technology Tip: To delete a single matrix, move the highlight there and press DEL; to delete every matrix in the catalog, press ◻ CLEAR. To move quickly to the *first* matrix (which may be out of view), press ◻ ▲; to jump down to the *last* matrix, press ◻ ▼.

Figure 7.53: MATRIX CATALOG

Figure 7.54: CREATE NEW matrix

Move the highlight to M1 and press [NEW] to create a new matrix with that name. Make this a Real matrix because all its elements are real numbers.

Tap [GO] until [GO→] is displayed so that the highlight will move automatically to the right after each entry. Input the top row by pressing 1 ENTER -x 4 ENTER 3 ENTER 5 ENTER. Now press ▼ to move down to the second row and back to the first column, then press -x 1 ENTER 3 ENTER -x 1 ENTER -x 3 ENTER 2 ENTER 0 ENTER -x 4 ENTER 6 ENTER to finish creating this matrix.

Technology Tip: You may delete any row (or column) by moving the highlight into that row (or column) and pressing DEL. Insert a row above (or a column to the left) of the highlight by pressing [INS].

Press ◻ MATRIX again and see that matrix M1 is now listed as a 3×4 real matrix. If you wish to change matrix M1, press [EDIT] and use the arrow keys to move directly to any element.

7.4.2 Row Operations: The HP 38G does not have row operations built-in.

7.4.3 Determinants: Enter this 3×3 square matrix as M1: $\begin{bmatrix} 1 & -2 & 3 \\ -1 & 3 & 0 \\ 2 & -5 & 5 \end{bmatrix}$. To calculate its determinant,

$\begin{Vmatrix} 1 & -2 & 3 \\ -1 & 3 & 0 \\ 2 & -5 & 5 \end{Vmatrix}$, move to the home screen and press down A...Z while tapping D E T. Continue with (A...Z M 1) ENTER. You should find that $|M_1| = 2$.

Figure 7.55: Determinant

You may also start by pressing MATH, then moving up to Matrix and right to DET.

7.5   Additional Topics

7.5.1 Iteration: The Ans feature enables you to perform iterations to evaluate a function repeatedly. As an example, calculate $\dfrac{n-1}{3}$ for $n = 27$. Then calculate $\dfrac{n-1}{3}$ for $n =$ the answer to the previous calculation. Continue to use each answer as n in the *next* calculation. Here are keystrokes to accomplish this iteration on the HP 38G calculator (see the results in Figure 7.56). Notice that when you use Ans in place of n in a formula, it is sufficient to press ENTER to continue an iteration.

Iteration	*Keystrokes*	*Display*
1	27 ENTER	27
2	(◻ ANSWER - 1) / 3 ENTER	8.66666666667
3	ENTER	2.55555555556
4	ENTER	.51851851852
5	ENTER	-.16049382716

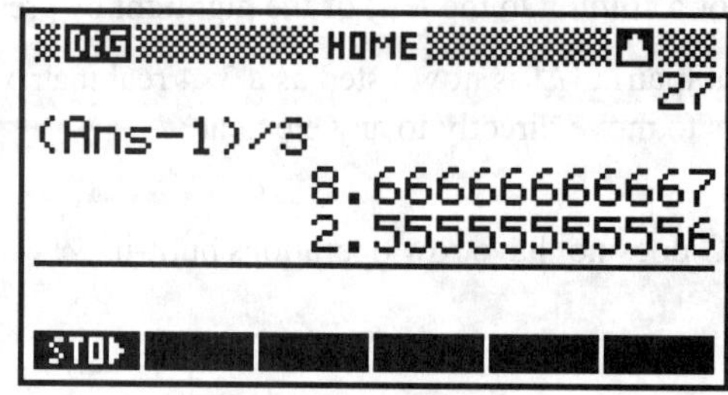

Figure 7.56: Iteration

Press ENTER several more times and see what happens with this iteration. You may wish to try it again with a different starting value.

7.5.2 Arithmetic and Geometric Sequences: Use iteration with the Ans variable to determine the n-th term of a sequence. For example, find the 18th term of an *arithmetic* sequence whose first term is 7 and whose common difference is 4. Set the first term by pressing 7 ENTER; then start the progression with the recursion formula, ◻

ANSWER + 4 ENTER. This yields the 2nd term, so press ENTER sixteen more times to find the 18th term. For a *geometric* sequence whose common ratio is 4, start the progression with ☐ ANSWER × 4 ENTER.

You can also define the sequence recursively with the HP 38G by pressing LIB and starting Sequence in the APLET LIBRARY (see Figure 7.7). Once again, let's find the 18th term of an *arithmetic* sequence whose first term is 7 and whose common difference is 4. You need to enter the first *two* terms and a formula for the *n*-th term. For the sequence U1, set the first term $u_1 = 7$ and the second term $u_2 = 11$ (Figure 7.57). Make $u_n = u_{n-1} + 4$ by moving the highlight to U1(N) and pressing [U1] [(N-1)] + 4 [OK]. Now press NUM to leave this menu and go to a numerical table. To find the 18th term u_{18} of this sequence, either scroll to the line where $n = 18$ or else enter 18 directly into the first column (see Figure 7.58).

Technology Tip: Up to ten different sequences may be entered in SEQUENCE SYMBOLIC VIEW. To move quickly to the *first* sequence (which may be out of view), press ☐ ▲; to jump down to the *last* sequence, press ☐ ▼.

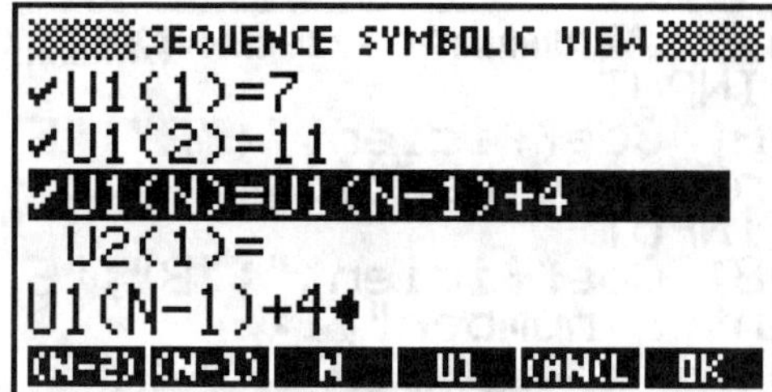

Figure 7.57: SEQUENCE SYMBOLIC VIEW

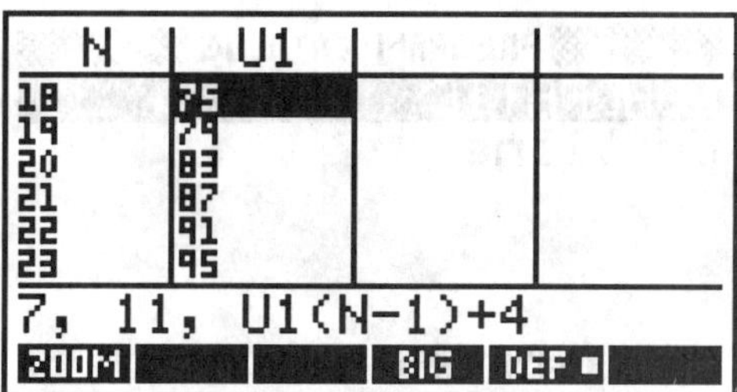

Figure 7.58: Sequence table

Technology Tip: While you are scrolling through the numerical table, press [DEF] to toggle between displaying the formula (as in Figure 7.59) and the numerical value at the bottom of the window.

Of course, you could use the *explicit* formula for the *n*-th term of an arithmetic sequence, $t_n = a + (n-1)d$. First enter values for the variables *a*, *d*, and *n* in the home screen, then evaluate the formula by pressing A...Z A + (A...Z N - 1) A...Z D ENTER. For a geometric sequence whose *n*-th term is given by $t_n = a \cdot r^{n-1}$, enter values for the variables *a*, *r*, and *n* in the home screen, then evaluate the formula by pressing A...Z A A...Z R ^ (A...Z N - 1) ENTER.

7.5.3 Permutations and Combinations: To calculate the number of *permutations* of 12 objects taken 7 at a time, $_{12}P_7$, press MATH ▲ (to Prob.) ▶ ▼ ▼ [OK] 12 , 7) ENTER. Thus $_{12}P_7 = 3{,}991{,}680$, as shown in Figure 7.59.

For the number of *combinations* of 12 objects taken 7 at a time, $_{12}C_7$, press MATH ▲ (to Prob.) ▶ [OK] 12 , 7) ENTER. So $_{12}C_7 = 792$.

Figure 7.59: $_{12}P_7$ and $_{12}C_7$

7.6   Programming

7.6.1 Entering a Program: The HP 38G is a programmable calculator that can store sequences of commands for later replay. Here's an example to show you how to enter a useful program that solves quadratic equations by the quadratic formula.

Press ◘ PROGRAM to access the PROGRAM CATALOG. The HP 38G has space for many programs, each called by a name you give it. The names of all your programs are listed alphabetically in the PROGRAM CATALOG. Create a new program now, so press [NEW].

Notice in Figure 7.61 that there is now a function key [A...Z] in addition to the calculator's A...Z key. Press [A...Z], which is like pressing CAPS LOCK on a computer keyboard, and then press all the letters you want. Remember to press [A...Z] when you are finished and want to restore keys to their primary functions. To lock in lowercase letters, press ◘ [A...Z]. To unlock from lowercase, press [A...Z] again.

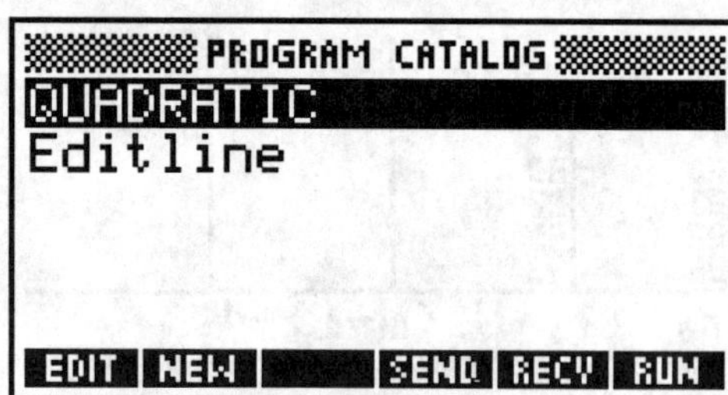

Figure 7.60: PROGRAM CATALOG

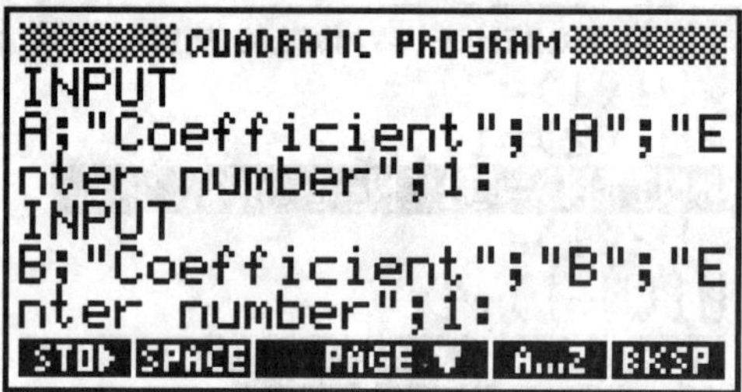

Figure 7.61: QUADRATIC PROGRAM

Enter a descriptive title for this program. To name it Quadratic, press A...Z Q ◘ [A...Z] U A D R A T I C and then [OK] or ENTER to move to the program editor.

Any command you could enter directly in the HP 38G's home screen can be entered as a line in a program. There are also special programming commands.

Some programming commands are obtained by pressing MATH [CMDS], then moving the highlight to a command category, then pressing ▶ and moving the highlight to a specific command. To simplify these directions, we use the notation MATH [CMDS/*category*/*command*] in the program listing below.

You may also type a command directly, instead of searching for it in the PROGRAM COMMANDS. For example, instead of all the keystrokes for MATH [CMDS/*Branch*/*If*] [OK], just press [A...Z] I F [A...Z].

Input the program Quadratic by pressing the keystrokes given in the listing below. Individual program commands are separated by : .You may interrupt program input at any stage. To return later for more editing, press ◘ PROGRAM, move the highlight down to this program's name, and press [EDIT].

Program Line	Keystrokes
INPUT A;"Coefficient";	MATH [CMDS/*Prompt*/*INPUT*] [OK] [SPACE] A...Z A ◘ ;
"A";"Enter number"; 1:	◘ CHARS ▲ [OK] A...Z C ◘ [A...Z] O E F F I C I E N T S [a...z■]
	◘ CHARS ▲ [OK] ◘ ;
	◘ CHARS ▲ [OK] A...Z A ◘ CHARS ▲ [OK] ◘ ;
	◘ CHARS ▲ [OK] A...Z E ◘ [A...Z] N T E R [SPACE]
	N U M B E R [a...z■] ◘ CHARS ▲ [OK] ◘ ; 1 ◘ : ENTER

waits for you to input a value that will be assigned to the variable A

                                     HP 38G Graphing Calculator

INPUT B;"Coefficient";	MATH [CMDS/*Prompt/INPUT*] [OK] [SPACE] A...Z B □ ;
"B";"Enter number";1:	□ CHARS ▲ [OK] A...Z C □ [A...Z] O E F F I C I E N T S [a...z▪]
	□ CHARS ▲ [OK] □ ;
	□ CHARS ▲ [OK] A...Z B □ CHARS ▲ [OK] □ ;
	□ CHARS ▲ [OK] A...Z E □ [A...Z] N T E R [SPACE]
	N U M B E R [a...z▪] □ CHARS ▲ [OK] □ ; 1 □ : ENTER
INPUT C;"Coefficient";	MATH [CMDS/*Prompt/INPUT*] [OK] [SPACE] A...Z C □ ;
"C";"Enter number";1:	□ CHARS ▲ [OK] A...Z C □ [A...Z] O E F F I C I E N T S [a...z▪]
	□ CHARS ▲ [OK] □ ;
	□ CHARS ▲ [OK] A...Z C □ CHARS ▲ [OK] □ ;
	□ CHARS ▲ [OK] A...Z E □ [A...Z] N T E R [SPACE]
	N U M B E R [a...z▪] □ CHARS ▲ [OK] □ ; 1 □ : ENTER
$B^2-4AC \rightarrow D$:	A...Z B □ x^2 - 4 A...Z A A...Z C [STO ▶] A...Z D □ : ENTER

calculates the discriminant and stores its value as D

CASE	MATH [CMDS/*Branch/CASE*] [OK] ENTER

begins a series of tests on the discriminant

IF D>0	MATH [CMDS/*Branch/IF*] [OK] [SPACE]
	A...Z D MATH [MTH/*Tests/>*] [OK] 0 [SPACE]

tests to see if the discriminant is positive

THEN MSGBOX	MATH [CMDS/*Branch/THEN*] [OK] [SPACE]
"Two real roots: "	MATH [CMDS/*Prompt/MSGBOX*] [OK] [SPACE]
(-B+√D)/(2A)", "	□ CHARS ▲ [OK] A...Z T □ [A...Z] W O [SPACE] R E A L
(-B-√D)/(2A): END	[SPACE] R O O T S [a...z▪] □ : [SPACE] □ CHARS ▲ [OK]
	(-x A...Z B + √x A...Z D) / (2 A...Z A)
	□ CHARS ▲ [OK] , [SPACE] □ CHARS ▲ [OK]
	(-x A...Z B - √x A...Z D) / (2 A...Z A) □ : [SPACE]
	MATH [CMDS/*Branch/END*] [OK] ENTER

displays the two real roots

IF D==0	MATH [CMDS/*Branch/IF*] [OK] [SPACE]
	A...Z D MATH [MTH/*Tests/==*] [OK] 0 [SPACE]

tests to see if the discriminant is zero

THEN MSGBOX	MATH [CMDS/*Branch/THEN*] [OK] [SPACE]
"Double root: "	MATH [CMDS/*Prompt/MSGBOX*] [OK] [SPACE]
-B/(2A): END	□ CHARS ▲ [OK] A...Z D □ [A...Z] O U B L E [SPACE]
	R O O T [a...z▪] □ : [SPACE] □ CHARS ▲ [OK]
	-x A...Z B / (2 A...Z A) □ : [SPACE]
	MATH [CMDS/*Branch/END*] [OK] ENTER

displays the double root

IF D<0	MATH [CMDS/*Branch/IF*] [OK] [SPACE]
	A...Z D MATH [MTH/*Tests/<*] [OK] 0 [SPACE]

tests to see if the discriminant is negative

THEN MSGBOX	MATH [CMDS/*Branch*/*THEN*] [OK] [SPACE]
"Complex conjugates: "	MATH [CMDS/*Prompt*/*MSGBOX*] [OK] [SPACE]
-B/(2A)" ± " √-D/(2A)"i":	□ CHARS ▲ [OK] A...Z C □ [A...Z] O M P L E X [SPACE]
END	C O N J U G A T E S [a...z■] □ : [SPACE] □ CHARS ▲ [OK]
	-x A...Z B / (2 A...Z A) □ CHARS ▲ [OK] [SPACE]
	□ CHARS ▶ ▶ ▶ ▶ ▶ ▶ ▶ [OK] [SPACE] □ CHARS ▲ [OK]
	√x -x A...Z D / (2 A...Z A) □ CHARS ▲ [OK]
	[SPACE] □ A...Z I □ CHARS ▲ [OK] □ : [SPACE]
	MATH [CMDS/*Branch*/*END*] [OK] ENTER

> displays the complex roots;
> since $D < 0$, we must use $-D$ as the radicand

| End | MATH [CMDS/*Branch*/*END*] [OK] |

> marks the end of a CASE group of commands

When you have finished, press HOME to leave the program editor.

You may remove a program from memory by pressing □ PROGRAM, then move the highlight to the program's name and press DEL to delete the entire program.

7.6.2 Running a Program: To run the program just entered, press □ PROGRAM, move the highlight to its name, and press [RUN]. Or in the HOME screen, type RUN Quadratic and press ENTER.

The program has been written to prompt you for values of the coefficients a, b, and c in a quadratic equation $ax^2 + bx + c = 0$. Input a value, then press ENTER to continue the program.

If you need to interrupt a program during execution, press ON.

The instruction manual for your HP 38G gives detailed information about programming. Refer to it to learn more about programming and how to use other features of your calculator.

Chapter 8

Sharp EL-9200/9300
Graphing Scientific Calculators

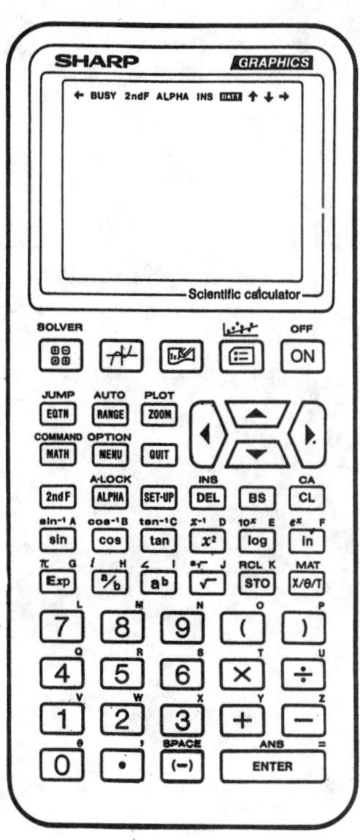

8.1   Getting started with the Sharp EL-9200/9300

8.1.1 Basics: Press the **ON** key to begin using your Sharp EL-9200/9300 calculator. If you need to adjust the display contrast, first press **2ndF** and then press **OPTION**. Next press **+** (the *plus* key) to increase the contrast or **−** (the *minus* key) to decrease the contrast. Leave this menu by pressing **QUIT**. When you have finished with the calculator, turn it off to conserve battery power by pressing **2ndF** and then **OFF**.

Figure 8.1: Operation mode keys

The four keys left of **ON** are used to set the Sharp EL-9200/9300's operation mode: for calculations, graphs, programming, statistics, statistical graphs, and solving equations (EL-9300 only). Press the first mode key, the one with arithmetic operators, for *calculation* mode. You need to press the calculation mode key before performing computations or evaluations.

Check the Sharp EL-9200/9300's settings by pressing **SETUP**. If necessary, use ▲ (the *up* arrow key) or ▼ (the *down* arrow key) to highlight a setting you want to change; you may also jump to a setting by pressing its letter. Next press **ENTER** or ▶ (the *right* arrow key) to move to a sub-menu of options; use an arrow key to move to your choice and press **ENTER** to put it into effect. Once again, you may just jump to an option by pressing its number. To start with, select these options as illustrated in Figure 8.2 by pressing the indicated keys: radian measure, press **B** 2; floating decimal point, press **C** 1; rectangular coordinates, **E** 1; one-line editing, **F** 2; decimal answers, **G** 1. Details on alternative options will be given later in this guide. For now, leave the **SETUP** menu by pressing **QUIT**. You may return to this menu at any time.

Figure 8.2: **SETUP** menu

Now press **MENU 1** for real-number calculation mode.

8.1.2 Editing: One advantage of one-line editing on the Sharp EL-9200/9300 is that up to 8 lines are visible at a time , so you can *see* a long calculation. For example, type this sum (see Figure 8.3):

$$1 + 2 + 3 + 4 + 5 + 6 + 7 + 8 + 9 + 10 + 11 + 12 + 13 + 14 + 15 + 16 + 17 + 18 + 19 + 20$$

Then press **ENTER** to see the answer, too.

Often we do not notice a mistake until we see how unreasonable an answer is. The Sharp EL-9200/9300 permits you to re-display an entire calculation, edit it easily, then execute the *corrected* calculation.

Suppose you had typed 12 + 34 + 56 as in Figure 8.3 but had *not* yet pressed **ENTER**, when you realize that 34 should have been 74. Simply press ◀ (the *left* arrow key) as many times as necessary to move the blinking cursor left to 3, then type 7 to write over it. On the other hand, if 34 should have been 384, move the cursor back to 4, press 2ndF INS (the cursor changes to a blinking arrow) and then type 8 (inserts at the cursor position and other characters are pushed to the right). Press 2ndF INS again to cancel insert mode. If the 34 should have been 3 only, either move the cursor *onto* 4 and press DEL to delete it, or move the cursor just *after* the 4 and press BS to back space over it.

Figure 8.3: Editing expressions

Technology Tip: To move quickly to the *beginning* of an expression you are currently editing, press 2ndF ◀ ; to jump to the *end* of that expression, press 2ndF ▶ .

Even if you had pressed ENTER, you may still edit the previous expression. Press CL and then any arrow key to *recall* the last expression that was entered. Pressing the *up* or *left* arrow key restores the previous expression with the cursor at the *end* of the line; pressing the *down* or *right* arrow key restores the last expression with the cursor at the *beginning* of the line. Now you can change it. In fact, the Sharp EL-9200/9300 retains many prior entries in a "last entry" storage area. Press 2ndF and an arrow key repeatedly to cycle through previous command lines that the calculator has remembered.

Technology Tip: When you need to evaluate a formula for different values of a variable, use the editing feature to simplify the process. For example, suppose you want to find the balance in an investment account if there is now $5000 in the account and interest is compounded annually at the rate of 8.5%. The formula for the balance is $P\left(1+\frac{r}{n}\right)^{nt}$, where P = principal, r = rate of interest (expressed as a decimal), n = number of times interest is compounded each year, and t = number of years. In our example, this becomes $5000(1+.085)^t$. Here are the keystrokes for finding the balance after t = 3, 5, and 10 years.

Years	Keystrokes	Balance
3	CL 5000 (1 + .085) a^b 3 ENTER	$6386.45
5	◀ ◀ 5 ENTER	$7518.28
10	◀ ◀ 10 ENTER	$11,304.92

Then to find the balance from the same initial investment but after 5 years when the annual interest rate is 7.5%, press these keys to change the last calculation above: ◀ ◀ DEL ◀ 5 ◀ ◀ ◀ ◀ ◀ 7 ENTER.

8.1.3 Key Functions: Most keys on the Sharp EL-9200/9300 offer access to more than one function, just as the keys on a computer keyboard can produce more than one letter ("g" and "G") or even quite different characters ("5" and "%"). The primary function of a key is indicated on the key itself, and you access that function by a simple press on the key.

To access the *second* function indicated in *yellow* above a key, first press 2ndF (an indicator appears at the top of the screen) and *then* press the key. For example, to calculate 5^{-1}, press 5 2ndF x⁻¹ ENTER.

When you want to use a letter or other character printed in *blue* above a key, first press ALPHA (another indicator appears at the top of the screen) and then the key. For example, to use the letter K in a formula, press ALPHA K. If

Sharp EL-9200/9300 Graphing Scientific Calculator

you need several letters in a row, press 2ndF A-LOCK, which is like CAPS LOCK on a computer keyboard, and then press all the letters you want. Remember to press ALPHA when you are finished and want to restore the keys to their primary functions.

8.1.4 Order of Operations: The Sharp EL-9200/9300 performs calculations according to the standard algebraic rules. Working outwards from inner parentheses, calculations are performed from left to right. Powers and roots are evaluated first, followed by multiplications and divisions, and then additions and subtractions.

Note that the Sharp EL-9200/9300 distinguishes between *subtraction* and the *negative sign*. If you wish to enter a negative number, it is necessary to use the (-) key. For example, you would evaluate $-5-(4\cdot-3)$ by pressing (-) 5 - (4 × (-) 3) ENTER to get 7.

Enter these expressions to practice using your Sharp EL-9200/9300.

Expression	Keystrokes	Display
$7-5\cdot3$	7 - 5 × 3 ENTER	-8
$(7-5)\cdot3$	(7 - 5) × 3 ENTER	6
$120-10^2$	120 - 10 x² ENTER	20
$(120-10)^2$	(120 - 10) x² ENTER	12100
$\dfrac{24}{2^3}$	24 ÷ 2 aᵇ 3 ENTER	3
$\left(\dfrac{24}{2}\right)^3$	(24 ÷ 2) aᵇ 3 ENTER	1728
$(7--5)\cdot-3$	(7 - (-) 5) × (-) 3 ENTER	-36

8.1.5 Algebraic Expressions and Memory: Your calculator can evaluate expressions such as $\dfrac{N(N+1)}{2}$ *after* you have entered a value for N. Suppose you want $N=200$. Press 200 STO N to store the value 200 in memory location N. (The STO key prepares the Sharp EL-9200/9300 for an alphabetical entry, so it is *not* necessary to press ALPHA also. And there is no need to press ENTER at the end.) Whenever you use N in an expression, the calculator will substitute the value 200 until you make a change by storing *another* number in N. Next enter the expression $\dfrac{N(N+1)}{2}$ by typing ALPHA N (ALPHA N + 1) ÷ 2 ENTER. For $N=200$, you will find that $\dfrac{N(N+1)}{2}=20100$.

The contents of any memory location may be revealed by typing just its letter name and then ENTER. Another way to recall the value of N is to press 2ndF RCL N. And the Sharp EL-9200/9300 retains memorized values even when it is turned off, so long as its batteries are good.

8.1.6 Repeated Operations with ANS: The result of your *last* calculation is always stored in memory location ANS and replaces any previous result. This makes it easy to use the answer from one computation in another computation. For example, press 30 + 15 ENTER so that 45 is the last result displayed. Then press 2ndF ANS ÷ 9 ENTER and get 5 because $\frac{45}{9}=5$.

With a function like division, you press the ÷ key *after* you enter an argument. For such functions, whenever you would start a new calculation with the previous answer followed by pressing the function key, you may press just the function key. So instead of 2ndF ANS ÷ 9 in the previous example, you could have pressed simply ÷ 9 to achieve the same result. This technique also works for these functions: + - × x^2 a^b % 2ndF x^{-1}.

Here is a situation where this is especially useful. Suppose a person makes \$5.85 per hour and you are asked to calculate earnings for a day, a week, and a year. Execute the given keystrokes to find the person's incomes during these periods (results are shown in Figure 8.4):

Pay period	Keystrokes	Earnings
8-hour day	5.85 × 8 ENTER	\$46.80
5-day week	× 5 ENTER	\$234
52-week year	× 52 ENTER	\$12,168

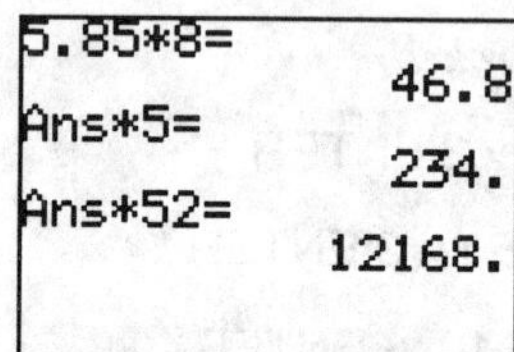

Figure 8.4: ANS variable

8.1.7 The MATH Menu: Operators and functions associated with a scientific calculator are available either immediately from the keys of the Sharp EL-9200/9300 or by 2ndF keys. You have direct key access to common arithmetic operations (x^2, $\sqrt{}$, 2ndF x^{-1}, a^b, 2ndF $\sqrt[a]{}$), exponential and logarithmic functions (log, 2ndF 10^x, ln, 2ndF e^x), and a famous constant (2ndF π).

A significant difference between the Sharp EL-9200/9300 and many scientific calculators is that the Sharp EL-9200/9300 requires the argument of a function *after* the function, as you would see a formula written in your textbook. For example, on the Sharp EL-9200/9300 you calculate $\sqrt{16}$ by pressing the keys $\sqrt{}$ 16 in that order.

Here are keystrokes for basic mathematical operations. Try them for practice on your Sharp EL-9200/9300.

Expression	Keystrokes	Display
$\sqrt{3^2 + 4^2}$	$\sqrt{}$ (3 x^2 + 4 x^2) ENTER	5
$2\frac{1}{3}$	2 + 3 2ndF x^{-1} ENTER	2.333333333
$\log 200$	LOG 200 ENTER	2.301029996
$2.34 \cdot 10^5$	2.34 × 2ndF 10^x 5 ENTER	234000
$\sqrt[3]{125}$	3 2ndF $\sqrt[a]{}$ 125 ENTER	5

Back in Section 8.1.1, you used the SETUP menu to select *one-line* editing. The Sharp EL-9200/9300 calculator also supports *equation* editing, so that mathematical expressions appear on the screen as they do in your textbook (see Figure 8.5 and Figure 8.6 for a comparison). Press SETUP F 1 ENTER to enable equation editing and once again execute the keystrokes listed above.

The equation editor displays "built-up" expressions and reduces the need for parentheses, but the calculator's response to keystrokes can be slower.

Sharp EL-9200/9300 Graphing Scientific Calculator

In equation editing, you terminate the scope of some functions by pressing ▶, instead of adding extra parentheses. For example, evaluate $\sqrt{3^2 + 4^2} + 5^2$ with the following keystrokes in one-line editing: $\sqrt{}$ (3 x² + 4 x²) + 5 x² ENTER. The answer is 50. Try these keystrokes again in equation editing and the answer is different because you are evaluating $\sqrt{(3^2 + 4^2) + 5^2}$ and not $\sqrt{3^2 + 4^2} + 5^2$ here. Now press these keys in the equation editor: $\sqrt{}$ 3 x² + 4 x² ▶ + 5 x² ENTER to get 50 again. In practice, simply watch the screen and the cursor to see when ▶ is needed during equation editing.

Additional mathematical operations and functions are available from the MATH menu (Figure 8.7). Press MATH to see the various options. You will learn in your mathematics textbook how to apply many of them. As an example, calculate |–5| by pressing MATH A 1 (-) 5 ENTER. To leave the MATH menu and take no other action, press QUIT.

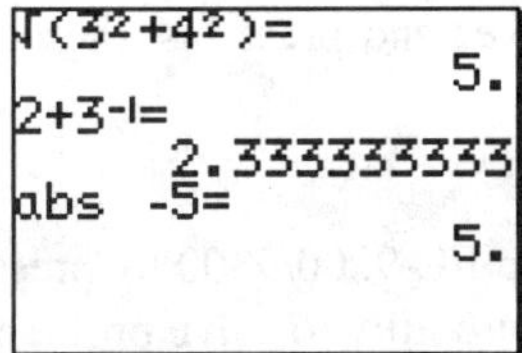

Figure 8.5: One-line editing

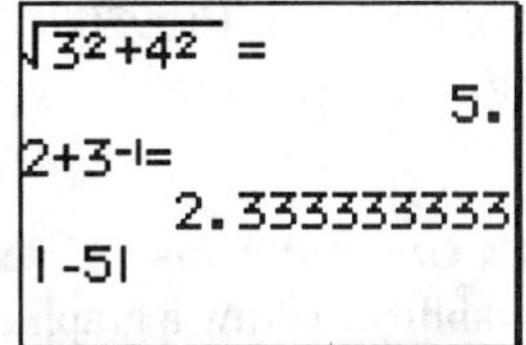

Figure 8.6: Equation editing

Figure 8.7: MATH menu

The *factorial* of a non-negative integer is the *product* of *all* the integers from 1 up to the given integer. The symbol for factorial is the exclamation point. So 4! (pronounced *four factorial*) is 1·2·3·4 = 24. You will learn more about applications of factorials in your textbook, but for now use the Sharp EL-9200/9300 to calculate 4! Press these keystrokes: 4 MATH A 5 ENTER.

8.2   Functions and Graphs

8.2.1 Evaluating Functions: Suppose you receive a monthly salary of $1975 plus a commission of 10% of sales. Let x = your sales in dollars; then your wages W in dollars are given by the equation $W = 1975 + .10x$. If your January sales were $2230 and your February sales were $1865, what was your income during those months?

Here's how to use your Sharp EL-9200/9300 to perform this task. Let x = 2230 by pressing CL 2230 STO X/θ/T. (The X/θ/T key lets you enter the variable x easily without having to use the ALPHA key.) Then evaluate the expression $1975 + .10x$ for January's wages by pressing these keys: 1975 + .10 X/θ/T ENTER. Now set x = 1865 by pressing 1865 STO X/θ/T. These steps are shown in Figure 8.8. Recall the expression $1975 + .10x$ by pressing 2ndF ▲ *twice*, then press ENTER (see Figure 8.9) to find the February wages.

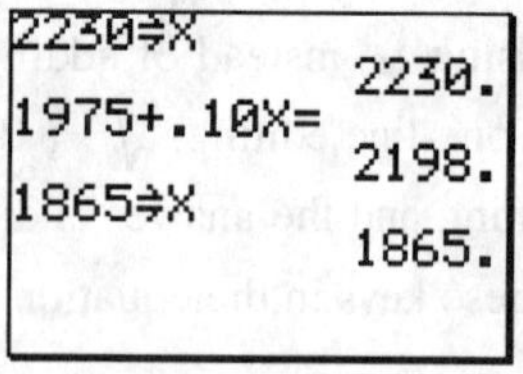

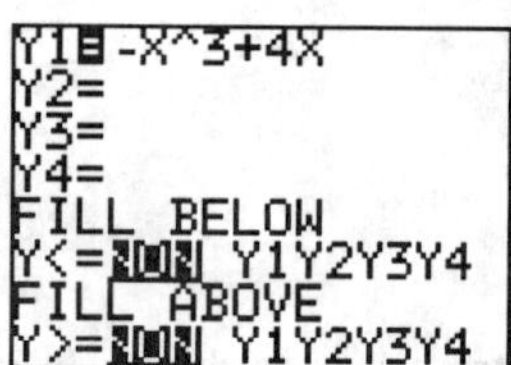

Figure 8.8: Evaluating a function

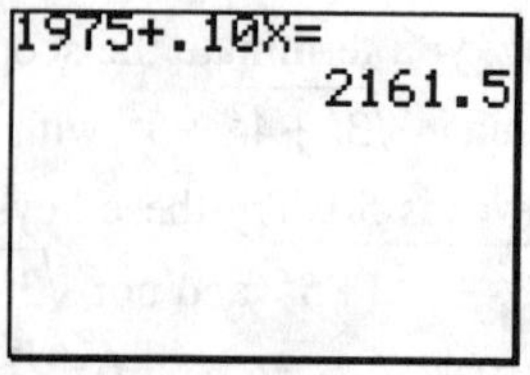

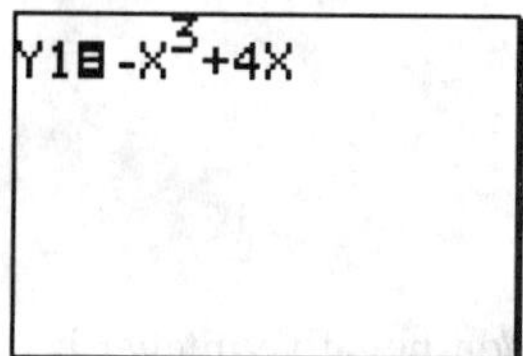

Figure 8.9: February's wages

Each time the Sharp EL-9200/9300 evaluates the function $1975 + .10x$, it uses the *current* value of x.

Technology Tip: The Sharp EL-9200/9300 does not require multiplication to be expressed between variables, so *xxx* means x^3. It is often easier to press two or three x's together than to search for the square key or the power key. Of course, expressed multiplication is also not required between a constant and a variable. Hence to enter $2x^3 + 3x^2 - 4x + 5$ in the Sharp EL-9200/9300, you might save keystrokes and press just these keys: 2 X/θ/T X/θ/T X/θ/T + 3 X/θ/T X/θ/T - 4 X/θ/T + 5.

8.2.2 Functions in a Graph Window: Enter the graph mode of the Sharp EL-9200/9300 by pressing the second key in the top row. The ability to draw a graph contributes substantially to our ability to solve problems.

For example, here is how to graph $y = -x^3 + 4x$. First press the graph mode key and delete anything that may be there by moving with the up or down arrow key (in equation editing, press 2ndF and then the arrow key) to Y1 or to any of the other functions and pressing CL wherever necessary. Then, with the cursor on the top line Y1, press (-) X/θ/T a^b 3 + 4 X/θ/T to enter the function (as in Figure 8.10 for one-line editing and Figure 8.11 for equation editing).

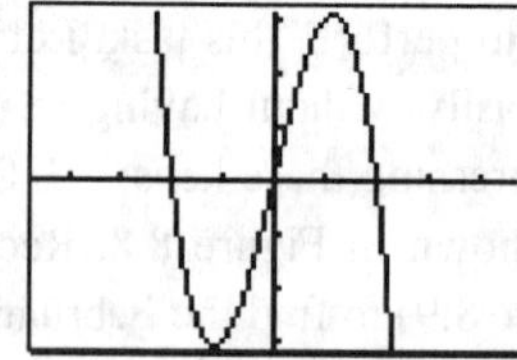

Figure 8.10: Graph entry - one-line editing

Figure 8.11: Graph entry - equation editing

Now press the graph mode key again and the Sharp EL-9200/9300 changes to a window with the graph of $y = -x^3 + 4x$. You may return to edit the function by pressing either EQTN or MENU A and a number.

Your graph window may look like the one in Figure 8.12 or it may be different. Since the graph of $y = -x^3 + 4x$ extends infinitely far left and right and also infinitely far up and down, the Sharp EL-9200/9300 can display only a piece of the actual graph. This displayed rectangular part is called a *viewing rectangle*. You can easily change the viewing rectangle to enhance your investigation of a graph.

Figure 8.12: Graph of $y = -x^3 + 4x$

The viewing rectangle in Figure 8.12 shows the part of the graph that extends horizontally from -4.7 to 4.7 and vertically from -3.1 to 3.1. Press RANGE to see information about your viewing rectangle; press arrow keys to move between the X RANGE and the Y RANGE screens. Figures 8.13 and 8.14 show the RANGE screens that correspond to the viewing rectangle in Figure 8.12. This is the *default* viewing rectangle for the Sharp EL-9200/9300.

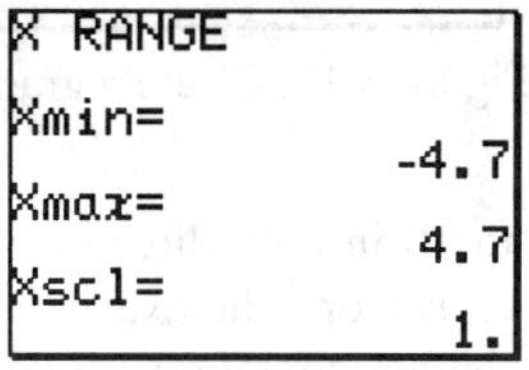

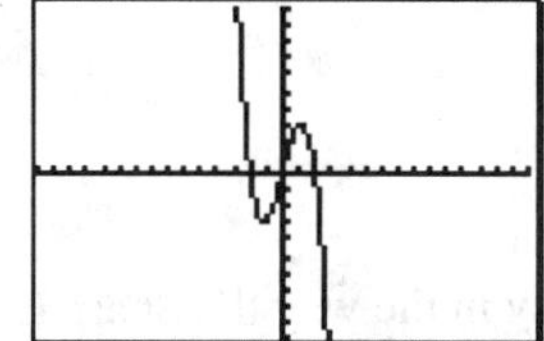

Figure 8.13: Default X RANGE

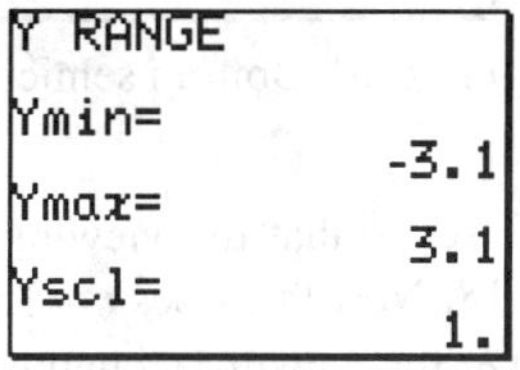

Figure 8.14: Default Y RANGE

The variables Xmin and Xmax are the minimum and maximum *x*-values of the viewing rectangle; Ymin and Ymax are its minimum and maximum *y*-values. Xscl and Yscl set the spacing between tick marks on the axes.

Use the arrow keys ▲ and ▼ to move up and down from one line to another in these lists; pressing the ENTER key will move down the list. Input a new value. The Sharp EL-9200/9300 will *not* permit a maximum that is *less* than the corresponding minimum. Also, remember to use the (-) key, not - (which is subtraction), when you want to enter a negative value. The following figures show different viewing rectangles with their ranges.

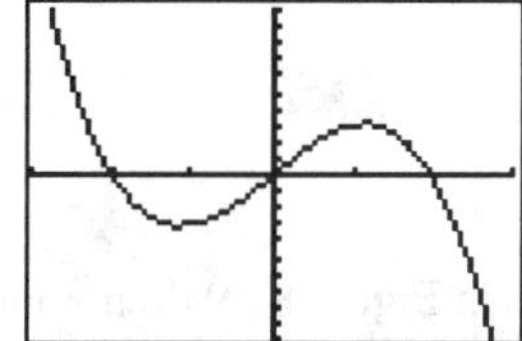

Figure 8.15: Window [-15, 15] by [-10, 10]

Figure 8.16: Window [-3, 3] by [-10, 10]

To set the range quickly to default values (see Figures 8.13 and 8.14), press RANGE MENU A ENTER. You may also set range values suitable for graphing particular functions, such as power and root functions (RANGE MENU B), exponential and logarithmic functions (RANGE MENU C), and trigonometric functions (RANGE MENU D).

Technology Tip: After you input a function, press 2ndF AUTO to draw the graph in a window with the current X RANGE values but automatically scaled in the vertical direction. This is an advantage when you are not sure how tall a viewing rectangle to set.

8.2.3 Graphing a Circle: Here is a useful technique for graphs that are not functions, but that can be "split" into a top part and a bottom part, or into multiple parts. Suppose you wish to graph the circle whose equation is $x^2 + y^2 = 36$. First solve for *y* and get an equation for the top semicircle, $y = \sqrt{36 - x^2}$, and for the bottom semicircle, $y = -\sqrt{36 - x^2}$. Then graph the two semicircles simultaneously.

The keystrokes to draw this circle's graph follow. Enter $\sqrt{36 - x^2}$ as Y1 and $-\sqrt{36 - x^2}$ as Y2 (see Figure 8.17) by pressing the graph mode key and then $\sqrt{\ }$ (36 - X/θ/T x²) ENTER (-) $\sqrt{\ }$ (36 - X/θ/T x²). Press the graph mode key again to draw them both.

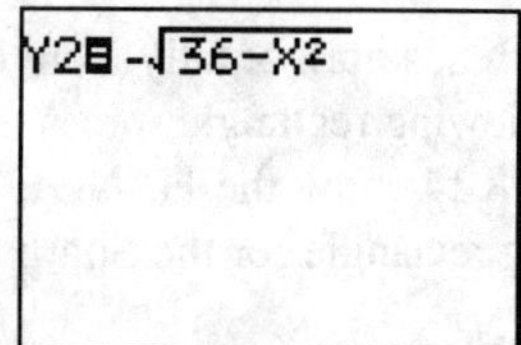

Figure 8.17: Bottom semicircle

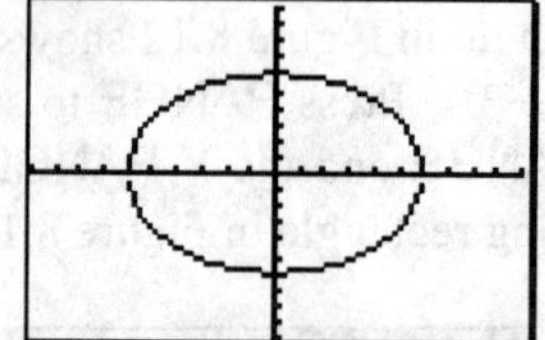

Figure 8.18: Circle's graph

If your range were set so that the viewing rectangle extends from -10 to 10 in both directions, your graph would look like Figure 8.18. Now this does *not* look like a circle, because the units along the axes are not the same. Press RANGE and change the viewing rectangle to extend from -12 to 12 in the horizontal direction and from -8 to 8 in the vertical direction and see a graph (Figure 8.19) that appears more circular.

Technology Tip: The way to get a circle's graph to look circular is to change the range variables so that the value of Ymax - Ymin is $\frac{2}{3}$ times Xmax - Xmin. The method works because the dimensions of the Sharp EL-9200/9300's display are such that the ratio of vertical to horizontal is approximately $\frac{2}{3}$.

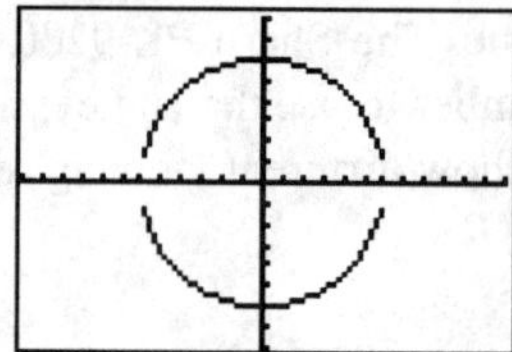

Figure 8.19: A circle

The two semicircles in Figure 8.19 do not meet because of an idiosyncrasy in the way the Sharp EL-9200/9300 plots a graph.

Technology Tip: A square viewing rectangle, in which units along both axes are the same, is also important when you want to judge whether two lines are perpendicular. The intersection of perpendicular lines will always *look* like a right angle in a square viewing rectangle.

8.2.4 TRACE: Graph $y = -x^3 + 4x$ in the default viewing rectangle. Press either of the arrow keys ◀ or ▶ and see the cursor move along the graph. The coordinates of the cursor's location are displayed at the bottom of the screen, as in Figure 8.20, in floating decimal format. The cursor is constrained to the function. The coordinates that are displayed belong to points on the function's graph, so the *y*-coordinate is the calculated value of the function at the corresponding *x*-coordinate.

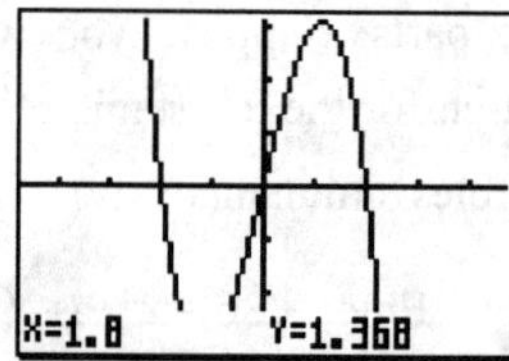

Figure 8.20: Trace on $y = -x^3 + 4x$

Press 2ndF ◀ or 2ndF ▶ to jump to the endpoints of the part of the graph that is displayed in a window. Remove the trace cursor and its coordinates from the graph window by pressing CL.

Sharp EL-9200/9300 Graphing Scientific Calculator

Now plot a second function, $y = -.25x$, along with $y = -x^3 + 4x$. Press **MENU A 2** and enter $-.25x$ for Y2, then press the graphing mode key.

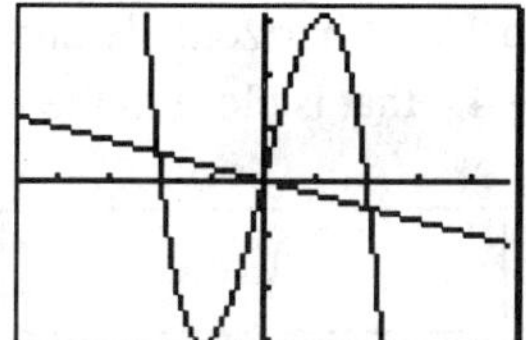

Figure 8.21: $y = -x^3 + 4x$ and $y = -.25x$

Note that the equal signs next to **Y1** and **Y2** are *both* highlighted. This means *both* functions will be graphed. Press **MENU A 1**, move the cursor directly on top of the equal sign next to **Y1** and press **ENTER**. This equal sign should no longer be highlighted. Now press the graph mode key and see that only **Y2** is plotted.

So up to 4 different functions may be stored in the **Y=** list and any combination of them may be graphed simultaneously. You can make a function active or inactive for graphing by pressing **ENTER** on its equal sign to highlight (activate) or remove the highlight (deactivate). Go back and do what is needed in order to graph **Y1** but not **Y2**.

Now activate **Y2** again so that both graphs are plotted. Press ◄ or ► and the cursor appears first on the graph of $y = -x^3 + 4x$ because it is **Y1**. Press ▲ to move the cursor vertically to the graph of $y = -.25x$; move the cursor back to $y = -x^3 + 4x$ by pressing ▼. Next press the right and left arrow keys to trace along the graph of $y = -.25x$. When more than one function is plotted, you can move the trace cursor vertically from one graph to another in this way.

Technology Tip: By the way, trace along the graph of $y = -.25x$ and press and hold either ◄ or ►. Eventually you will reach the left or right edge of the window. Keep pressing the arrow key and the Sharp EL-9200/9300 will allow you to continue the trace by panning the viewing rectangle. Check the **RANGE** screen to see that Xmin and Xmax are automatically updated.

The Sharp EL-9200/9300's display has 95 horizontal columns of pixels and 63 vertical rows. So when you trace a curve across a graph window, you are actually moving from **Xmin** to **Xmax** in 94 equal jumps, each called Δx. You would calculate the size of each jump to be $\Delta x = \dfrac{\text{Xmax} - \text{Xmin}}{94}$. Sometimes you may want the jumps to be friendly numbers like .1 or .25 so that, when you trace along the curve, the x-coordinates will be incremented by such a convenient amount. Just set your viewing rectangle for a particular increment Δx by making **Xmax** = **Xmin** + 94·Δx. For example, if you want **Xmin** = -5 and Δx = .3, set **Xmax** = -5 + 94·.3 = 23.2. Likewise, set **Ymax** = **Ymin** + 62·Δy if you want the vertical increment to be some special Δy.

To center your window around a particular point, say (h, k), and also have a certain Δx, set **Xmin** = h - 47·Δx and **Xmax** = h + 47·Δx. Likewise, make **Ymin** = k - 31·Δy and **Ymax** = k + 31·Δy. For example, to center a window around the origin, (0, 0), with both horizontal and vertical increments of .25, set the range so that **Xmin** = 0 - 47·.25 = -11.75, **Xmax** = 0 + 47·.25 = 11.75, **Ymin** = 0 - 31·.25 = -7.75, and **Ymax** = 0 + 31·.25 = 7.75.

The Sharp EL-9200/9300's standard window is already a friendly viewing rectangle, centered at the origin (0, 0) with $\Delta x = \Delta y = 0.1$.

See the benefit by first plotting $y = x^2 + 2x + 1$ in a graphing window extending from -5 to 5 in both directions. Trace near its y-intercept, which is (0, 1), and move towards its x-intercept, which is (-1, 0). Then initialize the range to the default window and trace again near the intercepts.

8.2.5 ZOOM: Plot again the two graphs, for $y = -x^3 + 4x$ and for $y = -.25x$. There appears to be an intersection near $x = 2$. The Sharp EL-9200/9300 provides several ways to enlarge the view around this point. You can change the viewing rectangle directly by pressing RANGE and editing the values of Xmin, Xmax, Ymin, and Ymax. Figure 8.22 shows a new window extending from 1 to 3 horizontally and from -2 to 1 vertically. Trace has been turned on and the coordinates of a point on $y = -x^3 + 4x$ that is close to the intersection are displayed.

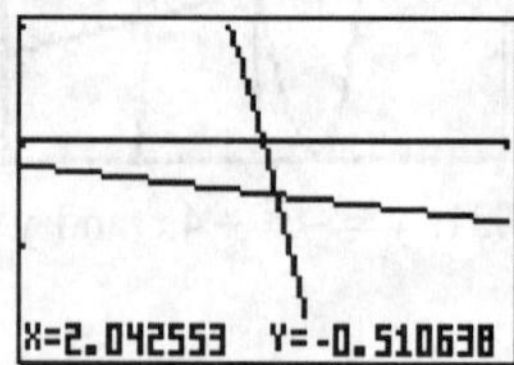

Figure 8.22: Closer view

A more efficient method for enlarging the view is to draw a new viewing rectangle with the cursor. Start again with a graph of the two functions $y = -x^3 + 4x$ and $y = -.25x$ in a default viewing rectangle (press RANGE MENU ENTER for the default window, from -4.7 to 4.7 along the x-axis and from -3.1 to 3.1 along the y-axis).

Now imagine a small rectangular box around the intersection point, near $x = 2$. Press ZOOM 1 (Figure 8.23) to draw a box to define this new viewing rectangle. Use the arrow keys to move the cursor, whose coordinates are displayed at the bottom of the window, to one corner of the new viewing rectangle you imagine.

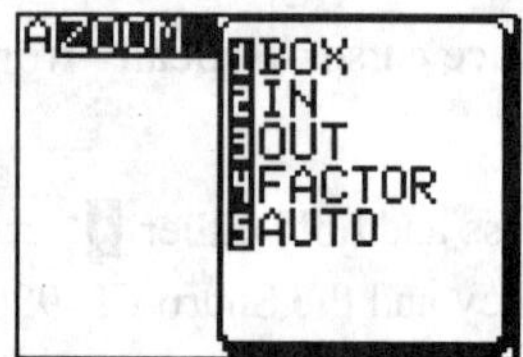

Figure 8.23: ZOOM menu

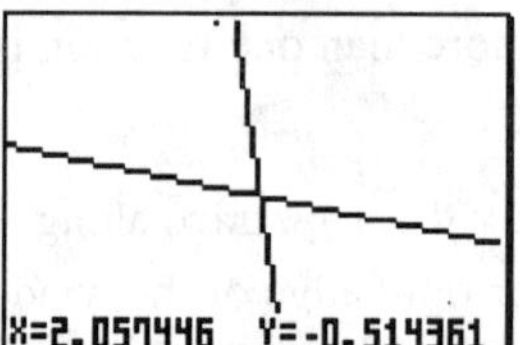

Figure 8.24: New viewing rectangle

Press ENTER to fix the corner where you have moved the cursor. Use the arrow keys again to move the cursor to the diagonally opposite corner of the new rectangle. If this box looks all right to you, press ENTER. The rectangular area you have enclosed will now enlarge to fill the graph window (Figure 8.24).

You may cancel the zoom any time *before* this last ENTER by pressing CL.

You can also gain a quick magnification of the graph around the cursor's location. Return once more to the default range for the graph of the two functions $y = -x^3 + 4x$ and $y = -.25x$. Trace as close as you can to the point of intersection near $x = 2$ (see Figure 8.21). Then press ZOOM 2 and the calculator draws a magnified graph, centered at the cursor's position (Figure 8.25). The range variables are changed to reflect this new viewing rectangle. Look in the RANGE menu to check.

As you see in the ZOOM menu (Figure 8.23), the Sharp EL-9200/9300 can zoom in (press ZOOM 2) or zoom out (press ZOOM 3). Zoom out to see a larger view of the graph, centered at the cursor position. You can change the horizontal and vertical scale of the magnification by pressing ZOOM 4 and editing X-FACTOR and Y-FACTOR, the horizontal and vertical magnification factors.

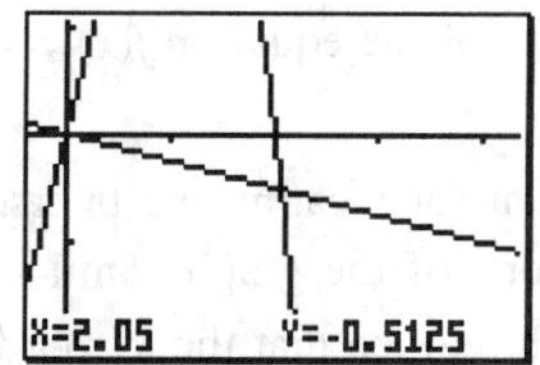

Figure 8.25: After a zoom in

It is not necessary for **X-FACTOR** and **Y-FACTOR** to be equal. Sometimes, you may prefer to zoom in one direction only, so the other factor should be set to 1. As usual, press **QUIT** to leave the **ZOOM** menu.

Technology Tip: If you should zoom in too much and lose the curve, press **ZOOM 5** for auto scaling and start again.

An advantage of zooming in from the default viewing rectangle or from a friendly viewing rectangle is that subsequent windows will also be friendly.

8.3   Solving Equations and Inequalities

8.3.1 Intercepts and Intersections: Tracing and zooming are also used to locate an x-intercept of a graph, where a curve crosses the x-axis. For example, the graph of $y = x^3 - 8x$ crosses the x-axis three times (see Figure 8.26). After tracing over to the x-intercept point that is furthest to the left, zoom in (Figure 8.27). Continue this process until you have located all three intercepts with as much accuracy as you need. The three x-intercepts of $y = x^3 - 8x$ are approximately -2.828, 0, and 2.828.

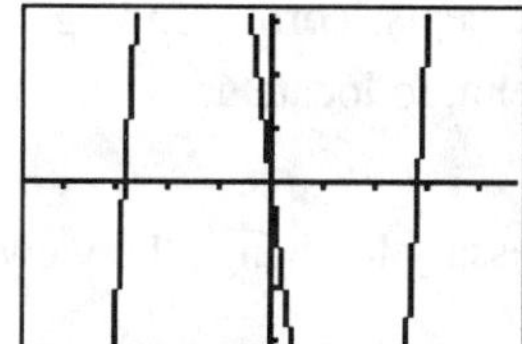

Figure 8.26: Graph of $y = x^3 - 8x$

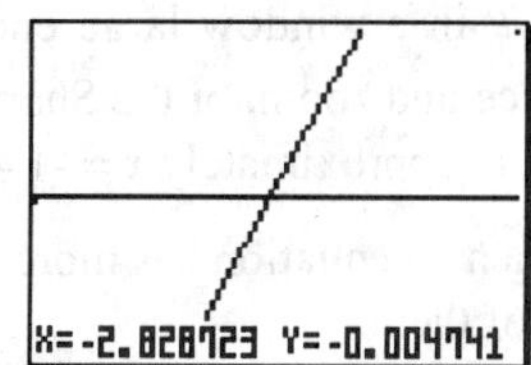

Figure 8.27: An x-intercept of $y = x^3 - 8x$

Technology Tip: As you zoom in, you may also wish to change the spacing between tick marks on the x-axis so that the viewing rectangle shows scale marks near the intercept point. Then the accuracy of your approximation will be such that the error is less than the distance between two tick marks. Change the x-scale on the Sharp EL-9200/9300 from the **RANGE** menu. Move the cursor down to **Xscl** and enter an appropriate value.

The Sharp EL-9200/9300 automates the search for x-intercepts. First trace along the graph until the cursor is just left of an x-intercept. Press **2ndF JUMP** (Figure 8.28) and choose 4 to find the next x-intercept of this function. Repeat until you have located all x-intercepts of this graph.

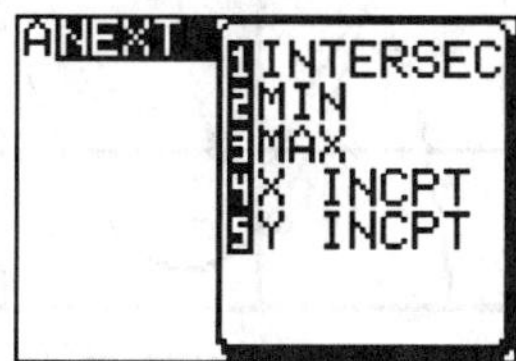

Figure 8.28: JUMP menu

An x-intercept of a function's graph is a *root* of the equation $f(x) = 0$. So these techniques for locating x-intercepts also serve to find the roots of an equation.

TRACE and ZOOM are especially important for locating the intersection points of two graphs, say the graphs of $y = -x^3 + 4x$ and $y = -.25x$. Trace along one of the graphs until you arrive close to an intersection point. Then press ▲ or ▼ to jump to the other graph. Notice that the x-coordinate does not change, but the y-coordinate is likely to be different (see Figures 8.29 and 8.30).

When the two y-coordinates are as close as they can get, you have come as close as you now can to the point of intersection. So zoom in around the intersection point, then trace again until the two y-coordinates are as close as possible. Continue this process until you have located the point of intersection with as much accuracy as necessary.

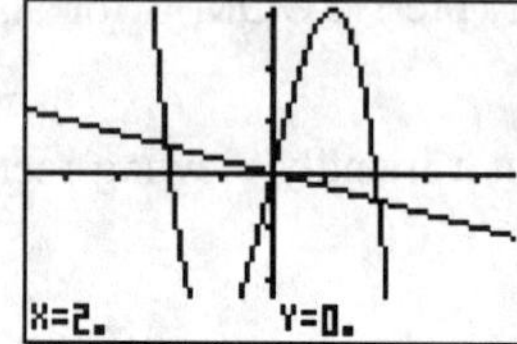

Figure 8.29: Trace on $y = -x^3 + 4x$

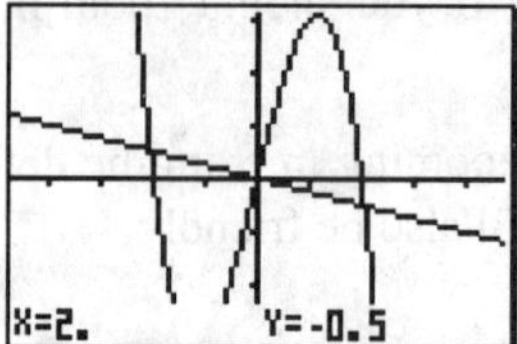

Figure 8.30: Trace on $y = -.25x$

Automate the search for points of intersection by tracing along one curve until you are left of an intersection. Then press 2ndF JUMP 1 to locate the next intersection point. The calculator displays *approximate* coordinates; zoom in to improve the approximation.

8.3.2 Solving Equations by Graphing: Suppose you need to solve the equation $24x^3 - 36x + 17 = 0$. First graph $y = 24x^3 - 36x + 17$ in a window large enough to exhibit *all* its x-intercepts, corresponding to all the equation's roots. Then use trace and zoom, or the Sharp EL-9200/9300's JUMP menu, to locate each one. In fact, this equation has just one solution, approximately $x = -1.414$.

Remember that when an equation has more than one root, it may be necessary to change the viewing rectangle a few times to locate all of them.

Technology Tip: To solve an equation like $24x^3 + 17 = 36x$, you may first transform it into standard form, $24x^3 - 36x + 17 = 0$, and proceed as above. However, you may also graph the *two* functions $y = 24x^3 + 17$ and $y = 36x$, then zoom and trace to locate their point of intersection.

8.3.3 Solving Systems by Graphing: The solutions to a system of equations correspond to the points of intersection of their graphs (Figure 8.31). For example, to solve the system $y = x^2 - 3x - 4$ and $y = x^3 + 3x^2 - 2x - 1$, first graph them together. Then zoom and trace, or 2ndF JUMP, to locate their point of intersection, approximately (-2.17, 7.25).

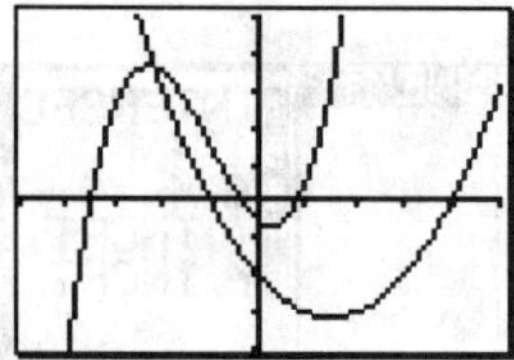

Figure 8.31: Solving a system of equations

You must judge whether the two current y-coordinates are sufficiently close for $x = -2.17$ or whether you should continue to zoom and trace to improve the approximation.

The solutions of the system of two equations $y = x^3 + 3x^2 - 2x - 1$ and $y = x^2 - 3x - 4$ correspond to the solutions of the single equation $x^3 + 3x^2 - 2x - 1 = x^2 - 3x - 4$, which simplifies to $x^3 + 2x^2 + x + 3 = 0$. So you may also graph $y = x^3 + 2x^2 + x + 3$ and find its x-intercepts to solve the system.

8.3.4 Solving Inequalities by Graphing: Consider the inequality $1 - \dfrac{3x}{2} \geq x - 4$. To solve it with your Sharp EL-9200/9300, graph the two functions $y = 1 - \dfrac{3x}{2}$ and $y = x - 4$ (Figure 8.32). First locate their point of intersection, at $x = 2$. The inequality is true when the graph of $y = 1 - \dfrac{3x}{2}$ lies *above* the graph of $y = x - 4$, and that occurs for $x < 2$. So the solution is the half-line $x \leq 2$, or $(-\infty, 2]$.

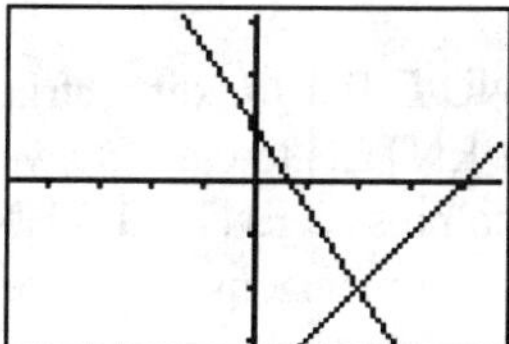

Figure 8.32: Solving $1 - \dfrac{3x}{2} \geq x - 4$

The Sharp EL-9200/9300 is capable of shading the region above or below a graph or between two graphs. For example, to graph $y \geq x^2 - 1$, first input the function $y = x^2 - 1$ as Y1. Then press MENU 5 (see Figure 8.33). Move the cursor to Y1 in the FILL ABOVE part and press ENTER to highlight it. These keystrokes instruct the calculator to shade the region *above* $y = x^2 - 1$. The result is shown in Figure 8.34.

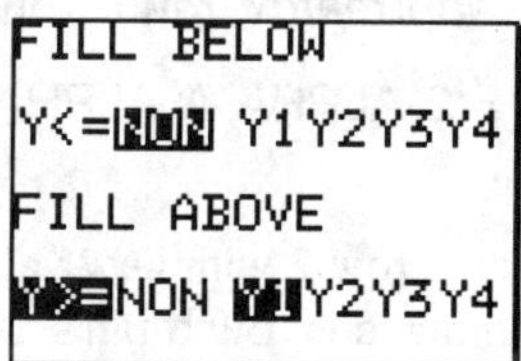

Figure 8.33: FILL menu

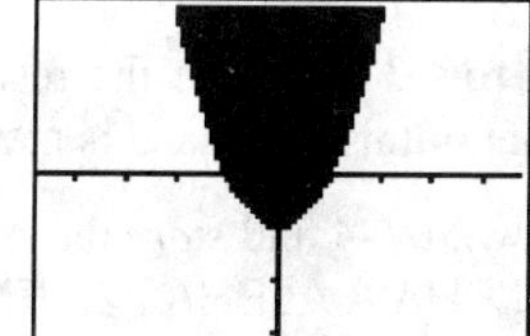

Figure 8.34: Graph of $y \geq x^2 - 1$

To clear the shading, press MENU 5 and highlight NON for both FILL BELOW and FILL ABOVE.

Now use shading to solve the previous inequality, $1 - \dfrac{3x}{2} \geq x - 4$. Input $y = 1 - \dfrac{3x}{2}$ as Y1 and $y = x - 4$ as Y2. Then press MENU 5 and highlight Y1 for FILL BELOW and Y2 for FILL ABOVE. The shading extends left from $x = 2$, hence the solution to $1 - \dfrac{3x}{2} \geq x - 4$ is the half-line $x \leq 2$, or $(-\infty, 2]$.

Figure 8.35: FILL menu

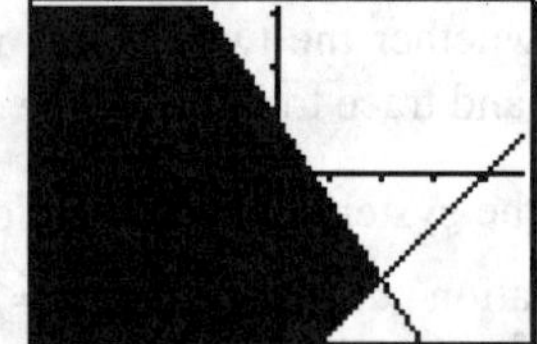

Figure 8.36: Graph of $1 - \dfrac{3x}{2} \geq x - 4$

8.4   Matrices

8.4.1 Making a Matrix: The Sharp EL-9200/9300 can display and use 26 different matrices, each identified by a letter of the alphabet. Here's how to create this 3×4 matrix $\begin{bmatrix} 1 & -4 & 3 & 5 \\ -1 & 3 & -1 & -3 \\ 2 & 0 & -4 & 6 \end{bmatrix}$ in your calculator.

Press MENU A 3 for matrix mode, then MENU B 0 1 to edit matrix A. If some other matrix A were already in the calculator's memory, first press MENU D 0 1 ENTER to clear it away, then MENU B 0 1 to create a new one. You will be prompted for matrix A's dimensions, so press 3 ENTER 4 ENTER. If you need to change the dimensions of matrix A, press MENU C 0 1 and input its new dimensions.

Use the arrow keys to move the cursor directly to a matrix element you want to change. If you press ENTER, you will move down a column and then right to the next row. Continue to enter all the elements of matrix A.

Leave matrix editing by pressing QUIT and return to the home screen.

8.4.2 Row Operations: Here are the keystrokes necessary to perform elementary row operations on a matrix. Your textbook provides more careful explanation of the elementary row operations and their uses.

To interchange the second and third rows of the matrix A that was defined above, press MATH F 1 ALPHA A ALPHA , 2 ALPHA , 3) ENTER. The format of this command is row swap(*matrix, row1, row2*).

To add row 2 and row 3 and store the results in row 3, press MATH F 2 ALPHA A ALPHA , 2 ALPHA , 3) ENTER. The format of this command is row plus(*matrix, row1, row2*).

And to multiply row 2 by -4 and *store* the results in row 2, thereby replacing row 2 with new values, press MATH F 3 (-) 4 ALPHA , ALPHA A ALPHA , 2) ENTER. The format of this command is row mult(*scalar, matrix, row*).

To multiply row 2 by -4 and *add* the results to row 3, thereby replacing row 3 with new values, press MATH F 4 (-) 4 ALPHA , ALPHA A ALPHA , 2 ALPHA , 3) ENTER. The format of this command is row m.p.(*scalar, matrix, row1, row2*).

Technology Tip: It is important to remember that your Sharp EL-9200/9300 does *not* store a matrix obtained as the result of any row operations. The calculator places a result only in the temporary ANS matrix. So when you need to perform several row operations in succession, it is a good idea to store the result of each one in a temporary place. You may wish to use matrix Z to hold such intermediate results.

For example, use elementary row operations to solve this system of linear equations: $\begin{cases} x - 2y + 3z = 9 \\ -x + 3y = -4 \\ 2x - 5y + 5z = 17 \end{cases}$.

First enter this *augmented matrix* as A in your Sharp EL-9200/9300: $\begin{bmatrix} 1 & -2 & 3 & 9 \\ -1 & 3 & 0 & -4 \\ 2 & -5 & 5 & 17 \end{bmatrix}$. Next store this matrix in C (press MATH A STO MAT C ENTER) so you may keep the original in case you need to recall it.

Here are the row operations and their associated keystrokes. At each step, the result is stored in C and replaces the previous matrix C.

Row Operation	Keystrokes
row plus(C, 1, 2)	MATH F 2 ALPHA C ALPHA , 1 ALPHA , 2) STO MAT C
row m.p.(-2, C, 1, 3)	MATH F 4 (-) 2 ALPHA , ALPHA C ALPHA , 1 ALPHA , 3) STO MAT C
row plus(C, 2, 3)	MATH F 2 ALPHA C ALPHA , 2 ALPHA , 3) STO MAT C
row mult(½, C, 3)	MATH F 3 1 ÷ 2 ALPHA , ALPHA C ALPHA , 3) STO MAT C

Thus $z = 2$, so $y = -1$ and $x = 1$.

8.4.3 Determinants: Enter this 3×3 square matrix as A: $\begin{bmatrix} 1 & -2 & 3 \\ -1 & 3 & 0 \\ 2 & -5 & 5 \end{bmatrix}$. To calculate its determinant, $\begin{vmatrix} 1 & -2 & 3 \\ -1 & 3 & 0 \\ 2 & -5 & 5 \end{vmatrix}$,

press MATH E 6 MAT A ENTER. You should find that $|A| = 2$.

8.5   Additional Topics

8.5.1 Iteration: The 2ndF ANS feature enables you to perform iterations to evaluate a function repeatedly. As an example, calculate $\dfrac{n-1}{3}$ for $n = 27$. Then calculate $\dfrac{n-1}{3}$ for n = the answer to the previous calculation. Continue to use each answer as n in the *next* calculation. Here are keystrokes to accomplish this iteration on the Sharp EL-9200/9300 calculator (see the results in Figure 8.37). Notice that when you use Ans in place of n in a formula, it is sufficient to press ENTER to continue an iteration.

Assure that you are in the correct mode by pressing the calculation mode key, then MENU 1.

Iteration	Keystrokes	Display
1	27 ENTER	27.
2	(2ndF ANS - 1) ÷ 3 ENTER	8.666666667
3	ENTER	2.555555556
4	ENTER	0.518518518
5	ENTER	-0.160493827

Press ENTER several more times and see what happens with this iteration. You may wish to try it again with a different starting value.

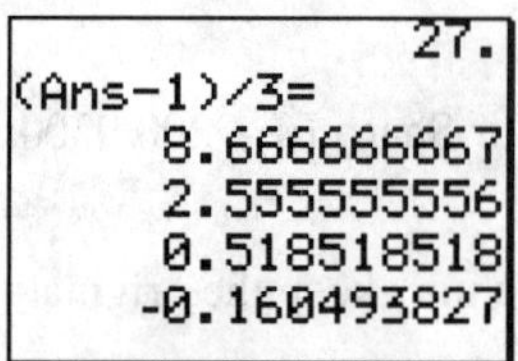

Figure 8.37: Iteration

8.5.2 Arithmetic and Geometric Sequences: Use iteration with the Ans variable to determine the n-th term of a sequence. For example, find the 18th term of an *arithmetic* sequence whose first term is 7 and whose common difference is 4. Enter the first term 7, then start the progression with the recursion formula, 2ndF ANS + 4 ENTER. This yields the 2nd term, so press ENTER sixteen more times to find the 18th term. For a *geometric* sequence whose common ratio is 4, start the progression with 2ndF ANS × 4 ENTER.

Of course, you could also use the *explicit* formula for the n-th term of an arithmetic sequence, $t_n = a + (n-1)d$. First enter values for the variables a, d, and n, then evaluate the formula by pressing ALPHA A + (ALPHA N - 1) ALPHA D ENTER. For a geometric sequence whose n-th term is given by $t_n = a \cdot r^{n-1}$, enter values for the variables a, r, and n, then evaluate the formula by pressing ALPHA A ALPHA R a^b (ALPHA N - 1) ENTER.

8.5.3 Permutations and Combinations: To calculate the number of *permutations* of 12 objects taken 7 at a time, $_{12}P_7$, press 12 MATH A 7 7 ENTER. Thus $_{12}P_7 = 3{,}991{,}680$.

For the number of *combinations* of 12 objects taken 7 at a time, $_{12}C_7$, press 12 MATH A 6 7 ENTER. So $_{12}C_7 = 792$.

8.6　Programming

8.6.1 Entering a Program: The Sharp EL-9200/9300 is a programmable calculator that can store sequences of commands for later replay. Here's an example to show you how to enter a useful program that solves quadratic equations by the quadratic formula.

Press the programming mode key (in the middle of the top row) to access the programming menu, where you will find a list of any programs that were input previously. The Sharp EL-9200 has space for up to 55 programs, and the Sharp EL-9300 has space for up to 99 programs.

To create a new program, press C ENTER, then 4 so this program will run in complex mode. The ALPHA indicator is on, so press letter keys to name this program quadratic. Then press ▼ to continue.

Notice that the name quadratic is in *lowercase* letters. In programming mode, pressing ALPHA or 2ndF A·LOCK allows you to enter a lowercase letter. For uppercase letters, press ALPHA 2ndF or 2ndF A·LOCK 2ndF.

A single *uppercase* letter, when used for a variable name, refers to a memory location. It is called a *global* variable. For any other program, or even outside programming mode, this memory location retains the value you store there until you store something else. However a *lowercase* letter names a *local* variable that exists only during the current program. Values stored in local variables cannot be passed to another program and are not available outside the program in which they are created.

Lowercase variable names can be longer than one letter. For example, length is a valid local variable name. So multiplication between local variables must be expressed: you must enter length × width for a product.

Any command you could enter directly in the Sharp EL-9200/9300's home screen can be entered as a line in a program. There are also special programming commands.

You *must* press ENTER or ⬇ after each line to complete the entry. Press CL to clear a single line; press 2ndF CA to delete an entire program.

Enter the program quadratic by pressing the keystrokes given in the listing below. You may interrupt program input at any time by pressing a mode key. To return later for more editing, press the programming mode key, then B, use the arrow keys to locate the program's name in the listing, and press ENTER. Take care, however, that the keystrokes given here assume that you are entering these lines of code sequentially. Frequently, for example, when you press 2ndF A·LOCK to put the calculator in alphabetic entry mode for one line of code, subsequent lines will assume that the calculator is already in that state.

Program Line	*Keystrokes*
Print "Enter a	2ndF COMMAND A 1 2ndF COMMAND 2 2ndF A·LOCK 2ndF E N T E R SPACE A ⬇

displays the words *Enter a* on the Sharp EL-9200/9300 screen

Input a	2ndF COMMAND 3 A ⬇

waits for you to input a value that will be assigned to the variable a

Print "Enter b	2ndF COMMAND 1 2ndF COMMAND 2 2ndF E N T E R SPACE B ⬇
Input b	2ndF COMMAND 3 B ⬇
Print "Enter c	2ndF COMMAND 1 2ndF COMMAND 2 2ndF E N T E R SPACE C ⬇
Input c	2ndF COMMAND 3 C ⬇
$d = b^2 - 4a*c$	D = B ALPHA x^2 – 4 ALPHA A × ALPHA C ⬇

calculates the discriminant and stores its value as d

$m = (-b+\sqrt{d})/(2a)$	ALPHA M ALPHA = ((-) ALPHA B + √ ALPHA D) ÷ (2 ALPHA A) ⬇

calculates one root and stores it as m

$n = (-b-\sqrt{d})/(2a)$	ALPHA N ALPHA = ((-) ALPHA B – √ ALPHA D) ÷ (2 ALPHA A) ⬇
If d<0 Goto 1	2ndF COMMAND B 3 ALPHA D 2ndF COMMAND C 2 0 ALPHA SPACE 2ndF COMMAND B 2 1 ⬇

tests to see if the discriminant is negative;

in case the discriminant is negative, jumps to the line Label 1 below;
if the discriminant is not negative, continues on to the next line

If d=0 Goto 2	2ndF COMMAND 3 ALPHA D 2ndF COMMAND C 1 0 ALPHA SPACE 2ndF COMMAND B 2 2 ⬇

tests to see if the discriminant is zero;

in case the discriminant is zero, jumps to the line Label 2 below;
if the discriminant is not zero, continues on to the next line

Print "Two real roots   2ndF COMMAND A 1 2ndF COMMAND 2 2ndF A·LOCK
                            2ndF T W O SPACE R E A L SPACE R O O T S ▼

Print m   2ndF COMMAND 1 M ▼

    displays one root

Print n   2ndF COMMAND 1 N ALPHA ▼

End   2ndF COMMAND 6 ▼

    stops program execution

Label 1   2ndF COMMAND B 1 1 ▼

    jumping point for the Goto command above

Print "Complex roots   2ndF COMMAND A 1 2ndF COMMAND 2
                            2ndF A·LOCK 2ndF C O M P L E X SPACE R O O T S ▼

    displays a message in case the roots are complex numbers

Print m   2ndF COMMAND 1 M ▼

    displays one root

Print n   2ndF COMMAND 1 N ALPHA ▼

End   2ndF COMMAND 6 ▼

Label 2   2ndF COMMAND B 1 2 ▼

Print "Double root   2ndF COMMAND A 1 2ndF COMMAND 2
                            2ndF A·LOCK 2ndF D O U B L E SPACE R O O T ▼

    displays a message in case there is a double root

Print m   2ndF COMMAND 1 M ▼

End   2ndF COMMAND 6 ▼

When you have finished, press any mode key to leave the program editor.

8.6.2 Running a Program: To run the program just entered, press the programming mode key and ENTER. Go to its name in the program listing, then press ENTER to select this program and to execute it.

The program has been written to prompt you for values of the coefficients *a*, *b*, and *c* in a quadratic equation $ax^2 + bx + c = 0$. Input a value, then press ENTER to continue the program.

If you need to interrupt a program during execution, press QUIT.

The instruction manual for your Sharp EL-9200/9300 gives detailed information about programming. Refer to it to learn more about programming and how to use other features of your calculator.

Chapter 9

Texas Instruments TI-83
Graphics Calculator

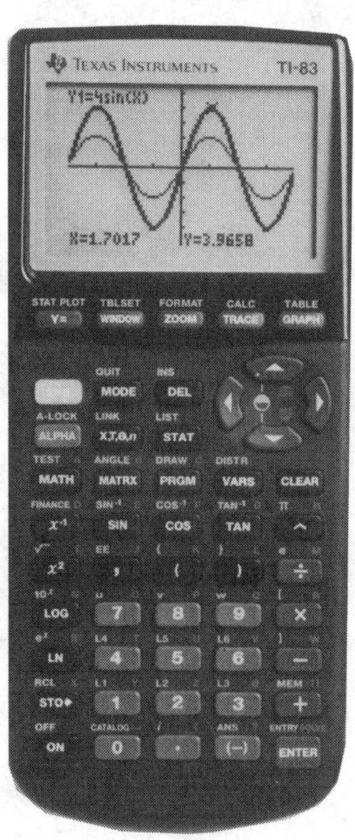

9.1 Getting started with the TI-83

9.1.1 Basics: Press the ON key to begin using your TI-83. If you need to adjust the display contrast, first press 2nd, then press and hold ▼ (the *down* arrow key) to lighten or ▲ (the *up* arrow key) to darken. As you press and hold ▼ or ▲, an integer between 0 (lightest) and 9 (darkest) appears in the upper right corner of the display. When you have finished with the calculator, turn it off to conserve battery power by pressing 2nd and then OFF.

Check your TI-83's settings by pressing MODE. If necessary, use the arrow keys to move the blinking cursor to a setting you want to change. Press ENTER to select a new setting. To start with, select the options along the left side of the MODE menu as illustrated in Figure 9.1: normal display, floating decimals, radian measure, function graphs, connected lines, sequential plotting, real numbers, and full screen display. Details on alternative options will be given later in this guide. For now, leave the MODE menu by pressing CLEAR.

Figure 9.1: MODE menu

Figure 9.2: Home screen

9.1.2 Editing: One advantage of the TI-83 is that up to eight lines are visible at one time, so you can *see* a long calculation. For example, type this sum (Figure 9.2):

$$1 + 2 + 3 + 4 + 5 + 6 + 7 + 8 + 9 + 10 + 11 + 12 + 13 + 14 + 15 + 16 + 17 + 18 + 19 + 20$$

Then press ENTER to see the answer too.

Often we do not notice a mistake until we see how unreasonable an answer is. The TI-83 permits you to redisplay an entire calculation, edit it easily, then execute the *corrected* calculation.

Suppose you had typed $12 + 34 + 56$ as in Figure 9.2 but had *not yet* pressed ENTER, when you realize that 34 should have been 74. Simply press ◄ (the *left* arrow key) as many times as necessary to move the blinking cursor left to 3, then type 7 to write over it. On the other hand, if 34 should have been 384, move the cursor back to 4, press 2nd INS (the cursor changes to a blinking underline) and then type 8 (inserts at the cursor position and the other characters are pushed to the right). If the 34 should have been 3 only, move the cursor to 4, and press DEL to delete it.

Technology Tip: To move quickly to the *beginning* of an expression you are currently editing, press ▲ (the *up* arrow key); to jump to the *end* of that expression, press ▼ (the *down* arrow key).

Even if you had pressed ENTER, you may still edit the previous expression. Press 2nd and then ENTRY to recall the last expression that was entered. Now you can change it. In fact, the TI-83 retains many prior entries in a "last entry" storage area. Press 2nd ENTRY repeatedly until the previous line you want replaces the current line.

Technology Tip: When you need to evaluate a formula for different values of a variable, use the editing feature to simplify the process. For example, suppose you want to find the balance in an investment account if there is now $5000 in the account and interest is compounded annually at the rate of 8.5%. The formula for the balance is

$P = \left(1 + \frac{r}{n}\right)^{nt}$, where P = principal, r = rate of interest (expressed as a decimal), n = number of times interest is compounded each year, and t = number of years. In our example, this becomes $5000(1+.085)^t$. Here are the keystrokes for finding the balance after t = 3, 5, and 10 years.

Years	Keystrokes	Balance
3	5000 (1 + .085) ∧ 3 ENTER	$6386.45
5	2nd ENTRY ◄ 5 ENTER	$7518.28
10	2nd ENTRY ◄ 10 ENTER	$11,304.92

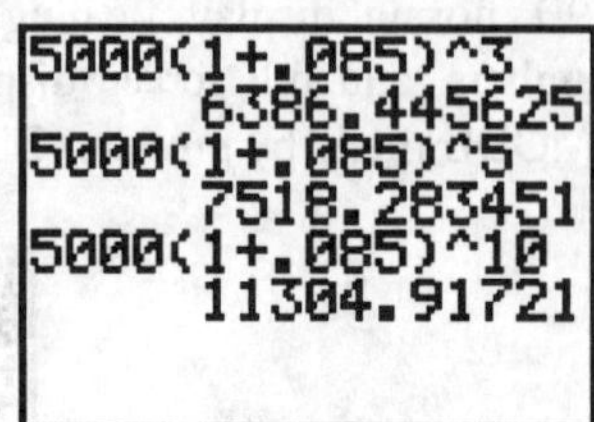

Figure 9.3: Editing expressions

Then to find the balance from the same initial investment but after 5 years when the annual interest rate is 7.5%, press the keys to change the last calculation above: 2nd ENTRY ◄ DEL ◄ 5 ◄ ◄ ◄ ◄ ◄ 7 ENTER.

9.1.3 Key Functions: Most keys on the TI-83 offer access to more than one function, just as the keys on a computer keyboard can produce more than one letter ("g" and "G") or even quite different characters ("5" and "%"). The primary function of a key is indicated on the key itself, and you access that function by a simple press on the key.

To access the *second* function indicated to the *left* above a key, first press 2nd (the cursor changes to a blinking ♦) and *then* press the key. For example to calculate $\sqrt{25}$, press 2nd $\sqrt{}$ 25 ENTER.

Technology Tip: The TI-83 automatically places a left parenthesis, (, after many functions and operators (including LOG, 2nd 10^x, LN, 2nd e^x, SIN, COS, TAN, and 2nd $\sqrt{}$). If no other calculations are being done, a matching right parenthesis does *not* need to be entered.

When you want to use a letter or other character printed to the *right* above a key, first press ALPHA (the cursor changes to a blinking **A**) and then the key. For example, to use the letter K in a formula, press ALPHA K. If you need several letters in a row, press 2nd A-LOCK, which is like the CAPS LOCK key on a computer keyboard, and then press all the letters you want. Remember to press ALPHA when you are finished and want to restore the keys to their primary functions.

9.1.4 Order of Operations: The TI-83 performs calculations according to the standard algebraic rules. Working outwards from inner parentheses, calculations are performed from left to right. Powers and roots are evaluated first, followed by multiplications and divisions, and then additions and subtractions.

Enter these expressions to practice using your TI-83.

Expression	Keystrokes	Display
$7 - 5 \cdot 3$	7 − 5 × 3 ENTER	−8
$(7 - 5) \cdot 3$	(7 − 5) × 3 ENTER	6
$120 - 10^2$	120 − 10 x² ENTER	20
$(120 - 10)^2$	(120 − 10) x² ENTER	12100
$\dfrac{24}{2^3}$	24 ÷ 2 ∧ 3 ENTER	3
$\left(\dfrac{24}{2}\right)^3$	(24 ÷ 2) ∧ 3 ENTER	1728
$(7 - -5) \cdot -3$	(7 − (−) 5) × (−) 3 ENTER	−36

9.1.5 Algebraic Expressions and Memory: Your calculator can evaluate expressions such as $\dfrac{N(N+1)}{2}$ *after* you have entered a value for N. Suppose you want $N = 200$. Press 200 STO◆ ALPHA N ENTER to store the value 200 in memory location N. Whenever you use N in an expression, the calculator will substitute the value 200 until you make a change by storing *another* number in N. Next enter the expression $\dfrac{N(N+1)}{2}$ by typing ALPHA N (ALPHA N + 1) ÷ 2 ENTER. For $N = 200$, you will find that $\dfrac{N(N+1)}{2} = 20100$.

The contents of any memory location may be revealed by typing just its letter name and then ENTER. And the TI-83 retains memorized values even when it is turned off, so long as its batteries are good.

9.1.6 Repeated Operations with ANS: The result of your *last* calculation is always stored in memory location ANS and replaces any previous result. This makes it easy to use the answer from one computation in another computation. For example, press 30 + 15 ENTER so that 45 is the last result displayed. Then press 2nd ANS ÷ 9 ENTER and get 5 because $45 \div 9 = 5$.

With a function like division, you press the ÷ *after* you enter an argument. For such functions, whenever you would start a new calculation with the previous answer followed by pressing the function key, you may press just the function key. So instead of 2nd ANS ÷ 9 in the previous example, you could have pressed simply ÷ 9 to achieve the same result. This technique also works for these functions: + − × ∧ x² x⁻¹.

Here is a situation where this is especially useful. Suppose a person makes $5.85 per hour and you are asked to calculate earnings for a day, a week, and a year. Execute the given keystrokes to find the person's incomes during these periods (results are shown in Figure 9.4).

Pay Period	Keystrokes	Earnings
8-hour day	5.85 × 8 ENTER	$46.80
5-day week	× 5 ENTER	$234
52-week year	× 52 ENTER	$12,168

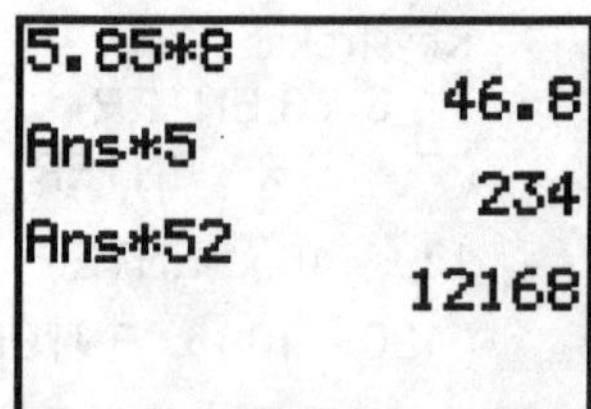

Figure 9.4: ANS variable

9.1.7 The MATH Menu: Operators and functions associated with a scientific calculator are available either immediately from the keys of the TI-83 or by the 2nd keys. You have direct access to common arithmetic operations (x^2, 2nd $\sqrt{}$, 2nd x^{-1}, $\wedge$), trigonometric functions (SIN, COS, TAN), and their inverses (2nd SIN^{-1}, 2nd COS^{-1}, 2nd TAN^{-1}), exponential and logarithmic functions (LOG, 2nd 10^x, LN, 2nd e^x), and a famous constant (2nd π).

A significant difference between the TI-83 graphing calculators and most scientific calculators is that TI-83 requires the argument of a function *after* the function, as you would see in a formula written in your textbook. For example, on the TI-83 you calculate $\sqrt{16}$ by pressing the keys 2nd $\sqrt{}$ 16 in that order.

Here are keystrokes for basic mathematical operations. Try them for practice on your TI-83.

Expression	Keystrokes	Display
$\sqrt{3^2+4^2}$	2nd $\sqrt{}$ (3 x^2 + 4 x^2) ENTER	5
$2\frac{1}{3}$	2 + 3 x^{-1} ENTER	2.333333333
$\log 200$	LOG 200 ENTER	2.301029996
$2.34 \cdot 10^5$	2.34 $\times$ 2nd 10^x 5 ENTER	234000

Additional mathematical operations and functions are available from the MATH menu. Press MATH to see the various options (Figure 9.5). You will learn in your mathematics textbook how to apply many of them. As an example, calculate $\sqrt[3]{7}$ by pressing MATH then *either* 4[$\sqrt[3]{}$] or ▼ ▼ ▼ ENTER; finally press 7 to see 1.912931183. To leave the MATH menu and take no other action, press 2nd QUIT or just CLEAR.

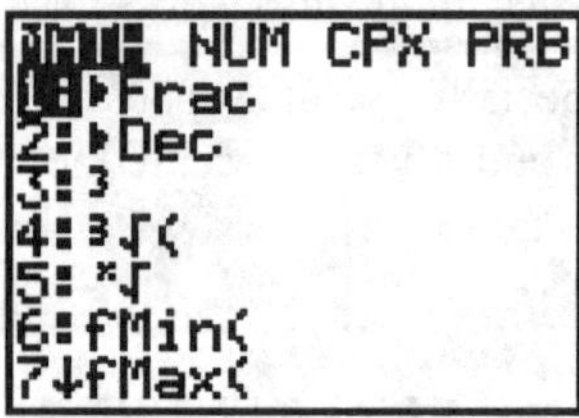

Figure 9.5: MATH menu

The *factorial* of a non-negative integer is the *product* of *all* the integers from 1 up to the given integer. The symbol for factorial is the exclamation point. So 4! (pronounced *four factorial*) is $1 \cdot 2 \cdot 3 \cdot 4 = 24$. You will learn more about applications of factorials in your textbook, but for now use the TI-83 to calculate 4! Press these keystrokes: 4 MATH ◄ 4[!] ENTER *or* 4 MATH ◄ ▼ ▼ ▼ ENTER ENTER.

9.2 Functions and Graphs

9.2.1 Evaluating Functions: Suppose you receive a monthly salary of \$1975 plus a commission of 10% of sales. Let x = your sales in dollars; then your wages W in dollars are given by the equation $W = 1975 + .10x$. If your January sales were \$2230 and your February sales were \$1865, what was your income during those months?

Here's one method to use your TI-83 to perform this task. Press the Y= at the top of the calculator to display the function editing screen (Figure 9.6). You may enter as many as ten different functions for the TI-83 to use at one time. If there is already a function Y_1 press ▲ or ▼ as many times as necessary to move the cursor to Y_1 and then press CLEAR to delete whatever was there. Then enter the expression $1975 + .10x$ by pressing these keys: 1975 + .10 X,T,θ,n. (The X,T,θ,n key lets you enter the variable X easily without having to use the ALPHA key.) Now press 2nd QUIT to return to the main calculations screen.

Assign the value 2230 to the variable x by these keystrokes (see Figure 9.7): 2230 STO▸ X,T,θ,n. Then press ALPHA : to allow another expression to be entered on the same command line. Next press the following keystrokes to evaluate Y_1 and find January's wages: VARS ▶ 1*[Function]* 1*[Y₁]* ENTER.

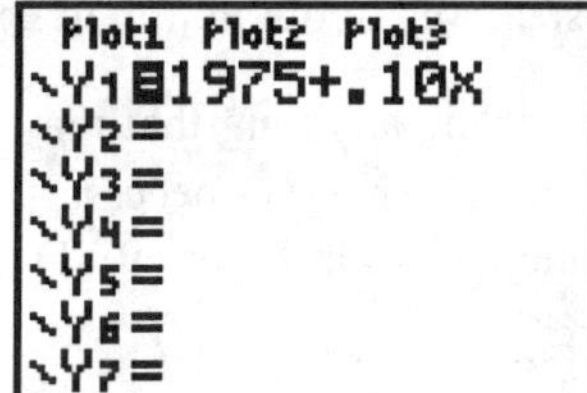

Figure 9.6: Y= screen

Figure 9.7: Evaluating a function

It is not necessary to repeat all these steps to find the February wages. Simply press 2nd ENTRY to recall the entire previous line, change 2230 to 1865, and press ENTER. Each time the TI-83 evaluates the function Y_1, it uses the *current* value of x.

Like your textbook, the TI-83 uses standard function notation. So to evaluate $Y_1(2230)$ when $Y_1(x) = 1975 + .10x$, press VARS ▶ 1*[Function]* 1*[Y₁]* (2230) ENTER (see Figure 9.8). Then to evaluate $Y_1(1865)$, press 2nd ENTRY to recall the last line and change 2230 to 1865.

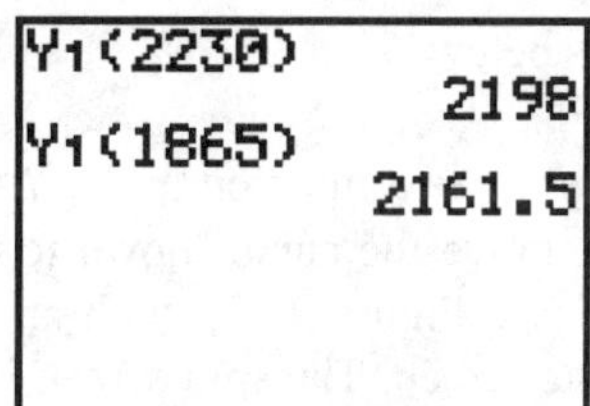

Figure 9.8: Function notation

You may also have the TI-83 make a table of values for the function. Press 2nd TBLSET to set up the table (Figure 9.9). Move the blinking cursor onto Ask beside Indpnt:, then press ENTER. This configuration permits you to input values for x one at a time. Now press 2nd TABLE, enter 2230 in the x column, and press ENTER (see Figure 9.10). Continue to enter additional values for x and the calculator automatically completes the table with corresponding values of Y_1. Press 2nd QUIT to leave the TABLE screen.

Figure 9.9: TBLSET screen

Figure 9.10: Table of values

Technology Tip: The TI-83 does not require multiplication to be expressed between variables, so *xxx* means x^3. It is often easier to press two or three *x*'s together than to search for the square key or the powers key. Of course, expressed multiplication is also not required between a constant and a variable. Hence to enter $2x^3 + 3x^2 - 4x + 5$ in the TI-83, you might save keystrokes and press just these keys: 2 X,T,θ,n X,T,θ,n X,T,θ,n + 3 X,T,θ,n X,T,θ,n − 4 X,T,θ,n + 5

9.2.2 Functions in a Graph Window: Once you have entered a function in the Y= screen of the TI-83, just press GRAPH to see its graph. The ability to draw a graph contributes substantially to our ability to solve problems.

For example, here is how to graph $y = -x^3 + 4x$. First press Y= and delete anything that may be there by moving with the arrow keys to Y$_1$ or to any of the other lines and pressing CLEAR wherever necessary. Then, with the cursor on the top line Y$_1$, press (−) X,T,θ,n $\wedge$ 3 + 4 X,T,θ,n to enter the function (as in Figure 9.11). Now press GRAPH and the TI-83 changes to a window with the graph of $y = -x^3 + 4x$ (Figure 9.12).

While the TI-83 is calculating coordinates for a plot, it displays a busy indicator at the top right of the graph window.

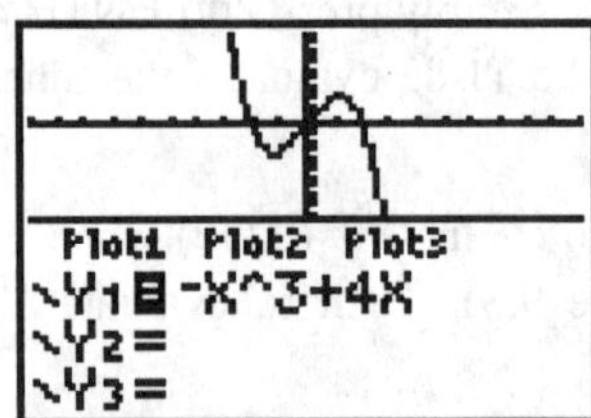

Figure 9.11: Split screen: Y= below

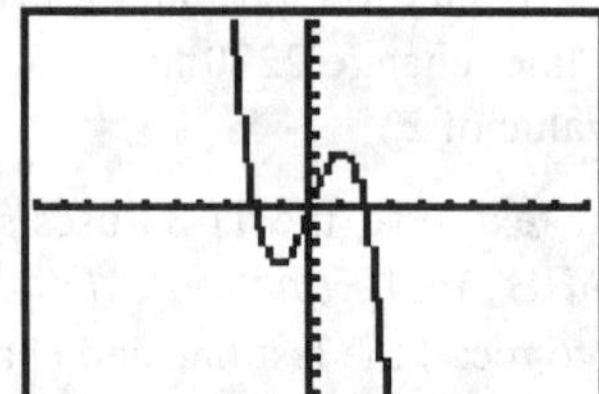

Figure 9.12: Graph of $y = -x^3 + 4x$

Technology Tip: If you would like to see a function in the Y= menu and its graph in a graph window, both at the same time, open the MODE menu, move the cursor down to the last line, and select Horiz screen. Your TI-83's screen is now divided horizontally (see Figure 9.11), with an upper graph window and a lower window that can display the home screen or an editing screen. The split screen is also useful when you need to do some calculations as you trace along a graph. For now, restore the TI-83 to Full screen.

Technology Tip: The TI-83 also can also show a vertically split screen with a graph on the left side and a table of values on the right side (the G-T option on screen display line of the MODE menu). This feature allows you to see both the graph and a corresponding table of values. Note that unless you use 2nd TBLSET to generate the table (as in Section 9.2.1), the table that is shown may not correspond to the current function.

TI-83 Graphics Calculator

Your graph window may look like the one in Figure 9.12 or it may be different. Since the graph of $y = -x^3 + 4x$ extends infinitely far left and right and also infinitely far up and down, the TI-83 can display only a piece of the actual graph. This displayed rectangular part is called a *viewing rectangle.* You can easily change the viewing rectangle to enhance your investigation of a graph.

The viewing rectangle in Figure 9.12 shows the part of the graph that extends horizontally from -10 to 10 and vertically from -10 to 10. Press WINDOW to see information about your viewing rectangle. Figure 9.13 shows the WINDOW screen that corresponds to the viewing rectangle in Figure 9.12. This is the *standard* viewing rectangle for the TI-83.

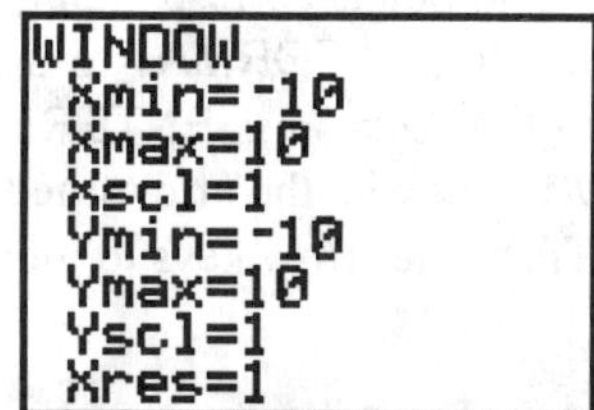

Figure 9.13: Standard WINDOW

The variables Xmin and Xmax are the minimum and maximum x-values of the viewing rectangle; Ymin and Ymax are the minimum and maximum y-values.

Xscl and Yscl set the spacing between tick marks on the axes.

Xres sets pixel resolution (1 through 8) for function graphs.

Technology Tip: Small Xres values improve graph resolution, but may cause the TI-83 to draw graphs more slowly.

Use the arrow keys ▲ and ▼ to move up and down from one line to another in this list; pressing the ENTER key will move down the list. Enter a new value to over-write a previous value and then press ENTER. Remember that a minimum *must* be less than the corresponding maximum or the TI-83 will issue an error message. Also, remember to use the (–) key, not – (which is subtraction), when you want to enter a negative value. Figures 9.12–13, 9.14–15, and 9.16–17 show different WINDOW screens and the corresponding viewing rectangle for each one.

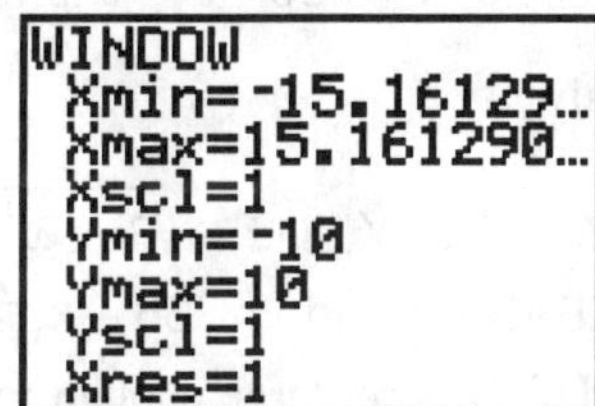

Figure 9.14: Square window

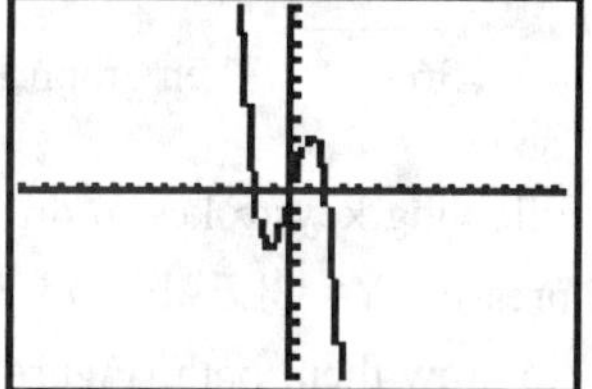

Figure 9.15: Graph of $y = -x^3 + 4x$

To initialize the viewing rectangle quickly to the *standard* viewing rectangle (Figure 9.13), press ZOOM 6[*ZStandard*]. To set the viewing rectangle quickly to a square (Figure 9.15), press ZOOM 5[*ZSquare*]. More information about square windows is presented later in Section 9.2.3.

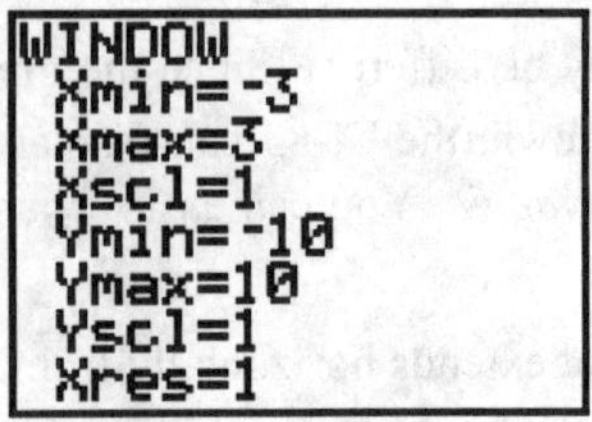

Figure 9.16: Custom window

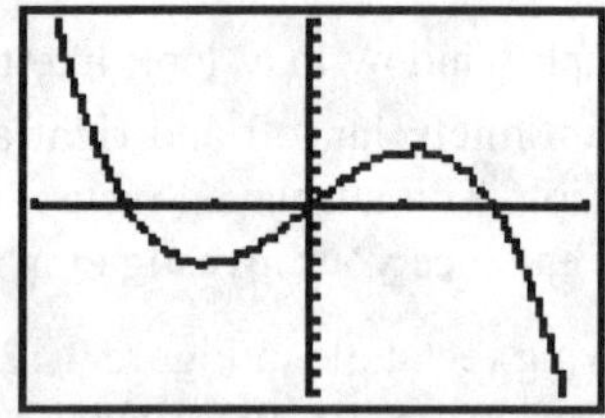

Figure 9.17: Graph of $y = -x^3 + 4x$

Sometimes you may wish to display grid points corresponding to tick marks on the axes. This and other graph format options may be changed by pressing 2nd FORMAT to display the FORMAT menu (Figure 9.18). Use arrow keys to move the blinking cursor to GridOn; press ENTER and then GRAPH to redraw the graph. Figure 9.19 shows the same graph as in Figure 9.17 but with the grid turned on. In general, you'll want the grid turned *off*, so do that now by pressing 2nd FORMAT, use the arrow keys to move the blinking cursor to GridOff, and press ENTER and CLEAR.

Figure 9.18: FORMAT menu

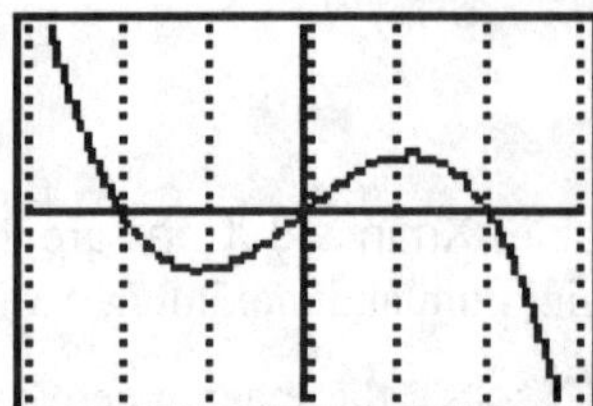

Figure 9.19: Grid turned on for $y = -x^3 + 4x$

Technology Tip: On the TI-83, the style of your graph can be changed by changing the icon to the left of Y_1 on the Y= screen. To change the icon press Y= ◄ ◄ and then ENTER repeatedly to scroll through the different styles available.

9.2.3 Graphing a Circle: Here is a useful technique for graphs that are not functions but can be "split" into a top part and a bottom part, or into multiple parts. Suppose you wish to graph the circle of radius 6 whose equation is $x^2 + y^2 = 36$. First solve for y and get an equation for the top semicircle, $y = \sqrt{36 - x^2}$, and for the bottom semicircle, $y = -\sqrt{36 - x^2}$. Then graph the two semicircles simultaneously.

Use the following keystrokes to draw this circle's graph. Enter $\sqrt{36 - x^2}$ as Y_1 and $-\sqrt{36 - x^2}$ as Y_2 (see Figure 9.20) by pressing Y= CLEAR 2nd $\sqrt{}$ 36 – X,T,θ,n x^2) ENTER CLEAR (–) 2nd $\sqrt{}$ 36 – X,T,θ,n x^2). Then press GRAPH to draw them both (Figure 9.21). Make sure that the WINDOW is set large enough to display a circle of radius 6.

Figure 9.20: Two semicircles

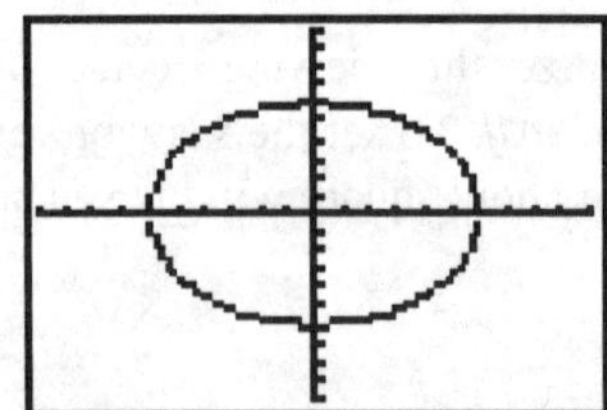

Figure 9.21: Circle's graph - standard WINDOW

TI-83 Graphics Calculator

Instead of entering $-\sqrt{36-x^2}$ as Y_2, you could have entered $-Y_1$ as Y_2 and saved some keystrokes. On the TI-83, try this by going into the Y= screen and pressing ▼ to move the cursor down to Y_2. Then press CLEAR (−) VARS ► 1*[Function]* ENTER (Figure 9.22). The graph should be as before.

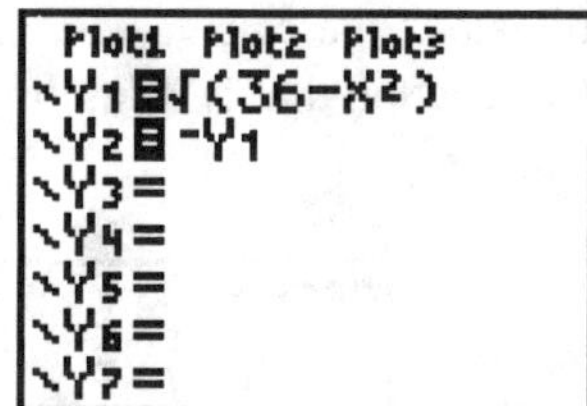

Figure 9.22: Using the VARS menu

If your range were set to a viewing rectangle extending from −10 to 10 in both directions, your graph would look like Figure 9.21. Now this does *not* look a circle, because the units along the axes are not the same. You need what is called a "square" viewing rectangle. Press ZOOM 5*[ZSquare]* and see a graph that appears more circular.

Technology Tip: Another way to get a square graph is to change the range variables so that the value of Ymax − Ymin is approximately $\frac{2}{3}$ times Xmax − Xmin. For example, see the WINDOW in Figure 9.23 to get the corresponding graph in Figure 9.24. This method works because the dimensions of the TI-83's display are such that the ratio of vertical to horizontal is approximately $\frac{2}{3}$.

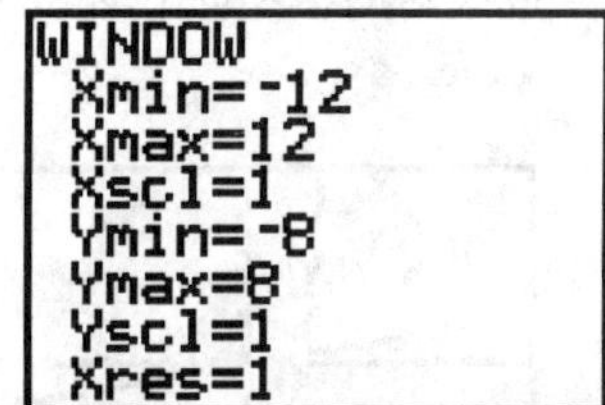

Figure 9.23: $\frac{\text{vertical}}{\text{horizontal}} = \frac{16}{24} = \frac{2}{3}$

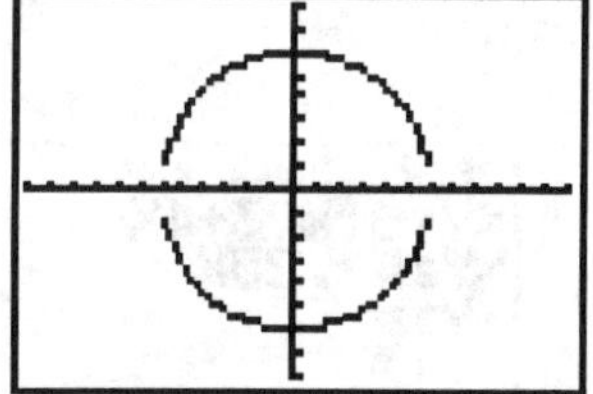

Figure 9.24: A "square" circle

The two semicircles in Figure 9.24 do not meet because of an idiosyncrasy in the way the TI-83 plots a graph.

9.2.4 TRACE: Graph the function $y = -x^3 + 4x$ from Section 9.2.2 using the standard viewing rectangle. (Remember to clear any other functions in the Y= screen.) Press any of the arrow keys ▲ ▼ ◄ ► and see the cursor move from the center of the viewing rectangle. The coordinates of the cursor's location are displayed at the bottom of the screen, as in Figure 9.25, in floating decimal format. This cursor is called a *free-moving cursor* because it can move from dot to dot *anywhere* in the graph window.

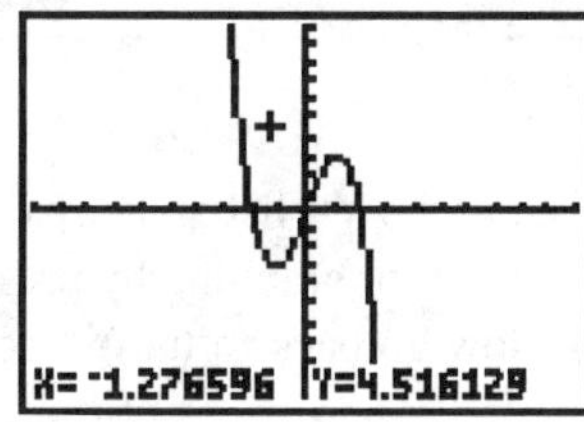

Figure 9.25: Free-moving cursor

Remove the free-moving cursor and its coordinates from the window by pressing GRAPH, CLEAR, or ENTER. Press an arrow key again and the free-moving cursor will reappear at the same point you left it.

Press TRACE to enable the left ◄ and right ► arrow keys to move the cursor along the function. The cursor is no longer free-moving, but is now constrained to the function. The coordinates that are displayed belong to points on the function's graph, so the y-coordinate is the calculated value of the function at the corresponding x-coordinate (Figure 9.26). The TI-83 displays the function that is being traced in the upper left of the screen while the TRACE feature is being used.

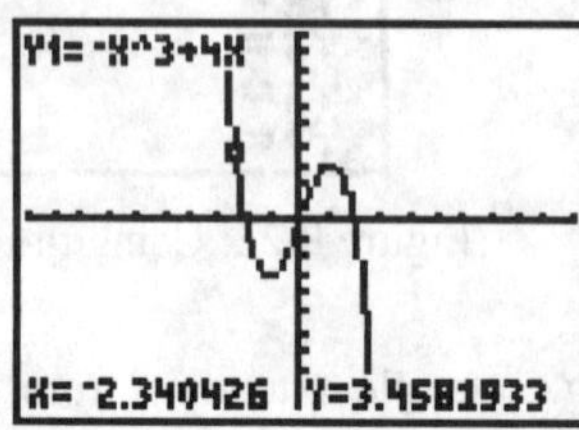

Figure 9.26: TRACE

Now plot a second function, $y = -.25x$, along with $y = -x^3 + 4x$. Press Y= and move the cursor to the Y_2 line and enter $-.25x$, then press GRAPH to see both functions (Figure 9.28).

Notice that in Figure 9.27 the equal signs next to Y_1 and Y_2 are *both* highlighted. This means that *both* functions will be graphed. In the Y= screen, move the cursor directly on top of the equal sign next to Y_1 and press ENTER. This equal sign should no longer be highlighted (Figure 9.29). Now press GRAPH and see that only Y_2 is plotted (Figure 9.30).

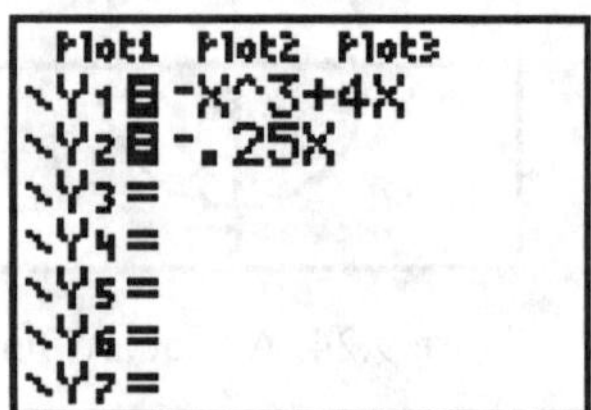

Figure 9.27: Two functions

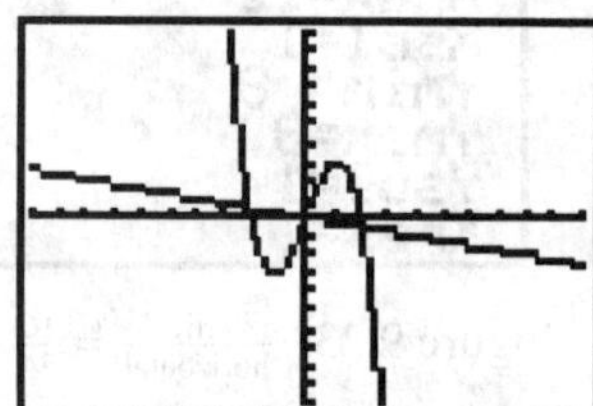

Figure 9.28: $y = -x^3 + 4x$ and $y = -.25x$

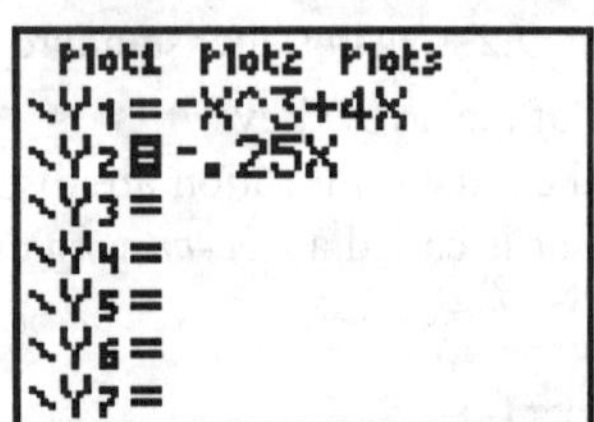

Figure 9.29: only Y_2 active

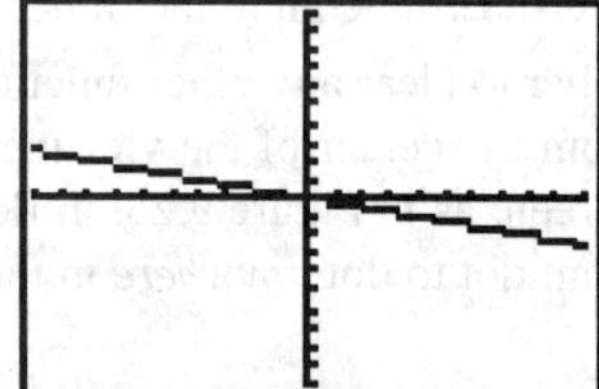

Figure 9.30: Graph of $y = -.25x$

Many different functions can be stored in the Y= list and any combination of them may be graphed simultaneously. You can make a function active or inactive for graphing by pressing ENTER on its equal sign to highlight (activate) or remove the highlight (deactivate). Now go back to the Y= screen and do what is needed in order to graph Y_1 but not Y_2.

Now activate both functions so that both graphs are plotted. Press TRACE and the cursor appears first on the graph of $y = -x^3 + 4x$ because it is higher up on the Y= list. You know that the cursor is on this function, Y_1, because this function is displayed in the upper left of the screen. Press the up ▲ or down ▼ arrow key to move the cursor vertically to the graph of $y = -.25x$. Now the function $Y_2 = -.25x$ is shown in the upper left of the screen. Next press the left and right arrow keys to trace along the graph of $y = -.25x$. When more than one function is plotted, you can move the trace cursor vertically from one graph to another with the ▲ and ▼ keys.

Technology Tip: By the way, trace the graph of $y = -.25x$ and press and hold either ◄ or ►. Eventually you will reach the left or right edge of the window. Keep pressing the arrow key and the TI-83 will allow you to continue the trace by panning the viewing rectangle. Check the WINDOW screen to see that the Xmin and Xmax are automatically updated.

The TI-83 has a display of 95 horizontal columns of pixels and 63 vertical rows, so when you trace a curve across a graph window, you are actually moving from Xmin to Xmax in 94 equal jumps, each called Δx. You would calculate the size of each jump to be $\Delta x = \dfrac{\text{Xmax} - \text{Xmin}}{94}$. Sometimes you may want the jumps to be friendly numbers like 0.1 or 0.25 so that, when you trace along the curve, the x-coordinates will be incremented by such a convenient amount. Just set your viewing rectangle for a particular increment Δx by making Xmax = Xmin + 94 · Δx. For example, if you want Xmin = −5 and $\Delta x = 0.3$, set Xmax = −5 + 94 · 0.3 = 23.2. Likewise, set Ymax = Ymin + 62 · Δy if you want the vertical increment to be some special Δy.

To center your window around a particular point, say (h, k), and also have a certain Δx, set Xmin = $h - 47 \cdot \Delta x$ and make Xmax = $h + 47 \cdot \Delta x$. Likewise, make Ymin = $k - 31 \cdot \Delta y$ and make Ymax = $k + 31 \cdot \Delta x$. For example, to center a window around the origin (0, 0), with both horizontal and vertical increments of 0.25, set the range so that Xmin = 0 − 47 · 0.25 = −11.75, Xmax = 0 + 47 · 0.25 = 11.75, Ymin = 0 − 31 · 0.25 = −7.75 and Ymax = 0 + 31 · 0.25 = 7.75.

See the benefit by first plotting $y = x^2 + 2x + 1$ in a standard graphing window. Trace near its y-intercept, which is (0, 1), and move towards its x-intercept, which is (−1, 0). Then press ZOOM 4[ZDecimal] and trace again near the intercepts.

9.2.5 ZOOM: Plot again the two graphs, for $y = -x^3 + 4x$ and $y = -.25x$. There appears to be an intersection near $x = 2$. The TI-83 provides several ways to enlarge the view around this point. You can change the viewing rectangle directly by pressing WINDOW and editing the values of Xmin, Xmax, Ymin, and Ymax. Figure 9.31 shows a new viewing rectangle for the range displayed in Figure 9.32. The cursor has been moved near the point of intersection; move your cursor closer to get the best approximation possible for the coordinates of the intersection.

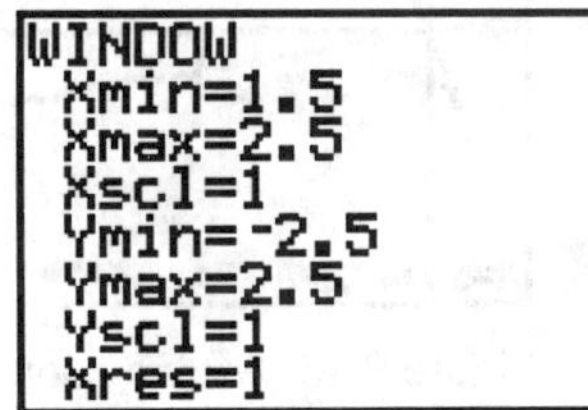

Figure 9.31: New WINDOW

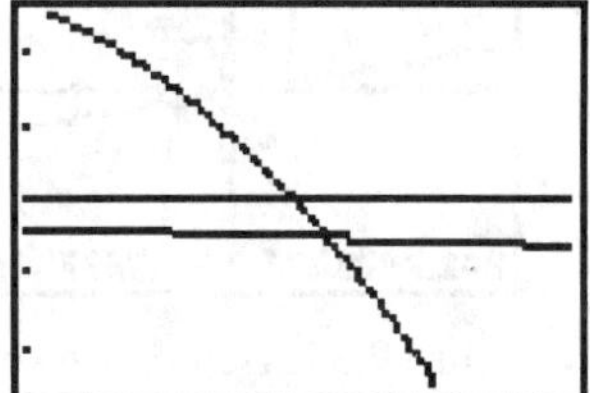

Figure 9.32: Closer view

A more efficient method for enlarging the view is to draw a new viewing rectangle with the cursor. Start again with a graph of the two functions $y = -x^3 + 4x$ and $y = -.25x$ in a standard viewing rectangle. (Press ZOOM 6[ZStandard] for the standard viewing window.)

Now imagine a small rectangular box around the intersection point, near $x = 2$. Press ZOOM 1*[ZBox]* (Figure 9.33) to draw a box to define this new viewing rectangle. Use the arrow keys to move the cursor, whose coordinates are displayed at the bottom of the window, to one corner of the new viewing rectangle you imagine.

Press ENTER to fix the corner where you moved the cursor; it changes shape and becomes a blinking square (Figure 9.34). Use the arrow keys again to move the cursor to the diagonally opposite corner of the new rectangle (Figure 9.35). If this box looks all right to you, press ENTER. The rectangular area you have enclosed will now enlarge to fill the graph window (Figure 9.36).

Figure 9.33: ZOOM menu

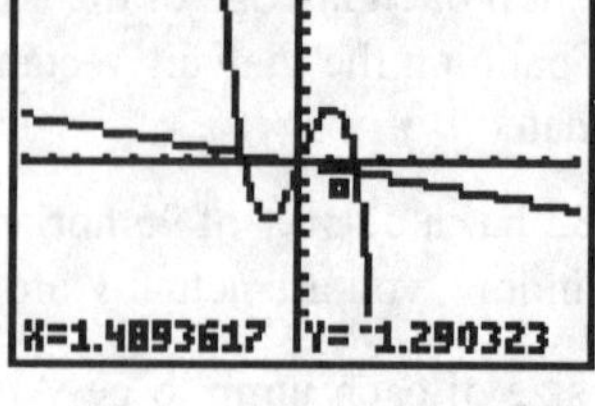

Figure 9.34: One corner selected

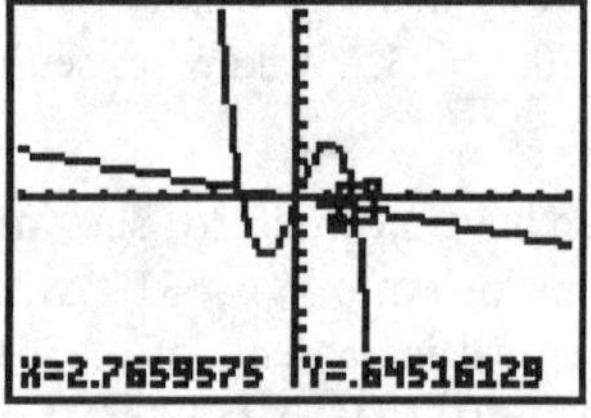

Figure 9.35: Box drawn

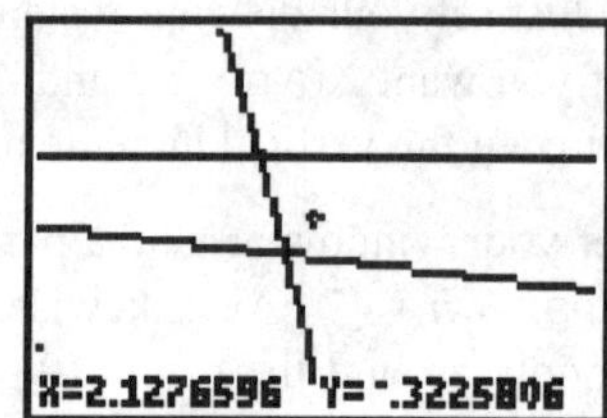

Figure 9.36: New viewing rectangle

You may cancel the zoom any time *before* you press this last ENTER. Press ZOOM once more and start over. Press CLEAR or GRAPH to cancel the zoom, or press 2nd QUIT to cancel the zoom and return to the home screen.

You can also quickly magnify a graph around the cursor's location. Return once more to the standard window for the graph of the two functions $y = -x^3 + 4x$ and $y = -.25x$. Press ZOOM 2*[Zoom In]* and then press arrow keys to move the cursor as close as you can to the point of intersection near $x = 2$ (see Figure 9.37). Then press ENTER and the calculator draws a magnified graph, centered at the cursor's position (Figure 9.38). The range variables are changed to reflect this new viewing rectangle. Look in the WINDOW menu to verify this.

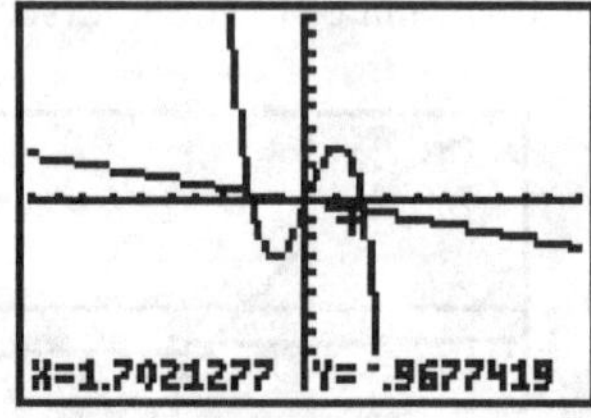

Figure 9.37: Before a zoom in

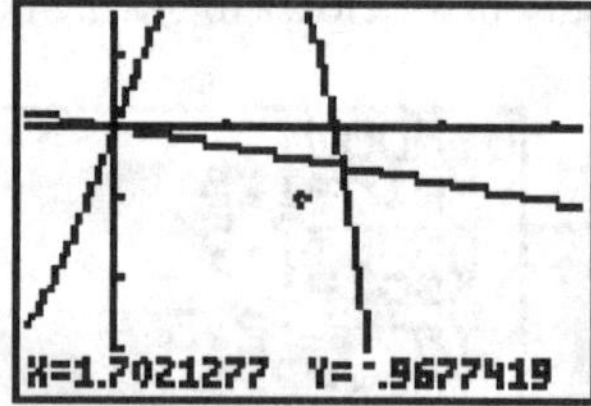

Figure 9.38: After a zoom in

As you see in the ZOOM menu (Figure 9.33), the TI-83 can zoom in (press ZOOM 2) or zoom out (press ZOOM 3). Zoom out to see a larger view of the graph, centered at the cursor position. You can change the horizontal and vertical scale of the magnification by pressing ZOOM ▶ 4*[SetFactors]* (see Figure 9.39) and editing XFact and YFact, the horizontal and vertical magnification factors (Figure 9.40).

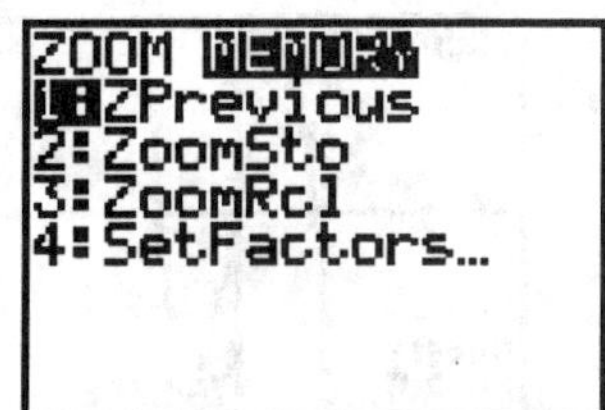

Figure 9.39: ZOOM MEMORY menu

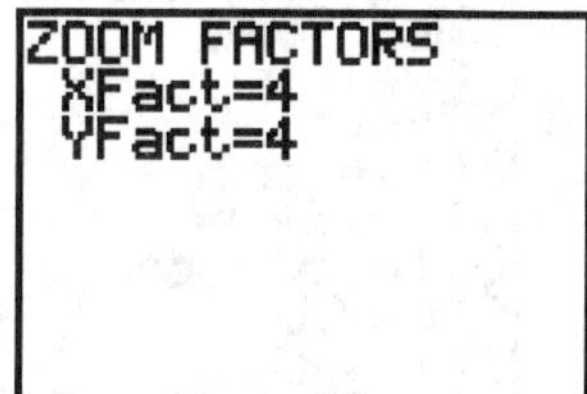

Figure 9.40: ZOOM MEMORY SetFactors

Technology Tip: An advantage of zooming in from square viewing window is that subsequent windows will also be square. Likewise, if you zoom in from a friendly viewing rectangle, the zoomed windows will also be friendly.

The default zoom factor is 4 in both direction. It is not necessary for **Xfact** and **Yfact** to be equal. sometimes, you may prefer to zoom in one direction only, so the other factor should be set to 1. As usual, press **2nd QUIT** to leave the **ZOOM** menu.

Technology Tip: The TI-83 remembers the window it displayed before a zoom. So if you should zoom in too much and lose the curve, press ZOOM ▶ 1*[ZPrevious]* to go back to the window before. If you want to execute a series of zooms but then return to a particular window, press ZOOM ▶ 2*[ZoomSto]* to store the current window's dimensions. Later, press ZOOM ▶ 3*[ZoomRcl]* to recall the stored window.

9.3   Solving Equations and Inequalities

9.3.1 Intercepts and Intersections: Tracing and zooming are also used to locate an x-intercept of a graph, where a curve crosses the x-axis. For example, the graph of $y = x^3 - 8x$ crosses x-axis three times (Figure 9.41). After tracing over to the x-intercept point that is farthest to the left, zoom in (Figure 9.42). Continue this process until you have located all three intercepts with as much accuracy as you need. The three x-intercepts of $y = x^3 - 8x$ are approximately −2.828, 0, and 2.828.

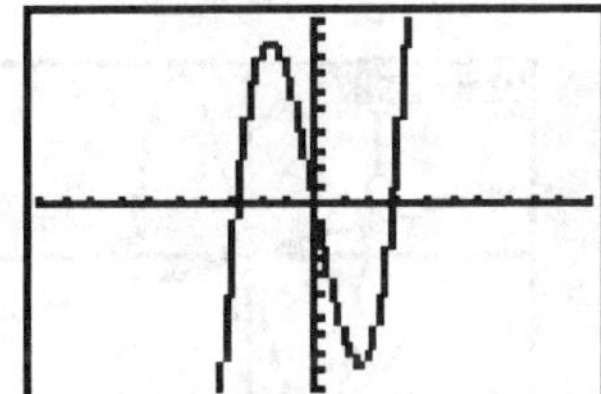

Figure 9.41: Graph of $y = x^3 - 8x$

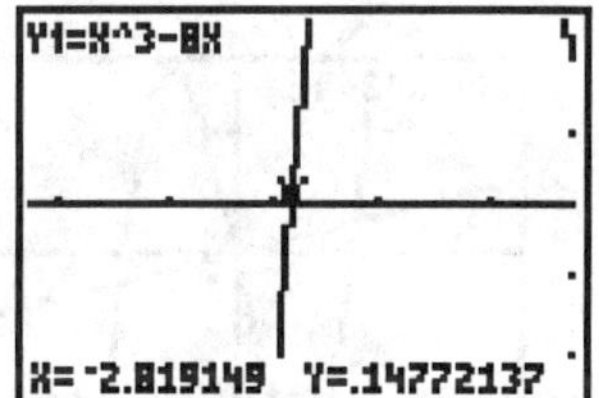

Figure 9.42: Near an x-intercept of $y = x^3 - 8x$

Technology Tip: As you zoom in, you may also wish to change the spacing between tick marks on the x-axis so that the viewing rectangle shows scale marks near the intercept point. Then the accuracy of your approximation will be such that the error is less than the distance between two tick marks. Change the x-scale on the TI-83 from the **WINDOW** menu. Move the cursor down to x**Scl** and enter an appropriate value.

The x-intercept of a function's graph is a *zero* of the function, so press **2nd CALC** to display the **CALCULATE** menu and choose **2 *[zero]*** to find a zero of this function (Figure 9.43). You will be prompted for a value left of the zero. Either trace the cursor to such a point or enter a value left of the zero. Press **ENTER**. Then you will be prompted for a value right of the zero. Either trace the cursor to such a point or enter a value right of the zero. Press **ENTER**. Note the two arrows near the top of the display marking the left and right bounds (Figure 9.44).

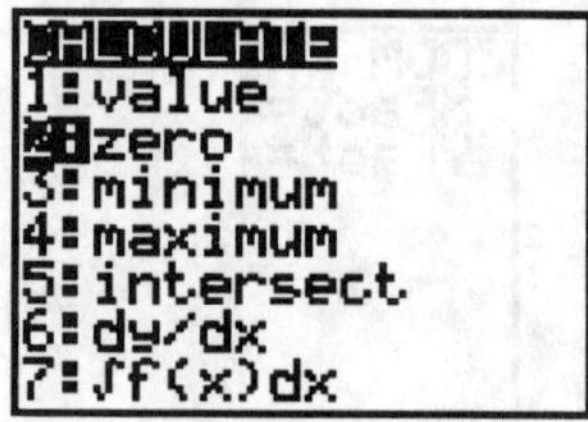

Figure 9.43: CALCULATE menu

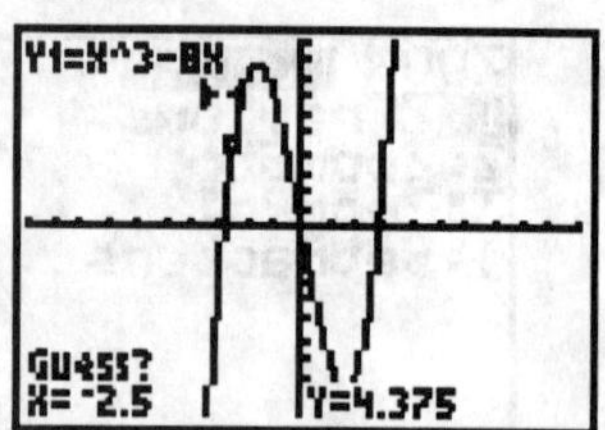

Figure 9.44: Finding a zero

Finally, you will be prompted for a guess of the zero. Either move the cursor near the zero or enter a guess for the zero. Good choices for the lower bound, upper bound, and guess can help the calculator work more efficiently and quickly. Press ENTER and the TI-83 shows the coordinates of the point and indicates that it is a zero (Figure 9.45).

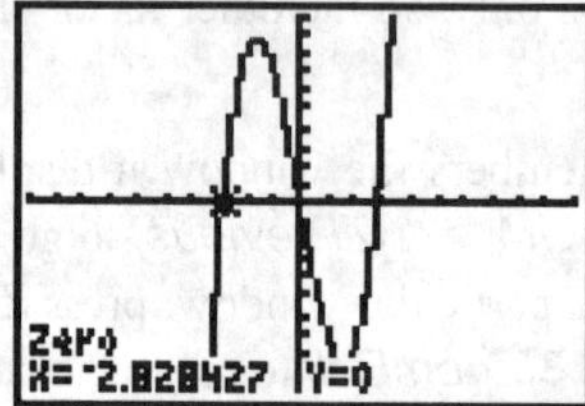

Figure 9.45: A zero of $y = x^3 - 8x$

TRACE and ZOOM are especially important for locating the intersection points of two graphs, say the graphs of $y = -x^3 + 4x$ and $y = -.25x$. Trace along one of the graphs until you arrive close to an intersection point. Then press ▲ or ▼ to jump to the other graph. Notice that the x-coordinate does not change, but the y-coordinate is likely to be different (Figures 9.46 and 9.47).

When two y-coordinates are as close as they can get, you have come as close as you now can to the point of intersection. So zoom in around the intersection point, then trace again until the two y-coordinates are as close as possible. Continue this process until you have located the point of intersection with as much accuracy as necessary.

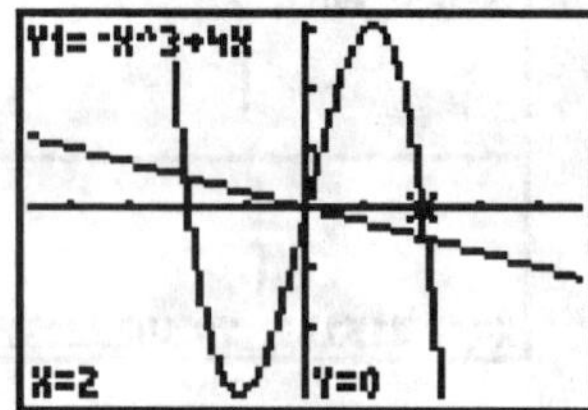

Figure 9.46: Trace on $y = -x^3 + 4x$

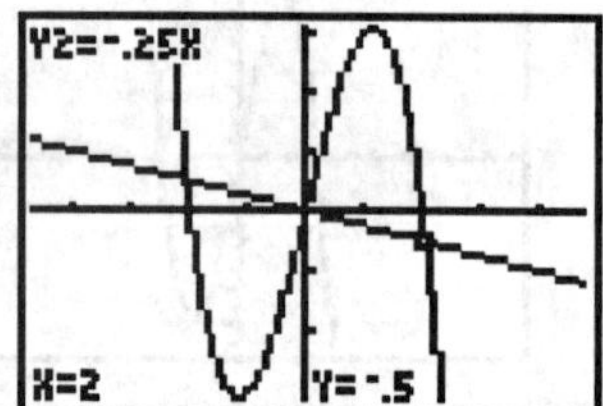

Figure 9.47: Trace on $y = -.25x$

You can also find the point of intersection of two graphs by pressing 2nd CALC 5 *[intersect]*. Trace with the cursor first along one graph near the intersection and press ENTER; then trace with the cursor along the other graph and press ENTER. Finally, move the cursor near the point of intersection and press ENTER again. Coordinates of the intersection will be displayed at the bottom of the window (Figure 9.48).

TI-83 Graphics Calculator

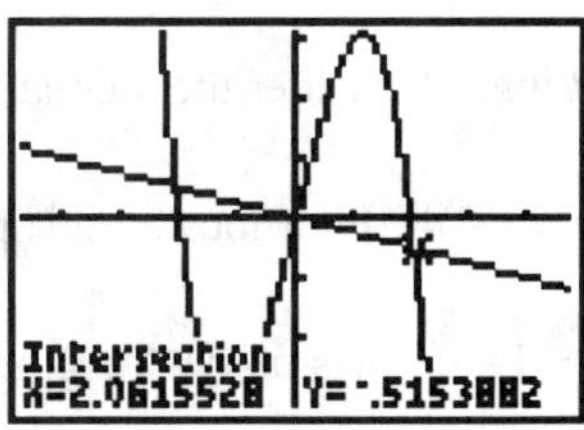

Figure 9.48: An intersection of $y = -x^3 + 4x$ and $y = -.25x$

9.3.2 Solving Equations by Graphing: Suppose you need to solve the equation $24x^3 - 36x + 17 = 0$. First graph $y = 24x^3 - 36x + 17$ in a window large enough to exhibit *all* its x-intercepts, corresponding to all the equation's zeros (roots). Then use trace and zooom, or the TI-83's zero feature, to locate each one. In fact this equation has just on soltuion, approximately $x = -1.414$.

Remember that when an equation has more than one x-intercept, it may be necessary to change the viewing rectangle a few times to locate all of them.

Technology Tip: To solve an equation like $24x^3 + 17 = 36x$, you may first transform it into standard form, $24x^3 - 36x + 17 = 0$, and proceed as above. However, you may also graph the *two* functions $y = 24x^3 + 17$ and $y = 36x$, then zoom and trace to locate their point of intersection.

9.3.3 Solving Systems by Graphing: The solutions to a system of equations correspond to the points of intersection of their graphs (Figure 9.49). For example, to solve the system $y = x^3 + 3x^2 - 2x - 1$ and $y = x^2 - 3x - 4$, first graph them together. Then use zoom and trace or the intersect option from the CALC menu to locate their point of intersection, approximately $(-2.17, 7.25)$.

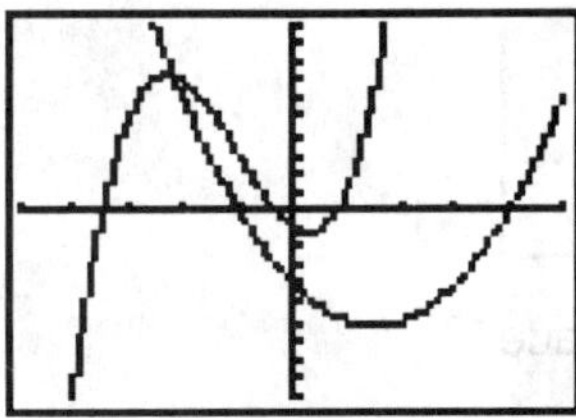

Figure 9.49: Graph of $y = x^3 + 3x^2 - 2x - 1$ and $y = x^2 - 3x - 4$

If you did not use the intersect feature, you must judge whether the two current y-coordinates are sufficiently close for $x = -2.17$ or whther you should continue to soom and trace to improve the approximation. The solutions of the system of two equations $y = x^3 + 3x^2 - 2x - 1$ and $y = x^2 - 3x - 4$ correspond to the solutions of the single equation $x^3 + 3x^2 - 2x - 1 = x^2 - 3x - 4$, which simplifies to $x^3 + 2x^2 + x + 3 = 0$. So you may also graph $y = x^3 + 2x^2 + x + 3$ and find its x-intercepts to solve the system.

9.3.4 Solving Inequalities by Graphing: Consider the inequality $1 - \dfrac{3x}{2} \geq x - 4$. To solve it with your TI-83, graph

the two function $y = 1 - \dfrac{3x}{2}$ and $y = x - 4$. First locate their point of intersection at $x = 2$ (Figure 9.50). The ine-

quality is true when the graph of $y = 1 - \dfrac{3x}{2}$ lies *above* the graph of $y = x - 4$, and that occurs when $x < 2$. So the

solution is the half-line $x \leq 2$, or $(-\infty, 2]$.

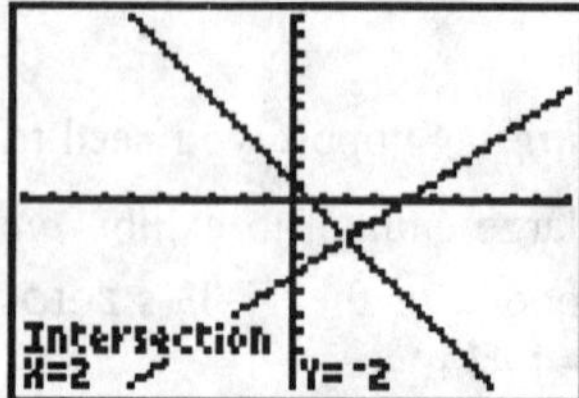

Figure 9.50: Solving $1 - \dfrac{3x}{2} \geq x - 4$

The TI-83 is capable of shading the region above or below a graph, or between two graphs. For example, to graph $y \geq x^2 - 1$, first graph the function $y = x^2 - 1$ as Y_1. Then press 2nd DRAW 7[Shade(] VARS ▶ 1[Function] 1[Y₁] , 100) ENTER (see Figure 9.51). These keystrokes instruct the TI-83 to shade the region *above* $y = x^2 - 1$ and *below* $y = 100$ (chosen because this is a y-value significantly above the graph window) using the default shading option. The result is shown in Figure 9.52.

Figure 9.51: DRAW Shade

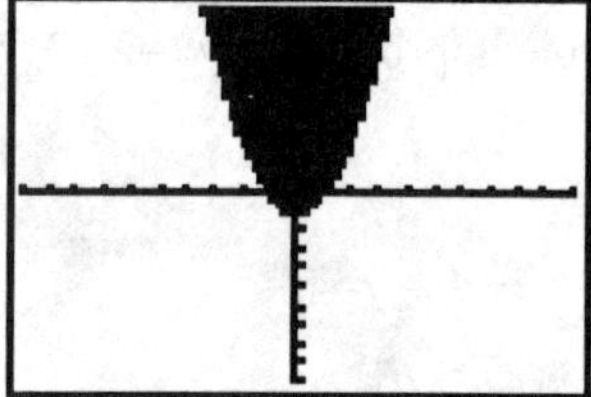

Figure 9.52: Graph of $y \geq x^2 - 1$

Now use shading to solve the previous inequality, $1 - \dfrac{3x}{2} \geq x - 4$. The function whose graph forms the lower

boundary is named *first* in the SHADE command (see Figure 9.53). To enter this in your TI-83, press these keys: 2nd DRAW 7[Shade(] X,T,θ,n − 4 , 1 − 3 X,T,θ,n ÷ 2) ENTER (Figure 9.54). The shading extends left from $x = -$

2, hence the solution to $1 - \dfrac{3x}{2} \geq x - 4$ is the half-line $x \leq 2$, or $(-\infty, 2]$.

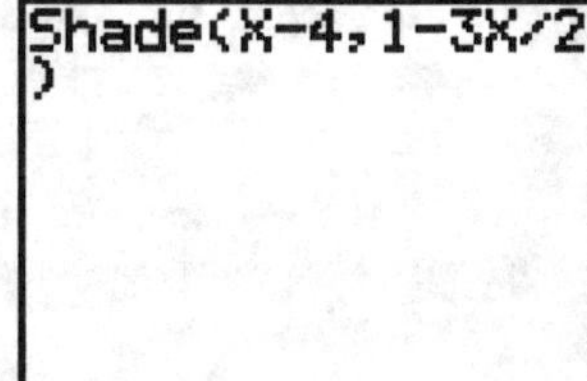

Figure 9.53: DRAW Shade command

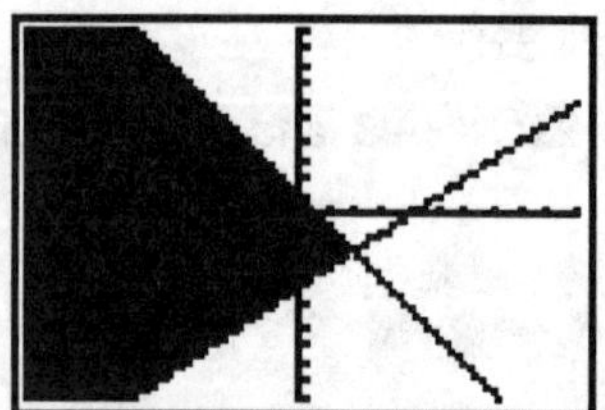

Figure 9.54: Graph of $1 - \dfrac{3x}{2} \geq x - 4$

TI-83 Graphics Calculator

More information about the DRAW menu is in the TI-83 manual.

9.4   Matrices

9.4.1 Making a Matrix: The TI-83 can work with 10 different matrices (A through J). Here's how to create this

3×4 matrix $\begin{bmatrix} 1 & -4 & 3 & 5 \\ -1 & 3 & -1 & -3 \\ 2 & 0 & -4 & 6 \end{bmatrix}$ in your calculator.

Press MATRX to see the matrix menu (Figure 9.55); then press ▶ ▶ or just ◀ to switch to the matrix EDIT menu. Whenever you enter the matrix EDIT menu, the cursor starts at the top matrix. Move to another matrix by repeatedly pressing ▼. For now, press ENTER to edit matrix [A].

The display will show the dimension of matrix [A] if the matrix exists; otherwise, it will display 1 × 1 (Figure 9.56). Change the dimensions of matrix [A] by pressing 3 ENTER 4 ENTER. Simply press ENTER or an arrow key to accept an existing dimension. The matrix shown in the window changes in size to reflect a changed dimension.

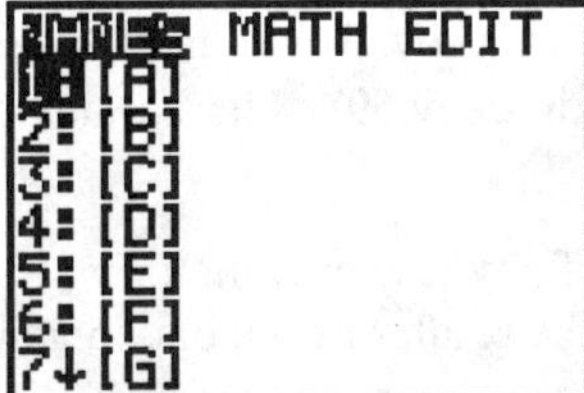

Figure 9.55: MATRX menu

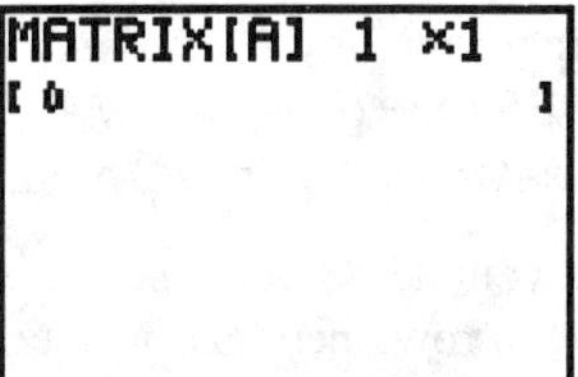

Figure 9.56: Editing a matrix

Use the arrow keys or press ENTER repeatedly to move the cursor to a matrix element you want to change. If you press ENTER, you will move right across a row and then back to the first column of the next row. At the right edge of the screen in Figure 9.57, there are dashes to indicate more columns than are shown. Go to them by pressing ▶ as many times as necessary. The ordered pair at the bottom left of the screen shows the cursor's current location within the matrix. The element in the second row and first column in Figure 9.57 is highlighted, so that the ordered pair at the bottom of the window is 2 , 1 and the screen shows that element's current value. Continue to enter all the elements of matrix [A]; press ENTER after inputing each value.

Figure 9.57: Editing a matrix

When you are finished, leave the editing screen by pressing 2nd QUIT to return to the home screen.

9.4.2 Row Operations: Here are the keystrokes necessary to perform elementary row operations on a matrix. Your textbook provides a more careful explanation of the elementary row operations and their uses.

To interchange the second and third rows of the matrix [A] that was defined above, press MATRX ▶ ALPHA C*[rowSwap(]* MATRX 1 , 2 , 3) ENTER (see Figure 9.58). The format of this command is rowSwap(*matrix, row1, row2*).

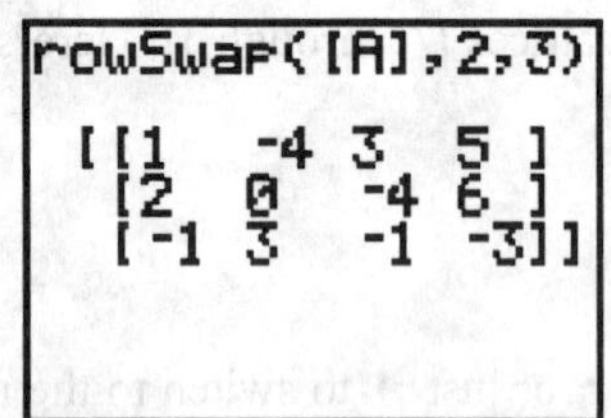

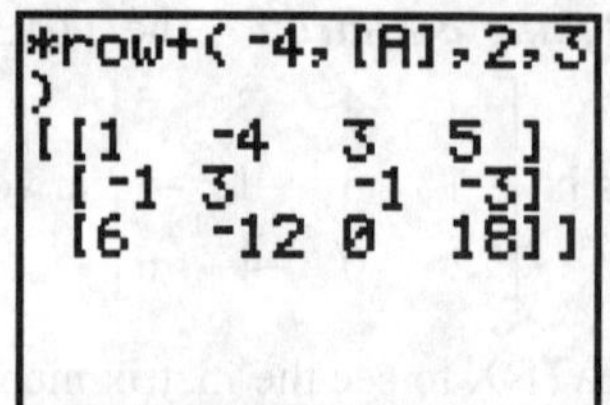

Figure 9.58: Swap rows 2 and 3
Figure 9.59: Add –4 times row 2 to row 3

To add row 2 and row 3 and *store* the results in row 3, press MATRX ▶ ALPHA D*[row+(]* MATRX 1 , 2 , 3) ENTER. The format of this command is row+(*matrix, row1, row2*).

To multiply row 2 by –4 and *store* the results in row 2, thereby replacing row 2 with new values, press MATRX ▶ ALPHA E*[*row(]* (–) 4 , MATRX 1 , 2) ENTER. The format of this command is *row(*value, matrix, row*).

To multiply row 2 by –4 and *add* the results to row 3, thereby replacing row 3 with new values, press MATRX ▶ ALPHA F*[*row+(]* (–) 4 , MATRX 1 , 2, 3) ENTER (see Figure 9.59). The format of this command is *row+(*scalar, matrix, row1, row2*).

Note that your TI-83 does *not* store a matrix obtained as the result of any row operation. So, when you need to perform several row operations in succession, it is a good idea to store the result of each one in a temporary place. You may wish to use matrix [J] to hold such intermediate results.

For example, use row operations to solve this system of linear equations: $\begin{cases} x - 2y + 3z = 9 \\ -x + 3y = -4 \\ 2x - 5y + 5z = 17 \end{cases}$.

First enter this *augmented matrix* as [A] in your TI-83: $\begin{bmatrix} 1 & -2 & 3 & 9 \\ -1 & 3 & 0 & -4 \\ 2 & -5 & 5 & 17 \end{bmatrix}$. Next store this matrix as [E] (press

MATRX 1 STO▸ MATRX 5 ENTER), so you may keep the original in case you need to recall it.

Here are the row operations and their associated keystrokes. At each step, the result is stored in [E] and replaces the previous matrix [E]. The completion of the row operations is shown in Figure 9.60.

Row Operations	*Keystrokes*
add row 1 to row 2	MATRX ▶ ALPHA D MATRX 5 , 1 , 2) STO▸ MATRX 5 ENTER
add –2 times row 1 to row 3	MATRX ▶ ALPHA F (–) 2 , MATRX 5 , 1 , 3) STO▸ MATRX 5 ENTER
add row 2 to row 3	MATRX ▶ ALPHA D MATRX 5 , 2, 3,) STO▸ MATRX 5 ENTER
multiply row 3 by $\frac{1}{2}$	MATRX ▶ ALPHA E 1 ÷ 2 , MATRX 5 , 3) STO▸ MATRX 5 ENTER

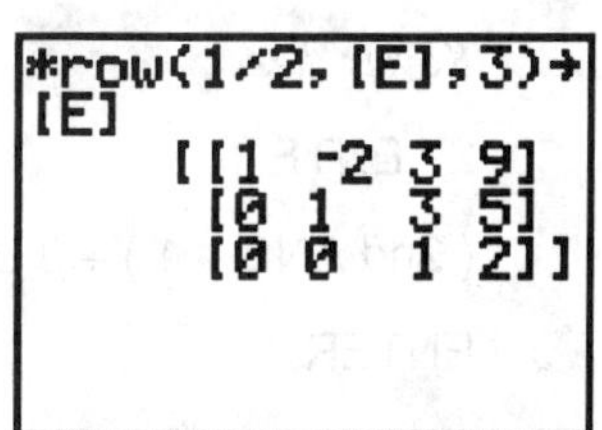

Figure 9.60: Final matrix after row operations

Thus $z = 2$, so $y = -1$ and $x = 1$.

Technology Tip: The TI-83 can produce a row-echelon form and the reduced row-echelon form of a matrix. The row-echelon form of matrix [A] is obtained by pressing MATRX ▶ ALPHA A*[ref(]* MATRX 1) ENTER and the reduced row-echelon form is obtained by pressing MATRX ▶ ALPHA B*[rref(]* MATRX 1) ENTER. Note that the row-echelon form of a matrix is not unique, so your calculator may not get exactly the same matrix as you do by using row operations. However, the matrix that the TI-83 produces will result in the same solution to the system.

9.4.3 Determinants: Enter this 3×3 square matrix as [A]: $\begin{bmatrix} 1 & -2 & 3 \\ -1 & 3 & 0 \\ 2 & -5 & 5 \end{bmatrix}$. To calculate its determinant $\begin{bmatrix} 1 & -2 & 3 \\ -1 & 3 & 0 \\ 2 & -5 & 5 \end{bmatrix}$, go to the home screen and press MATRX ▶ 1*[det(]* MATRX 1) ENTER. You should find that the determinant is 2 as shown in Figure 9.61.

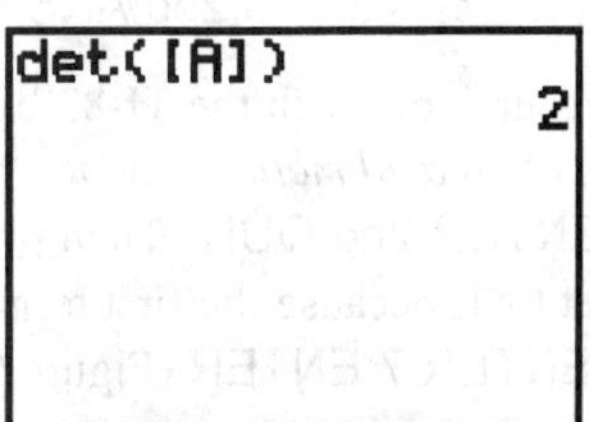

Figure 9.61: Determinant of [A]

9.5   Additional Topics

9.5.1 Iteration: The ANS key enables you to perform *iteration*, the process of evaluating a function repeatedly. As an example, calculate $\dfrac{n-1}{3}$ for $n = 27$. Then calculate $\dfrac{n-1}{3}$ for $n =$ the answer to the previous calculation. Continue to use each answer as n in the *next* calculation. here are keystrokes to accomplish this iteration on the TI-83 calculator. (See the results in Figure 9.62.) Notice that when you use ANS in place of n in a formula, it is sufficient to press ENTER to continue an iteration.

Iteration	Keystrokes	Display
1	27 ENTER	27
2	(2nd ANS − 1) ÷ 3 ENTER	8.666666667
3	ENTER	2.555555556
4	ENTER	.5185185185
5	ENTER	−.1604938272

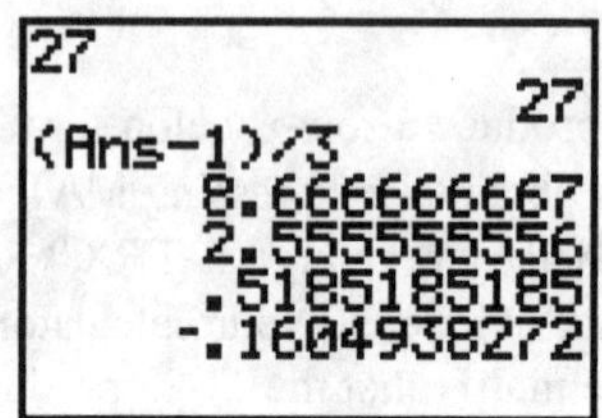

Figure 9.62: Iteration

Press ENTER several more times and see what happens with this iteration. You may wish to try it again with a different starting value.

9.5.2 Arithmetic and Geometric Sequences: Use iteration with the ANS variable to determine the n-th term of a sequence. For example, find the 18th term of an *arithmetic* sequence whose first term is 7 and whose common difference is 4. Enter the first term 7, then start the progression with the recursion formula, 2nd ANS + 4 ENTER. This yields the 2nd term, so press ENTER sixteen more times to find the 18th term. For a *geometric* sequence whose common ratio is 4, start the progression with 2nd ANS × 4 ENTER.

You can also define the sequence recursively with the TI-83 by selecting Seq in the MODE menu (see Figure 9.1). Once again, let's find the 18th term of an *arithmetic* sequence whose first term is 7 and whose common difference is 4. Press MODE ▼ ▼ ▼ ► ► ► ENTER 2nd QUIT. Then press Y= to edit any of the TI-83's three sequences, u_n, v_n, or w_n. Make sure that nMin is set to 1, because the first term is u_1 where $n = 1$. Make $u_n = u_{n-1} + 4$ and $u_1 = 7$ by pressing 2nd u (X,T,θ,n − 1) + 4 ENTER 7 ENTER (Figure 9.63). Now, when you press the variable key, X,T,θ,n, you get an n because the calculator is in sequence mode. Press 2nd QUIT to return to the home screen. To find the 18th term of this sequence, calculate u_{18} by pressing 2nd u (18) ENTER (Figure 9.64).

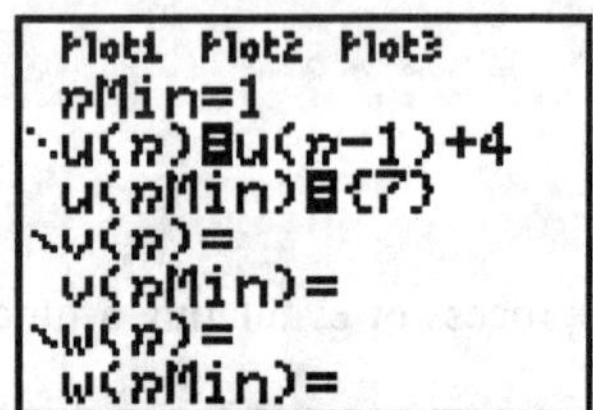

Figure 9.63: Sequential Y= menu

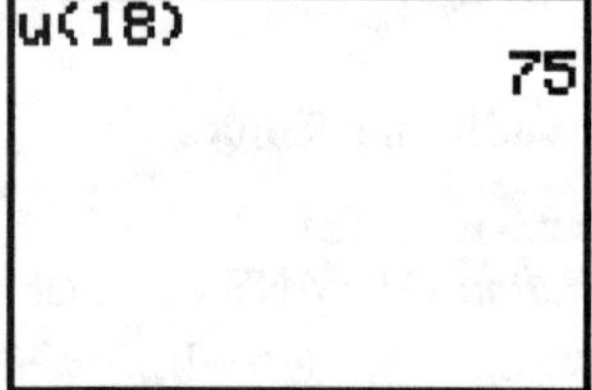

Figure 9.64: Sequence mode

Of course, you could also use the *explicit* formula for the n-th term of an arithmetic sequence $t_n = a + (n-1)d$. First enter values for the variables a, d, and n, then evaluate the formula by pressing ALPHA A + (ALPHA N − 1) ALPHA D ENTER. For a geometric sequence whose n-th term is given by $t_n = a \cdot r^{n-1}$, enter values for the variables a, d, and r, then evaluate the formula by pressing ALPHA A ALPHA R ∧ (ALPHA N − 1) ENTER.

                                                    TI-83 Graphics Calculator

To use the explicit formula in Seq MODE, make $u_n = 7 + (n-1) \cdot 4$ by pressing Y= 7 + (X,T,θ,n − 1) × 4 ENTER 2nd QUIT. Once more, calculate u_{18} by pressing 2nd u (18) ENTER.

9.5.3 Permutations and Combinations: To calculate the number of permutations of 12 objects taken 7 at a time, $_{12}P_7$, press 12 MATH ◄ 2*[nPr]* 7 ENTER (Figure 9.65). Thus $_{12}P_7 = 3{,}991{,}680$.

For the number of combinations of 12 objects taken 7 at a time, $_{12}C_7$, press 12 MATH ◄ 3*[nCr]* 7 ENTER (Figure 9.65). Thus $_{12}C_7 = 792$.

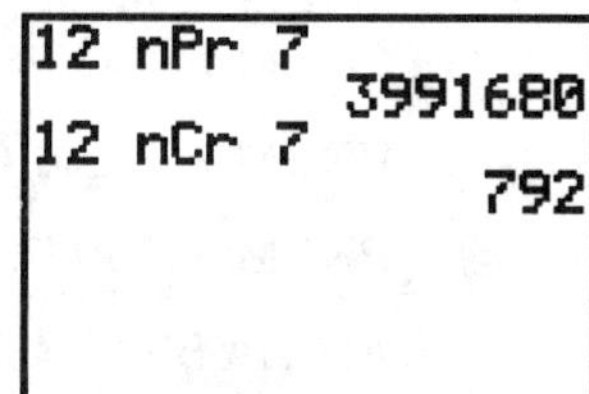

Figure 9.65: $_{12}P_7$ and $_{12}C_7$

9.6   Programming

9.6.1 Entering a Program: The TI-83 is a programmable calculator that can store sequences of commands for later replay. Here's an example to show you how to enter a useful program that solves quadratic equations by the quadratic formula.

Press PRGM to access the programming menu. The TI-83 has space for many programs, each named by a name you give it. To create a new program now, start by pressing PRGM ◄ 1*[Create New]*.

For convenience, the cursor is a blinking **A**, indicating that the calculator is set to receive alphabetic characters. Enter a descriptive title of up to eight characters, letter, or numerals (but the first character must be a letter or θ). Name this program QUADRAT and press ENTER to go to the program editor.

In the program, each line begins with a colon (:) supplied automatically by the calculator. Any command you could enter directly in the TI-83's home screen can be entered as a line in a program. There are also special programming commands.

Input the program QUADRAT by pressing the keystrokes given in the listing below. You may interrupt program input at any stage by pressing 2nd QUIT. To return late for more editing, press PRGM ►, move the cursor down to this program's name, and press ENTER.

Each time you press ENTER while writing a program, the TI-83 *automatically* inserts the : character at the beginning of the next line.

The instruction manual for your TI-83 gives detailed information about programming. Refer to it to learn more about programming and how to use other features of your calculator.

Note that this program makes use of the TI-83's ability to compute complex numbers. Make sure that the type of numbers in the MODE menu (Figure 9.1) is set to a+b*i*.

Enter the program QUADRAT by pressing the given keystrokes.

<table>
<tr><td>Program Line</td><td>Keystrokes</td></tr>
</table>

: Disp "ENTER A"   PRGM ▶ 3 2nd A-LOCK " E N T E R ␣ A " ENTER

displays the words ENTER A on the TI-83 screen

: Input A   PRGM ▶ 1 ALPHA A ENTER

waits for you to input a value that will be assigned to the variable A

: Disp "ENTER B"   PRGM ▶ 3 2nd A-LOCK " E N T E R ␣ B " ENTER

: Input B   PRGM ▶ 1 ALPHA B ENTER

: Disp "ENTER C"   PRGM ▶ 3 2nd A-LOCK " E N T E R ␣ C " ENTER

: Input C   PRGM ▶ 1 ALPHA C ENTER

: $B^2-4AC \to D$ ALPHA B x^2 – 4 ALPHA A ALPHA C STO▸ ALPHA D ENTER

calculates the discriminant and stores its value as D

: $(-B+\sqrt{(D)})/(2A) \to M$ ((–) ALPHA B + 2nd $\sqrt{\ }$ ALPHA D)) ÷ (2 ALPHA A) STO▸ ALPHA M ENTER

calculates one root and stores it as M

: $(-B-\sqrt{(D)})/(2A) \to N$ ((–) ALPHA B – 2nd $\sqrt{\ }$ ALPHA D)) ÷ (2 ALPHA A) STO▸ ALPHA N ENTER

: If D<0   PRGM 1 ALPHA D 2nd TEST 5 0 ENTER

tests to see if the discriminant is negative;

: Goto 1   PRGM 0 1 ENTER

if the discriminant is negative, jumps to the line Lbl 1 below; if the discriminant is not negative, continues on to the next line

: If D=0   PRGM 1 ALPHA D 2nd TEST 1 0 ENTER

tests to see if the discriminant is zero;

: Goto 2   PRGM 0 2 ENTER

if the discriminant is zero, jumps to the line Lbl 2 below; if the discriminant is not zero, continues on to the next line

: Disp "TWO REAL ROOTS", M   PRGM ▶ 3 2nd A-LOCK " T W O ␣ R E A L ␣ R O O T S " ALPHA , ALPHA M ENTER

: Pause   PRGM 8 ENTER

displays the message "TWO REAL ROOTS" and one root then pauses

:Disp N   PRGM ▶ 3 ALPHA N ENTER

displays the other root

: Stop   PRGM ALPHA F ENTER

stops program execution

| : Lbl 1 | PRGM 9 1 ENTER |

jumping point for the Goto command above

| : Disp "COMPLEX ROOTS", M | PRGM ▶ 3 2nd A-LOCK " C O M P L E X ˌ R O O T S "
ALPHA , ALPHA M ENTER |

| : Pause | PRGM 8 ENTER |

displays the message "COMPLEX ROOTS" and one root, then pauses

| :Disp N | PRGM ▶ 3 ALPHA N ENTER |

displays the other root

| : Stop | PRGM ALPHA F ENTER |

| : Lbl 2 | PRGM 9 2 ENTER |

| :Disp "DOUBLE ROOT", M | PRGM ▶ 3 2nd A-LOCK " D O U B L E ˌ R O O T "
ALPHA , ALPHA M ENTER |

displays a message in case there is a double root, and the solution (root)

When you have finished, press 2nd QUIT to leave the program editor and move on.

If you want to remove a program from memory, press 2nd MEM 2*[Delete]* 7*[Prgm]*. Then use the down arrow ▼ to move the indicator next to the name of the program you want to delete, and when the indicator is next to its name, press ENTER to remove it from the calculator's memory.

9.6.2 Executing a Program: To execute the program you have entered, press PRGM and the number corresponding to the program; and press ENTER to execute it. If you have forgotten its name, use the arrow keys to move through the program listing to find its description QUADRAT. Then press ENTER to execute it.

The program has been written to prompt you for values of the coefficients a, b, and c in a quadratic equation $ax^2 + bx + c = 0$. Input a value, then press ENTER to continue the program.

If you need to interrupt a program during execution, press ON 1.

Chapter 10

Texas Instruments TI-86 Graphics Calculator

10.1.1 Basics: Press the ON key to begin using your TI-86. If you need to adjust the display contrast, first press 2nd, then press and hold ▼ (the *down* arrow key) to lighten or ▲ (the *up* arrow key) to darken. As you press and hold ▼ or ▲, an integer between 0 (lightest) and 9 (darkest) appears in the upper right corner of the display. When you have finished with the calculator, turn it off to conserve battery power by pressing 2nd and then OFF.

Check your TI-86's settings by pressing 2nd MODE. If necessary, use the arrow keys to move the blinking cursor to a setting you want to change. Press ENTER to select a new setting. To start with, select the options along the left side of the MODE menu as illustrated in Figure 10.1: normal display, floating decimals, radian measure, rectangular coordinates, function graphs, decimal number system, rectangular vectors, and differentiation type. Details on alternative options will be given later in this guide. For now, leave the MODE menu by pressing EXIT or 2nd QUIT or CLEAR.

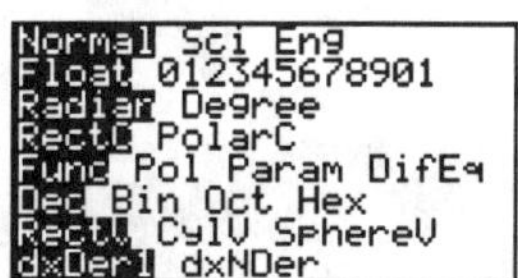

Figure 10.1: MODE menu

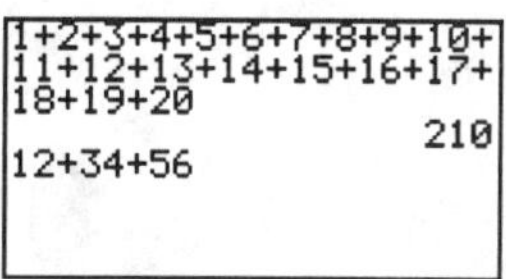

Figure 10.2: Home screen

10.1.2 Editing: One advantage of the TI-86 is that up to eight lines are visible at one time, so you can *see* a long calculation. For example, type this sum (Figure 10.2):

$$1 + 2 + 3 + 4 + 5 + 6 + 7 + 8 + 9 + 10 + 11 + 12 + 13 + 14 + 15 + 16 + 17 + 18 + 19 + 20$$

Then press ENTER to see the answer too.

Often we do not notice a mistake until we see how unreasonable an answer is. The TI-86 permits you to redisplay an entire calculation, edit it easily, then execute the *corrected* calculation.

Suppose you had typed $12 + 34 + 56$ as in Figure 10.2 but had *not yet* pressed ENTER, when you realize that 34 should have been 74. Simply press ◄ (the *left* arrow key) as many times as necessary to move the blinking cursor left to 3, then type 7 to write over it. On the other hand, if 34 should have been 384, move the cursor back to 4, press 2nd INS (the cursor changes to a blinking underline) and then type 8 (inserts at the cursor position and the other characters are pushed to the right). If the 34 should have been 3 only, move the cursor to 4, and press DEL to delete it.

Technology Tip: To move quickly to the *beginning* of an expression you are currently editing, press ▲ (the *up* arrow key); to jump to the *end* of that expression, press ▼ (the *down* arrow key).

Even if you had pressed ENTER, you may still edit the previous expression. Press 2nd and then ENTRY to recall the last expression that was entered. Now you can change it. In fact, the TI-86 retains many prior entries in a "last entry" storage area. Press 2nd ENTRY repeatedly until the previous line you want replaces the current line.

Technology Tip: When you need to evaluate a formula for different values of a variable, use the editing feature to simplify the process. For example, suppose you want to find the balance in an investment account if there is now $5000 in the account and interest is compounded annually at the rate of 8.5%. The formula for the balance is

$P\left(1+\frac{r}{n}\right)^{nt}$, where P = principal, r = rate of interest (expressed as a decimal), n = number of times interest is compounded each year, and t = number of years. In our example, this becomes $5000(1+.085)^{t}$. Here are the keystrokes for finding the balance after $t = 3$, 5, and 10 years.

Years	Keystrokes	Balance
3	5000 (1 + .085) ^ 3 ENTER	$6386.45
5	2nd ENTRY ◄ 5 ENTER	$7518.28
10	2nd ENTRY ◄ 10 ENTER	$11,304.92

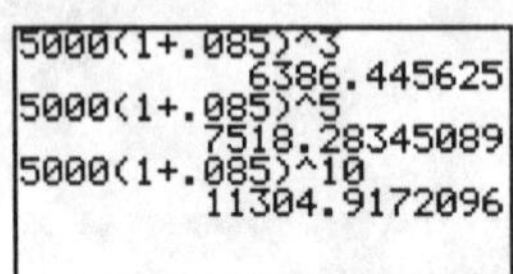

Figure 10.3: Editing expressions

Then to find the balance from the same initial investment but after 5 years when the annual interest rate is 7.5%, press the keys to change the last calculation above: 2nd ENTRY ◄ DEL ◄ 5 ◄ ◄ ◄ ◄ ◄ 7 ENTER.

10.1.3 Key Functions: Most keys on the TI-86 offer access to more than one function, just as the keys on a computer keyboard can produce more than one letter ("g" and "G") or even quite different characters ("5" and "%"). The primary function of a key is indicated on the key itself, and you access that function by a simple press on the key.

To access the *second* function indicated to the *left* above a key, first press 2nd (the cursor changes to a blinking ↑) and *then* press the key. For example to calculate $\sqrt{25}$, press 2nd $\sqrt{}$ 25 ENTER.

When you want to use a capital letter or other character printed to the *right* above a key, first press ALPHA (the cursor changes to a blinking **A**) and then the key. For example, to use the letter K in a formula, press ALPHA K. If you need several letters in a row, press ALPHA twice in succession, which is like the CAPS LOCK key on a computer keyboard, and then press all the letters you want. Remember to press ALPHA when you are finished and want to restore the keys to their primary functions. To type lowercase letters, press 2nd alpha (the cursor changes to a blinking **a**). To lock in lowercase letters, press 2nd alpha 2nd alpha or 2nd alpha ALPHA. To unlock from lowercase, press ALPHA ALPHA (you'll see the cursor change from blinking **a** to blinking **A** and then to the standard blinking rectangle).

10.1.4 Order of Operations: The TI-86 performs calculations according to the standard algebraic rules. Working outwards from inner parentheses, calculations are performed from left to right. Powers and roots are evaluated first, followed by multiplications and divisions, and then additions and subtractions.

Enter these expressions to practice using your TI-86.

TI-86 Graphics Calculator

Expression	Keystrokes	Display
$7 - 5 \cdot 3$	7 – 5 × 3 ENTER	–8
$(7 - 5) \cdot 3$	(7 – 5) × 3 ENTER	6
$120 - 10^2$	120 – 10 x^2 ENTER	20
$(120 - 10)^2$	(120 – 10) x^2 ENTER	12100
$\dfrac{24}{2^3}$	24 ÷ 2 ∧ 3 ENTER	3
$\left(\dfrac{24}{2}\right)^3$	(24 ÷ 2) ∧ 3 ENTER	1728
$(7 - -5) \cdot -3$	(7 – (–) 5) × (–) 3 ENTER	–36

10.1.5 Algebraic Expressions and Memory: Your calculator can evaluate expressions such as $\dfrac{N(N+1)}{2}$ *after* you have entered a value for N. Suppose you want $N = 200$. Press 200 STO⬦ N ENTER to store the value 200 in memory location N. (The STO⬦ key prepares the TI-86 for alphabetical entry, so it is not necessary to press ALPHA also.) Whenever you use N in an expression, the calculator will substitute the value 200 until you make a change by storing *another* number in N. Next enter the expression $\dfrac{N(N+1)}{2}$ by typing ALPHA N (ALPHA N + 1) ÷ 2 ENTER. For $N = 200$, you will find that $\dfrac{N(N+1)}{2} = 20100$.

The contents of any memory location may be revealed by typing just its letter name and then ENTER. And the TI-86 retains memorized values even when it is turned off, so long as its batteries are good.

A variable name in the TI-86 can be a single letter, or a string of up to eight characters that begins with a letter followed by other letters, numerals, and various symbols. Variable names are case sensitive, which means that length and Length and LENGTH may represent *different* quantities.

10.1.6 Repeated Operations with ANS: The result of your *last* calculation is always stored in memory location ANS and replaces any previous result. This makes it easy to use the answer from one computation in another computation. For example, press 30 + 15 ENTER so that 45 is the last result displayed. Then press 2nd ANS ÷ 9 ENTER and get 5 because $45 \div 9 = 5$.

With a function like division, you press the ÷ *after* you enter an argument. For such functions, whenever you would start a new calculation with the previous answer followed by pressing the function key, you may press just the function key. So instead of 2nd ANS ÷ 9 in the previous example, you could have pressed simply ÷ 9 to achieve the same result. This technique also works for these functions: + – × ∧ x^2 x^{-1}.

Here is a situation where this is especially useful. Suppose a person makes $5.85 per hour and you are asked to calculate earnings for a day, a week, and a year. Execute the given keystrokes to find the person's incomes during these periods (results are shown in Figure 10.4).

Pay Period	Keystrokes	Earnings
8-hour day	5.85 × 8 ENTER	$46.80
5-day week	× 5 ENTER	$234
52-week year	× 52 ENTER	$12,168

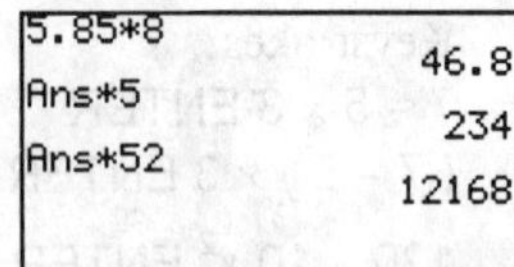

Figure 10.4: ANS variable

10.1.7 The MATH Menu: Operators and functions associated with a scientific calculator are available either immediately from the keys of the TI-86 or by the 2nd keys. You have direct access to common arithmetic operations (x^2, 2nd $\sqrt{\ }$, 2nd x^{-1}, ^), trigonometric functions (SIN, COS, TAN), and their inverses (2nd SIN^{-1}, 2nd COS^{-1}, 2nd TAN^{-1}), exponential and logarithmic functions (LOG, 2nd 10^x, LN, 2nd e^x), and a famous constant (2nd π).

A significant difference between the TI-86 graphing calculators and most scientific calculators is that TI-86 requires the argument of a function *after* the function, as you would see in a formula written in your textbook. For example, on the TI-86 you calculate $\sqrt{16}$ by pressing the keys 2nd $\sqrt{\ }$ 16 in that order.

Here are keystrokes for basic mathematical operations. Try them for practice on your TI-86.

Expression	*Keystrokes*	*Display*
$\sqrt{3^2 + 4^2}$	2nd $\sqrt{\ }$ (3 x^2 + 4 x^2) ENTER	5
$2\frac{1}{3}$	2 + 3 2nd x^{-1} ENTER	2.33333333333
log 200	LOG 200 ENTER	2.30102999566
$2.34 \cdot 10^5$	2.34 × 2nd 10^x 5 ENTER	234000
	or 2.34 × 10 ^ 5 ENTER	

Additional mathematical operations and functions are available from the MATH menu. Press 2nd MATH to see the various options that are listed across the bottom of the screen (Figure 10.5). These options are activated by pressing corresponding menu keys, F1 through F5.

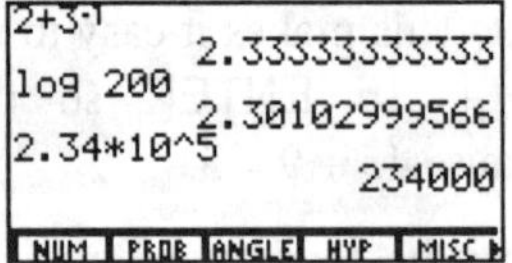

Figure 10.5: Basic MATH menu

For example, pressing F1 brings up the NUM menu of numerical functions. You will learn in your mathematics textbook how to apply many of them. Note that the basic MATH menu items have moved up a line; these options are now available by pressing 2nd M1 through 2nd M5. As an example, determine |−5| by pressing 2nd MATH F1 and then F5 (−) 5 ENTER (see Figure 10.6).

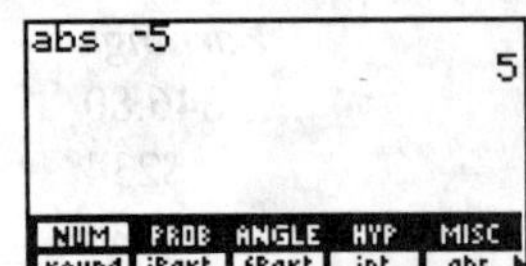

Figure 10.6: MATH NUM menu

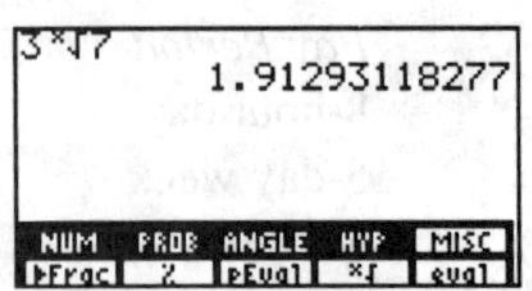

Figure 10.7: MATH MISC menu

Next calculate $\sqrt[3]{7}$ by first pressing 2nd MATH F5 (when the MATH NUM menu is displayed, as in Figure 10.6, just press 2nd M5) to access the MISC menu of miscellaneous mathematical functions. The arrow at the right end of this menu indicates there are more items that you can access. You may press the MORE key repeatedly to move down the row of options and back again. To calculate $\sqrt[3]{7}$, press 2nd MATH F5 MORE 3 F4 $[\sqrt[x]{\ }]$ 7 ENTER; this will result in 1.91293118277 (Figure 10.7). To leave the MATH menu and take no other action, press EXIT a couple of times.

The *factorial* of a non-negative integer is the *product* of *all* the integers from 1 up to the given integer. The symbol for factorial is the exclamation point. So 4! (pronounced *four factorial*) is $1 \cdot 2 \cdot 3 \cdot 4 = 24$. You will learn more about applications of factorials in your textbook, but for now use the TI-86 to calculate 4! Press these keystrokes: 2nd MATH F2 *[PROB]* 4 F1 *[!]* ENTER.

10.2   Functions and Graphs

10.2.1 Evaluating Functions: Suppose you receive a monthly salary of $1975 plus a commission of 10% of sales. Let x = your sales in dollars; then your wages W in dollars are given by the equation $W = 1975 + .10x$. If your January sales were $2230 and your February sales were $1865, what was your income during those months?

Here's one method to use your TI-86 to perform this task. Press the GRAPH key and then F1 to select y(x)= to get access to the function editing screen (Figure 10.8). Press F4 *[DELf]* as many times as necessary to delete any functions that may be there already. Then with the cursor on the top line to the right of y1= enter the expression $1975 + .10x$ by pressing these keys: 1975 + .10 F1. As you see, the TI-86 uses lowercase letters for its graphing variables, just like your mathematics textbook. Note that pressing F1 in this situation is the same as pressing either x-VAR or 2nd alpha X. The x-VAR key lets you enter the variable x easily without having to use the ALPHA key. Now press 2nd QUIT to return to the main calculations screen.

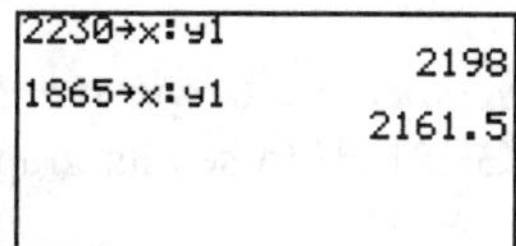

Figure 10.8: y(x)= screen   Figure 10.9: Evaluating a function

Assign the value 2230 to the variable x by using these keystrokes (see Figure 10.9): 2230 STO⬧ x-VAR. Then press 2nd : to allow another expression to be entered on the same command line. Next press the following keystrokes to evaluate y1 and find January's wages: 2nd alpha Y 1 ENTER.

It is not necessary to repeat all these steps to find the February wages. Simply press 2nd ENTRY to recall the entire previous line, change 2230 to 1865, and press ENTER. Each time the TI-86 evaluates the function y1, it uses the *current* value of x.

Like your textbook, the TI-86 uses standard function notation. So to evaluate $y_1(2230)$ when $y_1(x) = 1975 + .10x$, 2nd alpha Y 1 (2230) ENTER (see Figure 10.10). Then to evaluate $y_1(1865)$, press 2nd ENTRY to recall the last line and change 2230 to 1865.

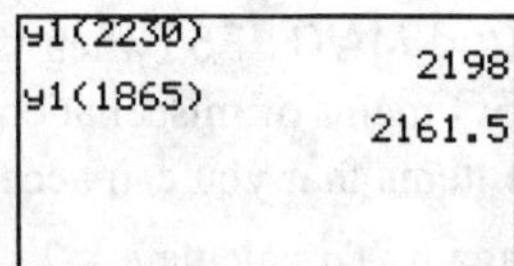

Figure 10.10: Function notation

You may also have the TI-86 make a table of values for the function. Press TABLE to get the TABLE menu across the bottom of the screen and then press F2 *[TBLST]* to set up the table (Figure 10.11). Move the blinking cursor onto Ask beside Indpnt:, then press ENTER. This configuration permits you to input values for x one at a time. Now press F1 *[TABLE]*, enter 2230 in the x column, and press ENTER (see Figure 10.12). Continue to enter additional values for x and the calculator automatically completes the table with corresponding values of y1. Press 2nd QUIT to leave the TABLE screen.

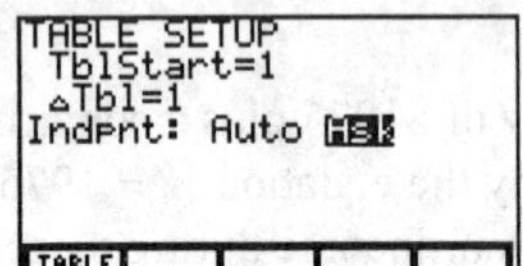

Figure 10.11: TBLSET screen

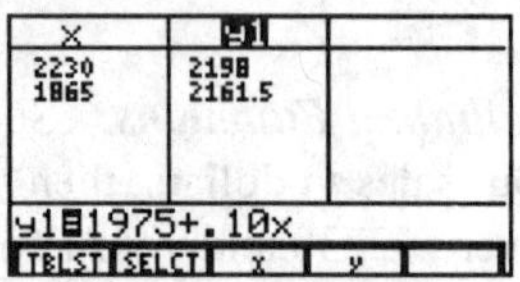

Figure 10.12: Table of values

Technology Tip: The TI-86 does not require multiplication to be expressed between variables, so *xxx* means x^3. It is often easier to press two or three x's together than to search for the square key or the powers key. Of course, expressed multiplication is also not required between a constant and a variable. Hence to enter $2x^3 + 3x^2 - 4x + 5$ in the TI-86, you might save keystrokes and press just these keys: 2 x-VAR x-VAR x-VAR + 3 x-VAR x-VAR – 4 x-VAR + 5.

10.2.2 Functions in a Graph Window: Once you have entered a function in the y(x) screen of the TI-86, just press 2nd M5 *[GRAPH]* to see its graph. The ability to draw a graph contributes substantially to our ability to solve problems.

For example, here is how to graph $y = -x^3 + 4x$. First press GRAPH y(x)= and delete anything that may be there by moving with the arrow keys any of the existing functions and pressing F4 *[DELf]*. Then, with the cursor on the top line to right of y1, press (–) x-VAR ∧ 3 + 4 x-VAR to enter the function (as in Figure 10.13). Now press 2nd M5 *[GRAPH]* and the TI-86 changes to a window with the graph of $y = -x^3 + 4x$ (Figure 10.14). To remove the menu from bottom of the display screen, press CLEAR.

While the TI-86 is calculating coordinates for a plot, it displays a busy indicator at the top right of the graph window.

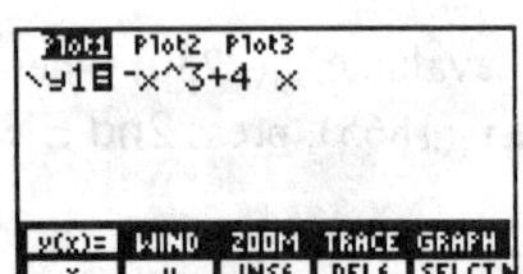

Figure 10.13: y(x)= screen

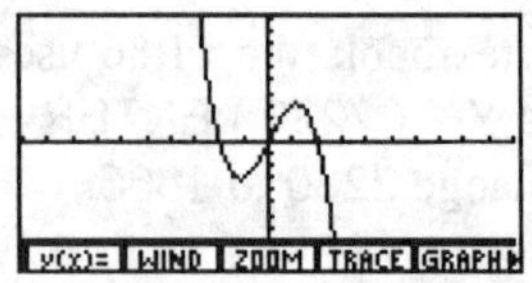

Figure 10.14: Graph of $y = -x^3 + 4x$

Your graph window may look like the one in Figure 10.14 or it may be different. Since the graph of $y = -x^3 + 4x$ extends infinitely far left and right and also infinitely far up and down, the TI-86 can display only a piece of the actual graph. This displayed rectangular part is called a *viewing rectangle*. You can easily change the viewing rectangle to enhance your investigation of a graph.

The viewing rectangle in Figure 10.14 shows the part of the graph that extends horizontally from -10 to 10 and vertically from -10 to 10. Press F2 *[WIND]* to see information about your viewing rectangle. Figure 10.15 shows the WINDOW screen that corresponds to the viewing rectangle in Figure 10.14. This is the *standard* viewing rectangle for the TI-86.

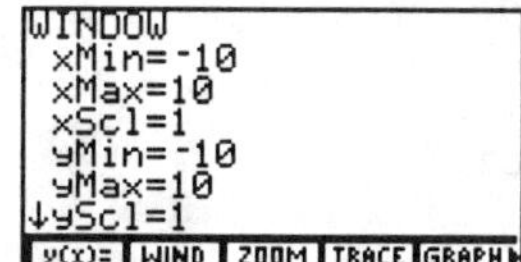

Figure 10.15: Standard WINDOW

The variables xMin and xMax are the minimum and maximum x-values of the viewing rectangle; yMin and yMax are the minimum and maximum y-values.

xScl and yScl set the spacing between tick marks on the axes.

Scrolling to the bottom of the screen, xRes sets pixel resolution (1 through 8) for function graphs.

Technology Tip: Small Xres values improve graph resolution, but may cause the TI-86 to draw graphs more slowly.

Use the arrow keys ▲ and ▼ to move up and down from one line to another in this list; pressing the ENTER key will move down the list. Enter a new value to over-write a previous value and then press ENTER. Remember that a minimum *must* be less than the corresponding maximum or the TI-86 will issue an error message. Also, remember to use the (−) key, not − (which is subtraction), when you want to enter a negative value. Figures 10.14-15, 10.16-17, and 10.18-19 show different WINDOW screens and the corresponding viewing rectangle for each one.

To initialize the viewing rectangle quickly to the *standard* viewing rectangle (Figure 10.15), press F3 *[ZOOM]* F4 *[ZSTD]*. To set the viewing rectangle quickly to a "square" window (Figure 10.16), press F3 *[ZOOM]* MORE F2 *[ZSQR]*. More information about square windows is presented later in Section 10.2.3.

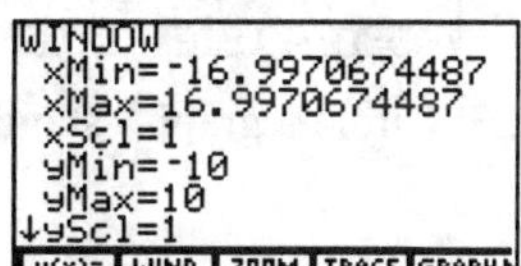

Figure 10.16: Square window

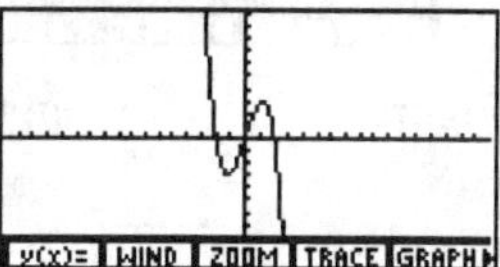

Figure 10.17: Graph of $y = -x^3 + 4x$

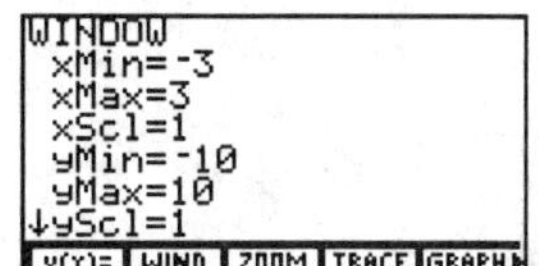

Figure 10.18: Custom window

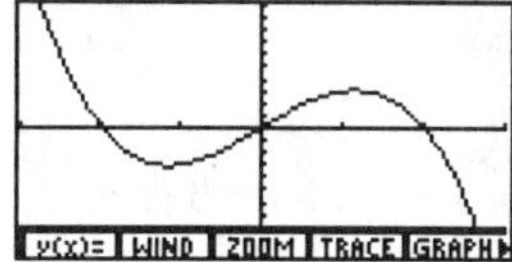

Figure 10.19: Graph of $y = -x^3 + 4x$

Sometimes you may wish to display grid points corresponding to tick marks on the axes. This and other graph format options may be changed by pressing GRAPH MORE F3 *[FORMT]* to display the FORMAT menu (Figure 10.20). Use arrow keys to move the blinking cursor to GridOn; press ENTER and then F5 *[GRAPH]* to redraw the graph. Figure 10.21 shows the same graph as in Figure 10.19 but with the grid turned on. In general, you'll want the grid turned *off*, so do that now by pressing GRAPH MORE F3 *[FORMT]*, using the arrow keys to move the blinking cursor to GridOff, and pressing ENTER and EXIT.

Figure 10.20: FORMAT menu

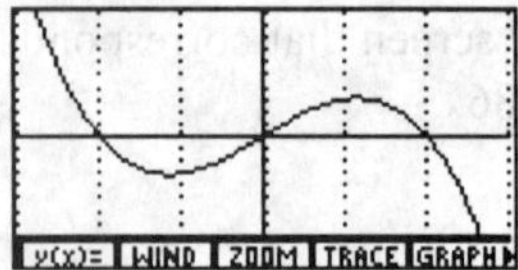

Figure 10.21: Grid turned on for $y = -x^3 + 4x$

Technology Tip: On the TI-86, the style of your graph can be changed by changing the icon to the left of **y1** on the **y(x)=** screen. To change the icon enter the **y(x)=** screen and move your cursor onto the line of the function whose style you want to change. Then press **MORE** and F3 *[STYLE]* repeatedly to scroll through the different styles available.

10.2.3 Graphing a Circle: Here is a useful technique for graphs that are not functions but can be "split" into a top part and a bottom part, or into multiple parts. Suppose you wish to graph the circle of radius 6 whose equation is $x^2 + y^2 = 36$. First solve for y and get an equation for the top semicircle, $y = \sqrt{36 - x^2}$, and for the bottom semicircle, $y = -\sqrt{36 - x^2}$. Then graph the two semicircles simultaneously.

Use the following keystrokes to draw this circle's graph. Enter $\sqrt{36 - x^2}$ as **y1** and $-\sqrt{36 - x^2}$ as **y2** (see Figure 10.22) by pressing **GRAPH** F1 *[y(x)]* **CLEAR 2nd** $\sqrt{\ }$ (36 – x-VAR x^2) **ENTER CLEAR** (–) **2nd** $\sqrt{\ }$ (36 – x-VAR x^2). Then press **2nd M5** *[GRAPH]* to draw them both (Figure 10.23). Make sure that the **WINDOW** is set large enough to display a circle of radius 6.

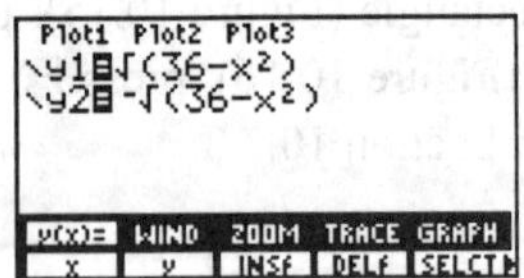

Figure 10.22: Two semicircles

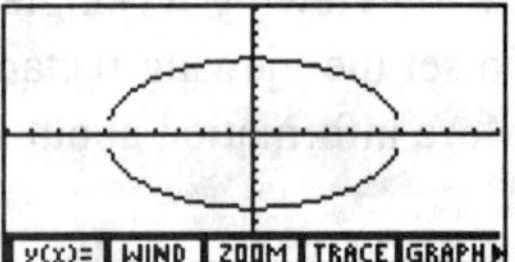

Figure 10.23: Circle's graph - standard WINDOW

Instead of entering $-\sqrt{36 - x^2}$ as **y2**, you could have entered –**y1** as **y2** and saved some keystrokes. On the TI-86, try this by going into the **y(x)=** screen and pressing ▼ to move the cursor down to **y2**. Then press **CLEAR** (–) **2nd alpha Y 1** (Figure 10.24). The graph should be as before.

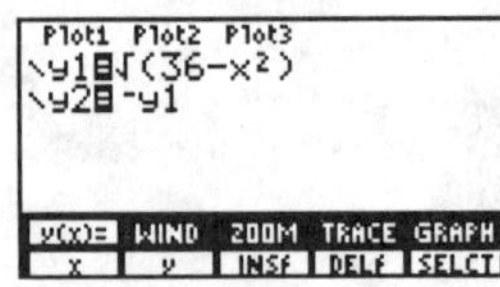

Figure 10.24: Using **y1**

If your range were set to a viewing rectangle extending from -10 to 10 in both directions, your graph would look like Figure 10.23. Now this does *not* look a circle, because the units along the axes are not the same. You need what is called a "square" viewing rectangle. Press F3 *[ZOOM]* MORE F2 *[ZSQR]* and see a graph that appears more circular.

Technology Tip: Another way to get a square graph is to change the window variables so that the value of yMax − yMin is approximately $\frac{10}{17}$ times xMax − xMin. For example, see the WINDOW in Figure 10.25 to get the corresponding graph in Figure 10.26. This method works because the dimensions of the TI-86's display are such that the ratio of vertical to horizontal is approximately $\frac{10}{17}$.

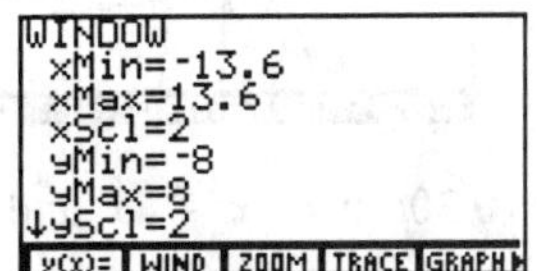

Figure 10.25: $\frac{\text{vertical}}{\text{horizontal}} = \frac{16}{27.2} = \frac{10}{17}$

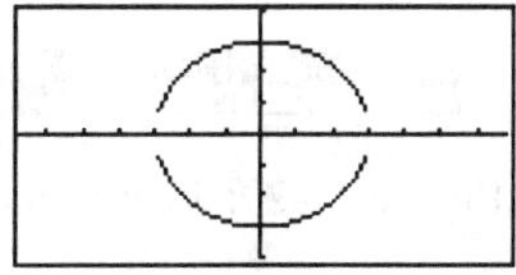

Figure 10.26: A "square" circle

The two semicircles in Figure 10.26 do not meet because of an idiosyncrasy in the way the TI-86 plots a graph.

10.2.4 TRACE: Graph the function $y = -x^3 + 4x$ from Section 10.2.2 using the standard viewing rectangle. (Remember to clear any other functions in the Y= screen.) Press any of the arrow keys ▲ ▼ ◄ ► and see the cursor move from the center of the viewing rectangle. The coordinates of the cursor's location are displayed at the bottom of the screen, as in Figure 10.27, in floating decimal format. (Recall that if you have a menu at the bottom of the screen, you can remove it by pressing CLEAR.) This cursor is called a *free-moving cursor* because it can move from dot to dot *anywhere* in the graph window.

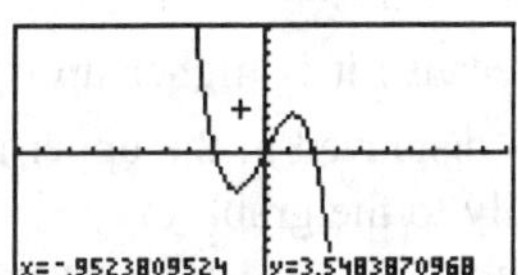

Figure 10.27: Free-moving cursor

Remove the free-moving cursor and its coordinates from the window by pressing CLEAR, ENTER, or GRAPH (this also restores the GRAPH menu). If you press an arrow key once again, the free-moving cursor will reappear at the same point you left it.

With the GRAPH menu active at the bottom of the screen, press F4 *[TRACE]* to enable the left ◄ and right ► arrow keys to move the cursor along the function. The cursor is no longer free-moving, but is now constrained to the function. The coordinates that are displayed belong to points on the function's graph, so the y-coordinate is the calculated value of the function at the corresponding x-coordinate (Figure 10.28).

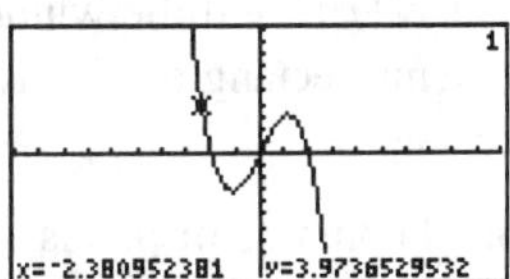

Figure 10.28: TRACE

Now plot a second function, $y = -.25x$, along with $y = -x^3 + 4x$. Press GRAPH F1 *[y(x)=]* and enter $-.25x$ for y2, then press 2nd M5 *[GRAPH]* to see both functions (Figure 10.30).

Notice that in Figure 10.29 the equal signs next to Y_1 and Y_2 are *both* highlighted. This means that *both* functions will be graphed. In the y(x)= screen, move the cursor to y1 and press F5 *[SELCT]* to turn off the selection of the function. The equal sign besides y1 should no longer be highlighted (Figure 10.31). Now press 2nd M5 *[GRAPH]* and see that only y2 is plotted (Figure 10.32).

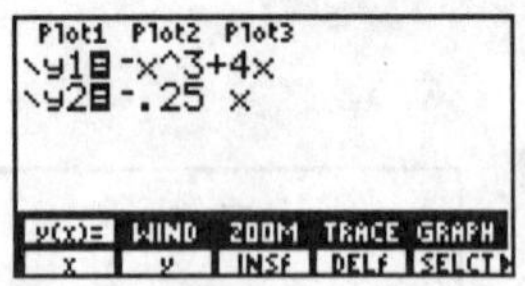

Figure 10.29: Two functions

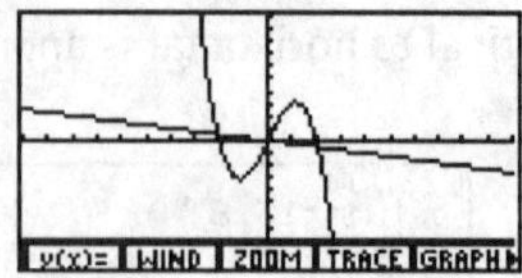

Figure 10.30: $y = -x^3 + 4x$ and $y = -.25x$

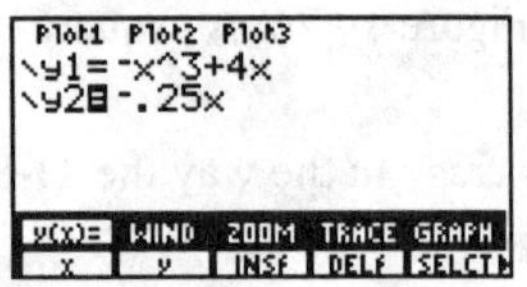

Figure 10.31: only Y_2 active

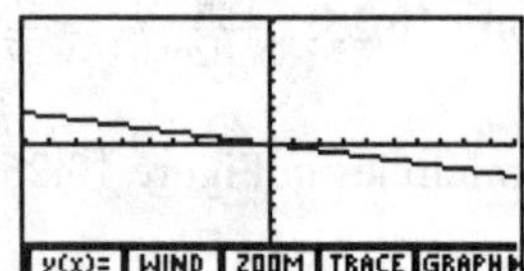

Figure 10.32: Graph of $y = -.25x$

Many different functions can be stored in the y(x)= list and any combination of them may be graphed simultaneously. You can make a function active or inactive for graphing by pressing SELCT to highlight (activate) or remove the highlight (deactivate) from the equal sign. Now go back to the y(x)= screen and do what is needed in order to graph y1 but not y2.

Now activate both functions so that both graphs are plotted. Press GRAPH F4 *[TRACE]* and the cursor appears first on the graph of $y = -x^3 + 4x$ because it is higher up on the y(x)= list. You know that the cursor is on this function, y1, because the number 1 is displayed in the upper right corner of the screen. Press the up ▲ or down ▼ arrow key to move the cursor vertically to the graph of $y = -.25x$. Now the function the number 2 is displayed in the upper right corner of the screen. Next press the left and right arrow keys to trace along the graph of $y = -.25x$. When more than one function is plotted, you can move the trace cursor vertically from one graph to another with the ▲ and ▼ keys.

Technology Tip: By the way, trace the graph of $y = -.25x$ and press and hold either ◀ or ▶. Eventually you will reach the left or right edge of the window. Keep pressing the arrow key and the TI-86 will allow you to continue the trace by panning the viewing rectangle. Check the WINDOW screen to see that the xMin and xMax are automatically updated.

If you trace along the graph of $y = -x^3 + 4x$, the cursor will eventually move *above* or *below* the viewing rectangle. The cursor's coordinates on the graph will still be displayed, though the cursor itself can no longer be seen.

When you tracing along a graph, press ENTER and the window will quickly pan over so that the cursor's position on the function is centered in a new viewing rectangle. This feature is especially helpful when you trace near or beyond the edge of the current viewing rectangle.

The TI-86 has a display of 127 horizontal columns of pixels and 63 vertical rows, so when you trace a curve across a graph window, you are actually moving from xMin to xMax in 126 equal jumps, each called Δx. You would calculate the size of each jump to be $\Delta x = \dfrac{\text{xMax} - \text{xMin}}{126}$. Sometimes you may want the jumps to be friendly numbers like 0.1 or 0.25 so that, when you trace along the curve, the x-coordinates will be incremented by such a convenient amount. Just set your viewing rectangle for a particular increment Δx by making xMax = xMin + 126 · Δx. For example, if you want xMin = −15 and Δx = .25, set xMax = −15 + 126 · .25 = 16.5. Likewise, set yMax = yMin + 62Δy if you want the vertical increment to be some special Δy.

To center your window around a particular point, say (h, k), and also have a certain Δx, set xMin = h − 63 · Δx and make xMax = h + 63 · Δx. Likewise, make yMin = k − 31 · Δy and make yMax = k + 31 · Δx. For example, to center a window around the origin (0, 0), with both horizontal and vertical increments of 0.25, set the range so that xMin = 0 − 63 · 0.25 = −15.75, xMax = 0 + 63 · 0.25 = 15.75, yMin = 0 − 31 · 0.25 = −7.75 and yMax = 0 + 31 · 0.25 = 7.75.

See the benefit by first plotting $y = x^2 + 2x + 1$ in a standard graphing window. Trace near its y-intercept, which is (0, 1), and then move towards its x-intercept, which is (−1, 0). Then change to a viewing rectangle that extends from −6.3 to 6.3 horizontally and from −3.1 to 3.1 vertically (center at the origin, Δx and Δy both .1), and trace again near its y-intercept. The TI-86 makes it easy to get this particular viewing window: press GRAPH F3 *[ZOOM]* MORE F4 *[ZDECM]*.

10.2.5 ZOOM: Plot again the two graphs, for $y = -x^3 + 4x$ and $y = -.25x$. There appears to be an intersection near $x = 2$. The TI-86 provides several ways to enlarge the view around this point. You can change the viewing rectangle directly by pressing WINDOW and editing the values of xMin, xMax, yMin, and yMax. Figure 10.34 shows a new viewing rectangle for the range displayed in Figure 10.33. The trace feature has been turned on and the coordinates are displayed for a point on $y = -x^3 + 4x$ close to the intersection.

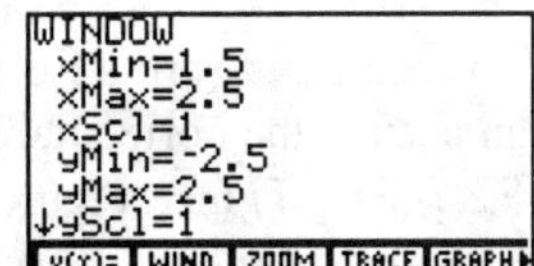

Figure 10.33: New WINDOW

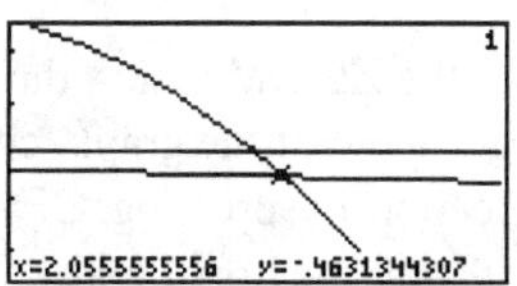

Figure 10.34: Closer view

A more efficient method for enlarging the view is to draw a new viewing rectangle with the cursor. Start again with a graph of the two functions $y = -x^3 + 4x$ and $y = -.25x$ in a standard viewing rectangle. (Press GRAPH F3 *[ZOOM]* F4 *[ZSTD]* for the standard viewing window.)

Now imagine a small rectangular box around the intersection point, near $x = 2$. Press GRAPH F3 *[ZOOM]* F1 *[BOX]* to draw a box to define this new viewing rectangle. Use the arrow keys to move the cursor, whose coordinates are displayed at the bottom of the window, to one corner of the new viewing rectangle you imagine.

Press ENTER to fix the corner where you moved the cursor; it changes shape and becomes a blinking square (Figure 10.35). Use the arrow keys again to move the cursor to the diagonally opposite corner of the new rectangle (Figure 10.36). If this box looks all right to you, press ENTER. Then press CLEAR to remove the menu from the bottom of the screen. The rectangular area you have enclosed will now enlarge to fill the graph window (Figure 10.37).

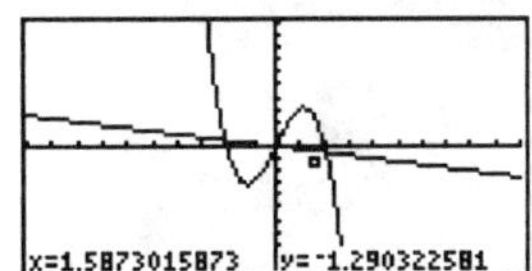

Figure 10.35: One corner selected

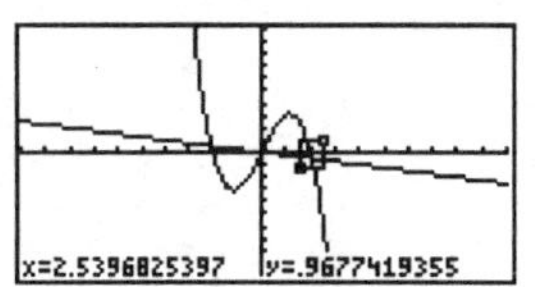

Figure 10.36: Box drawn

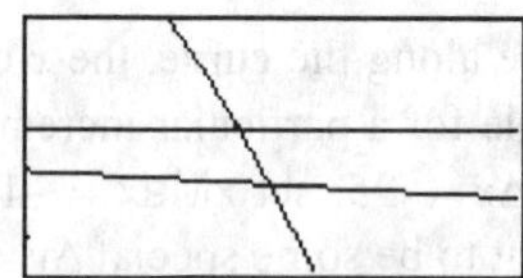

Figure 10.37: New viewing rectangle

You may cancel the zoom any time *before* you press this last ENTER. Press EXIT or GRAPH to interrupt the zoom and return to the current graph window. Even if you did execute the zoom, you may still return to the previous viewing rectangle by pressing F5 *[ZPREV]* in the ZOOM menu.

You can also quickly magnify a graph around the cursor's location. Return once more to the standard window for the graph of the two functions $y = -x^3 + 4x$ and $y = -.25x$. Start the zoom by pressing GRAPH F3 *[ZOOM]* F2 *[ZIN]*; next use arrow keys to move the cursor as close as you can to the point of intersection near $x = 2$ (see Figure 10.38). Then press ENTER and the calculator draws a magnified graph, centered at the cursor's position (Figure 10.39). The range variables are changed to reflect this new viewing rectangle. Look in the WINDOW menu to verify this.

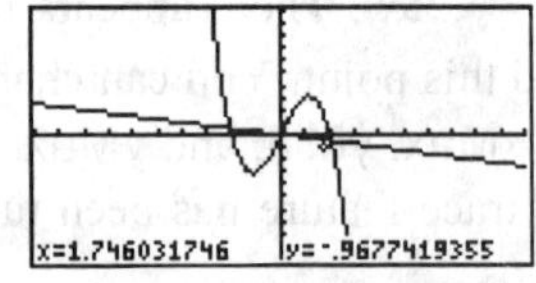

Figure 10.38: Before a zoom in

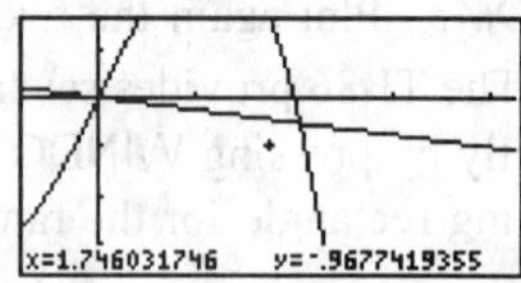

Figure 10.39: After a zoom in

Selecting in the ZOOM menu, the TI-86 can zoom in (press F2 *[ZIN]*) or zoom out (press F3 *[ZOUT]*). Zoom out to see a larger view of the graph, centered at the cursor position. You can change the horizontal and vertical scale of the magnification by pressing GRAPH F3 *[ZOOM]* MORE MORE F2 *[ZFACT]* (see Figure 10.40) and editing xFact and yFact, the horizontal and vertical magnification factors.

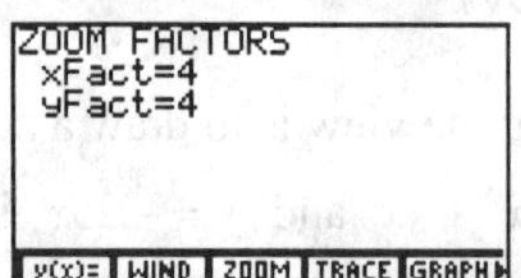

Figure 10.40: Set zoom factors

The default zoom factor is 4 in both direction. It is not necessary for xFact and yFact to be equal. sometimes, you may prefer to zoom in one direction only, so the other factor should be set to 1. As usual, press GRAPH or EXIT to leave the ZOOM FACTORS menu.

Technology Tip: If you should zoom in too much and lose the curve, zoom back to the standard viewing rectangle and start over or return to the previous viewing rectangle by pressing F5 *[ZPREV]* in the ZOOM menu.

10.3.1 Intercepts and Intersections: Tracing and zooming are also used to locate an x-intercept of a graph, where a curve crosses the x-axis. For example, the graph of $y = x^3 - 8x$ crosses x-axis three times (Figure 10.41). After tracing over to the x-intercept point that is farthest to the left, zoom in (Figure 10.42). Continue this process until you have located all three intercepts with as much accuracy as you need. The three x-intercepts of $y = x^3 - 8x$ are approximately –2.828, 0, and 2.828.

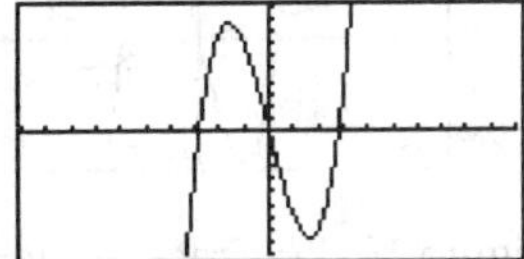

Figure 10.41: Graph of $y = x^3 - 8x$

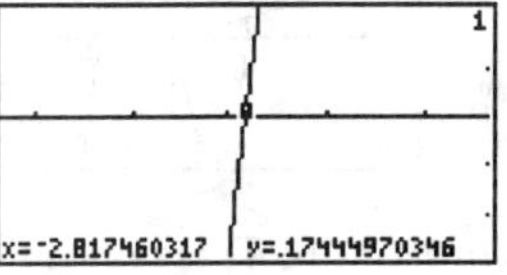

Figure 10.42: Near an x-intercept of $y = x^3 - 8x$

Technology Tip: As you zoom in, you may also wish to change the spacing between tick marks on the x-axis so that the viewing rectangle shows scale marks near the intercept point. Then the accuracy of your approximation will be such that the error is less than the distance between two tick marks. Change the x-scale on the TI-83 from the WINDOW menu. Move the cursor down to xScl and enter an appropriate value.

The x-intercept of a function's graph is a *root* of the function. Press GRAPH MORE F1 *[MATH]* to display the MATH menu across the bottom of the screen (Figure 10.43). Choose F1 *[ROOT]* to find a zero of this function. You will be prompted to trace the cursor along the graph first to a point *left* of the root (press ENTER to set this *left bound*). Then move to a point *right* of the root and set a *right bound* by pressing ENTER. Note the two arrows near the top of the display marking the left and right bounds (as in Figure 10.44).

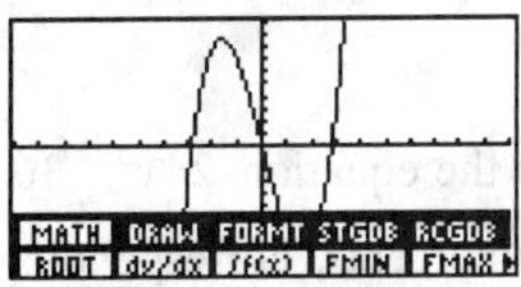

Figure 10.43: MATH menu

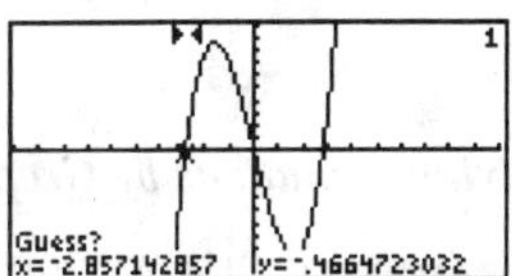

Figure 10.44: Finding a root

Next move the cursor along the graph between the two bounds and as close to the root as you can; this serves as a *guess* for the TI-86 to start its search. Good choices for the lower bound, upper bound, and guess can help the calculator work more efficiently and quickly. Press ENTER and the coordinates of a root will be displayed (Figure 10.45). Repeat this process to find the coordinates of any other root the function may have.

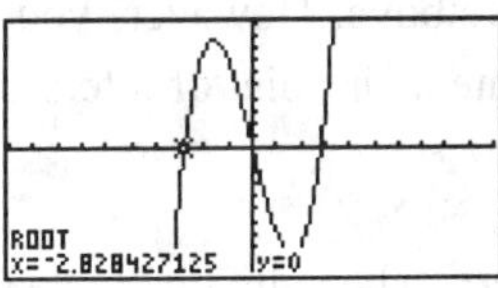

Figure 10.45: A root of $y = x^3 - 8x$

TRACE and ZOOM are especially important for locating the intersection points of two graphs, say the graphs of $y = -x^3 + 4x$ and $y = -.25x$. Trace along one of the graphs until you arrive close to an intersection point. Then press $\blacktriangle$ or $\blacktriangledown$ to jump to the other graph. Notice that the x-coordinate does not change, but the y-coordinate is likely to be different (Figures 10.46 and 10.47).

When two y-coordinates are as close as they can get, you have come as close as you now can to the point of intersection. So zoom in around the intersection point, then trace again until the two y-coordinates are as close as possible. Continue this process until you have located the point of intersection with as much accuracy as necessary.

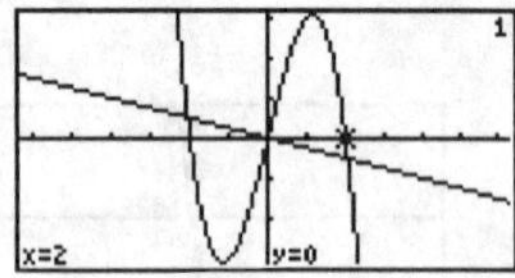

Figure 10.46: Trace on $y = -x^3 + 4x$

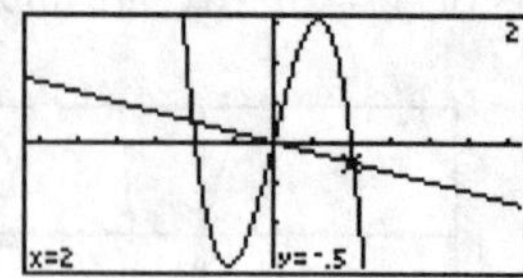

Figure 10.47: Trace on $y = -.25x$

You can also find the point of intersection of two graphs by pressing GRAPH MORE F1 *[MATH]* MORE F3 *[ISECT]*. Trace with the cursor first along one graph near the intersection and press ENTER; then trace with the cursor along the other graph and press ENTER. Marks are placed on the graphs at these points. Finally, move the cursor near the point of intersection and press ENTER again. Coordinates of the intersection will be displayed at the bottom of the window (Figure 10.48).

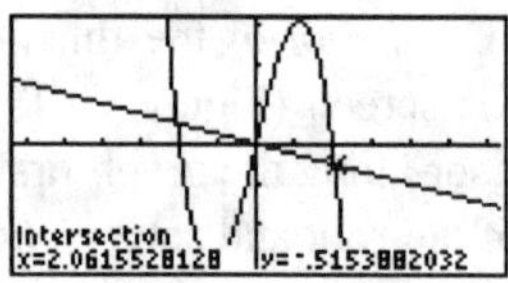

Figure 10.48: An intersection of $y = -x^3 + 4x$ and $y = -.25x$

10.3.2 Solving Equations by Graphing: Suppose you need to solve the equation $24x^3 - 36x + 17 = 0$. First graph $y = 24x^3 - 36x + 17$ in a window large enough to exhibit *all* its x-intercepts, corresponding to all the equation's zeros (roots). Then use trace and zoom, or the TI-86's root finder, to locate each one. In fact this equation has just on solution, approximately $x = -1.414$.

Remember that when an equation has more than one x-intercept, it may be necessary to change the viewing rectangle a few times to locate all of them.

Technology Tip: To solve an equation like $24x^3 + 17 = 36x$, you may first transform it into standard form, $24x^3 - 36x + 17 = 0$, and proceed as above. However, you may also graph the *two* functions $y = 24x^3 + 17$ and $y = 36x$, then zoom and trace to locate their point of intersection.

10.3.3 Solving Systems by Graphing: The solutions to a system of equations correspond to the points of intersection of their graphs (Figure 10.49). For example, to solve the system $y = x^3 + 3x^2 - 2x - 1$ and $y = x^2 - 3x - 4$, first graph them together. Then use zoom and trace or the ISECT option from the MATH menu to locate their point of intersection, approximately $(-2.17, 7.25)$.

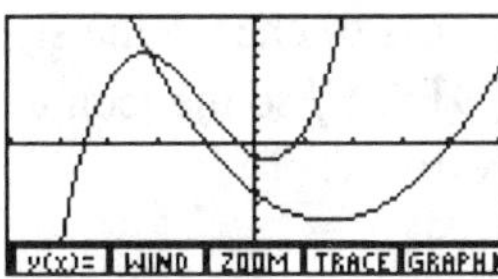

Figure 10.49: Graph of $y = x^3 + 3x^2 - 2x - 1$ and $y = x^2 - 3x - 4$

If you did not use the ISECT option, you must judge whether the two current y-coordinates are sufficiently close for $x = -2.17$ or whether you should continue to zoom and trace to improve the approximation. The solutions of the system of two equations $y = x^3 + 3x^2 - 2x - 1$ and $y = x^2 - 3x - 4$ correspond to the solutions of the single equation $x^3 + 3x^2 - 2x - 1 = x^2 - 3x - 4$, which simplifies to $x^3 + 2x^2 + x + 3 = 0$. So you may also graph $y = x^3 + 2x^2 + x + 3$ and find its x-intercepts to solve the system.

10.3.4 Solving Inequalities by Graphing: Consider the inequality $1 - \dfrac{3x}{2} \geq x - 4$. To solve it with your TI-86, graph the two functions $y = 1 - \dfrac{3x}{2}$ and $y = x - 4$ (Figure 10.50). First locate their point of intersection, at $x = 2$. The inequality is true when the graph of $y = 1 - \dfrac{3x}{2}$ lies *above* the graph of $y = x - 4$, and that occurs when $x < 2$. So the solution is the half-line $x \leq 2$, or $(-\infty, 2]$.

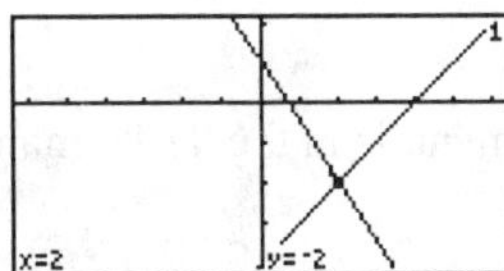

Figure 10.50: Solving $1 - \dfrac{3x}{2} \geq x - 4$

The TI-86 is capable of shading the region above or below a graph, or between two graphs. For example, to graph $y \geq x^2 - 1$, first graph the function $y = x^2 - 1$ as y1 in the GRAPH y(x)= screen. Then press GRAPH MORE F2 *[DRAW]* F1 *[Shade]* 2nd alpha Y 1 , 100) ENTER (see Figure 10.51). These keystrokes instruct the TI-86 to shade the region *above* $y = x^2 - 1$ and *below* $y = 100$ (chosen because this is the greatest y-value in the graph window). The result is shown in Figure 10.52.

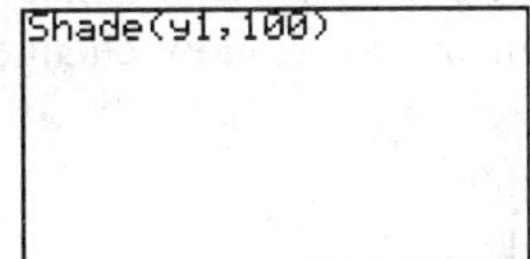

Figure 10.51: DRAW Shade

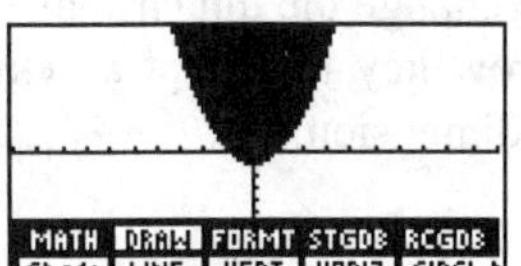

Figure 10.52: Graph of $y \geq x^2 - 1$

To clear the shading when you are already in the DRAW menu, press MORE MORE F1 *[CLDRW]*.

Another method for graphing $y \ge x^2 - 1$ is to change the style of y1 in the y(x)= screen. To do this, press GRAPH F1 *[y(x)=]* MORE F3 *[STYLE]* F3 *[STYLE]* so the icon to the left of y1 is an upper right triangle (Figure 10.53). Then press 2nd M5 *[GRAPH]* (Figure 10.54).

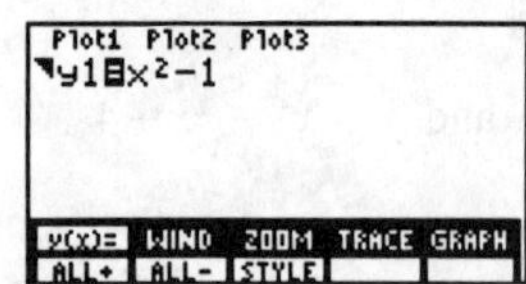

Figure 10.53: Shade above STYLE

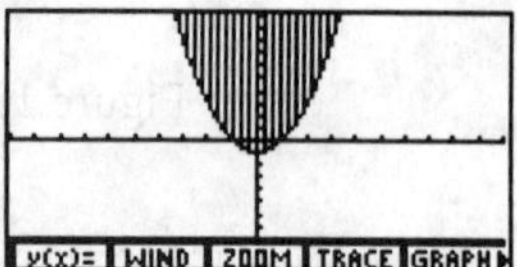

Figure 10.54: Graph of $y \ge x^2 - 1$

Now use shading to solve the previous inequality, $1 - \dfrac{3x}{2} \ge x - 4$. The function whose graph forms the lower boundary is named *first* in the SHADE command (see Figure 10.55). To enter this in your TI-86, press these keys: GRAPH MORE F2 *[DRAW]* F1 *[Shade]* x-VAR – 4 , 1 – 3 x-VAR ÷ 2) ENTER (Figure 10.56). The shading extends left from $x = -2$, hence the solution to $1 - \dfrac{3x}{2} \ge x - 4$ is the half-line $x \le 2$, or $(-\infty,\ 2]$.

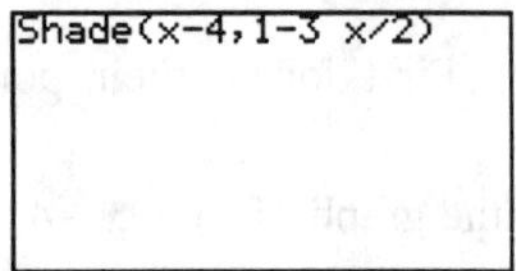

Figure 10.55: DRAW Shade command

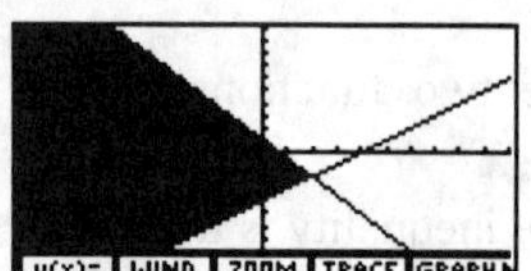

Figure 10.56: Graph of $1 - \dfrac{3x}{2} \ge x - 4$

More information about the DRAW menu is in the TI-86 manual.

10.4   Matrices

10.4.1 *Making a Matrix:*   The TI-86 can display and use many different matrices, each with up to 255 rows and up to 255 columns! Here's how to create this 3×4 matrix $\begin{bmatrix} 1 & -4 & 3 & 5 \\ -1 & 3 & -1 & -3 \\ 2 & 0 & -4 & 6 \end{bmatrix}$ in your calculator.

Press 2nd MATRX F2 *[EDIT]* to see the matrix edit menu (Figure 10.57). You must first name the matrix; let's name this matrix A (the TI-86 is already set for alphabetic entry) and press ENTER to continue.

You may change the dimensions of matrix A to 3×4 by pressing 3 ENTER 4 ENTER. Simply press ENTER or the down arrow key to accept an existing dimension. The matrix shown in the window changes in size to reflect a changed dimension.

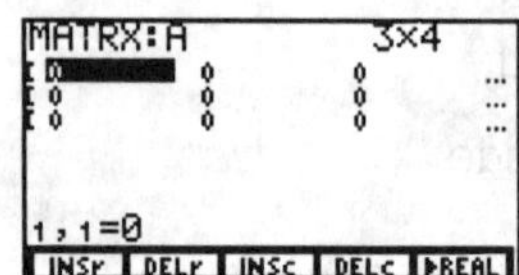

Figure 10.57: Editing a matrix

Use the arrow keys or press ENTER repeatedly to move the cursor to a matrix element you want to change. If you press ENTER, you will move right across a row and then back to the first column of the next row. At the right edge of the screen in Figure 10.58, there are dashes to indicate more columns than are shown. Go to them by pressing ▶ as many times as necessary. The ordered pair at the bottom left of the screen shows the cursor's current location within the matrix. The element in the second row and first column in Figure 10.58 is highlighted, so that the ordered pair at the bottom of the window is 2,1 and the screen shows that element's current value. Continue to enter all the elements of matrix A; press ENTER after inputting each value.

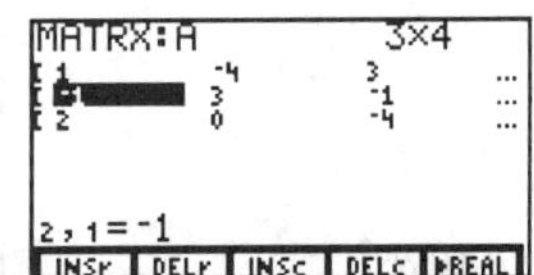

Figure 10.58: Editing a matrix

When you are finished, leave the editing screen by pressing 2nd QUIT to return to the home screen.

10.4.2 Row Operations: Here are the keystrokes necessary to perform elementary row operations on a matrix. Your textbook provides a more careful explanation of the elementary row operations and their uses.

To interchange the second and third rows of the matrix A that was defined above, press 2nd MATRIX F4 *[OPS]* MORE F2 *[rSwap]* ALPHA A , 2 , 3) ENTER (see Figure 10.59). The format of this command is rSwap(*matrix, row1, row2*).

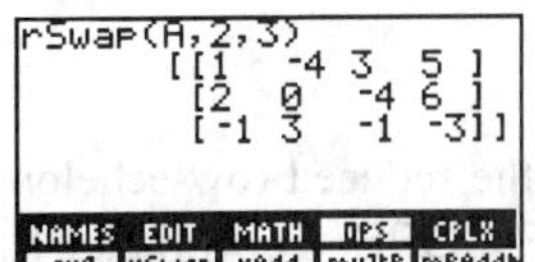

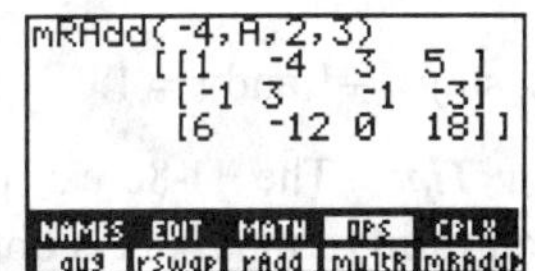

Figure 10.59: Swap rows 2 and 3

Figure 10.60: Add −4 times row 2 to row 3

To add row 2 and row 3 and *store* the results in row 3, press 2nd MATRX F4 *[OPS]* MORE F3 *[rAdd]* ALPHA A , 2 , 3) ENTER. The format of this command is rAdd(*matrix, row1, row2*).

To multiply row 2 by −4 and *store* the results in row 2, thereby replacing row 2 with new values, press 2nd MATRX F4 *[OPS]* MORE F4 *[multR]* (−) 4 , ALPHA A , 2) ENTER. The format of this command is multR(*scalar, matrix, row*).

To multiply row 2 by −4 and *add* the results to row 3, thereby replacing row 3 with new values, press 2nd MATRX F4 *[OPS]* MORE F5 *[mRAdd]* (−) 4 , ALPHA A , 2 , 3) ENTER (see Figure 10.60). The format of this command is mRAdd(*scalar, matrix, row1, row2*).

Note that your TI-86 does *not automatically* store a matrix obtained as the result of any row operation. So, when you need to perform several row operations in succession, it is a good idea to store the result of each one in a temporary place.

For example, use row operations to solve this system of linear equations: $\begin{cases} x - 2y + 3z = 9 \\ -x + 3y = -4 \\ 2x - 5y + 5z = 17 \end{cases}$.

First enter this *augmented matrix* as A in your TI-86: $\begin{bmatrix} 1 & -2 & 3 & 9 \\ -1 & 3 & 0 & -4 \\ 2 & -5 & 5 & 17 \end{bmatrix}$. Next store this matrix as C (press ALPHA A STO▸ C ENTER), so you may keep the original in case you need to recall it.

Here are the row operations and their associated keystrokes. At each step, the result is stored in C and replaces the previous matrix C. The completion of the row operations is shown in Figure 10.61.

Row Operations	*Keystrokes*
add row 1 to row 2	2nd MATRX F4 MORE F3 ALPHA C, 1, 2)
STO▸ C ENTER	
add −2 times row 1 to row 3	F5 (−) 2 , ALPHA C , 1 , 3) STO▸ C
ENTER	
add row 2 to row 3	F3 ALPHA C , 2, 3) STO▸ C ENTER
multiply row 3 by $\frac{1}{2}$	F4 1 ÷ 2 , ALPHA C , 3) STO▸ C ENTER

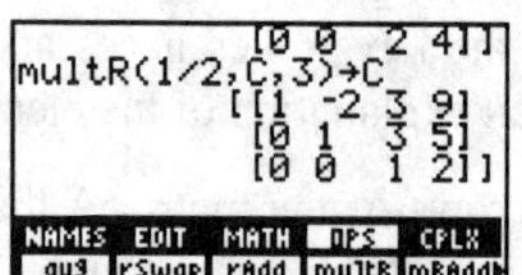

Figure 10.61: Final matrix after row operations

Thus $z = 2$, so $y = -1$ and $x = 1$.

Technology Tip: The TI-86 can produce a row-echelon form and the reduced row-echelon form of a matrix. A row-echelon form of matrix A is obtained by pressing 2nd MATRX F4 *[OPS]* F4 *[ref]* ALPHA A ENTER and the reduced row-echelon form is obtained by pressing 2nd MATRX F4 *[OPS]* F5 *[rref]* ALPHA A ENTER. Note that a row-echelon form of a matrix is not unique, so your calculator may not get exactly the same matrix as you did by using row operations. However, the matrix that the TI-86 produces will result in the same solution to the system.

10.4.3 Determinants: Enter this 3×3 square matrix as A: $\begin{bmatrix} 1 & -2 & 3 \\ -1 & 3 & 0 \\ 2 & -5 & 5 \end{bmatrix}$. To calculate its determinant $\begin{vmatrix} 1 & -2 & 3 \\ -1 & 3 & 0 \\ 2 & -5 & 5 \end{vmatrix}$, go to the home screen and press 2nd MATRX F3 *[MATH]* F1 *[det]* ALPHA A ENTER. You should find that the determinant is 2 as shown in Figure 10.62.

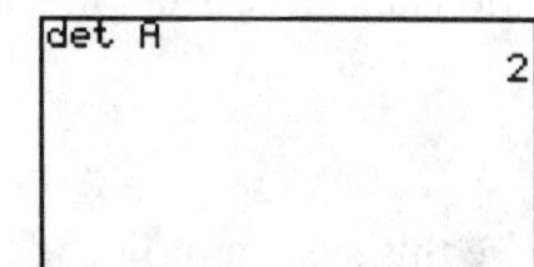

Figure 10.62: Determinant of A

TI-86 Graphics Calculator

10.5.1 Iteration: The ANS key enables you to perform *iteration*, the process of evaluating a function repeatedly. As an example, calculate $\dfrac{n-1}{3}$ for $n = 27$. Then calculate $\dfrac{n-1}{3}$ for n = the answer to the previous calculation. Continue to use each answer as n in the *next* calculation. here are keystrokes to accomplish this iteration on the TI-86 calculator. (See the results in Figure 10.63.) Notice that when you use ANS in place of n in a formula, it is sufficient to press ENTER to continue an iteration.

Iteration	Keystrokes	Display
1	27 ENTER	27
2	(2nd ANS – 1) ÷ 3 ENTER	8.66666666667
3	ENTER	2.55555555556
4	ENTER	.518518518519
5	ENTER	–.16049382716

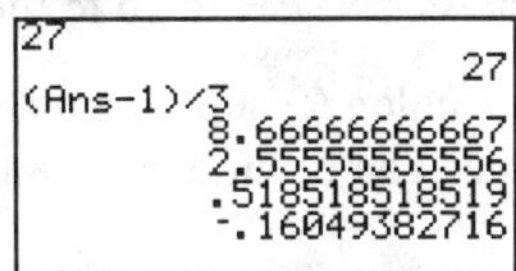

Figure 10.63: Iteration

Press ENTER several more times and see what happens with this iteration. You may wish to try it again with a different starting value.

10.5.2 Arithmetic and Geometric Sequences: Use iteration with the ANS variable to determine the n-th term of a sequence. For example, find the 18th term of an *arithmetic* sequence whose first term is 7 and whose common difference is 4. Enter the first term 7, then start the progression with the recursion formula, 2nd ANS + 4 ENTER. This yields the 2nd term, so press ENTER sixteen more times to find the 18th term. For a *geometric* sequence whose common ratio is 4, start the progression with 2nd ANS × 4 ENTER.

Of course, you could also use the *explicit* formula for the n-th term of an arithmetic sequence $t_n = a + (n-1)d$. First enter values for the variables a, d, and n, then evaluate the formula by pressing 2nd alpha a + (2nd alpha n – 1) 2nd alpha d ENTER. For a geometric sequence whose n-th term is given by $t_n = a \cdot r^{n-1}$, enter values for the variables a, d, and r, then evaluate the formula by pressing 2nd alpha a 2nd alpha r ∧ (2nd alpha n – 1) ENTER.

10.5.3 Permutations and Combinations: To calculate the number of permutations of 12 objects taken 7 at a time, $_{12}P_7$, press 2nd MATH F2 *[PROB]* 12 F2 *[nPr]* 7 ENTER (Figure 10.64). Thus $_{12}P_7 = 3{,}991{,}680$.

For the number of combinations of 12 objects taken 7 at a time, $_{12}C_7$, press 2nd MATH F2 *[PROB]* 12 F3 *[nCr]* 7 ENTER (Figure 10.64). Thus $_{12}C_7 = 792$. Note that you do not have to press 2nd MATH F2 *[PROB]* again if the MATH PROB menu is active.

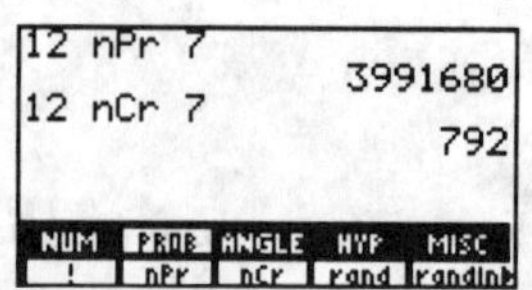

Figure 10.64: $_{12}P_7$ and $_{12}C_7$

10.6 Programming

10.6.1 Entering a Program: The TI-86 is a programmable calculator that can store sequences of commands for later replay. Here's an example to show you how to enter a useful program that solves quadratic equations by the quadratic formula.

Press PRGM to access the programming menu. The TI-86 has space for many programs, each named by a name you give it. To create a new program now, start by pressing PRGM F2 *[Edit]* and enter its name.

For convenience, the cursor is a blinking **A**, indicating that the calculator is set to receive alphabetic characters. Enter a descriptive title of up to eight characters, letters, or numerals (but the first character must be a letter or θ). Name this program QUADRAT and press ENTER to go to the program editor.

In the program, each line begins with a colon (:) supplied automatically by the calculator. Any command you could enter directly in the TI-86's home screen can be entered as a line in a program. There are also special programming commands.

Input the program QUADRAT by pressing the keystrokes given in the listing below. You may interrupt program input at any stage by pressing 2nd QUIT. To return later for more editing, press PRGM F2 *[EDIT]*, select the program name using the appropriate function key, and press ENTER.

Each time you press ENTER while writing a program, the TI-86 *automatically* inserts the : character at the beginning of the next line.

The instruction manual for your TI-86 gives detailed information about programming. Refer to it to learn more about programming and how to use other features of your calculator.

Enter the program QUADRAT by pressing the given keystrokes.

Program Line	*Keystrokes*
: Disp "Enter A"	F3 F3 MORE MORE F1 ALPHA E 2nd alpha ALPHA N T E R ⌴ ALPHA A F1 ENTER

displays the words Enter A on the TI-86 screen

| : Input A | MORE F1 ALPHA A ENTER |

waits for you to input a value that will be assigned to the variable A

: Disp "Enter B"	F3 MORE MORE F1 ALPHA E 2nd alpha ALPHA N T E R ⌴ ALPHA B F1 ENTER
: Input B	MORE F1 ALPHA B ENTER
: Disp "ENTER C"	F3 MORE MORE F1 ALPHA E 2nd alpha ALPHA N T E R ⌴ ALPHA C F1 ENTER

: Input C	MORE F1 ALPHA C ENTER
: ClLCD	MORE F5 ENTER

clears the calculator's display

| : $B^2-4A*C \rightarrow D$ | ALPHA B x^2 – 4 ALPHA A × ALPHA C STO⬥ D ENTER |

calculates the discriminant and stores its value as D

| : If D>0 | EXIT F4 F1 ALPHA D 2nd TEST F3 0 ENTER |

tests to see if the discriminant is positive

| : Then | EXIT F2 ENTER |

in the case the discriminant is positive, continues on to the next line;
if the discriminant is not positive, jumps to the comman after Else below

| : Disp "Two real roots" | EXIT F3 F3 MORE MORE F1 ALPHA T 2nd alpha ALPHA W O ⌴ R E A L ⌴ R O O T S F1 ENTER |
| : $(-B+\sqrt{(D)})/(2A) \rightarrow M$ | (((–) ALPHA B + 2nd $\sqrt{\ }$ ALPHA D) ÷ (2 ALPHA A) STO⬥ M ENTER |

calculates one root and stores it as M

| : Disp M | MORE F3 ALPHA M |

displays one root

: $(-B-\sqrt{(D)})/(2A) \rightarrow N$	(((–) ALPHA B – 2nd $\sqrt{\ }$ ALPHA D) ÷ (2 ALPHA A) STO⬥ N ENTER
: Disp N	MORE F3 ALPHA N
: Else	EXIT F4 F3 ENTER

continues from here if the discriminant is not positive

| : If D==0 | F1 ALPHA D 2nd TEST F1 0 ENTER |

tests to see if the discriminant is zero

| : Then | EXIT F2 ENTER |

in the case the discriminant is zero, continues on to the next line;
if the discriminant is not zero, jumps to the command after Else below

| : Disp "Double root" | EXIT F3 F3 MORE MORE F1 ALPHA D 2nd alpha ALPHA O U B L E ⌴ R O O T F1 ENTER |
| : $-B/(2A) \rightarrow M$ | (–) ALPHA B ÷ (2 ALPHA A) STO⬥ M ENTER |

the quadratic formula reduces to $\dfrac{-b}{2a}$ when $D = 0$

| : Disp M | MORE F3 ALPHA M ENTER |

: Else	EXIT F4 F3 ENTER
: Disp "Complex roots"	EXIT F3 F3 MORE MORE F1 ALPHA C 2nd alpha ALPHA O M P L E X ⎵ R O O T S F1 ENTER

displays a message in case the roots are complex numbers

: Disp "Real part"	MORE F3 MORE MORE F1 ALPHA R 2nd alpha ALPHA E A L ⎵ P A R T F1 ENTER
: –B/(2A)→R	(–) ALPHA B ÷ (2 ALPHA A) STO◆ R ENTER

calculates the real part $\dfrac{-b}{2a}$ of the complex roots

: Disp R	MORE F3 ALPHA R ENTER
: Disp "Imaginary part"	F3 MORE MORE F1 ALPHA I 2nd alpha ALPHA M A G I N A R Y ⎵ P A R T F1 ENTER
: $\sqrt{\ }$ –D/(2A)→I	2nd $\sqrt{\ }$ (–) ALPHA D ÷ (2 ALPHA A) STO◆ I ENTER

calculates the imaginary part $\dfrac{\sqrt{-D}}{2a}$ of the complex roots;

since $D < 0$, we must use $-D$ as the radicand

: Disp I	MORE F3 ALPHA I ENTER
: END	EXIT F4 F5 ENTER

marks the end of an If-Then-Else group of commands

: END	F5

When you have finished, press 2nd QUIT to leave the program editor and move on.

10.6.2 Executing a Program: To execute the program you have entered, press PRGM F1 *[NAME]* and look for QUADRAT. The names of the available programs are displayed alphabetically at the bottom of the screen; press MORE to advance through the listing. Press the function key corresponding to QUADRAT to select the program, and the press ENTER to execute it.

The program has been written to prompt you for values of the coefficients a, b, and c in a quadratic equation $ax^2 + bx + c = 0$. Input a value, then press ENTER to continue the program.

If you need to interrupt a program during execution, press ON.